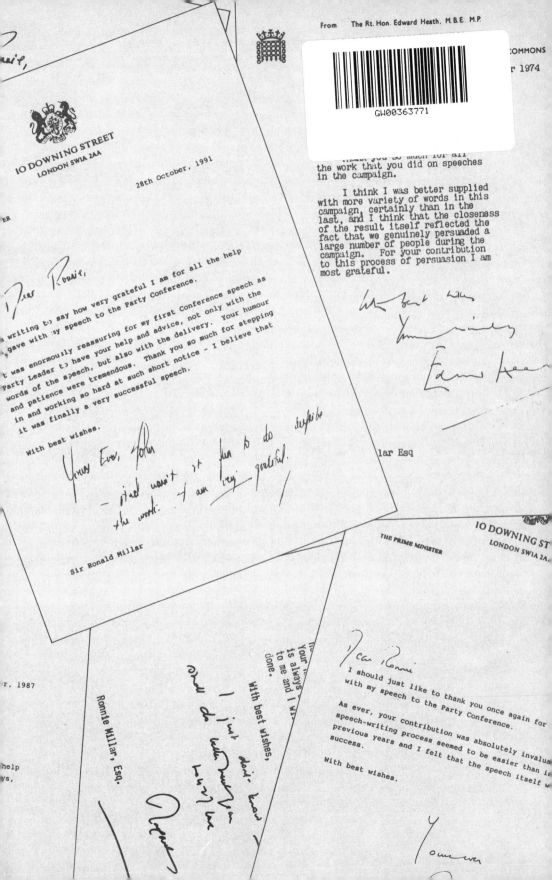

From   The Rt. Hon. Edward Heath, M.B.E. M.P.

COMMONS

r 1974

...k you so much for all
the work that you did on speeches
in the campaign.

I think I was better supplied
with more variety of words in this
campaign, certainly than in the
last, and I think that the closeness
of the result itself reflected the
fact that we genuinely persuaded a
large number of people during the
campaign.   For your contribution
to this process of persuasion I am
most grateful.

With best wishes
Yours sincerely
Edward Hea...

...lar Esq

---

10 DOWNING STREET
LONDON SWIA 2AA

28th October, 1991

Dear Ronnie,

...writing to say how very grateful I am for all the help
...gave with my speech to the Party Conference.

...t was enormously reassuring for my first Conference speech as
Party Leader to have your help and advice, not only with the
words of the speech, but also with the delivery. Your humour
and patience were tremendous. Thank you so much for stepping
in and working so hard at such short notice – I believe that
it was finally a very successful speech.

With best wishes.

Yours Ever, John

— and wasn't it fun to do despite
the work. I am very grateful.

Sir Ronald Millar

---

10 DOWNING ST
LONDON SWIA 2A

THE PRIME MINISTER

Dear Ronnie

I should just like to thank you once again for
with my speech to the Party Conference.

As ever, your contribution was absolutely invalua...
speech-writing process seemed to be easier than i...
previous years and I felt that the speech itself w...
success.

With best wishes.

Yours ever,

---

r. 1987

Ronnie Millar, Esq.

With best wishes,

...your...
...is always...
to me and I wi...
done.

I just don't know h...
we do without you
Ronnie

...help
...s,

A VIEW FROM THE WINGS

A VIEW
FROM
THE WINGS

WEST END, WEST COAST,
WESTMINSTER

· · · · · · · · · · · · · · · · · · · ·

Ronald Millar

WEIDENFELD & NICOLSON
London

First published in Great Britain in 1993 by
Weidenfeld & Nicolson
The Orion Publishing Group Ltd
Orion House,
5 Upper Saint Martin's Lane,
London WC2H 9EA.

ISBN 0 297 81301 3

British Library Cataloguing in Publication Data is available for this
title.

Typeset by Selwood Systems, Midsomer Norton
Printed in Great Britain by Butler & Tanner Ltd, Frome, Somerset

To Chris who said 'You must do it'
and my friends of the Dramatists' Club
who gave the final thrust.

Contents

. . . .

Illustrations

Between pages 150 and 151

The illustrations come from the author's own collection.

Acknowledgements

From a long and grateful list I am especially indebted to:

Lavinia Trevor, of the William Morris Agency, who took a light-hearted remark of mine seriously, introduced me to the world of publishing and thereby set in train all that followed.

My editor, Ion Trewin, distinguished son of a distinguished father, whose unobtrusive expertise, encouragement and easy friendship made my journey into books so much less arduous than it might have been.

Margaret Thatcher, whose permission I sought to include one or two of the remarkable letters she wrote to me during our long association and who gave it unreservedly.

John Major, who equally readily allowed me to include one of his.

Mary Lally, secretary of secretaries, who travelled all the way with me and processed a mountain of words with a miracle of a machine which did everything but actually write them. (Only a matter of time, of course.)

Peter Hennessy and Anthony Seldon, joint editors of *Ruling Performance: British Governments from Attlee to Thatcher* – an invaluable reference book for pinning down the precise date of political history.

My old friend and former colleague, Martin Landau (aka the Putney guru), who never doubted that this book would happen and whose enthusiastic bullying did much to make sure that it did.

To them and all those others who urged me on down the long road to hard covers, my lasting thanks.

Ronald Millar

Programme Note

. . . .

Shortly after the tearful, damp November morning when Margaret Thatcher left Downing Street for the last time as Prime Minister my telephone began ceaselessly to ring.

Literary agents – British, American, European, even a Japanese ('Goodbye, may I ask question, please?') – wanted to know where the lady could be found, as she had let it be known – or someone had – or they had guessed that in due course she would be writing her memoirs and they would be only too happy to be her representative and see them through to publication.

I didn't doubt that for a moment, but I kept saying in different ways 'I don't know where she is', which they appeared not to believe, though it was true. Finally, I said to one of them, 'If you don't land the lady's memoirs, how about mine?' It was a jest, a light-hearted quip to relieve the negative monotony.

The following morning I reached wearily for the receiver for the umpteenth time and a woman's voice said, 'My boss was talking to you yesterday about Mrs Thatcher's memoirs and you said, "How about mine?" Well – how about them?'

I explained that I had not meant it, it was just a joke. 'Why?' Because, I said, I had never written a book of any kind and further-more I had not the slightest intention. 'Why not?' she persisted. 'You're a writer, aren't you?'

'Yes, but –'

'Well, then.'

To get her off the line I promised to think about it, at the same time promising myself not to, but I reckoned without her tenacity and the urging of my friends ...

This, then, is the story of how two worlds, disparate but not dissimilar, came together, touched history and changed my life.

1

Overture and Beginners
1983
. . . .

They stop you at the checkpoint at the side entrance to the grounds. They may know you – your face, your voice, your car, your registration number – you get the treatment just the same.

These are country police, not capital city police, and at first glance appear relaxed and easy-going. They are in fact highly trained professionals. That morning they were cheerful. They are always cheerful.

'Hello, sir. Carrying any bombs today?'

'Bother. I forgot.'

'No sense taking a look then, is there?'

I passed them my car keys and they went through the familiar routine, unlocking the boot, rummaging around inside, using the mirror-on-the-long-pole device that enables you to see the full length of a car's undercarriage, finally ramming the boot shut, locking it, handing back the keys.

'Right, sir. All clear.'

'Better luck next time.'

'Cheers.'

I waved acknowledgement and drove on slowly, carefully up the path, turning first right then left, passing a couple of uniformed guards patrolling the grounds, rifle slung over right shoulder, into the quiet gravelled square with the high hedge that is the immediate approach to the house itself.

A feeling of total peace descends and you know at once why all Prime Ministers love Chequers. Since 1921, when Lord Lee of Fareham, encouraged by his wife, gave it to the nation, it has been the official country residence of the Queen's First Minister, his – or her – point of calm and quiet, away from the ferment of political life. America's Presidents have Camp David. Britain's Prime Ministers have Chequers.

Built in 1565, endowed by Lord and Lady Lee and administered by the Government, Chequers, in estate agent's jargon, combines size with intimacy. Flowers abound, bees hum, lawns are manicured, trees are tended, birds sing and if you stay overnight in spring or summer you waken to the dawn chorus (I'm a Londoner but if I ever moved to the country and wrote a book about it, 'Birdsong in the Morning' would be the title).

3

At Chequers a small herd of cows contributes to the rural scene but they are discreet as pre-war civil servants and the deliberations of visiting statesmen are not disturbed by a single moo.

'The stately homes of England, how beautiful they stand
To prove the upper classes have still the upper hand,'

sang Noël Coward in the early thirties.
No longer. Get to be Prime Minister and, whatever your origins, Chequers and all that goes with it is yours for the duration.

She was standing in the doorway, no coat, no scarf, the wind blowing her hair about. In London it's lacquered for the ever-intrusive camera, but here in rural England, although the business of the nation continues discreetly to be conducted, life is as mellow, casual and relaxing as it can be made. Even so, standing in open doorways, an easy target for the hidden sharpshooter, probably breaches strict security. But the lady has no physical fear.

'In this job you can't afford it, you wouldn't get anything done.'

I parked in the usual place and walked over to her. She is not a tactile person. She doesn't care to be kissed, opting for a sort of over-the-shoulder clasp, quite affectionate but avoiding frontal contact. However, for once she refrained from evasive action. (Mr Heath is even less tactile. He doesn't like shaking hands.)

'Here you are at last. Good. I rang as soon as I heard. We've been looking for you since Thursday.'

I nodded. 'Your chauffeur told me.'

He'd been waiting beside my car, which had been parked on a yellow line just off Kensington Church Street. This was as near as I could get to my London flat. Parking *permits* do not guarantee a parking *space*, as the leaflet kindly informs you.

She looked at me closely. 'All right?'

'Yes. I'm fine.'

'Come on in. There's a cold wind.'

It was February 1983.

The Great Hall was warm and welcoming. There was a large log fire burning in the grate. The grand piano glistened with the flames' reflection though the keyboard was closed (had it been like that since Ted's time?) and the usual superb paintings hung from the walls.

A Wren Petty Officer came forward with a whisky and soda already poured out. I could tell the Scotch was strong from the colour.

The three Services staff Chequers in turn. I was glad it was the

4

Navy that weekend. It made me feel specially at home.

'Thanks.' I took a swig. It was strong all right. The drinks weren't usually that potent at Chequers. Someone had said something.

'I asked Number Ten to keep trying your number. Where were you, dear?'

'A girlfriend lives just down the road from me. I went there for a couple of days. I didn't fancy being on my own. Not right away.'

'That's how I thought you might feel.'

The message delivered by the chauffeur had been, 'If you're a bit down, drop everything and come straight to Chequers.'

'How old was your mother?'

'Three weeks off ninety.'

'Those are the kind of genes to have.'

The tone was just right: crisp, unsentimental. I didn't want words of sympathy. The sympathy was in the invitation.

By now I'd been to Chequers a number of times but usually to work on a speech, not simply to be cheered up because cheering-up was probably what you needed most at the time.

'Was it peaceful?'

'Extraordinary. She just turned over and went to sleep.'

'That's the way to go, if you can manage it.'

The Wren came up. Not at the double, naval-style. Discreetly. Everything is discreet at Chequers.

'Luncheon is ready, Prime Minister.'

'Let Mr Thatcher know, will you? Shall we go in, dear? Bring your glass.'

There were no other guests. We walked through to the dining room: dark panelled oak and a side view of the swimming-pool building, forever associated in my mind with that most gallant of consorts, Mrs Runcie, the wife of the former Archbishop of Canterbury. On a famous occasion she had done a series of belly-flops at a lunch party for Nancy Reagan. Unabashed by the whiplash sound, and no doubt pain, of belly smacking water like a rifle shot and echoing out beyond the terrace until it died away in the Chilterns, she had dived bravely on for the glory of the Church Militant.

We sat at the small round table by the window, used for meals when there are only a few guests. Through it Denis Thatcher could be seen practising putting while a Special Branch man solemnly fielded the little white balls. When he came in the first course was being served.

'Hello, my old. Good to see you. Understand your mum's moved on to better things.'

'That's right?'

'All in order?'

'Absolutely.'

'Well done.' He sat down, inspected his plate. 'I say, Thatcher, what's this?'

'An omelette, dear.'

'I can see that. What's it made of?'

'Eggs, dear.'

'Good heavens, woman, I know that. What I'm trying to establish is what's this grey stuff sloshing about inside?'

'Mushroom, dear.'

'Now we're getting somewhere.' He looked at me and winked. I had the feeling he'd staged this little impromptu for my benefit to lift the gloom, if any. There wasn't, but he couldn't know that. A thoroughly decent human being, Denis Thatcher, shrewd, watchful, loyal to a fault and, although he referred to his wife as 'The Boss', unchallenged master of his household.

Later she said, 'We thought perhaps you might have gone back to Reading.'

Reading? For a moment I was puzzled.

'When there's a loss in the family people do rather tend to return to their roots.'

Well, perhaps. It hadn't occurred to me but she is *au courant* on family matters as, indeed, on one or two others.

'Anyway, I'm glad we found you.'

I too was glad and wondered how many other Prime Ministers, with the daily, hourly pressures upon them, would have found the time to take the trouble.

I stayed through tea and drinks at six and let the peace of Chequers work its magic. English through and through, Chequers is balm for the troubled soul. When they came to the front door to see me off it was dark outside.

'Take care now.'

'I'll do that. And thank you. Thank you for today.'

Driving back to London, I thought about personal warmth and human kindness, and how the private view and public vision of this most unexpected woman, about whom it's impossible to be neutral, reflected two entirely different personalities. The thought was to return to me many times, when the anti-Thatcher industry was in full swing and she came under sustained personal attack. But playing the woman instead of the ball is for after the interval.

Come with me, then, if you will, on a journey that's theatrical before becoming political but which sets the scene for what is to follow, as the unconnected strands of an accidental life rendezvous and fall gradually into focus.

'Only connect,' said E. M. Forster. Yes. And if chance passes you the surprise baton, take it from the outstretched hand. Make the connection and run with it, run all the way until – but wait. Someone's pressed Fast Forward. Stop. Reverse. Now, sequentially, please, from Letter A. One ... two ...

ACT I

1916–42

1

. . . .

I Only Knew the Photograph

Reading, Berkshire, is a town in southern England that, if conceivably possible, one should try not to be born in. This is in no way to denigrate the inhabitants who are – or were, for it's some time since I had the privilege of visiting there – as reasonable, or unreasonable, as the rest of the human race. Nor is it the one-way traffic system (from which, having entered, it is, or was, virtually impossible to exit) that makes Reading a less than ideal trampoline for life.

No, the trouble with Reading is there is nothing to do in the evenings. Nevertheless I am, as Mrs Thatcher would say, a bit wet about Reading. For it was there, a few years before the turn of the century, when the old Queen Victoria was nearing the end of her long journey through life, that my parents began theirs. As, in due course, did I.

My father was a Scot by descent, though not by nature. His family had come south from Dumfries. The brighter Scots of each generation tend to head south across the border to show the English how to run England. (Considering the bloodstained picture Shakespeare painted of them in 'the Scottish Play' this is generous.)

My mother, on the other hand, was quintessentially English. Offhand I can't think of any Englishwoman – or man, for that matter – as quintessential as my mother, and what she would have said about the Channel Tunnel doesn't bear thinking about. Her maiden name was Dacre-Hill which, as you see, was hyphenated. The Dacre element she would pronounce Dacré when she felt in the mood. I don't know why she did this. To cheer herself up on a wet day, perhaps, or improve her accent. I only know that until she was married Dacre-Hill would periodically become Dacré-Hill. 'French, you know,' she would say. My mother was about as French as Harrods.

She was twenty-three and my father twenty-five when they met. They liked one another a lot and laughed together at the same things and finally loved one another a lot. I said there was nothing to do in Reading in the evenings but of course there is always that. My parents' first meeting had been at a rehearsal of an amateur dramatic society called The Merrythoughts.

The century was still young – it was 1916 – and despite the war to end wars of 1914–18 ('now in its third year' as the diagonal strips proclaim on West End theatrical posters) innocence had not yet departed the land. Music was still musical, there were even tunes to be heard if you cared for melody, and television as we know it had not been invented. Second only to his love for my mother, my father loved rowing, a sport at which he excelled and acquired a number of silver cups, most of them at Henley Regatta. He also acquired a 'rowing heart' that he was assured was nothing to worry about and which he ignored, so my mother did the worrying for him. When it caused him to fail his army medical he was hugely embarrassed. She, on the other hand, was delighted and made no bones about it. She was too honest to dissemble. Now she wouldn't lose her husband because someone had murdered an Archduke in some place called Sarajevo she had never heard of. But for my father's passion for rowing he would probably have died in the trenches along with more than half his generation and I would not be here.

Turned down by the Army, my father decided to go into business. He set up a paintworks on a hill just outside Reading (it's still there), appointed himself its managing director and began to sell paint to industry, notably a special kind of paint called 'Reading Green'. What with the paintworks and The Merrythoughts and the war that he felt deeply he should be a part of, life was full and varied. But there was one thing missing, and so one evening after work he rode down the hill on his motorbike and dropped in on my mother.

Dorothy Dacre-Hill was much sought after, not only for her beauty which was considerable – the long brown tresses only just stopped short of the carpet – but for the singing lessons which she gave for almost no money to the aspiring daughters of the middle class. When she opened the door to my father that evening she knew at once what was coming. Indeed she had known since the third rehearsal of *The Second Mrs Tanqueray*, which is hardly surprising since half Reading knew about Ronnie and Dorothy. However, when he put the question she went through the hoops of gasping 'Who – me?' and 'Oh' and 'What a surprise!', as respectable young ladies were expected to do until the free-and-easy twenties. Some even felt obliged to swoon as their socially more exacting mothers had before them. Mine toyed with the idea but decided against it. When I asked her why – she was, after all, a budding actress with a talent for the dramatic (which was not always confined to the stage) – she said The Merrythoughts had not yet taught her to do a stage fall.

However, my mother could always push the button marked 'Down-to-earth' when it was called for. So when my father asked eagerly, 'Will you think about it?' she said at once, 'I don't have to. Of course I'll marry you. When shall we do it? In the summer?' At which he held her close and kissed her with passion and the loving certainty that he had found his girl. 'Let's not wait,' he said. 'Let's do it just as soon as we can publish the banns.'

'But, darling boy, I've nothing to wear!'

'We'll find some old rag. Please. I've a feeling there's no time to lose.'

She said simply, 'Dear, I'm not pregnant if that's what you mean.'

But he didn't mean that.

And so Dorothy Ethel married Ronald Hugh and wore white at the wedding and looked a picture, as does every young girl who gets married in white whatever she may have looked before, and some-times even after. The wedding and reception over, they travelled to London and saw *Chu Chin Chow* at His Majesty's Theatre and spent their honeymoon night in the bridal suite of the Savoy Hotel and half the orchestra came in and played the big waltz from *The Chocolate Soldier* that begins with the words 'Come, come, I love you truly' and ends with 'O happy, happy wedding day' – which it had been, despite the rain – and my mother worried about the cost (like most people who have never had serious money, and some who do, she always worried about it) and kept saying, 'I'm sure we can't afford all this' until finally my father said, 'Of course we can't. We'll have to do a moonlight flit, but let's go to bed first, shall we?'

When I was a child my mother must have told me a hundred times the story of how she married my father but I could never hear it too often, not only because it was better than any fairy story but because my father was in it and the way she told it he had all the best lines. And so she would tell it all over again with minor variations, but not too many because I knew it by heart and would correct her if she went wrong and make her start again.

After the honeymoon my parents returned to Reading and life on an even keel, or as even as a keel can be for two people who, according to those who knew them, were blessed by the gods.

The only problem was money. It was still wartime and my father had sunk all his savings in the business and had not yet begun to recoup his investment. But lovers don't measure paradise in financial terms. He worked with his men on the factory floor and covered himself in paint and came home to my mother at night, to the house on the river at Shiplake which his father had given them as a wedding present, and cleaned himself up and after dinner he would put his feet up and my mother would play the piano and sing the Josie Collins' song from *The Maid of the Mountains*, the one about 'that sunlit mountainside', and life was loving and gentle and good.

To complete a happiness that must have been almost tangible only one thing was needed: a child. Appropriate prayers were despatched, and presumably received, because in the second week of November 1919, exactly a year after Armistice Day – no, a year and a *day* after Armistice Day, I always get it wrong – they were answered. It's strange, I can recite at the drop of a hat 'Please to remember the *fifth* of November, gunpowder, treason and plot', but every year when my birthday comes round I have to stop and think, Which came first – the Armistice or me?

In due course I was christened, with the same initials as my father's business, R.G.M. standing both for Reading, Green and Marvell and Ronald Graeme Millar. When friends or relatives asked my mother, somewhat unnecessarily, if she were happy (I'm told you had to be blind not to marvel at it) she would say, 'So happy I'm scared.'

'Scared?'

'You see, I have the best man that ever lived – no, truly – and a child and a lovely home, and the war's over at last, thank God, and oh, everything is perfect.'

'So?'

'I'm scared to death it won't last.'

One Thursday after work – it was Maundy Thursday – when they had been married not quite four years, my father said 'I shan't be long' and kissed my mother and promised to be back in time for dinner. Then he hopped on his motorbike and rode over to Boulter's Lock near Maidenhead to inspect a new boat. About halfway home a heavy-duty truck came fast round a bend in a narrow lane on the wrong side of the road. Truck and motorbike met head-on. The truck was the larger and heavier of the two ... They said, but for his 'rowing heart' he might have made it. As it was he died instantly, not of injuries but from shock.

I was all of eighteen months when it happened so it was some little time before I knew I would never get to know my father. When finally my mother decided I was old enough to be told I didn't say anything. I didn't cry. I just stood there. Then I walked away. I wanted to be alone to try and figure out what I ought to feel about someone I only knew from a photograph.

2

. . . .

Coloured Lights that Came and Went

In the early twenties mourning in the provinces was high-profile. Anything less would be frowned upon by the neighbours. So my mother, having lost a husband, was obliged to wear a long, black crepe dress with a veil and a kind of headdress affair which made her look like a novice nun. Her whole nature, which was sunny and resilient, rebelled at this permanent reminder of grief. She knew that the man she had loved and married and whose nature was equally unrepining would not have wished it. If men must work and women must weep, well and good, but privately into the pillows was both her need and her philosophy. For the rest, she had a child on her hands and the sooner the challenge of an unpredictable future was taken up the better.

So, after just one week, dress and veil were banished to the boxroom and when she went to the bank to find out what was in the kitty, it was a fine day and she wore a bright blue dress to go with it. What was in the kitty was very little. But there was the house by the river and the factory on the hill, surely they were worth a penny or two, so how about a mortgage?

'You mean a second mortgage? I wouldn't advise it.' The bank manager who had known my mother since her teens had put on a black tie to acknowledge her mourning, only to find that she was dressed for spring.

No, she didn't mean a second mortgage, Mr Littlewood, she didn't even know what a second mortgage was. She meant a straightforward mortgage on the house.

'Ah, you mean a first mortgage.'

But it seemed this had already been taken out to cover the weekly wage bill at Reading, Green and Marvell and the interest on the initial investment, which had only partly been paid off.

'But my husband is – was a successful businessman.'

'Yes, indeed, your late husband had excellent prospects. But an initial outlay takes time to recoup and meanwhile your late husband – '

'I do wish you wouldn't use that expression. Sorry, but he wasn't *late*. He was never late. If anything he was early – especially dying on me in his twenties, bless his heart.'

'His heart. Of course. A rowing man, as I remember. The strain on the cardiac muscle. I am so very sorry. You must be devastated, left a widow at your age.'

'Widow is another awful word, isn't it? Please. Let's not go into all this now or we shall both end up in floods.'

In accordance with the bank's advice, the house on the river was disposed of to the bank which held the mortgage, the factory on the hill was taken over by my father's brother Max, some nominal financial help was offered by my father's family by way of a loan but my mother's independence asserted itself, she didn't like to be beholden. What was needed now was a job of some kind, but she'd married young and hadn't trained for anything.

Well, all right, she'd start. She could sing and play the piano and she had done some amateur dramatics.

The Royal Academy of Dramatic Art is situated at 62 Gower Street, London WC2. A week later she had travelled to London with her son and taken a room almost opposite. After some intricate manoeuvres and a little bribery she managed to get an audition for the autumn term.

I don't have a verbatim record of these proceedings but I understand they went something like this:

'Miss Hill, please.'

(Miss Hill enters from the wings. Voices in the darkened stalls stop chattering. One takes over the audition.)

'Good morning, Miss Hill.'

'Dacre-Hill, actually.'

'I'm sorry, it says here – '

'Not at all.'

'So, Miss Dacre-Hill – '

'Unless you'd prefer Dacré – '

'Why should I do that?'

'Because it's my name.'

'Which is? Hill or Dacre-Hill or Dacré-Hill?'

17

'All three, actually. The accent is optional.'

'I see. So Miss – er – you'd like to be a student at the Royal Academy?'

'Yes, please.'

'Do you have any theatrical experience?'

'I know Owen Nares and how to breathe.'

'I beg your pardon?'

'I have a good pair of lungs and my husband went to school with Owen Nares.' (Nares was the matinée idol of the day.)

'Well, that's nice.'

'Yes, he is, he's lovely and a wonderful friend. I just thought I'd mention it.'

'We're glad you did. Anything else you'd like to tell us?'

'Yes. About my lungs. I'm a singer, you see.'

'Ah. Would you like to sing something for us now?'

'Not really.'

'Why is that?'

'I have a cyst on my epiglottis.'

'I beg your pardon?'

'It's nothing to worry about. Quite a simple operation.'

'I'm so glad.'

'Thank you.'

'Perhaps you'd like to come back and sing something for us when you've had it done.'

'Not really.'

'Young lady, what *would* you like to do?'

'Learn to act. I mean *really* act, not just amateur acting. I've done that and it was fun, but I want to be a professional and eventually earn some money so that I can look after my son and have him educated. Then, when he's a man, he can get a proper job, not something – you know – here today and gone tomorrow like the theatre.'

'I see. You want to get into the theatre to keep him out of it.'

'That's very well put.'

'Thank you.'

'Not at all.'

(An assistant stage manager appears from the wings.)

ASM: 'Excuse me. Anyone here name of Millar?'

(Heavy breathing from the stalls.)

'No. There is no one here name of Millar. There are several people here name of Hill or Dacre-Hill or Dacré-Hill or Primrose Hill I shouldn't wonder and one of them has a cyst on her epiglottis though

I'm not sure which but there's no one name of Millar. That at least is clear.'

'I'm awfully sorry but – my name is Millar.'

Silence. Finally: 'Are you entirely sure?'

'Yes.'

'You're not making this up?'

'No, Millar is my married name.'

'You seem to have quite a string of names. Is that the lot or are there more to come?'

'There's Dorothy Ethel. Dorothy Ethel Dacre – or Dacré – Millar or Hill or Dacre-Hill or Dacré-Hill. I hope I'm not confusing you.'

'I'm hanging on by my fingernails.'

ASM: 'Excuse me, there's a call for you, Miss.'

'Mrs, actually. Mrs Millar. I'm sorry but would you excuse me. Thank you for your time, it's been lovely, but I'd better go. I've got a neighbour looking after my son, that's her on the line now I think. She leaves at one but I could pop back any time. I only live across the way.'

'Er, no, I don't think that will be necessary.'

'Well, anyway, goodbye and thank you again.'

(False exit. Muttering in the stalls.)

'Wait. One second. Miss – er – Mrs – have you ever played comedy?'

'Oh yes. And I'm pretty good at accents, too. We did *Abie's Irish Rose* in The Merrythoughts and I was Rose and then in *The Belle of New York* – '

'You were the Belle.'

'You saw me!'

'No, but who else would it be?'

'Well, thank you. That's one of the nicest – '

'Yes, all right, some other time. If there is one.'

'What does that mean?'

'It means that when you've gone we'll have a little talk and maybe, just maybe – '

'But that's wonderful!'

'I don't know. It may not be. Don't count on anything. But good luck. And Dorothy – may I call you Dorothy?'

'Please. Feel free.'

'Don't call us. We'll call you.'

When my mother first told me this tale of her RADA audition I said it was a pretty daring ploy, carrying on like a circus clown to persuade them she was a comedienne. She denied this, maintaining it wasn't a ploy, it was panic.

'I was so petrified I thought I was going to faint, but maybe if I kept on talking – I didn't know what I was saying – it might be all right.'

And it was. Two days later they called her and that autumn Dorothy Dacre-Hill (accent optional) became a student at the Royal Academy of Dramatic Art.

Life at RADA was brisk and cheerful and instructive and the student with a string of names learnt how to move and stand still and not to direct traffic with her hands and if you make a gesture to emphasise a point make it clear-cut and precise, not any old how, and hold your head up and listen, and this is how you throw your voice without raising it, now you try it, no, dear, not like that, like this, that's better and always remember that the eyes have it, they have it all the way and you have quite a pair so use them. Her fellow students were mostly her contemporaries which meant that passes were made and when she said sorry but she had a child, they said 'Oi – Oi!' and took it for granted that it was out of wedlock and when they found it wasn't they were disappointed but took her under their wing and were happy to babysit when she had classes and one of them was available. All of which was fine and floral while the money lasted.

Now there was a hard-and-fast rule at RADA that, whilst you were a student, you might not during term-time take a professional job. This is not unreasonable. To have completed a two-year course at RADA, even if one hasn't won the Gold, is a cachet and a guarantee that you're not just a social butterfly playing at being an actress but are sufficiently serious about your profession to have gone the distance.

My mother was fully aware of this, but needs must, so, using her married name, when she heard they were looking for a second understudy in a light comedy about to open in Shaftesbury Avenue she auditioned for the job and got it. It seemed like a stroke of luck. As second understudy she wasn't seen on stage nor was she listed in the programme. However, she'd forgotten about the mid-week matinée. When she let it be known that she had trouble with a wisdom tooth three Wednesdays running, eyebrows were raised and she found herself in the Principal's office.

'Come in, my dear. Now what did I want to see you about? Oh yes. Yes, we're all very happy with your work, Dorothy, and of course you always look pleasing.'

'Thank you, Mr Barnes.'

'There's just one thing – do sit down – I just wondered if there was anything I don't know that you felt I ought to.'

'I don't quite follow.'

'Well, why don't you go away and think about it and then come back and – I say, look at the clock. You mustn't be late for your matinée.'

Silence. 'How did you find out?'

'My dear, I have been in this business quite a while, you know, and when a wisdom tooth acts up only on Wednesday afternoons... Almost every West End show has a Wednesday matinée. Which one is it?'

'*Lord Richard in the Pantry.*'

'Ah yes. Well, I hope you get a chance to play – Laura, isn't it – one of these days.'

'Who told you?'

'Goodbye, Dorothy. We shall miss you and good luck.'

'Who was it?'

'All the very best.'

'But surely you're not going to kick me out just for – I was broke. I needed the money.'

'Don't we all, my dear. But rules, as they say, are rules.'

And that, as they say, was that.

Kenneth Barnes had done his student a good turn. She did play Laura for a whole week when the star was off and the first understudy had the flu. This led to walk-ons, to small parts, to not-quite-so-small parts and eventually to playing the lead in Number Two and then in Number One touring companies of famous West End hits like *White Cargo* in which she played the native girl Tondeleyo with lashings of brown make-up and very little else, and the Yvonne Arnaud part in that famous forerunner of the Ben Travers farces, *Tons of Money.*

This meant travelling on Sundays from one town to the next and living in digs – which were sometimes tolerable and sometimes terrible – with a small son, now aged five, in tow, who found the backstage life wildly exciting but whose mother thought dragging a small boy all over the United Kingdom was the worst possible way to bring up a child but he couldn't be left so what could she do?

The child knew what she could do. Nothing. Stay with it. The entire cast of first *White Cargo* and then *Tons of Money* was spoiling him outrageously, as were the backstage staff, taking him up in the 'flies', showing him how the curtain went up and down and how the coloured lights came and went while the most marvellous stories were going on below which he didn't understand but his mother had something to do with them because there she was brown all over with a funny accent poisoning everyone in sight in *White Cargo* and making them laugh their heads off with another funny accent in

Tons of Money so it must be all right and anyway it was far better than real life.

Sometimes I would stand in the wings and watch the actors moving about under the lights and I would have the curious sensation that whatever story was being told out there I was both observing it and a part of it. When I became involved in politics, I was to have that sensation again. But my life at the edges and then at the centre of political power was light years later.

What was worrying my mother while she toured the land with a child on her hands was that he was falling hopelessly in love with the theatre and that was not at all what she had in mind for him when he grew up. I could choose for myself then, of course, but the choice was to be grounded in a solid education that was practical and down-to-earth and would provide a steady income. A precarious life in the theatre, with two-thirds of the profession out of work nine-tenths of the time, failed to qualify on every possible count. She realised I was stage-struck but at five years old it was easy to change a child's mind, the chances were he'd change it himself, after all he'd wanted to be a bus conductor and that no longer rang a bell. The first thing was to get him away from the backstage atmosphere (what she hadn't realised was that, as Alan Coren nearly said, 'You can take the boy out of the theatre but you cannot take the theatre out of the boy').

I was packed off to an elderly aunt who lived in a small flat in the middle of Glasgow. Aunt Maggie McNichol gave me a warm welcome, all the love in the world, and acute colitis. In that order. I didn't know what colitis was and I certainly couldn't spell it but my stomach told me that food came into it – and out of it.

My aunt was bewildered. 'Och, you puir wee thing,' she cried when the doctor had gone. 'Cross my heart and hope to die, I can't for the life of me think how you picked up that "itis" thing.'

I could. I knew exactly how I picked up that 'itis' thing. My aunt loved onions. So we had bacon and egg and onions for breakfast, liver and bacon and onions for lunch, and grilled herring and onions for supper. It was clear to me that at this rate of onion consumption my aunt's regular hope to die was likely to receive a positive answer. What's more, one more onion and I'd be going with her, if I hadn't gone ahead of her. Which is how I came to be whisked away from Glasgow and the loving care of Aunt Maggie McNichol and sent to a boarding school on the south coast at the advanced age of five and a half.

Bexhill-on-Sea in the 1920s was the mecca of preparatory schools for middle-class offspring, mostly from the south of England with a sprinkling from India and Ceylon. At that time Bexhill had more prep schools, boys' and girls', to the square foot than any other seaside resort. Today it has more old-age pensioners. The boys' school where I was sent – Normandale in Collington Avenue, a few miles from Hastings where the Normans fought and won the battle in 1066 – was typical of its time.

There was a girls' school, Thornbank, to the left of us; Harewood, another boys' school, to the right; and St John's, yet another girls' school, opposite. Then there was Seafield and Garth Place about a mile away, both for boys. (No mixed bathing in those days.) We played soccer with Seafield and cricket with Garth Place and put our tongues out at our rival academies when we passed on our school walks, crocodile fashion two by two, getting a privileged education. Normandale was run by a Mr and Mrs Salmon, who were friends of friends of my Uncle Jack and Aunt Cis and were willing to take a small child of five and a half whose mother was a widow and had gone on the stage, which was still not considered the thing in the 1920s but never mind so long as the fees were paid, more grist to a new cricket pavilion, and it wasn't the child's fault, poor little chap, if his mother chose to traipse about all over England, Scotland and Wales 'acting', if you please, and with next to nothing on, they said, what kind of a play was that, but lips closed, no one need know about his mother.

For the first few days I was desperate with homesickness and, like Aunt Maggie, wanted to die. I couldn't understand why I'd been sent to this peculiar place. Didn't my mother care about me any more? She behaved as though she cared so what was I doing here? Had love been just another of her performances? It was years before I understood: that without my father she had been afraid of caring too much, that school and letting go the apron strings were synonymous.

I used to howl my head off whenever term began, but children, especially very young children, adjust with the speed of light. Mrs Salmon, who was kind enough in a headmaster's wife sort of way, told me all Normandale boys had to learn to stand on their own two feet and when I asked why, she said that was what life was all about. I didn't see how they could stand on anyone else's so decided to give it a whirl.

As I was too young to have proper lessons in a classroom I was treated as though I was at nursery school and given paint and brushes to make a mess with in the sanitorium, and great big copies of the *Illustrated London News*, with photographs in sepia of the Great War of 1914–18, which had ended exactly a year and a day before I was born and apparently was all the fault of a man who went about scowling at everyone in a huge helmet with a pointed thing on top which must have made sleeping difficult and who for years I thought was called Caesar but who turned out to be the Kaiser. The photographs, which fascinated me, were of men in tin hats and brown uniforms caked in mud who for some reason, Matron's pert young assistant told me, were all called Tommy Atkins.

'Why?'

'No idea, love.'

'It's silly.'

'Never mind. Press on regardless.'

They were everywhere, in places with funny names which apparently were French, splashing through more and more mud in something called trenches (no sign of Harold Macmillan reading Aeschylus in his but then I didn't know about him and Aeschylus at the time) with guns going off all round them and Tommy Atkins covered in blood and bandages marching cheerfully on and announcing that it was a long, long way to Tipperary, wherever that might be, but to keep the home fires burning till the boys came home. But they didn't. Most of them didn't come home. When you turned the page they were being blown to pieces in a variety of close-ups. All of which any psychiatrist could have told you could scar a child for life and was the very last thing to be shown to it, whether the child liked it or not, which this one did and screamed when they took his war away.

The future being happily concealed from us, I was unaware that some fourteen years later there would be a second world war with the same enemy and I would be up to my seaboots in it, which gave one a rather different perspective.

One day without warning the Salmons were gone, a new headmaster named Insley and his wife had taken over, the copies of the *Illustrated London News* had been burned amid a lot of 'Good Gods' and 'Bless my Souls' and I was placed in the bottom of the first form to begin a normal education.

3

· · · · · · · · · · · ·

What Sort of Ship is a Scholarship?

As a small boy I did not have an inquiring mind. I did as I was told when young – and made up for it later. I knew we had very little money and that my mother had to work hard to get what we had. I also discovered that my Uncle Jack, who was married to my father's sister, Aunt Cis, and was 'something in the City', had had a hand in sending me to Normandale and more than a hand in seeing that the fees were paid.

John Sell Cotman, descended from the painter and named after him, was a small man with a huge heart and a grand house in Pyrford, Surrey, with a staff of domestics and a great big Daimler with a drinks cabinet and a chauffeur named Conway and a farm and a dairymaid named Rosa with red cheeks and a lovely disposition.

I fell in love with Rosa and asked her to wait for me and she promised she would but she didn't, she married Conway and I was pageboy at their wedding in the village church and when the Vicar declared them man and wife I howled and had to be led away. Uncle Jack Cotman was a man of means with a strong sense of social responsibility which had a lot to do with helping to pay for my education. He and Aunt Cis had no children of their own and so I used to go to The Old House at Pyrford in the holidays whenever my mother was away on tour and be treated as though I were their son. When possible my mother would come on Sundays on her way to the next touring date.

One Sunday after lunch my uncle, who had a fine tenor voice, sang something in a strange language. (It was in fact Greig's 'Ich lieber dich' – 'I love you' – though it might have been 'Yes, we have

25

no bananas' for all I knew.) He sang it straight at my mother. When he began to follow it with something about a pair of sparkling eyes my aunt, who had been accompanying him on the Steinway, got the message, lowered the piano lid and suggested a brisk walk. At this my uncle said rain was forecast, my aunt muttered 'Just what you need. Cool you down', my mother spluttered into her handkerchief and I was bundled out of the room and up to the nursery before I could clarify the position.

The Old House was Georgian. It had a priest's hole and secret panels where one could imagine almost anything happening and I used to wish I could stay there for ever. This wish was very nearly granted because my aunt told my mother on one of her visits that she had decided to adopt me. She had no children of her own and had come to love this odd child who was of course wilful and disobedient but it wasn't his fault that he hadn't been properly brought up. At this my mother, who was not an actress for nothing, gave her temperament full rein and 'There was a blazing row that rattled the windows' she told me as soon as I was old enough to take such dramas in my stride and thoroughly enjoy them.

When my uncle learnt what his wife had proposed he told my mother that while he would like nothing better than to have an adopted son and I would do very nicely for the role, he had a proposal of his own, which sounds like a plot for a play of the period (late Pinero or Henry Arthur Jones). Why didn't he leave my aunt, he said, marry my mother, adopt me and make me his heir? My mother thought about it for all of five minutes, then sent him back to his wife and told him not to be silly. As she was very fond of him and it would have solved all our financial problems, I thought when I learnt about it later that she was an even more generous and independent spirit than I already knew her to be.

Uncle Jack was South African (white of skin and gold of heart) and belonged to the tribe of life-enhancers. He was loved by everyone and by no one more than my mother, but not – as they used to say in those days – 'in that way'.

My uncle said not a word of this to my aunt but her sixth sense sounded the alarm and during dinner one evening when her husband was unusually silent she said, 'What's the matter, Jack? Missing that woman?'

At this my uncle, stung because it was true, for once lost his cool and flared, 'If by any chance you're referring to the person I think you're referring to, it's entirely due to "that woman", as you call her, that I'm sitting here tonight. So you can stop calling her "that woman". Her name is Dorothy.'

This was a mistake. My aunt, who should have let the ball go through to the wicket-keeper, came back with 'And what is that supposed to mean?'

'It's short for Dorothea which means "a gift from God",' said my uncle, which wasn't bad for a defensive shot into the covers but didn't really help matters all that much.

Whereupon my aunt, who would have made a useful relief bowler and whom I was secretly rather fond of (when my uncle lost his money and they had to move to a smaller house she called it Brickwall because, she said, it was something to be got over) rose, threw down her napkin and walked from the room.

'Cis, come back, dear. Please. I'm sorry. I apologise,' said my uncle like the gentleman he was.

So, tall and thin which gave her a natural dignity, my aunt came slowly back, sat down and said, 'Well?'

And then – foolishly, I'm afraid – my uncle told her.

Not being a woman I can't be sure but I don't imagine many wives care to feel they owe their husband's continued presence under the marital roof to a rival's generosity. For over twenty years my aunt never spoke to my mother except through a third person and whenever she referred to her, which was as little as possible, always called her 'that woman'. At least she didn't call her 'that *bloody* woman' (a charming soubriquet that would one day be applied to another lady who was just about to be born in the town of Grantham, England).

My aunt need not have worried. She was never in danger of losing her husband.

My mother had a host of admirers and numerous proposals. I always knew there was something in the wind when whoever was the latest beau insisted on taking me to the circus or teaching me bezique. One of the most ardent was Louis Hayward who showered me with presents until he suddenly rushed in one evening clutching his stomach, cried 'Gastric flu! Sam Goldwyn! What a break!' and went to Hollywood and became a film star. Then there were Kenneth Birrell and Clifford Bartlett, both actors, who told a bewitched youngster wondrous tales about the theatre when his mother was out of the room, and a Spanish millionaire who used to telephone her from Madrid in the middle of the night and shriek 'Carissima, I loove you!' I rather think I put the boot in there, without really meaning to, by picking up the phone one night, saying in my mother's voice 'Oh, don't be an ass' and replacing the receiver and then taking it off the hook.

Were any of these gentlemen-callers her lovers? I never inquired.

27

At the time I didn't know the meaning of the word and when I did it seemed unimportant. But my mother was naturally generous and affectionate and I think it unlikely that a young, unattached actress of the twenties who was something of a beauty (Dorothy Wilding, the photographer, was always asking her to sit for her) would have gone through her heyday without an affair or two with someone she was fond of. But marriage? That was something else again. For my mother there was no one like my father, the depth of her love for him was such that there never could be, and so it remained for the rest of her long and happy life.

Years later, when my mother and my aunt were both in their seventies, my uncle turned to me one day and whispered, 'Old chap, do you realise how alike our two girls have become?' It was true, although 'our two girls' would have gone to the stake before admitting it. However, after my uncle's death they became firm friends.

It's never easy for a mere male to master the intricate female code. In that respect, I sometimes think I'm still at school.

At Normandale, the Insleys turned out to be very different from their predecessors, especially the new headmaster. F. P. Insley was a 'Character'. (Are all schoolmasters Characters or is it just in retrospect, when the fear has gone?) Insley – tallish, thickset, with a bald and bumpy skull – was known as Pi (initials FPI, schoolboy shorthand, very subtle). Also the Mad Major. He had, we learnt, been something of a force on the Western Front. If they hadn't burned my *Illustrated London News* I could have looked him up.

'Storm'd at with shot and shell, boldly they rode and well, into the jaws of Death, into the mouth of – ' Well, anyway, he was a born leader and got shell-shocked for his pains, poor man. This no doubt accounted for his habit of starting a sentence and losing the thread, e.g. 'Right. Now turn to your Tacitus, page – er – thing, line – er – there. Millar will translate for us.'

'Where from, sir?'

'I've just told you, boy. Stand up straight and pay attention.'

(Oh, the injustice of not hitting back – but a serviceable lesson for life after school, if any.)

For all his verbal disjunctions, as a teacher of the classics for the young Pi wasn't half bad. A tremendous enthusiast, he was fond of quoting Samuel Johnson: 'Greek, sir, is like lace. Every man gets as much of it as he can', and echoed Matthew Arnold's paean to 'The Grand, Old, Fortifying Classical Curriculum'. (No longer the alpha and omega of modern teaching, more's the pity.)

I owe Pi much, but for a long time I couldn't for the life of me fathom the point of a classical education. My mother, as I knew by heart, had insisted on a course of practical instruction that would ensure her son 'a future with a steady income'. Fair enough, but how, I wondered, was a knowledge of Latin and Ancient Greek – which were called 'dead' languages – to ensure any income at all, let alone a steady one, for the living? I mean, I was only a schoolboy and who was I to talk but no one I had ever met spoke so much as a syllable of the confounded stuff.

The trouble was, I was no good at maths or science but for some strange reason had an aptitude for Latin and Greek. That is, according to my school reports, which I used to open in the train going home for the holidays and stick down again with glue that oozed on to my short trousers and all but gave the game away. (No Sellotape in those days, dammit.)

'What's this sticky stuff, darling?'

'Treacle, Mum.'

'Doesn't look like treacle to me, dear.'

Gradually, as through a glass darkly, I began to see why the works of Tacitus and Cicero, of Sophocles and Aeschylus had survived the centuries and given the name Classics to 'the classics'. It was much more than a lesson in economy of language, it opened the door to a kind of truth and rhythm and beauty of expression that, for all its concern with silly old wars and battles long ago, reflected the age that I was living in, as they must have every generation that had gone before.

Pi was a man of many parts. On Sundays he would put on a lay preacher's white gown and conduct interdenominational matins for the entire school ('In the name of the Father and of the Son and of the Holy – er – thing') and the scattering of parents who were taking their offspring out for a decent meal by way of a change would listen to Pi's sermon, then with relief join in singing 'Onward, Christian Soldiers' with tremendous gusto. (Never mind the bit about marching as to war, it's a marvellous tune.) The service took place in what on weekdays was the gym, except for Wednesday afternoons when it became Miss Purrot's dancing academy, in which we boys danced with one another with a kind of stiff abandon that was more comical than stimulating and probably cured for life any burning desire for carnal knowledge of one's fellow man that might have been kindling in the formative breast. Happily the sexual bigots of the past can no longer persecute the nonconformist but I'm bound to say that once round the gym with Mayhew Minor clutched in my arms, exuding an odour that indicated he had cut Matron's weekly dose of castor oil, and the opposite sex could count on me for exclusive attention till the cows came home or, if that is an unhappy allusion, *ad* most definitely *aeternitatem*.

As I move up the school, I notice that a strange word begins to crop up in adult conversation. 'The boy must get a scholarship' starts to sound like a gramophone record on which the needle has stuck. At first I have no idea what a scholarship is. I assume it is some sort of naval vessel. Then all of a sudden I am twelve and into long trousers – and now I know what a scholarship is.

A scholarship is hard slog in hot rooms. A scholarship is competition in education. Is this a good idea? I never thought about it at the time but yes, I'm afraid it is. It's necessary agony if you're even halfway bright, because a scholarship is money for lift-off to the next rung on the ladder of enlightenment and without it, unless your family is flush, your chance of going onward and upward is likely to be circumscribed.

'YUWΘI GEAUTOV' ('Know thyself') says my Greek textbook. I'm all in favour of knowing myself so I try to make an honest assessment. I know that I'm not entirely stupid, that I've begun to appreciate Latin and Greek and to respond to most kinds of music. I can even play a tolerable piano ('Golliwog's Cakewalk' at Hastings Music Festival, Honourable Mention and Diploma). I am tall and thin and have long legs and have won the hundred yards' on sports day three years running and I captain the Second Eleven at cricket and score well for the First but in the scorer's box, not at the crease, a major disappointment.

I am, in fact, a thoroughly conventional, middle-class (it's 1932) English schoolboy who takes life's carousel as it comes round – home, school, theatre, home, school, theatre – and finds it more amusing than alarming and has no thought of writing anything more serious than the weekly letter home but is apparently expected to get a scholarship to somewhere or other, though where is not clear, and anyway, don't worry about it, love, if you get it you get it and if not, it doesn't matter one little bit (blessed liar) and yes, dear, you *were* a memorable Lady Macbeth in the school play, I can safely say I shall never forget it. Dorothy Millar (née Hill or Dacre-Hill or Dacré-Hill) was quite a lady.

4

. . . .

Onward and Upward?

A scholarship from a preparatory to a public school is not only a feather in the school cap of the boy who gets one and a useful windfall for his parents, whose fees are commensurately reduced, it's one up for the school and its headmaster who have trained him for it like a Derby colt and can put 'Winchester or Charterhouse scholarship obtained' on the prospectus if the preppy pulls it off. By the way, in England a public school is a private school. (If you know, forgive me. If not, it's one of our funny little ways.)

At Normandale, if a boy won a scholarship the entire school was given the day off and went on a picnic to Beachy Head. The idea was to have the whole school rooting for you and for you to know how much was riding on your success – a whole day off work – so better not let the side down (I have reason to believe that bets were laid with the gardener's boy but I have no proof).

At all events, one might not sweat too much about one's parents' opinion, or even what the masters said, but a whole day off work for one's mates – oh, cunning, artful Pi. When he saw that all this was making me nervous as a jumping bean – I was to go flat out for a Winchester classical scholarship because it was the most prestigious – Pi had another of his bright thoughts.

'Hello? Mrs Millar? Insley here. About the boy. No, he's not dead, he's fine. Just wanted to put you in the picture. The Harrow exam is before the Winchester, so I'm putting him in for that. No, no, just a trial run. Get him used to the idea of a strange hall, invigilators walking up and down, eye on the clock, heavy breathing down candidates' necks and so forth. Do his nerves a power of thing. By

31

the time Winchester comes round he should walk it. All right with you?'

A boy named Burn, a boarder at Normandale, lived in Harrow near the school. It was arranged that I should stay with his parents for the week of the scholarship exam. Each morning I bade goodbye to Dr and Mrs Burn, gave a cheery wave and wandered happily up the hill. I'd slept like a top and had a jolly good breakfast (not an onion in sight). As for nerves, what was there to be nervous about? Nothing was expected of me so I could relax and sail through the papers with a light heart. My heart was so light that when the English paper asked 'Who was Karl Marx?' – the kind of thing that could slip a chap's mind if he was tensed up but I was millpond calm – I had no hesitation in answering, 'One of the Marx Brothers.' (I did mention that it was light years before I dipped my toe in the political stream.)

I've often wondered if it was the *fons et origo* of Communism himself that caused the subsequent upheaval. It would have been in character. Did some examiner with a sense of humour, eyes alight with glee, cry 'One of the Marx Brothers! Ye Gods! This is just the sort of lad we need at Harrow'? All I know is they gave me a scholarship and instantly the cat was among the pigeons.

'Excuse me, sir, but wasn't the object of the exercise to prepare me for Winchester?'

'Of course, old chap, but you've done a bit too well too soon. Carry on swotting. We're turning Harrow down.'

Turning it down? Were they mad? What if I flunked Winchester? The bird in hand would have gone to roost, and there'd only be one class item left in the current scholarship round. Admittedly Charterhouse was a pretty good 'only', but by that time – three scholarship exams on the trot? You might as well ask a rank outsider to win the Derby, the King George & Queen Elizabeth and the Prix de l'Arc de Triomphe and still expect the poor beast to be upstanding at the finish. I went around in a daze. Pi, however, was in his heaven. Waving a single sheet of paper as though it were the Treaty of Versailles he announced my triumph to the whole school after morning prayers: 'Just shows what you slackers can do if you put your – er – thing into the – er – there' – and in accordance with tradition gave the school the day off work.

Thundering cheers. I'm man of the match and hero of the hour and we all trot off to Beachy Head with sardine sandwiches and Matron, in case the excitement proves too much for the smaller fry and one of them goes over the cliff. For my part I feel like jumping. Not only because Harrow has been handed back ('thanks but no thanks'), not even because Winchester is now the second leg of a potential triple nightmare, but because I've suddenly realised that Harrow is only half an hour on the tube from Shaftesbury Avenue and all those lovely London theatres, whereas Winchester is God knows where and, not to put too fine a point upon it, does anyone care?

I had begged my mother to let me go to Harrow. Among other inducements there was the annual cricket match with Eton at Lord's. More of a social than a cricketing event but she could wear that floating chiffon thing with the matching hat that drove the gentlemen-callers out of their minds and I'd look pretty snazzy in a Harrow boater, so come on, Mum, let's grab the kettle while it's boiling.

At first she was on my side. The thought of the Brain of Bexhill having to go through it all again when he'd surprisingly scored at the first chukka was, she had to admit, asking a lot.

But Pi was adamant. 'My dear Mrs – er, if Harrow is what the boy can do at the dress rehearsal, imagine how he'll come through when it's the first night.'

The metaphor reminded me once more of the proximity of Harrow to the West End theatres and like an ass I pointed it out to my mother. 'So that's it, is it? Oh no you don't.' It was one of her Dacre-Hill days.

'*Please*, Mum.'

'No, and that's final.' I looked suitably crushed and was gathered to the maternal bosom. She was Dorothy Millar again. 'Cheer up, love, Pi says Winchester will be a walkover. And it's a lovely sleepy country town.'

As I set off by car for this lovely sleepy country town and – despite a hair-raising, cross-country drive in the Mad Major's prehistoric Morris Cowley (known to the boys of Normandale as the Flying Bedstead), Mad Major at the wheel driving like Malcolm Campbell in Bluebird, quite impervious to the occasional kerb or bump in the road and car and occupants becoming airborne for several yards before making a crash-landing – actually got there, I knew I was going down with something.

So did my mother, who was waiting for us at the God-Begot Hotel in the High Street, where, after running out of petrol, we eventually arrived an hour late. I gave a special whoop at the sight of her, part relief, part exhaustion and part involuntary bark.

She took one look at me and said, 'That boy's got whooping cough.'

'Just a tickle,' said Pi airily. 'It's the heat. Hot lemon and thing, right as rain in the morning.'

He dumped my suitcase on the pavement. 'Good luck, boy. Nothing

33

to it. Downhill all the way. Remember Harrow,' and with a wave
and a couple of backfires from the Flying Bedstead he was gone in a
cloud of dust. As we passed through the hotel reception area I let off
a barrage of whoops which caused a couple of women with small
boys in attendance, who were wolfing sandwiches and cake, to look
round sharply. My mother gave one of her curtain-call smiles and
pushed me quickly into the lift.

During the night I'm not sure which made the most noise, my
whoops or the traffic in the High Street. Didn't anyone ever go to
bed in this lovely sleepy country town?

The following morning we arrived at the examination hall to find
candidates and parents, mostly mothers, gathered outside the door. I
spotted the two women from the God-Begot with their offspring and
moved towards them, letting out what seemed to me a friendly whoop
of recognition. They drew back as though stung by a swarm of wasps,
hauling their two candidates with them. I tried to say 'Good morning,
lovely day' but was seized by a paroxysm of whoops that caused the
rest of the assembled parenthood to turn and stare in alarm. The two
from the hotel looked at each other, then marched in unison up to
my mother.

'Your boy's got whooping cough,' said one.

'Yes, indeed,' said the other.

'Just a tickle,' said my mother. 'It's the heat, isn't it, darling?'

I drew breath to come in on cue but choked and whooped instead.

'He *has*!' they chorused.

'Listen to that!' they appealed to the rest of the group.

I struggled with the giggles, lost and set off another barrage. With
every whoop my competitors' parents clutched their young tighter
and shied away further.

When we were finally admitted to the examination room I was led
quietly away by the invigilator to a desk apart from the others and
a small screen was placed around me as though I had beriberi or
yellow fever. For all I know, my papers were sterilised before they
were marked and the examiners warned to wear surgical gloves.

At every session throughout the week I remained in semi-quar-
antine, coughing and wheezing behind my screen like La Traviata
on her way out but with one aria still to go. Now, in a play, or better
still a silent movie, the ending would have been as you like it. The
curtain rises on the final scene. I am back in the San, still coughing
my heart out, as with my last breath I gasp 'I did it' – whoop, croak –
'for you, Pi' – croak – 'and the boys of the old' – gasp – 'alma' –
gulp – 'mater' – whoop – ('Quick, Nurse, get Doctor.') 'Give them
my' – gasp, pant – 'best' – cough, whoop – 'and tell them I hope

they have a lovely, lovely' – whoop, gasp, choke, pant, gulp – ('He's going, Doctor!') – 'picnic' ... (Pianist plays Chopin's Funeral March.)

Winchester gave twenty-one scholarships that year. I came twenty-second. Can I help it if life's not 'Cinderella'?

The Charterhouse exam was set for a fortnight later, so instead of going back to school I went home, which for the moment was London: my mother's digs in George Street, off Baker Street, consisted of a fair-sized room with a gas ring and a minute bathroom but no kitchen. The idea was to rest from my exertions and finally to shake off my fell disease, so I stayed in bed and wrote a play based on Rafael Sabatini's *The Lion's Skin*.

When the day arrived for my third and final round in the scholarship stakes, to be held at Charterhouse-in-Southwark in London's East End, I was better but still able to manage a whoop at a pinch, though less frequently. Armed with a pharmacopoeia of syrups, lozenges and pills, we set off by Tube and arrived in tolerable spirits. However, one of the hopefuls who had, like me, failed to make Winchester and, like me, was hoping for Charterhouse, recognised my foghorn instantly.

'Look! Look! It's him! It's him!' cried this particularly obnoxious ginger-haired monster.

A lot of pointing and whispering went on and once again a number of my fellow competitors and their parents shied away like a team of horses backing off to a highwayman.

My mother decided the best method of defence was attack. 'Even if your boy did catch it,' she said in a voice trained to hit the back of the gallery, 'most children go down with it some time, don't they? Better to get it over and done with while they're young, don't you agree?'

No. They didn't. Far from it. It was clear they felt if anything would be better over and done with, it was me. So once again, as we trooped into the examination room, I was led firmly to a desk in a far corner of the hall with a screen round it.

'This is getting monotonous.'

'What was that?'

'Nothing, sir.'

It occurred to me, as once more I became invisible to the rest of the room, that if only I'd known this would happen I could have stuffed an Anglo-Latin dictionary into my trousers and had a high old time looking up all the words I couldn't translate. As it was I was sweating, not from fever but the knowledge that this was the last-chance saloon.

'It's madness,' I'd whispered to my mother, 'I'll never make it, I know I won't. You should have said yes to Harrow, I told you, I told you but you wouldn't listen. We had it in the bag and you blew it.'

'Ssh, love. Do your best. That's all anyone can ask.' I did my best, but I knew it wasn't.

On the last day there was a viva voce conducted by the then headmaster of Charterhouse, Sir Frank Fletcher. Each candidate saw him in turn. At first glance he seemed incredibly old – well, at least sixty – and rather frail.

'Ah yes. Millar. Come in, come in. You're the one with the cough, aren't you?'

I thought, if he catches it he'll be done for. I gave him a quick bark to warn him to stay clear.

'Come and sit down over here beside me.'

Well, at least if he was frail, he was game. I began to warm to him.

'Do you know, the same thing happened to me when I went for a scholarship, only mine was mumps. I remember looking at myself in the mirror and seeing an outsize melon staring back at me. Have you had mumps?'

'Yes, sir.'

'I rather enjoyed mine. Had to stay in the San for a fortnight. Much better food, I remember. Did they put you in the San?'

'No, sir. Just a room on my own but I had a wireless and the food wasn't that bad. Better than the awful stuff you usually get at school. Oh, I don't mean Charterhouse of course.'

'Of course you don't.'

We had a pleasant talk, punctuated by the occasional whoop, about everything under the sun except Latin and Greek. I knew Sir Frank was a distinguished classical scholar but he seemed to me nice and ordinary and altogether unalarming. At the end of quite a long conversation he said, 'Well now, you'd like to come to Charterhouse, would you? What put that idea into your head?'

'Well, sir, Charterhouse is the only one left. To be frank.'

'No, I'm Frank. You're – let me see' – he consulted his list of candidates – 'you're Ronald.' This seemed to amuse him no end.

Schoolmasters have a sense of humour all their own and much of it is not all that hilarious but they've been of tremendous value to me and I've always been fond of them, even the dottier ones, in fact especially the dottier ones.

Sir Frank was a lovely, gentle old boy. (I reckoned he could even be sixty-five, a tremendous age.) At the end of the viva he shook hands and said, 'Well, goodbye, young man. And in case we don't meet again, good luck.'

Blown it again, I thought, as I made for the door, and this was the end of the line. I could see the headlines: 'Schoolboy found Gassed in Garage by Flying Bedstead'.

'Oh, Millar. Am I right in thinking your mother's an actress?'

'Yes, sir.'

'Do you know, I saw her once in a play called "White something".'

'Cargo, sir.'

'That's the one. Jolly good she was, too. She took the part of a native girl called – now what was her name – it began with a T.'

'Tondeleyo.'

'Tondeleyo.' He savoured the word. 'What a beautiful name. She was frightfully wicked, I remember. Poisoned her lover. Cleopatra was always doing it, you know. Your mother's not really wicked, is she?'

'Not a bit, sir. She's a smasher.'

He muttered something.

'Sir?'

'*Sic dicunt omnes*. And so say all of us.' He needn't have translated, my Latin went that far. 'By the by, is she here today?'

'Yes, sir.'

'I thought I recognised her in the corridor. I'd have introduced myself but I wasn't certain it was she. You see, I'd never seen her with her clothes on.'

They gave thirteen scholarships that year. I remember the exact number because I was number thirteen. I still believe I only made Charterhouse because the headmaster of the day fancied my mother in the buff.

One of the more amusing misconceptions of the class-conscious twenties and thirties was this: that while a working-class lad was familiar from birth with the mystery of sex and more than happy to instruct his parents on the subject if requested, the so-called middle- and upper-class offspring was presumed to know nothing of such matters until he was knocking at the doors of puberty and frequently not even then. It wasn't true, of course, except on the surface. But at prep schools in the twenties the surface was what mattered and sex was no part of the curriculum.

'Remember, you're English, most of you, and those who aren't will *think* English by the time we've done with you, and that means you'll be a leader. No time for the flesh and the – er – thing, if you're a leader, there's a great big Empire out there waiting to be governed, so remember, with the possible exception of Saturday nights, straight bat, clean shirt, and control is good for the soul.' That was roughly the theory. It didn't always work out that way. Pi had his own methods.

On the last night of term at Normandale it was the custom for those boys who were leaving and going on to higher things to be summoned to the headmaster's bedroom in pyjamas and dressing gown for a ritual known as 'a mug of cocoa and a little chat'. The choice of bedroom and pyjamas instead of study and school uniform was presumably because they were thought to be more appropriate to the subject about to be discussed. They set the scene, as it were. So on my last night I found myself, as head boy, ushering some half-dozen other leavers into Pi's bedroom, where we were instructed to 'grab a mug and take a pew'.

When we had grabbed and were seated, Pi, standing hands clasped behind back, back to unlit gas fire, got straight to business.

'Now you boys who are leaving, you're all thirteen or thereabouts which means that unless there's something seriously wrong you've reached the age of – er – thing. Now you didn't come here just to lark about, you came to be prepared for life. That's why your people sent you here. So before I wave you on your way there's something I want to make sure you've got buttoned up and that's this business of making babies. Battersby, do you want to pump ship?'

'No, sir.'

'Then stop fidgeting, boy. Where was I?'

'Making babies, sir.'

'Right. Now you've all been babies in your time.' This was indisputable. Indeed one could think of some who were babies still. 'So I take it you're old enough to know that when you were born you weren't dropped down your people's chimney by a passing – er – thing.'

Muted hysteria.

Battersby: 'Excuse me, sir, what thing would that be?'

Pi: 'A stork, boy, a stork. I just told you. So. How did you arrive, eh? How did you get here?' Silence. 'Bit of a puzzle, hm? All right, Battersby, you seem to be on the ball, any ideas?'

Battersby had this sort of idea by the gross and had regaled us with a wide selection nightly after lights-out since he was twelve. However, being good-natured as well as naturally dirty-minded he wasn't out to spoil Pi's sexual sermon. So he thrust a fist in his mouth and stared at the floor. Pi pressed on.

Pi: 'Now there'll come a time when you'll probably have babies yourself. That is to say, your wife will actually have the baby but she can't be expected to do it all on her own, can she?'

Emphatic male chorus: 'No, sir!'

Pi: 'No. So that's where you come in with your little – er, contribution.'

Some of us looked out of the window, others at the ceiling. I settled for an intense study of a pair of sculls that crisscrossed the wall above Pi's bed. They were marked 'Insley. Keble College. Stroke'.

Pi (finally): 'Well, I think that's perfectly clear. Just wanted to put you in the picture. Any questions?' Battersby appeared to be about to disintegrate. 'Yes, boy, out with it. What's the problem?' Battersby shook his head in disbelief and succumbed to an elaborate fit of coughing.

'Right. That's it, then. Cherchez la thing and happy landings.'

We rose as a man is perhaps *le mot juste* in the circumstances. As we reached the door Pi called after us.

'Oh, one more thing.' We halted. 'Here's a tip I've always found useful. Any time you're a bit flummoxed and don't know whether you're on your head or your thing, say to yourself 'it's just funny old nature' and think of the *accouchement* of a cow.'

For years afterwards, whenever I saw a herd of dairy cattle standing at anchor in a field, staring at nothing, I would think of Pi's valedictory address and a wave of symbiotic understanding would come over me. Truly, an English education is a wonderful thing.

The BC (Before Charterhouse) hols were spent, at my insistence, seeing as many of the London shows as my mother could afford. She had not changed her attitude to my fascination with the theatre which she could discourage but scarcely deny since she knew precisely where and from whom I got it. However, things were going her way. I was off to Charterhouse for five years in the autumn to continue a formal education and in that time I would grow up and, with luck, grow out of it.

So every Saturday night we would join a gallery queue, hiring a stool for sixpence from the man who had the concession to be sure of a seat, going away for a quick meal and returning half an hour before the curtain. I would then drag Dacre-Hill up the seemingly endless steep stone steps to the gallery ('Come on, come *on!*'), where she would pay eight shillings for a couple of seats in the gods.

All the plays of that era seemed to me marvellous and some of them actually were pretty good. A man called C. L. Anthony, who turned out not to be a man at all but a saleslady at Heal's in Tottenham Court Road named Dodie Smith, wrote a string of hits: *Autumn Crocus, Service, Touch Wood, Call It a Day, Dear Octopus* – I remember them vividly along with my huge enjoyment. In those days audiences had not yet been introduced to kitchen-sink drama by George Devine and the Royal Court Theatre so the plays all had middle- to upper-class backgrounds, were beautifully observed and brilliantly acted by, among many, Fay Compton, Flora Robson, Marie Tempest, John Gielgud, Jack Hawkins and Owen Nares.

We always went to see Owen wherever he was playing, not only because he was a fine actor and my father had been at school with him and my mother worked with him but because he always tipped me a ten-bob note, which at that time was riches and was spent at once on more climbs to the London galleries.

Excited by this bout of theatre-going I made a few minor revisions to my dramatisation of Sabatini's *The Lion's Skin* and declared it ready for production. My mother's agent was a good friend and former actor named Haddon Mason and I decided, after careful thought, that he should have the privilege of becoming my agent, too, and launching my first play. Haddon was a successful agent but I felt that an additional ten per cent to his income from my royalties worldwide would not come amiss. My mother duly gave Haddon the play and he promised to read it at once, or as soon after that as was possible.

Meanwhile I decided that the great impresario, C. B. Cochran, should have the privilege of presenting the piece and, lying on the bed with the *Spotlight* casting directory, immediately began casting. To play Deirdre I chose a promising young newcomer named Celia Johnson with whom I had fallen in love when I had seen her in a play by H. M. Harwood called *Cynara* ('I have been faithful to thee, Cynara, in my fashion'). She was my first love since Rosa the dairymaid but Rosa had betrayed me with the chauffeur and my emotions had long curdled. I swore I would indeed be faithful to Celia (having regretfully turned down Marie Tempest as a shade too old) and as evidence of my constancy she was to be my very first leading lady.

A week went by and no word from Haddon. I couldn't understand it but my mother said he was a very busy man and not to be impatient. After a second week's silence I asked her to telephone the agency. It was clear that he must be seriously ill. No other explanation was possible. After all, he was not just an agent but a family friend and perhaps we should send flowers. Dacre-Hill said she would think about it.

That afternoon, while she was still thinking, a letter arrived by hand. It had been slipped under the door. Every word is written on my heart. It ran:

My dear Dorothy,
I have read Ronnie's play with the greatest interest. You
do realise, don't you, that its running time is exactly
twelve minutes? I know this because that is how long it
took me to read all seventeen pages.

I'm sure he will write a fine play one day. May I keep
this copy as a memento? I promise to return it to him on
his first big first night.

With my fond love to you both, Haddon

PS: There is rather a good joke on page 6. Is that Ronnie
or Sabatini?

It was clear that my life was over but my mother said she wouldn't
go that far and how about the gallery at Drury Lane, where a musical
play called *Glamorous Night* by one Ivor Novello had just opened? I
decided I might as well go along and, after seeing *Glamorous Night*, I
suddenly realised that there *was* something wrong with *The Lion's
Skin*. Well, not exactly *wrong* but missing.

The following morning I took my sole remaining copy to Drury
Lane stage door addressed to Mr Novello, with a note suggesting that
he might care to set it to music. I added that if by any chance he wasn't
available, would he be kind enough to let me know immediately as
my second choice was Elgar and I didn't want to keep him waiting.
A few days later the play came back with a charming note from Ivor
(I already thought of him as a fellow author and therefore first names
were in order) saying that it was very kind of me to think of him but
he was afraid he only wrote music to his own libretti and he hoped
I wouldn't be too upset by this reply as from the handwriting he had
an idea I might be rather young.

I wrote back a brief acknowledgement saying I wasn't in the least
upset and that I wasn't young, I was thirteen years, four months
and two days, and I hoped his show would have some sort of a run
and that he wouldn't be too upset if it didn't, yours ever.

I then turned to Elgar but could find no trace of him in *Spotlight*
and had no idea where he was. Dacre-Hill said he was probably at
that very moment conducting an angel choir in a spirited rendering
of 'Land of Hope and Glory'.

I said coldly I didn't find that very funny and why hadn't she told
me Elgar had died and she said she hadn't known he was my second
choice and I said yes, she did, I'd told her, *I'd told her* and now she'd
made me look a complete idiot with Ivor and she said that by all

41

accounts he was a darling man and she thought he'd have the sophistication to rise above it.

We had quite a spat and I suddenly got fed up with the whole thing and chucked *The Lion's Skin* in a bottom drawer from which it somehow disappeared. I assume Dacre-Hill sent it to the British Museum.

5

. . . .

'Deo Dante Dedi'

In Britain, from the Renaissance onwards, foreign visitors have remarked on the strange native custom of sending ordinary, well-behaved children away from home as soon as possible to the public schools . . . they usually conclude that the English prefer their animals to their children. — The Times *leader*

Charterhouse School, some forty miles from London, is to be found on a hilltop above Godalming in Surrey, one of the more prosperous and, in the thirties, politically Conservative counties in the south of England. (Nowadays the boundaries of political allegiance can't be so readily taken for granted.)

The majestic old stone buildings that are the main school have been so since Charterhouse came down from London in 1872. They seem untouched by time and should be good for several centuries yet. There are still eleven houses, named after their original house-masters, as in my time, but those that were outside the school grounds (including mine) have been moved inside and modernised. This has the advantage of making them more practical and functional but also more uniform which in my view – I'm sorry. One tends to want things to be as they were when one was young. They cannot and, indeed, should not be.

The school motto – 'Deo Dante Dedi' ('God giving I gave') – like most moral prescriptions, is simply devised but hard to live up to. I'm not sure how much, or even whether, I 'gave' at the time. I would like to think I did because my five years on Charterhouse Hill gave me much that I value and cherish with a deep affection. That this would be so was by no means apparent on the evening of 21 September 1933 when I arrived at Pageites (original housemaster one Dr Page – stern of aspect, white of beard, straight out of Central Casting's Edwardian section if the ancient lithograph was to be believed) for the Oration Quarter, or winter term.

At thirteen and a half I was the archetype of your typical 'new

43

bug' – like a midshipman in the Navy, the lowest form of animal life. To go from head boy at one's 'T'otherun', as one's prep school was known, to less than the dust virtually overnight is quite a shock to the system. It's also a useful introduction (if you haven't already had the pleasure) to life's little ups and downs. By the way, any notion you might have that being a 'hash pro' (Carthusian for scholarship boy) gave one some kind of special status can be instantly dismissed. On the contrary, to be a 'hash pro' was felt to be a deliberate reflection on the intellectual capacity of one's fellows. One was regarded as a sort of snooty, superior swot (definitely 'au-de-sus-de-sa-Gare' as the Englishman said in Rattigan's *French Without Tears*) and therefore an object of distaste if not aversion.

I explained there was nothing superior about me, quite the reverse, because my scholarship was the last awarded. 'God, I don't know what this house is coming to. I say, Blomfield, did you hear that? Our hash pro's the bottom of the bunch.' When I said I might not have come bottom if I hadn't been stricken with my fell disease they grabbed a handbell, rang it and cried 'Plague! Plague! The hash pro's got the plague! Bring out your dead!' and various other admonitions before rushing screaming from the Long Room.

This ragging went on for about a week and then stopped as suddenly as it had started. In a strange way I'd rather enjoyed it, I think because it was clearly a tribal ritual and therefore meant that I was being admitted (albeit gradually and grudgingly and at the very bottom of the ladder) to that traditional institution of the Establishment, an English public school. Whether this was, or was not, a good idea was too early for me to judge. The thing was to conform or be walloped. I conformed.

Charterhouse in the thirties, like most of its kind, was pretty spartan. Matthew Arnold's basic concept, unstated but implicit and imported from Rugby by its principal competitors, was that the way to turn that graceless and amorphous animal, a boy, into the collector's piece of Society, an English gentleman, was not to be gentle but to knock the stuffing out of him, start from scratch, and in the vacuum thus created to implant the unique qualities that went to make up that incomparable nonpareil.

For the benefit of the multiracial society in which we now live I am not saying that this always works; I'm saying that Matthew Arnold said it should and that his methods, though immoderate, have not been altogether unsuccessful. Certainly the Armed Forces, adding the word 'officer' to 'gentleman' and omitting the word 'English', had long since adopted them to considerable effect.

The key to it was, of course, discipline – self and enforced by others.

In my time, discipline at Charterhouse, though strict – and stricter when imposed by seniors on juniors than by the masters – was by no means excessive. We fagged for the monitors and kept the best seats for them at school entertainments and were whacked intermittently with a light cane for various misdemeanours of a harmless nature but not – at least not in the house of Dr Page who observed the proceedings dispassionately from above the fireplace – with any particular relish. A caning was symbolic rather than sadistic. What's more, it gave the recipient who endured it without a murmur a certain status and, according to a chum of mine with a positive approach to all misfortune, was at least something to fill up his bally letter home with.

Far harder to take, in my view, was Greek composition on an empty stomach at what seemed like well before dawn. Despite my growing appreciation of the classics, a freezing dark winter's morning and a mug of lukewarm cocoa to get to class on is not, I suggest, all that conducive to a love of ancient literature and I would like to add that, without gloves, the moving finger writes and, having writ, freezes. However, no doubt it was all, as Pi would say, 'preparation for life', which is not, I have since discovered, altogether without pain.

My first glimpse, not of pain exactly, but of the other side of the social coin, came in my second year.

A group of us from Charterhouse-near-Godalming used to go up from time to time to old Charterhouse-in-Southwark (where I had sat my scholarship exam) to kick a football around and have tea and buns with less privileged boys from London's East End. We weren't patronising the disadvantaged and I don't think they thought we were. If they did, they didn't show it. They were tough and cheerful and good hosts and these expeditions were not only a total contrast to our sheltered Carthusian existence but something of a social eye-opener, which is no doubt what they were meant to be. I had not been particularly conscious that the education I was receiving was especially privileged. If it was, I felt – when I thought about it at all because in those days I just got on with things instead of dissecting them – that I had worked hard to be where I was and that anyone else could have had the same advantages if they had done as I had and taken an exam that had given me a ticket to ride.

What was missing, of course, in this superficial analysis of the less fortunate was the prep school years that had prepped me for Charterhouse, just as Charterhouse was prepping me for university.

My mother had had no money to start the ball rolling but my Uncle Jack had and so the all-important first step on the ladder was made possible for me. Without that kick-start I might well have stayed on the ground indefinitely. Luck, a helping hand, and just enough money to get by are necessary for lift-off. All three were granted to me – and thanks are very much in order.

Those East End visits not only jolted me awake, they opened eyes on both sides of the coin and when the war came and the country came together as one nation it was that unity that found the strength to hold out for six years and ultimately led to victory. Am I hinting that a united nation stems only from a Socialist society? The reverse. The one-nation concept was Disraeli, not Karl Marx.

At this point it would be neat and tidy to say that political awareness began for me at Charterhouse but it wouldn't be true. Social studies and the inequality of opportunity of pre-war society were not a part of the curriculum and I was more concerned with obtaining a senior scholarship (which without a single whoop I managed rather more comfortably than the junior one) and appearing in school productions of Ǩarel Capek's *R.U.R.*, Auden and Isherwood's *The Ascent of F6* and a light-hearted revue *All Alight at Scholar's Court* which I co-wrote and appeared in. I also conducted the orchestra wearing a pair of white gloves.

My friends told me the gloves were quite unnecessary and that even Sir Thomas Beecham managed without them but I insisted, explaining that I needed to be seen in the dark. The revue was a great success and the school loved every minute, but the highly regarded Robert Birley, who had come from Eton to succeed my dear Sir Frank Fletcher as headmaster, didn't care for it. 'This must never happen again,' he said. Since it was clean as a whistle I think he must have been rehearsing for his future job of re-educating the German people after Hitler's war.

Another disapproving voice was that of my housemaster, A. L. Irvine, who was also form master of the Classical Sixth, so his influence upon me was all-embracing. Pink, plump, shy, and Dickensian, with a head like an egg and known to all as The Uncle, Irvine was a 'Character' in the Pi class, though entirely different. When Pi turned up one day in the Flying Bedstead and invited himself to lunch, The Uncle sat speechless and bewildered throughout the meal while Pi held forth in animated discourse, sentence after sentence trailing off into 'er – thing' and 'er – there' so that it was impossible even for an experienced Pi-listener like me to make out what on earth he was talking about. After we'd waved him off down the hill, the Bedstead backfiring as usual, The Uncle turned to me and said, 'He's mad, of course.' It was a statement not a question. As Pi had said much the same to me about The Uncle who had scarcely spoken ('Is he quite right in the er – thing?') I felt discretion was the better part of eccentricity and gave an enigmatic shrug.

Despite his constant discouragement of my theatrical activities – how was I to know that he was acting under orders from my adored but ridiculous Dacre-Hill? – I loved The Uncle. (How appalled he would have been to hear one of his former pupils speak of love.) His pronunciation of certain words was, to me at least, unique. In The Uncle's world you heard with your 'years', you played 'larn tennis' and of course golf wasn't golf, it was 'goff'.

I only once defeated him in verbal conflict and that was when I was a new bug. During prep (known as 'Banco') I licked my finger to turn a page. He tapped me on the shoulder and said with the utmost gravity, 'Have you ever seen a gentleman do that?' 'Yes, sir. My uncle Jack Cotman does it all the time and he's the finest gentleman I know.' Uncle Irvine gave a sigh to shatter windows, hid his face behind the thumb and forefinger of his left hand and moved on.

He was a strange mixture, The Uncle. For all his eccentricities and suppressed emotions which we, his charges, were encouraged to emulate, he had the classicist's almost childlike sense of humour. In spite of his habitual reserve, this occasionally burst forth. There was an ancient ex-Bursar known as The Colonel (he had probably been a colonel in the Wars of the Roses) who still lived near the school and The Uncle was fond of telling and retelling over and over how one day the Colonel needed a new pair of shoes. 'So where did he go for them?' We had heard the answer a thousand times but would have strangled anyone who dared to utter.

'Where, sir?'

'Boots!' cried The Uncle. 'Boots, Boots, Boots!'

At which he would convulse with mirth until his eyes swam and the water poured down his cheeks and mopping-up began with a huge coloured handkerchief. (One day some years later when he had come to London for a matinée of a play of mine and we were having tea at the Waldorf he confessed he had made the Boots story up.)

The Uncle loved the classics and, along with Charterhouse and cricket, seemed to live for them but his innate reserve made it hard for him to communicate his burning enthusiasm unless a boy shared that love already so he was not quite the first-class teacher that he might have been. He also appeared to dislike the theatre unless it was Sophocles (*Antigone*) or Aristophanes (*The Birds* or *The Frogs*) but perhaps it was just that my mother had got at him and he was merely pretending.

He had a charming wife whom he adored but in front of us liked to pretend was a scatterbrain ('My dear, if you really think Glasgow is the capital of Wales there's no more to be said') and three spirited children. On one occasion they dragged him to London to see the long-running musical *Me and My Girl*, starring Lupino Lane, at the Victoria Palace. I asked him if he had enjoyed it.

Deep sigh. 'No.'

'Sorry about that, sir. What was wrong with it?'

'The title. Bad grammar, you know.'

It's 1936 and the whole of Pageites is assembled in Matron's room to listen to Edward VIII's abdication on the wireless. History is happening before our very ears. '... *I have found it impossible to carry the heavy burden of responsibility and to discharge my duties as King without the help and support of the woman I love* ... '

A. L. Irvine, housemaster, covers his face with the thumb and forefinger of his left hand, as he does in class when listening to one of his pupils murder the classics. What, if any, are his emotions? Is he moved? Is he bored? Has the King let the side down? There is no way of knowing, which of course is his intention.

We Pageites are on the side of the King to a man, or rather a growing and ignorant boy. To us, Baldwin is a cold heartless cad without an ounce of charity or romance in his soul.

'How *could* he?' asks one of the juniors in tears.

'He's a politician,' I answer with disdain. 'What else can one expect?' Mrs Simpson wasn't my cup of coffee, but if she was the King's, why not?

From which it can safely be concluded that my heart ruled my head and that my knowledge of politics and the rights and wrongs of the grave constitutional issues involved was nonexistent.

It's the last term of my last year and God, if there is one, is benignly in his heaven, all is most decidedly right with my world.

Thanks to seniority and my senior scholarship I'm head of the house, a school monitor and among the higher echelons of the Classical Sixth. In addition I have a Greek Exhibition to King's College, Cambridge, in the bag, so there's very little work to do. There's cricket on Green, and O. C. Day, and white flannels and strawberries and cream from Crown, the tuckshop, where old Ma D behind the counter inquires of her daughter, 'How much are these tuppenny bars, Floss?'

Late at night, long after lights-out during those last weeks at Charterhouse, a group of my special friends – among them Ben Travers Junior, son of playwright Ben, and J. D. P. ('Hoppy') Tanner who was to become an international soccer star – broke every rule in the school book and gathered in my study to listen to Noël Coward and Gertrude Lawrence on gramophone records with handkerchiefs stuffed down the soundbox to cushion the volume: *Private Lives* – the balcony scene from Act I plus 'Some Day I'll Find You' – and the same immaculate couple in *To-Night at 8.30*, nine playlets full of the inimitable clipped dialogue laced with Coward lyrics and music. Feeling wildly sophisticated and clandestine we sip cheap smuggled wine out of toothmugs.

This is the life. 'Floreat aeterna Carthusiana Domus.' Not a cloud on the horizon. Not one? Think. It's the summer of 1938. Well, yes, of course, there's that bloody man Hitler. Apparently, throughout my time at Charterhouse, Germany has been rearming and now the European dominoes have begun to fall. The Rhineland has been reoccupied, the Sudetenland has gone, it looks like Czechoslovakia will follow and what's all this about something called an Anschluss? Perhaps the Austrians *want* to be part of the German empire. After all, they were part of Hungary's or was it the other way round?

I realise that if there's a war I'm just the age for it, but it would be false to pretend I've seen it coming. No shame in that. Practically no one else has either, except Mr Churchill, who keeps calling for Britain and the United States and the rest of the free world to wake up and rearm against the growing German menace, but he's in the wilderness and few are listening. It's Mr Chamberlain at Number Ten and he seems to have everything, as Pi would say, buttoned up.

However, the public schools have not entirely ignored the situation. Here at Charterhouse we've been playing at soldiers once a week for five years in the Officers Training Corps, though I fancy if Hitler could see us he wouldn't be all that alarmed. Still, the OTC is a start and the second-hand khaki uniforms take me back to my childhood and the sepia snaps of World War I. Only the mud and the blood are missing. For the moment, that is.

And now it's the last night of the summer term and there's sweet singing in the choir at the final service in the magnificent Memorial Chapel to those who gave their lives in the War of 1914–18. It's three years since I was confirmed here and took my first communion. Confirmed in what? In wanting to believe. *Wanting* to. That at least, and surely that's something, or am I to be weighed in the balance and found – yes, precisely – wanting?

As we go in I stand a moment and look at the names of the fallen on the walls at the north entrance and wonder, idly, if mine will one day soon be up there with them. Are we to be the successors of that doomed generation that died in the war to end all wars? The thought passes and I take my seat in the choirstalls.

We're in fine voice tonight. The long summer holidays lie ahead and this final service is always moving, especially for those who aren't coming back. They say you blub when Tippy Fielden at the organ starts the final chords of the final hymn, 'Lord, dismiss us with thy blessing'. Oh, come on, don't be wet. You're far too old to be awash with sentimental schoolboy tears. But when the time comes – confound that blasted tune, I can hold out against the words, it's the music that gets me every time – I blub with the best of them.

Not for long, though. As we come out into the early summer evening of 1938 and I start slowly down the road to Pageites for the last time as a member of the school I stop and linger a moment on the bridge at the top of Charterhouse Hill and look down over the valley. It's been a pretty good five years and I'm deeply grateful to this privileged place for what it has given me and which I've learnt to love, but there's Cambridge to come and the prospect delights (they say the Cambridge girls have smashing legs).

Meanwhile it may be calendar summer on Charterhouse Hill but for me and my generation it's spring time, the only pretty ring time, as the Bard observed. It won't last, of course, but while it does, with a hey and a ho and a hey nonny no, the hell with Hitler. We're young and alive and there ain't gonna be no war and we're not going to die, not at his behest anyway, and not while the sun shines strong on our fleeting and more than a little ridiculous youth.

Who says the best is yet to come? Why, I do. *I* do.

6

. . . .

Light Blue and Light Hearted

Autumn 1938 – and a chill in the air.

I'd been to the cinema: Bing Crosby and Donald O'Connor in *Pennies from Heaven* ('Every time it rains it rains... don't you know each cloud contains' et cetera). A tuneful piece of Hollywood Americana, typically optimistic, that normally would have had me humming all the way home but as I came out of the Plaza into Piccadilly music and movie had gone from my mind.

What remained, and still remains, was the Gaumont-British newsreel of Neville Chamberlain coming down the aircraft steps at Heston Airport on his return from Munich and the tall, increasingly haggard figure of the Prime Minister with his old-fashioned wing collar, bushy moustache and umbrella waving his already famous piece of paper (it had been front and centre of every national newspaper that morning).

During September, accompanied by Sir Horace Wilson, his special adviser, and Alec Douglas-Home, his Parliamentary Private Secretary, he had flown to Berchtesgaden and Bad Godesberg, seeking a settlement with Adolf Hitler that would meet the German dictator's territorial requirements and dissuade him from seizing any more of Europe than he had already acquired. Each time he had come back empty-handed.

But now apparently, on the last day of September, it was third time lucky. With the so-called Munich Agreement in his pocket he clearly believed he had pulled it off. 'It bears Herr Hitler's signature as well as mine,' he cried, proudly waving his piece of paper before

51

returning to Downing Street and proclaiming 'Peace in our time' from an upstairs window.

I shuddered. I'm not being wise after the event. All the adolescent optimism of my last night at Charterhouse had vanished and I felt, with that certainty about a future happening that comes occasionally in a lifetime, that World War II was now a fixture. Only the date was missing.

A fortnight later I went up to Cambridge to begin my Freshman year. By the time I had checked in at that most beautiful of colleges, King's, built on the banks of the Cam with a chapel even more beautiful than the Charterhouse Memorial, what I saw as the coming conflict had completely changed my attitude to my time at university.

My thoughts went something like this:

(a) Wars are for young men and if you're young and fit they'll send for you.

(b) Since there's going to be a war there's little point in preparing oneself for peace.

(c) As an Exhibitioner of the College a respectable minimum of work will be expected. I'll meet that minimum but I won't strive beyond it. For my first year I'll take it easy. If war has not come within twelve months and the danger has passed or at worst receded, then for the rest of my university career I'll make up for lost time and go flat out for the best degree I can manage.

Meanwhile, I would enjoy life while the going was good, and by all accounts there was a rich variety of ways in which enjoyment could be practised at the University of Cambridge. And that's how it was for one whole year.

A brief digression.

A Colonel Jardine, who had a small son at Pageites, had told The Uncle that if he knew of a scholarship boy worth sending to university whose family would still be short of funds with which to do so, he would like to help. On one condition: *that the boy knew nothing about it.* It was not until long after the war that I learnt of my unknown benefactor. It's not cruelty that brings tears to the eyes, it's goodness, unadulterated secret goodness.

As with all Freshmen, leaflets inviting one to join this, that and the other club, society or union were slid under one's door almost daily. I signed them with a fine abandon, half the time scarcely bothering to read them, determined as I was to plunge headlong into the traffic of Cambridge life, with special reference to the traffic of the stage.

Within a week I had joined three dramatic clubs: the Footlights, the ADC and the Marlowe (which included Shakespeare). I had had rules and regulations up to here since I was five and a half. Suddenly the sense of freedom was prodigious. I thought of Rupert Brooke at King's before World War I, trying to concentrate on the classics. Knowing nothing of Colonel Jardine, I wasn't even going to try. My mind was on the theatre and girls and books, not Latin and Greek books but modern English authors of whom I knew next to nothing.

After a month I went home for the weekend and told my mother as much about my carefree existence as I thought was good for her peace of mind – and mine. When I came to the theatrical side of my activities she looked hard at me, then shrugged. She had tried to point me in a different direction and had partially succeeded, but that didn't matter now. She could read the runes as well as the next mum. It was *my* life now and please God it lasted. All that mattered was my survival.

It was a brave performance but when I realised that her defences were almost down I gave them one last gentle push.

'Would you believe it,' I murmured, 'three of the senior dons at King's are theatre-minded to their fingertips. There's Dadie Rylands who runs the Marlowe [a Shakespearian producer of repute so high that he'd actually directed John Gielgud at the Haymarket], and the Senior Tutor, Donald Beves [a wealthy bachelor and keen actor who with Dadie was an integral part of the annual Footlights Revue], not to mention Provost Jack Sheppard who produces the Greek play every four years. How about that then?' I didn't gloat, at least not openly. 'A happy accident, one might say. Of course, there are those – I'm not saying I'm one of them – but there are people who might feel that, far from an accident, the hand of Fate had intervened, pointing to a future that's beginning to appear – how should I put it? – fractionally preordained?'

I managed to duck just in time as, for some extraordinary reason, a woman I would have regarded as second only to Mother Teresa, had I known of Mother Teresa at the time, began hurling the cushions at me.

The ADC had its own theatre and when they found I could play piano after a fashion they put me in the orchestra pit for the Christmas pantomime with Donald McWhinnie (later to become a leading television director). We may not have been Rawicz and Landauer but we kept together some of the time and when we did, a not unpleasing sound emerged.

On the third night at the interval, as I was about to go to the pub for a beer, I received a note summoning me to the Provost's Lodge 'quam celerime'. I dropped the note on Donald's music stand and biked off through the rain to King's, wondering if I was about to be sent down and if so, why. The drawing room of the Lodge was crammed with undergraduates from various colleges, each holding a text of something in his hand.

'What's this?' I hissed at one of them.

'Audition for you know what,' he hissed back.

I didn't, but before I could inquire further the Provost, a kind of academic Father Christmas in a black gown and mortarboard – plumpish, medium height, flowing silver locks, horn-rimmed spectacles – spotted me.

'Ah, they found you, dear boy. Bless you, bless you.'

The Provost blessed everyone indiscriminately. I had seen little of him in the eight weeks since I came up but whenever we had passed in the Quad I'd been beamed at and blessed, though the benign exterior could be deceptive. So was his age: somewhere in the fifties and agile as a monkey, he played eighty, padding about with a rubber-pointed stick which he would instantly discard if he needed to chase somebody. Provost Sheppard was the Character of Characters and, incidentally, the second-best theatrical director I have ever worked with.

'You've got your *Antigone* with you?'

'No, sir, I – '

'Here, take mine.'

'No, no – '

'I know it by heart, bless you.'

He thrust the text at me and the penny dropped. This was an audition for the Greek play.

'Now, my dears, settle. As you know, or ought to know, Sophocles wrote for a large cast so I'm going to get each of you to read a few lines of this immortal tragedy so that we can decide which of you shall be in the chorus, which shall carry a spear and which shall play Antigone and Ismene and the rest, including of course Creon, tyrant of Thebes, who has some of the loveliest poetry which he certainly doesn't deserve because he was a monster of authority but that's poetic licence, many of the worst people have the best lines in literature as in life, as you'll discover when you go down and if you don't believe me have a word with Master Shakespeare who knew all about these things.

'Now, hands up those who can sing? Because over there at the piano is Paddy Hadley who has written some glorious music for us. Four years ago when we did *The Frogs* Vaughan Williams was our composer, as some of you will remember. Well, this time it's Paddy and he's just as good as V.W. if not better, aren't you, Paddy?' (Paddy was a youngish don whose lectures on the great composers were already famous.) 'Right, we'll sort out the singers later. First the principals. Now, let me see, page eleven. You read Antigone' (pointing at a good-looking fair-haired boy) 'and you read Ismene, bless you' (pointing at me) 'and *you* read Creon' (pointing at a huge undergraduate with a Saddam Hussein moustache who looked as if he should be auditioning for the Boat Race). 'Good. Off we go.'

I glanced at my watch. The second half must have started.

'Excuse me, Provost.'

'Yes, dear boy?'

'I'm playing in the pit at the panto and – '

'You're doing what, my dear?'

'The pantomime at the ADC. I'm second piano.'

'Let me be the first to congratulate you.'

'The thing is, I'm terribly sorry but I have to go.'

'Go? Dear boy, I don't want to seem presumptuous but life does have its little priorities and in the hierarchy of dramatic art I can't help feeling *Antigone* takes precedence over *Mother Goose*. Or are you a Socialist?' No, I wasn't a Socialist. 'That's all right then. Now if someone would close the door, may we begin?'

I managed to make it back to the panto in time for the national anthem in which I played several harmonies that had never been heard before. McWhinnie took off his glasses and polished them.

'Nice to see you again. What happened?'

'Don't ask.'

What had happened was the Provost's original casting hadn't worked and he kept shuffling the pack this way and that between blessings. 'Saddam Hussein' had long gone and in fact did row in the Cambridge boat that year (we won). At one point I was Antigone and Antigone was Ismene, then we swapped and finally both wound up in the chorus. I kept looking pointedly at my watch but the Provost pretended not to notice.

Finally when he'd settled on Antigone and Ismene but was still without a tyrant of Thebes he murmured, 'I wonder. I just ... ' (long pause) 'wonder. Come here, dear boy.'

Nobody moved. He beckoned in my direction. I looked behind and on either side of me. 'No, you, dear boy. Here.'

'Me?'

'Yes, you. Come.'

I edged very slowly forward.

'Read Creon's opening speech for me, would you?'

Oh, no. No, I wouldn't. I'd rather be sent down. Creon was the largest part and anyway I looked about as tyrannical as Mother Goose's pet rabbit.

'Read, dear boy.'

I read, choked, stumbled.

'Again.'

I read it again. He let everyone go except Paddy Hadley. Eventually: 'What do you think, Paddy?'

I signalled a furious 'no' at Paddy but he winked and gave a thumbs-up. The Provost poured a glass of sherry and handed it to me. I gulped it down.

'It's going to need a lot of work, but we'll try, we'll try.'

'No. Please. I'd be delighted to carry a spear for you but – '

'What's the matter? Scared?'

'Terrified.'

'So am I but someone must carry the flag and you're our Greek Exhibitioner.'

That was no reason for making an exhibition of myself, I thought but didn't say.

'And you have a voice which carries. Isn't your mother an actress?' He frowned with sudden concentration. 'Could I by any chance have seen her as Titania in *The Dream* at the Open Air Theatre?'

My heart sank. I guessed what was coming. Yes, he could have.

'Brave lady. I remember thinking at the time she must have been so cold out there, without so much as a bay leaf.'

First the headmaster of Charterhouse, now the Provost of King's. Was there no end to this academic pursuit of my mother in a state of nature?

'Cheer up, bless you. You can handle it. Paddy, play him his entrance music. You'll love this.'

I did indeed love the music. It was brilliant, powerful, tremendous. But when someone has just signed a warrant for your execution I doubt if Verdi's *Requiem* is much of a help.

'Bene, bene! Benissimo!' cried Sheppard, embracing Paddy in an ecstasy. 'Let me paint the picture for you. There's this great procession filing slowly in, with Paddy at the Hammond organ and the orchestra building the excitement as the mighty King of Thebes approaches and the chorus hails him and summons him and the music hails him and summons him and the excitement builds until at last everyone turns and makes their obeisance and suddenly – suddenly – there he is! Or rather, there you are, bless you. On your personal rostrum. Quite alone. Lord of all you survey ... A silence falls. You wait, holding the audience in the palm of your hand ... and then at last

56

you begin that first great speech. Slowly, very slowly at first but gradually gathering pace.' He took off into the speech which I thought he was going to give in its entirety but he suddenly stopped.

'Miraculous. On and on you go, one magical iambic pentameter following another until the superb climacteric.' He took out a handkerchief. My God, he was weeping. 'Oh, Sophocles was a mighty poet. A mighty poet and a mighty dramatist. Yes, indeed, he knew his stuff, did Sophocles.'

I never doubted that Sophocles knew his stuff. My problem was, would *I* ever know his stuff?

During the Christmas holidays, wherever I go, Creon goes. It's like James Stewart and that rabbit Harvey. I recite the opening speech in bed, in the bath, over breakfast, at the cinema, in the gallery on our theatre nights. Whatever is happening on stage, whatever play the actors are performing, up in the gallery another one is going on in my head or a desperate undertone.

'Ssh!' goes half the gallery.

'Ssh!' goes my mother.

'Really, love,' she says on the bus going home, 'you can't go on like this.'

'That's the point, I don't want to go on. Nunc dimittis. Please! I'll never learn the damn thing.'

'Yes, you will, don't be silly.'

'But I don't look remotely like a tyrant!'

'Oh I don't know. Well, not yet perhaps, but you will. Yes, come to think of it, you'll make rather a good tyrant. Dig deep and find the walk. That's the way to find the part.'

This enthusiasm is weird. Particularly since, to Dorothy a son, Dacre-Hill has been the antithesis of Mrs Worthington. Suddenly I realise what has happened. The theatre and the classics have come together and now – now, when the last thing I want is to act, now she is tickled pink at the prospect. How Greek. How unspeakably, in every sense, Greek.

I recite Creon in my sleep. Sleep? MacProvost hath murdered sleep.

I have this nightmare. Paddy gives me the build-up with his grand chorale. The chorus and the spear-carriers process. And suddenly there's my cue and there I am on my personal blasted rostrum looking pretty damned magnificent. In shimmering full-length costume, a belt with diamond-studded daggers at my waist and on my head the golden crown of Thebes. What happens next? Silence, that's what happens next. Everyone waits for the great man to utter. Not a word, not a syllable. I stand there, turned to stone. Finally I open my mouth and a croak comes out. A truly ghastly croak. I give a glazed smile and the chorus stares at me aghast. So does the audience. I break out in a cold sweat and stumble, still croaking, into the wings – where I wake up with the bedclothes in a twisted heap on the floor.

I tell Dacre-Hill about it. 'If only I could get started. I might, I just might – be able to continue. But I can't begin. I dry every time at the first hurdle. It's sheer terror, of course. Panic. But I blow. I dry. What *am* I to do if I dry?'

'What everyone else does when they dry. Ad-lib.'

'In Greek??'

Back at Cambridge for my second term I tried to chicken out. Dadie Rylands had offered me Malcolm in his production of 'the Scottish Play' which was to follow *Antigone* at the Arts Theatre. There were still six weeks to go. Time to find another Creon and beat the Spaniards too. Dadie promised to press his prior claim but the Provost pulled rank.

I suddenly realised why he had chosen me to play Creon. As a Kingsman, I'd be on site to rehearse 'whenever I can find a spare minute, bless you'. He found a lot of spare minutes, usually at the end of the day which extended into the night as he coached me tirelessly in the diction, authority, stress, accent, emphasis and variety of tone required for 'this mighty masterpiece of ancient drama I have entrusted to your care, dear boy. You do understand what's required?'

'Yes, I know, I know what you want, but I can't get it, I'll never get the bloody thing!'

'You're beginning to persuade me. Have a chocolate.'

I could see he was becoming as desperate as I was. Whenever he was desperate I got a chocolate, which did nothing for me except make me feel sick.

He ran a hand through his white locks for the nth time. 'Now listen, my dear.' He was off again, very soft and gentle which meant an outburst was coming any minute. 'Try, if you'll be so kind, to grasp the fact that ninety-five per cent of your audience won't understand a word you're saying. They'll just about know the plot because it's in the programme but that's all. There'll be schoolboys and schoolgirls and Boy Scouts and Girl Guides and all sorts of peculiar people like that so you have to learn to get across to them the *essence* of what you are saying by – by the *intensity* of your interpretation – by the, heaven help us, sheer force of your *personality*, dear heart. Now do you by any chance follow a fraction of what I am trying to convey to you or shall we both go down on our knees and pray to Almighty Zeus, Apollo, Neptune, Mars and if all else fails, Aphrodite, for divine assistance?'

Silence. 'I'll try again.'

I tried again.

'No, no, no, no, *no!*' He tore off his gown, sat on a sofa and held his head in his hands. Having three or four wisdom teeth extracted would be preferable to this.

'I'm very sorry, Provost,' I said oh so quietly, 'but if you don't mind I'd like to resign.'

'What was that, dear boy?'

'I think it's best. Truly. You'll find someone. Goodnight, sir.'

As I came out of the Lodge, dawn was breaking over the river. Homer was right. It *was* rosy-fingered.

I thought of throwing myself in the water, decided against and wandered back to my rooms where I threw myself on the bed instead. Sophocles saw life as ceaseless suffering and mankind as the plaything of the gods. Plaything of the Provost more like, plaything of the Provost. As for all that bloody old Greek carnage, who needed it? Not I, not I, not I . . . Three hours later I was woken by a knocking at the door. I staggered up.

'Morning, sir. Lovely morning. Draw the curtains for you, shall I?' It was the Provost's hearty manservant in nerve-shattering form. 'Provost's compliments, sir, and he looks forward to seeing you at lunch, sir. Just a reminder.'

'But he never said anything about lunch. You must have made a mistake.'

'No mistake, sir. One o'clock at the Lodge. Thank you, sir.'

Reminder my foot. Not all the wheedling in the world or all the chocolates would change my mind. No, *sir*. If the Greeks had a word for it, I had a word for *them*.

When I arrived at the Lodge I was surprised to find two other guests.

'Ah, dear boy. There you are. Bravo. Come in, bless you, come in. You know our distinguished Bursar, Maynard Keynes, of course, and Mrs Keynes, the former, and never to be equalled as Giselle, Lopokova. Ronald here is a passionate balletomane so you'll have lots to talk about.' (I wasn't, so blow that for a lark.) 'I've been telling Lydia and Maynard how excited I am about your Creon and they can't wait for the first night. In fact, we've just opened a bottle of Louis Roederer as a little advance celebration. You do like champagne? Of course you do. You know, Maynard, I've produced not a few undergraduates in my time and I think I know one or two little things about actors and acting but I have no hesitation in saying that Ronald here is quite the most ... now what's the word I'm after? ... remarkable, that's it ... most remarkable performer I have encountered. The great thing about him is, if I venture a small suggestion, he's on to it like a flash. On to it? He's ahead of me. By Jove, he's fast. We're having the greatest fun working together, aren't we, dear boy? Do sit down, I hope you like oysters. You deserve them, indeed you do, my dear, bless you.'

One of the things I learnt at university was to know when one is beaten. This was the moment that I learnt it.

Dress parades are depressing things and I wandered on to the stage of the Arts Theatre and stood there feeling self-conscious and foolish.

Sheppard: 'Oh, dear me, dear boy, whatever's happened? You look about as malevolent as our illustrious founder, Henry the Good.' One look in the mirror and I knew that. Lorenz Hart probably had me in mind when he asked

Is your figure less than Greek
Is your mouth a little weak
When you open it to speak
Are you smart?

That at least would not be a problem. When I opened it to speak nothing would come out.

It was Donald Beves who came to the rescue. 'He'll be fine when he's made up. Leave him to me.' By the time Donald had done I looked a cross between Charles Laughton as Bligh of the *Bounty* enjoying the flogging of a mutineer while chewing on a lobster claw and Alastair Sim as Captain Hook licking his lips and chortling delight as the pirates closed on Peter Pan.

I cannot pass by Donald Beves without mentioning that he was posthumously reported – by *The Times*, no less – as possibly 'the Fourth Man' (Burgess and Maclean being two of the other three) in the notorious Russian spy affair. The Fourth Man was known to be a senior Cambridge figure whose surname consisted of five letters and began with a 'B'. The solution was of course Blunt, not Beves, but if Blunt had not survived to be named and exposed the late Donald, lovely man, could have gone down in history branded as a traitor.

The final dress rehearsal before an invited audience of friends went well, often a bad sign. It's the paying customers, who are neutral, that you have to please. I had the beginning of a headcold which made me slightly hoarse but my nerves were under control and I kept going without a prompt.

The Provost was moderately satisfied but warned the company that tomorrow would be a much more critical audience, he wanted more emotion and more bite, and might he remind us that what we were engaged in performing was a Greek tragedy, not *Showboat?* After which he wished us a good night's sleep and departed with a cascade of benedictions.

I hardly slept, the opening speech going into automatic pilot which I couldn't switch off, and by morning my cold was a lot worse. I reached the theatre at least an hour too early and sat staring at myself in the dressing-room mirror with a sense of impending disaster. I never felt or looked less tyrannical. My voice, affected by my cold, sounded unrecognisable. Paddy Hadley also arrived early to check his Hammond organ and looked in on me.

'All right?'

'No. Something's happened to my voice. Listen.' I spoke my opening lines. 'What the devil am I going to do?'

Paddy stared. 'But that's marvellous! Don't do anything! That's it! That's Creon! How did you manage it?'

'I caught a cold.'

'Well, hang on to it. It's deepened your voice by at least four semitones. Just what the doctor ordered. Good luck, you idiot.'

From that moment I knew it was going to be all right, except that standing in the wings in a trance, waiting for my cue which was the first chord of the last four bars of Paddy's majestic entrance music, I was thinking what a friend the man was and what a marvellous composer when I missed the damn cue and would have been off if I hadn't been goosed in the right buttock by the leader of the Palace Guard immediately behind me with the point of his spear. (None of your plastic rubbish in those days, this was the real McCoy.) First-aid and Elastoplast were administered at the interval and I was obliged whenever I sat on my throne to lean on the other buttock for the rest of the run.

Was *Antigone* a success? Well, my mother came and said, 'You were very masterful but the tip of your nose looked red and you sounded as if you had a cold' which wasn't quite the effect I'd been aiming for. The Greek Ambassador came twice and said we were all wonderful several times in Ancient Greek. Pi came by train – the Bedstead having finally been put to bed – and told the Provost that the whole thing was absolutely thing.

Finally, The Uncle came and sat in the second row at the Saturday matinée, hand and forefinger covering face throughout so that absolutely nothing of his reaction could be detected. However, when he came round to my minute dressing room under the stage he uncovered long enough to murmur, 'Well, no doubt you're glad that's over' in a voice that made clear he shared my presumed emotion. As he made to leave he turned suddenly and said, 'You weren't too bad in the final scene. Almost moving. Does your mother know you're performing?'

'Of course.'

He sighed. 'Tell her I did my best, will you?' and departed, hand and forefinger clapped across face and mouth as though he had said too much already.

My own view is that *Antigone* '39 at Cambridge had more pluses going for it than minuses, due largely to the Provost's perceptive direction – he could be as professionally sensitive as personally fierce (in which theatrically speaking he is not alone) – and Paddy Hadley's marvellous score. The applause when Paddy limped on stage – he had a wooden leg – to take a reluctant curtain call topped even the Provost's.

As for that remarkable Character, on the last night after blessing everyone in sight he threw his arms around me and embraced me, crying for all to hear, 'I *knew* you could be absolutely beastly if you tried, bless you! O what *brutes* we mortals be! One only has to tap the right vein – and I tapped yours, didn't I? Indeed I did. I know you thought me the most fearful bully and I probably am but I had to get rid of Reading, Berkshire, and release the murderous monster that lies lurking in the soul of man,' and a whole lot more in similar strain interspersed with blessings and embraces until suddenly he came down to earth with, 'And now, dear boy, we must put the ever-beguiling theatre behind us and do some real work.'

Somehow I failed to find the time.

From the sublime to the sublimely innocent. At Cambridge, May Week is the first week in June, which was also the title of the Footlights Revue of 1939. With the German army poised to strike, the mood was light-hearted and light-headed even by undergraduate standards. If it was not quite the Duchess of Richmond's Ball, it was the Last of the Summer Wine before once again the lights went out all over Europe.

Among its attractions were the future Attorney-General in Edward Heath's Government, Lord Rawlinson, who played my wife in one sketch, and in the second half a remarkable tour-de-force by one

Jimmy Edwards (undergraduate) in which he played the fool with the trombone and brought the house down. Further evidence of his talent was manifest even before the Footlights Revue. Donald Wolfit had brought his production of *Julius Caesar* to Cambridge and called for undergraduates to supply the Roman mob (well, it saved money, you see, and Donald, extravagant as your aunt on stage, was inclined to be rather less so off it).

Wearing plain white shifts and a funereal mien J. Edwards and I carried the bier of the dead Caesar in procession downstage, preceded and guided, with his back to the audience, by Donald as Mark Antony. At the opening performance James lost his sense of direction and headed for the orchestra pit. When Donald asked in a stage whisper what the hell he thought he was doing, Edwards replied in his normal voice, 'I'm only here for the bier.' The audience roared and Donald looked daggers. Shakespeare, I think, would definitely have cared for it.

The summer holidays came and went under a cloud of foreboding which finally burst with Hitler's invasion of Poland on 1 September, followed, at eleven o'clock on the morning of Sunday 3 September, by Britain's declaration of war with Germany.

My mother and I were up ninety-four stairs in the top-floor flat at 64 Pont Street, immediately opposite the Scottish church (subsequently reduced to rubble in the Blitz) when, a few minutes after eleven, the air-raid siren warning of imminent attack began to wail. They haven't wasted much time, I thought. Well, at least we'd have a first-class view of the bombers when they arrived. I climbed up the emergency exit on to the roof with a pair of binoculars but the sky was silent and clear of aircraft; only a canopy of barrage balloons hung like inflated sausages over London. Outwardly it was just like any other peaceful Sunday morning. All was still, as though the great city was holding its breath.

Twenty minutes later the all-clear sounded. It was a false alarm. As were the months of 'the Phoney War' that followed.

When word came for undergraduates to return to their studies and carry on as usual it seemed extraordinary. Poland had fallen to the German army. Surely, if one wasn't actually required to fight yet, what one should be studying was Clausewitz or Napoleon or Alexander, not Aeschylus and Tacitus and Homer. I telephoned my aged tutor who listened politely and said, 'You don't feel Thucydides on war might possibly prove illuminating?' He was a dear old duck and I liked him so I went back to King's.

Within a few days I received a typed letter from something called a Joint Selection Board, thanking me for my declaration, requesting me to report for interview the following week at such-and-such an address and to bring a birth certificate and any medical records that might be relevant.

Relevant to what? And what declaration was I being thanked for? I didn't remember declaring anything. I asked around and found that several friends had received similar communications. Was this some kind of Fifth Column activity? Or a joke, perhaps? Undergraduates were given to this kind of leg-pull. In wartime? There was no war this side of the Channel. Not yet.

The only way to get to the bottom of it was to follow instructions. So on the appointed day at the appointed hour – 'Ten a.m. and please be prompt' – I duly turned up at a large first-floor suite of rooms in a building near the Senate House. The rooms, which were full of undergraduates milling about, were bare of furniture apart from a series of desks on which were pen and paper and what looked like a form of some kind with wastepaper baskets stationed at strategic intervals.

There were also half-a-dozen older men moving about in a vaguely reassuring manner answering questions and requesting people to sit down and fill in something. Amongst them I suddenly spotted a familiar figure with a limp.

'Paddy!'

'Hello, King of King's.' It was the nickname I had been tagged with during *Antigone*, linking Thebes and my college in semi-blasphemous conjunction.

'Paddy, what are you doing here?'

'Helping to sort out all you eager beavers. I didn't know you'd volunteered.'

I didn't know either. 'What am I supposed to have volunteered for?'

'Kicking Der Führer in the balls.'

'I never volunteered to do that. I mean, I'm quite happy to but no one's asked me.'

'In that case, there's been a cock-up, which wouldn't surprise me. Hang on a second.' He vanished and returned in a moment, waving a piece of pink paper.

'That your signature?'

I stared. 'How did that get there?'

'You put it there, I imagine. Soon after Munich leaflets were shoved under college doors, you must have had one, asking for volunteers in the event of a war. Well, there seems to be one.'

So that was it. Of *course*, I'd practically never read the stuff that came whizzing under my door. I'd just signed blindly in my desire to be in the thick of Cambridge life.

'Okay, I'll play. What do I do?'

'Sit down and read that.'

Paddy pushed me into a chair. The form in front of me requested particulars of my birth, age and occupation, and if accepted for training as an officer in His Majesty's Forces, state which Service preferred though such choice could not be guaranteed. It took me half a second to tick 'Navy'.

Paddy peered over my shoulder. 'Any relatives in the Navy, alive or dead?'

'Does it help?'

'It might.'

'Afraid not,' I said, adding, 'Well, I do have an uncle who's a commander in – '

'Commander, eh? Follow me.'

'No, wait, Paddy, he's – '

But before I could stop him he'd grabbed my form and, limping at remarkable speed so that I could barely keep up, cut a swathe through several rooms full of people at desks filling in forms until he came to some trestle-tables joined together at the far end of the last room. Behind the tables sat three top brass in full uniform: a naval officer with several rings on his sleeve, an air force officer with a similar number and an army officer with equivalent pips on either shoulder. The naval man was in the centre.

'Excuse me, gentlemen,' said Paddy. 'Millar, sir. The Navy, I think you'll agree.' He handed the navy man my form and, leaning across the table, started whispering. All three officers' heads closed on Paddy, ears cocked. I strained mine and managed to catch a few words.

'Relatives galore ... massive potential ... naval family ... Commander Millar ... Dardanelles.'

Dardanelles? So far as I knew, Uncle Leslie had never been nearer the Dardanelles than Potters Bar. I even thought I caught something about Drake and the *Golden Hinde*. I began to feel slightly hysterical.

'Well, Millar,' said the Navy, welcome written all over his face. 'I gather you come from a long line of naval officers.'

'Er – not exactly, sir. There seems – '

At this point I received a sharp crack on the shin-bone. I don't know if you've ever been kicked by a wooden leg. It's much harder than a real one. In fact, between you and me and the Bolivian rainforests it hurts like hell.

'Many thanks, Paddy,' said the Navy. 'Well found.'

Paddy nodded and vanished. 'You know, Millar,' said the Navy, 'I have a feeling I've met this uncle of yours somewhere or other but I can't quite put my finger on it. Commander Millar ... Commander Millar ... ' he chewed on his pipe.

My uncle, a first-class accountant, was a pay commander in the Royal Naval Reserve and had recently been called up to a shore establishment somewhere in the North to keep the books in order.

'It'll come to me in a minute. Anyway, not surprised you've chosen the Senior Service, Millar – if you get a choice, that is, and I think, gentlemen, in your case we can safely say – '

'Just a minute, Tommy,' said the Brigadier. 'Young man, what have you got against the Army?'

'Not a thing, sir. Only I did five years in the OTC at Charterhouse and to be honest – '

'Five years, eh?' said the Army and turned to his colleagues. 'Five years' army training in the bag, gentlemen, how about that?'

'Yes, Dickie old thing,' said the Navy, 'but no relatives. No ancestry. No genealogical table d'hôte. Blood will out and this chap's blood goes all the way back through a third cousin of Nelson to – '

The Air Force cut in: 'Ever thought of flying with the RAF?'

'Yes, sir. I thought about it.'

'And?'

'I'd be scared stiff.'

'You? Scared? Never. Listen, we may be the junior service but for sheer excitement – '

'Absolutely, sir, but the fact is – '

'No, no, no,' said the Army. 'No experience. I tell you, five years in the OTC – '

I couldn't believe it. The Army, the Navy and the Air Force were fighting – actually fighting – over *me*. Was I that valuable? Perhaps I was.

'Got it!' cried the Navy suddenly. 'Commander Millar – *of course*! I remember Commander Millar! Took his submarine under the Dardanelles in World War One. Cut his way clear through the nets, came up the other side and sank half the Turkish fleet.'

'Sir, it's not quite like that. I do have a cousin, John Millar, who's a lieutenant, RN – '

'Cousin too, eh? Sorry, Dickie, bad luck, Jacko, but this one's got seawater coming out of his elbows.'

I watched closely as he wrote my name and put three ticks and a sort of star thing after it. Without a doubt I was pretty damned special. 'Well, Millar, it's been a pleasure. You'll love the Navy.

My very best to your uncle. Bravest man I ever met. Don't forget now.'

I promised I wouldn't.

On my way out I looked for Paddy. There was no trace of him. Then through a window I saw a limping figure hurrying down a side-street. I dashed down the stairs, gratitude bubbling out of me like a freshly opened bottle of the Widow.

'Paddy! Hey, Paddy!' I caught up with him. 'My dear chap, how can I ever thank you?'

He stared at me as though not only had he never met me before but should he have the misfortune to do so again it would be the worst day of his life.

'Can I help you, sir?'

'Man, you just did! And I want to say you're the most marvellous – '

'I think you have me confused, sir, with another.'

'Don't be an idiot. I don't know how you swung it – at least I do and you're raving mad but that doesn't alter the fact that it was your influence – '

'Influence? I, sir, have no influence with anyone. I merely hand out forms and empty wastepaper baskets. The rest, as they say, is silence. *Absolute* silence. Do I make myself clear? Good day to you, sir.'

And he was gone on his one good leg twice as fast as I could go on two.

Within a week I received confirmation from the Admiralty that I'd been selected for training as a sub-lieutenant in the Royal Naval Volunteer Reserve. I would be notified in due course when and where to report. Meanwhile I was to carry on with civilian life and whoever this letter was from begged to remain, on behalf of their Lords of Admiralty, mine faithfully, I couldn't make out the signature but it looked like Hobnail.

Carry on with civilian life? Didn't this chap Hobnail or whatever his name was know there was a war on? I bet if Churchill heard about this he'd grab one of his famous red stickers – 'Action This Day' – and stick it up this chap's quarterdeck.

After my interview I'd expected something better. A summons to HQ Pompey perhaps or Scapa Flow for immediate training with the Home Fleet. Even this Hobnail character must know one could hardly acquire the Nelson touch in a punt on the Cam. Nothing positive happened except my Medical which I sailed through. It was the only sailing I did for some time. I appeared to be on the back burner. I couldn't understand it.

Perhaps I should explain my impatience to enter the fray. It certainly did not stem from any outstanding heroic qualities. I am neither spectacularly brave nor, I hope, unduly craven. It was partly that I found the conflict with Hitler's Germany the most confounded nuisance, interfering as it did with what I saw as my future career at a crucial moment – i.e. before it had started. But there was another reason for wanting to get into the war, something more personal.

I remembered my mother telling me how my father's failure to pass his Medical in the First World War, though it set her mind at rest, had deeply embarrassed him. My passing mine and joining up in the Second was 'one for my dad'. (Sentimental foolishness? It's how I saw it at the time.)

I fretted through the Christmas holidays and sulked back to King's. Still no word from the Navy. This was getting ridiculous. If it'd been World War I I'd have had a drawer full of white feathers by now.

Dacre-Hill said, 'Do some work for a change, it'll take your mind off things' but I couldn't concentrate. Still, she was right about taking my mind off things.

The Footlights Club was touring the camps entertaining the troops and needed money for a scenery van. I decided to organise a charity concert on a Sunday at the Arts Theatre, Cambridge, in aid of the club, with as many celebrities from London's theatre world as I could muster. I wasn't too optimistic but at least I had an entrée through a few stage doors thanks to my mother, who seemed to know everyone.

After her touring days she had returned to the West End and understudied (and frequently played for) Tallulah Bankhead in *Let Us Be Gay* (as in 'gay as a lark') at the Lyric, Marie Tempest in *Passing Brompton Road* at the Criterion, Mary Ellis in *Double Harness* at the Apollo, Laura Cowie in Maugham's *Sheppey* at Wyndham's and Madeleine Carroll in Galsworthy's *The Roof* at the Vaudeville.

To my surprise and delight not a single artist I invited to Cambridge turned me down. John Gielgud, Peggy Ashcroft, Fay Compton, Hermione Gingold, Stephane Grappelli, Arthur Young, Bryan Michie, they couldn't wait. Theatre people are wonderfully generous about giving their time for a good cause and the wartime mood helped.

Was there anyone else I knew or at least had a nodding acquaintance with?

Glancing through a Cambridgeshire paper I came across an advertisement:

EMBASSY THEATRE, PETERBOROUGH

IVOR NOVELLO, ISABEL JEANS AND DOROTHY DICKSON

in a new comedy

'SECOND HELPING'

by

IVOR NOVELLO

Preceded by

'SONG PARADE'

Did I have the nerve? And, if so, would he remember *The Lion's Skin* and my letter offering him the chance of a lifetime turning my twelve-minute masterpiece into a musical? No, even if my name rang a bell, which was unlikely, it was nearly ten years since *Glamorous Night* at Drury Lane, which had been followed by *Careless Rapture* which had been followed by *The Dancing Years*, all of which I had watched from the gallery, *The Dancing Years* seven times.

Nothing venture, so I took the train to Peterborough in time for the evening performance of *Second Helping*. There were just two seats left and I got one of them by swearing I was only in Peterborough for one evening and Mr Novello was an old friend and would never forgive me if I didn't drop in and tell him what I thought of the show.

Song Parade was a curtain-raiser, a series of Novello's numbers, some from André Charlot revues of the twenties, and one new one. The curtain rose on the classic Novello profile, an incredibly handsome, godlike creature with sweeping dark hair, shrewd brown eyes and a full mouth, in a white dinner jacket, spotlit at a grand piano playing and sort of singing a new number called 'We'll Remember'.

I learnt subsequently that he hoped it would do for the Second World War what 'Keep the Home Fires Burning' did for the First. (It didn't, though 'We'll Gather Lilacs' which he wrote at the very end of the war came close.)

I enjoyed the nostalgic *Song Parade* which featured, apart from Novello himself, Peter Graves and Olive Gilbert, especially Graves who sang Jack Buchanan's old hit, 'And Her Mother Came Too'.

I didn't much care for *Second Helping*, one would have been enough, but what did it matter, it was an excuse for the women who

69

worshipped Novello to see him on stage and who would have braved the blackout and an air raid in full swing to hear him read the telephone directory.

After the play I went round to the stage door, manoeuvred a path through a swirl of fans waiting with autograph books and approached the stage-door keeper. I'd come over from Cambridge to see Mr Novello, I said, striking what I felt was a note of casual assurance. It was an important matter connected with the university and if he wasn't totally exhausted I'd be greatly obliged if he could spare me a few minutes.

The doorkeeper looked me up and down with dour suspicion. 'Shouldn't think so,' he said. 'What's yer name?'

'Millar,' I said, enunciating carefully. 'Millar with an "a": Ronald Millar with an "a".'

He rang through to what was presumably the star dressing room. 'I've got a Mr Robin Taylor 'ere from Cambridge. 'E says it's important but I dunno. What shall I do with 'im? Right.' He hung up. 'They'll ring down if 'e can see you,' he said. 'Personally I doubt it.'

While I waited more fans arrived with more autograph books. One of them asked if I was an actor. 'Only in Greek,' I said with a slight accent.

'Ooh! Are you famous?'

'Desperately.' I'd swapped the Greek accent for Noël Coward in *Private Lives*.

By the time the stage-door keeper muttered ''E says you can go up. First floor' in a voice that for hand-washing left Pontius Pilate at the post, I'd signed half the autograph books 'Dadie Rylands' and the other half 'Maynard Keynes' and promised to send a photograph if they'd leave their name and address at the stage door.

As I went in, Novello was seated at his dressing table slapping cream on his face, removing his make-up, his dresser standing by with towels. He saw me in the mirror.

'Hello. Come and sit down.' The dresser went out. 'Were you in front?'

'Yes.'

'How did you like our little play?'

'Er – '

'I know. But I wrote it in a rush to cheer people up. It'll be all right.'

'Yes, of course.'

'Or not, as the case may be.'

He slipped on a dressing gown. 'Do you smoke?'

70

'No, thanks.'

'I do. Far too much.' He lit a cigarette and threw himself into a chair. 'Now, Robin, what's all this about Cambridge?'

I let the Robin go, at least *The Lion's Skin* would go with it, and told him about the Footlights concert and who was coming.

'That's quite a cast.'

'Yes, but if you came it would be – well, it would put the cherry on the cake.'

'What would I have to do?'

'Play the piano.'

'How long for?'

'As long as you liked. Your own stuff, of course. I mean, your own music. Incidentally I think it's – I like it a lot.'

'So do I.' He said it quite objectively, as though the music just happened and all he had to do was write it down.

'Would you – will you come?' A pause.

'Let's talk about it over dinner, shall we?'

'Dinner? Oh but I have a train to catch. It's extremely kind of you, Mr Novello, but – '

'Nonsense. You must meet Isabel and Dotty and the others and tell us all about Cambridge and the Footlights.' He called for the dresser who reappeared like lightning. 'Ring the hotel, will you, and tell them we want a room for tonight for Mr Robin Taylor.'

'But I don't have so much as a toothbrush with me.'

'And a toothbrush.'

'No, Mr Novello, I couldn't possibly – '

'No, of course you couldn't and do stop calling me Mr Novello.'

Dinner was in a private sitting room. The food was fair and the wine was fine and most of the company were there and were charming and friendly and easy to talk to and I thought how right I'd been about a life in the theatre. If it was always like this (it's not, but never mind) and I survived the war at sea (if I ever got into it) this was the profession for me.

After the others had gone to bed Ivor went on chatting and chain-smoking.

'Do you always smoke as much as that?'

'Yes, when I'm working, which is nearly always. Tell me about you. Are you going into the war?'

'Yes.'

'When?'

'I don't know. I'm waiting to be sent for. It's all set.'

'You've done your audition, have you?'

'Yes.'

71

'Which Service?'

'Navy.'

'Don't go and get yourself killed or drowned or anything silly.'

'I'll try not to. My mother wouldn't like it.'

'I was in the last business. The Royal Flying Corps, as it was then. I got the planes up all right – well, more or less – it was when I came in to land there was a slight problem – wings came off and things like that – and as they didn't have all that number of spares they suggested I do something else for the war effort so I wrote "Home Fires" and everyone was happy. What are you going to do with your life when the war's over?'

'Act.'

'I thought so.'

'If I come through.'

'You're stage-struck.'

'Always have been.'

'Where do you get it from?'

'My mother's an actress.'

'What's her name?'

'It varies. Sometimes it's Dorothy Millar. Sometimes it's Dacre-Hill. Sometimes it's Dacré-Hill.'

'Well, it makes a change. But why is your name Taylor?'

'Actually it's not.'

'Really? Robin who, then?'

'It's not Robin either.'

'Are you a spy?'

'Yes. No. I'm Ronald Millar and I'm not a spy. It was your stage-door keeper. I think he's deaf.'

'Well, I'm glad we've got that cleared up. Good Lord, it's half past two.' He rose. 'Time for bed. Coming?'

For a split second alarm bells rang and I wondered if by any chance he meant... because if he did I'd better make it clear... He read my thoughts instantly and laughed.

'No, my dear, I know you're not. More's the pity.'

'How did you – '

'One always knows. But that doesn't mean ne'er the twain shall meet again. On the contrary. See you Sunday.'

'You don't mean you're coming?' I couldn't believe it.

'Don't you want me to?'

'Good Lord, yes!'

'Then I'll be there.'

But when I opened the curtains on that Sunday morning it was snowing heavily and obviously had been all night. King's College

72

Chapel was white all over and there was an almighty gale blowing. As I switched on the wireless for the news bulletin the phone went.

'Ronnie. This is Ivor. Look out of the window.'

'I just did.'

'It's all over the country and the forecast is more to come. My dear, I'm most frightfully sorry but I daren't risk it. We open at Liverpool tomorrow night and I have to be there by teatime at the latest. Will you forgive me?'

'I'll try.'

'You do understand?'

'Yes, of course. And thank you for the other evening. It was… very special.'

'Good luck with the concert. I'm sure the others will make it if they're coming from London. I'm leaving now for the train. Goodbye, dear. Keep in touch. I rather think we're on the same wavelength. Theatre-wise, I mean.'

There was a chuckle and he hung up.

Despite the weather all but one of my cast turned up. Only Bryan Michie fell by the wayside. Literally. A huge man, he ran the BBC radio programme *Youth Takes a Bow* and was due to compere a stage performance for us but he slipped and twisted his ankle on the wet pavement getting into his car. Gielgud volunteered to take over and did so wearing a hat tilted over one eye and an overcoat slung across his shoulders. It wasn't cold in the theatre and he was partly invisible but he looked very stylish. Then he and Peggy Ashcroft did their John Worthing and Cecily Cardew scene from Wilde's *The Importance of Being Earnest*, Hermione Gingold asked 'Why was I born a Bacchante?' as she had in a Gate revue and Stephane Grappelli played jazz violin like the unique musician he was – and still is.

All through the Blitz he and Arthur Young, the pianist and composer, drew the town, and those of us on leave, to Hatchett's Club in Piccadilly, most of which was fortunately underground. These days Grappelli plays with the LSO at the Barbican and his recordings with Yehudi Menuhin are a lasting joy.

In spite of the snowstorm raging outside the all-star cast gave the audience a time and vice versa and we overran by an hour. They stayed the night in Cambridge and over supper La Gingold, who indeed looked as you'd imagine a Bacchante and whose inimitable drawl had a touch of Edith Evans crossed with Maggie Smith but deeper-toned than either and whose vocabulary was a unique kind of mock-camp, was discussing 'the conflagration in which we appear to be embroiled. Without my permission, I may say. Which reminds me,' she suddenly turned to me, 'Darling, are you on the verge or does that come under the heading of reckless apostrophe?'

'On the verge of what?'

'Being called up or down or whatever it is.'

'Yes, I'm on the verge.'

'How close does it loom?'

'I'm not sure. I'm going into the Navy but they seem to be taking their time. Why?'

'Well, I was thinking – as one does from time to time if one has nothing better to do – I'm about to plunge into what is laughingly called an intimate revue to be known far and wide as *Swinging the Gate*. The title, I need hardly tell you, refers to the minuscule Gate Theatre under the arches by Charing Cross Station and you can't get much more intimate than that. Although we're being greatly daring and venturing into the wicked West End where we shall almost certainly sink without trace. Be that as it may, the revue has a cast of nine supporting me (my dear, if only they were!), people like delectable Madge [Elliott] and delicious Roberta [Huby] and a strange young man I saw at the Player's Theatre called Peter Ustinov who's quite brilliant but has never appeared in a company show before, preferring to fly solo, he says it's safer, one does knows what he means and I was wondering' – she looked me up and down – 'we need one more youth and there aren't many about and your acne seems under control – I suppose you're staying up – if that's the correct rather indelicate expression – until you're summoned?'

'I haven't decided. We come down next week, anyway.'

'Well, when you have descended, let me know. I might just have a little something for you.'

Three weeks later and sworn to secrecy about the Navy by Gingold – 'If you tell Norman [Norman Marshall, the producer] that you're on the verge he won't touch you with a butterfly net' – I went into rehearsal for *Swinging the Gate*. My introduction to Marshall, who despite a succession of Gate revues looked rather sinister, had been typical Gingold. His first question had hit the nail on the head.

'But aren't you likely to be called up?'

Before I could utter she intervened, 'Down, dear. He's a con-scientious defector and if he goes anywhere it'll be down a mine.' This seemed to satisfy Norman, if not me.

Swinging the Gate, which was written by Robert McDermott and Diana Morgan, composed mostly by Charles Zwar and built around Gingold, opened at the Ambassadors Theatre off Cambridge Circus at the end of June 1940. The notices were ecstatic.

In addition to her Bacchante inquiring the way to Chorleywood, Gingold was seen as a south coast woman with every ailment known to the medical profession and several which were not, prostrate on a *chaise-longue* as 'La Grande Amoureuse' and directing a class of spies in Upper Tooting among a variety of increasingly outrageous creations.

Peter Ustinov, who was new to all but the Player's public, scored an immediate success as Dr Hyprocitoff, the first of a long line of elderly eccentrics with which he began his acting career. He also appeared as James, the silent butler, to a gallant wartime Lady of the Manor, keeping her chin up and adapting to circumstances by riding an ancient penny-farthing bicycle. ('Petrol rationing means goodbye to the Rolls. We're all in it together' was the message.)

At the final dress rehearsal Peter had been asked not to join in the ensembles as his feet were said to be wayward and had trouble keeping time with the music. As he subsequently directed opera all over Europe with immense distinction this has always puzzled me.

My contribution was in a number of concerted items and various odds and ends long forgotten, with the exception of one 'Bert' in a sketch called 'The Conquering Hero' in which the moustache I wore to make me look older actually made me look about twelve and a half. I also understudied the other four male members of the cast.

The only one I didn't cover was Robert Helpmann, who only appeared when he wasn't dancing at Covent Garden and felt in the mood for giving his party piece, which was impersonations, notably the actress Margaret Rawlings reciting in a deep baritone 'The Owl and the Pussycat' by Edward Lee-ee-ee-ar. It was all witty, inconsequential, very English, and beautifully tailored to Gingold's growing public.

Among them was Ivor (Novello), who turned up one evening with a party of friends including Beatrice Lillie and Peter Graves and Dorothy Dickson and sent round a note inviting me to supper after the show at the Moulin d'Or.

I took to Bea Lillie on the spot and vice versa when she discovered that I was waiting to go into the Navy. Apparently her son Robert (Sir Robert Peel) had just been called up and was an Ordinary Seaman, she didn't know where but would I look after him when I ran into him as I was bound to, we'd probably be on the same boat or ship or whatever, wouldn't we? I thought it highly unlikely but promised anyway.

During those early days of the war Bea asked me to escort her here, there and everywhere; on one occasion to Lady Diana Cooper's, hostess of immense fame and beauty who had once appeared at the Theatre Royal, Haymarket, as the star of Max Reinhardt's production of *The Miracle*. Diana Cooper thanked me profusely for coming and begged, 'Do be nice to Duff, won't you? He's desperately tired.' As Duff Cooper, her husband, was Minister of War in charge of the Army and I was a sub-lieutenant-in-waiting not in charge of so much as a dinghy, I promised to be nice to Duff, despite the fact that I had fallen instantly in love with his beautiful wife who had the most perfect manners of any hostess I had ever met and I envied her husband to the top of my bent.

All of which was a long way from Cambridge and Creon and the Provost of King's, and heady mountain air for a young man waiting to go to war and who had already been exceptionally fortunate in his first encounter with the professional theatre.

7

. . . .

A Piece of Gin

My mother, who had long abandoned hope of diverting me into the Diplomatic after university (anything of a political nature was not for me, I said firmly) took *Swinging the Gate* in her stride and, although she never said so, was clearly delighted that the Navy was taking its time before availing itself of my services.

I rather think she hoped that Paddy's intervention had been counter-productive and that perhaps my 'naval ancestry' had been subject to a routine check and duly rumbled (for a time I had wondered about this myself). In any case, she regarded my love-affair with the theatre as preferable to a more intimate involvement with the war effort, and what was more, she claimed someone had told her (not surprisingly she couldn't remember who) that paperwork had never been the Navy's strong point and it wouldn't surprise her if they'd forgotten all about me.

It would, however, have surprised me. I had received a note, about which I had thought it best to say nothing, instructing me to present the enclosed chit to Gieves, the official tailors to the Navy, who would provide me with uniform, greatcoat, cap and any ancillary equipment that a junior officer might require. The note appeared to be signed Bluebottle or Blankcartridge.

I had an interesting afternoon at Gieves spending the Navy's money and smuggled my outfit into the theatre and locked it in a cupboard in Gingold's dressing room, who threatened to wear it in the finale.

Ten days later I was ordered – again by someone whose signature was indecipherable, Bluebottle or Blankcartridge had been superseded by Goasyouplease or Gooseberrypie (these chaps seemed to squiggle their signatures while being keel-hauled at five fathoms in a force ten) – to report to HMS *King Alfred* on 7 August 1940 at 0900 hours precisely. The necessary travel pass and train ticket to my destination was in a large sealed envelope marked TOP SECRET in red lettering and the whole package enclosed in an even larger envelope franked with the wartime instruction: CARELESS TALK COSTS LIVES. Clearly I was to be trained on board some pretty high-powered ship of the line.

Deeply impressed and excited, I moved about London imagining Gestapo on every street corner, disguised as ice-cream vendors or bootlace pedlars. Well, let them do their worst, neither thumbscrew nor rack nor the burning cigarette under thumbnail and forefingers would get my destination out of me.

'So,' said my mother, suddenly very still and quiet when I finally showed her my sailing orders. 'You'd better call Ging and Norman Marshall, hadn't you?' Norman was stoical and Gingold typical. 'Have you told Derry & Toms?' she inquired gravely. (Derry & Toms was a Kensington store.)

'Not yet. Should I?'

'But of course. With you at the helm the conflagration is bound to be over before you can say Peter Robinson and then they can go ahead with Outsize Week after all.' This was followed by her usual deep-throated chuckle at her own singularity.

I gave my two final performances in *Swinging the Gate* on the Saturday night, kissed and was kissed ceaselessly by the company and personally launched by Gingold cracking a bottle of champagne over my head and presenting me with a toy telescope ('should any blind-eye work be necessary').

On the Monday morning I was bathed and dressed in my uniform by 0600 hours. Suppressing the feeling that this was just another outfit for a number in the revue, I said I'd better be off.

'Shall I come to the station?' said Dacre-Hill.

'Please not.'

'Whatever you say. Goodbye, my darling.' A close hug. I was suddenly moved. This wouldn't do. 'Come back, won't you.'

'I promise.'

'I love you.'

'Me too.'

A massive final hug and I raced down the ninety-four stairs and into a taxi.

As I stroll through the main concourse of Victoria Station with no more than a hint of a swagger a couple of Ordinary Seamen going the other way salute smartly. I look behind me to see whom they are saluting, discover it's me and realise I must get used to this sort of thing. I return the salute with the merest suggestion of a smile which I rather doubt if Tyrone Power could have improved upon and slide easily into a first-class compartment which is empty and stretch out with the *Times* crossword as the 0700 takes me at last into the war. Slightly over an hour later we arrive at our destination. Looking around to make sure I'm not being observed by alien eyes I make my way to the station forecourt where I'm glad to see a couple of taxis drawn up plying for hire.

After letting an RAF type take the first – the Navy is of course the Senior Service but I am in a generous mood, besides, he's a wing commander – I give him a smart salute which seems to surprise him and he returns it with a rather sloppy mechanical sort of half-wave as the cab moves off. (Glad he's not a navy man.)

The driver of the second taxi chucks the butt of his cigarette out of the window. It lands at my feet. He yawns and lights another. I climb swiftly into the back like David Niven in a hurry to get to Navarone. At length: 'Right, guv. And where do I 'ave the pleasure of conveyin' you?'

There's a supercilious something about this chap's manner that I don't altogether care for. I'm wondering who Warner Brothers would cast for the part – Alan Jenkins, perhaps, no, he's too nice, when the cabby says, 'Are you with me, guv?' I come to.

'Yes, of course. Harbour, please, and make it snappy. I have to be on board at 0900 hours.'

'You 'ave to be where what?'

'On board my ship. I don't want to be late so do you mind casting off and taking me down to the harbour?'

'Takin' you down to the *what?*'

'The harbour, man, the harbour. You know what a harbour is, don't you? It's where ships sail from in wartime. Peacetime, too, for that matter. Right. Off you go.' And I sit back and concentrate on my crossword.

'Er, excuse me, guv. But you do know this is Brighton Station?'

'I'm fully aware that this is Brighton Station. Now will you get on down to the harbour, please.'

'I would if I could, guv. Straight up I would. Only, you see, I got a littul problem. It just so 'appens Brighton don't 'ave a bleedin' 'arbour.'

This man is obviously living in a time warp. Either that or he's been drinking.

'Don't be absurd, of course you 'ave a bleedin' – of course you have a harbour. I stayed at Brighton several times when I was a child. You have, in fact, a couple of harbours – one east and one west.'

'Oh, you mean a coupla *piers*. Yerss, we got a coupla piers all right, but a pier ain't an 'arbour, is it? Strewth. Which one do you want?'

'Look, cabby, I don't know what sort of game you're playing but I'm due on board my ship at 0900 hours *precisely* so kindly take me to where she rides at anchor.'

'What sort of ship?'

'Yes, I thought you might ask me that. Well, I'm not telling you.'

As it happens I'm not sure myself but I remember seeing a battle-wagon – or was it an aircraft carrier? – in *Jane's Fighting Ships* that I'm almost sure is called *King Alfred*.

'Well, if you ain't gonna tell me what to look for we'll just 'ave to sit 'ere, won't we, twiddlin' our bleedin' thumbs.'

'Now look here, you know perfectly well there's a war on and careless talk costs lives.'

'Gawdamighty!' he cries. "E wants a bleedin' 'arbour and we ain't got a bleedin' 'arbour and 'e wants a bleedin' ship and 'e won't say what bleedin' ship 'e wants!' A thought strikes him. 'Sure you don't want the Ship 'Otel? We got one o' those.'

At this point the passenger door is opened by a figure dressed identically to myself in wavy-navy sub-lieutenant's uniform.

'Going to the King Alfred by any chance?'

I heave a sigh of relief. 'Am I glad to see you! Yes, jump in. This cab's being driven by a nutter but at least we're two to one.'

'Why, what's wrong? King Alfred, please, driver.'

'King Alfred? Right, sir.'

And he lets in the clutch and we shoot down the hill towards the seafront.

'How did you do that?' I ask. 'He wouldn't budge for me. Mind you' – I lower my voice – 'I'm not entirely sure you should have named the – er – vessel. Top secret, my letter said.'

'That's just navy bull, old man. Good Lord, there's nothing secret about a swimming baths.'

'I'm sorry, what was that you said?'

'The Prince Albert Swimming Baths at Hove. They're HMS *King Alfred*, cocky. All His Majesty's shore establishments are HMS this, that or t'other. Wouldn't fool a fly, of course, but that's Whitehall for you. I say, you look a bit off. Care for a nip?'

He has produced a brandy flask from his hip pocket.

'Er – no. No, thanks.'

In front of me the driver's shoulders have begun to heave.

"E's not goin' to tell me!' he sobs, gasping for breath. 'Careless bleedin' talk costs bleedin' lives 'e says so 'e's not goin' to tell me that the King bleedin' Alfred is the bleedin' swimmin' baths at poor bleedin' bloody 'Ove!!' He chokes and, seeing me watching him in the driving mirror, gives a two-fingered salute before blowing a raspberry and giving vent to gales of mocking laughter.

There is an interesting silence.

Finally: 'On second thoughts,' I murmur softly, before accepting the bleedin' brandy flask and takin' a bleedin' swig.

For the next eight weeks a group of about thirty of us, all sub-lieutenants, RNVR, marched and wheeled and counter-marched in and out of the Albert Swimming Baths and up and down the front at Hove – the beach was mined and cordoned off with rolls of heavy-duty barbed wire all along the south coast – each of us taking charge of the squad in turn and being taught signals and knots and boat drill and naval terminology and all the nuts and bolts of seamanship by petty officers RN and chief petty officers RN with a patience that they did not hesitate to tell us they marvelled at and, when asked if we were ever going to sea, replied that since we were all at sea on land, with all due respect, gentlemen, it was bloody unlikely.

We were billeted in local boarding houses and fed and watered in the naval mess attached to HMS Swimming Baths. In the evening we had leave to do what we liked where we liked and to whom we liked provided we were back on parade by 0700 hours the following a.m. and if not we'd be court-martialled which would probably be the best thing that ever happened to the Royal Navy seeing as how, gentlemen, we were a hopeless shower and it would almost certainly shorten the war. I should like to place on record that these POs and CPOs were the salt of the seven seas and without them the Royal Navy would have long since returned to port and stayed there.

Most evenings I took the 6.10 to Victoria. When I turned up at the end of the show at the Ambassadors Theatre I was greeted like a conquering hero and had to field a barrage of questions. What was my ship like? Superb. No, that wasn't her name, simply my opinion of her. Was she big or small? Top secret. How many guns? So many you couldn't count them. Ah, battleship. Did I say so? No, but, well, one could put two and two together.

Enigmatic smile.

Gingold (sotto voce): 'Have you any top secrets you'd care to sell or swap?'

A View From the Wings

R.M.: 'Nothing sensational.'

Gingold: 'I have one or two. For example, I could slip you last week's box-office figures for a small donation.'

R.M.: 'Can't afford it.'

Gingold: 'What you need is promotion, deeah. I chance to be on terms with one or two admirals who owe me, for reasons we will not discuss, the odd favour. The next time one of them makes an approach, I shall make one on your behalf.'

London was awash with young men in uniform, and not a few young women. The Rivoli Bar beneath the Ritz Hotel was a popular haunt and there one evening I suddenly ran into a delightful young girl I had known as a teenager when we were both on regular summer holidays at Westgate-on-Sea on the Kentish coast. Subsequently at Cambridge letters had flown to and fro and romance was very much in the air when it was interrupted by the war. Now suddenly here she was again, a young woman and ravishing. When her companion had to leave I bought her a drink and asked her what Service she was about to join and she said she was in a reserved occupation.

R.M.: 'How interesting. Munitions factory? Don't answer if you shouldn't.'

Delightful Young Girl: '*Vogue.*'

R.M.: 'I beg your pardon?'

D.Y.G.: '*Vogue* magazine. You know. Models. Pretty clothes. That sort of thing.'

R.M.: 'You jest, of course.'

But she didn't. Churchill or someone had said that keeping up morale was terribly important, you see, and looking at women putting on nice clothes was recognised as a great morale-booster. I said looking at women taking them off wasn't all that bad either, at which she blushed and looked even more delightful. I felt it my duty to give her a pep talk, and took her back to the Pont Street flat where I usually stayed overnight before returning to Hove on the milk train (Dacre-Hill had joined ENSA and was away touring the camps in Ivor Novello's *Fresh Fields*, playing the Lilian Braithwaite part, so we were alone). There, to recover from the ninety-four stairs, I opened a bottle of wine and plumped up the cushions on the divan and when we had made ourselves comfortable I pointed out as politely as possible that to call a job on *Vogue* magazine a reserved occupation was bordering on the indecent and the sooner she did something respectable like making bombs or joining one of the Services the better.

As she just smiled and was clearly going to do nothing about it, there was little mileage in pressing the point so I changed the subject and we drank the wine and one way and another had a remarkably pleasant time together.

We met frequently when I was on leave. It was as though we had never lost touch. She was always joyful to be with and we laughed a lot and drank a little and danced and went to the movies and I began to ponder the classical wartime conundrum: is it selfish or sensible to think of getting married, bearing in mind that when the war was over it was more than possible that one would not be around to enjoy the peace? There were days when I felt it would be unfair even to raise the subject (my Scottish caution) and others when I thought Coward was right in *To-Night at 8.30*: 'Grab it while you can: grab every scrap of happiness while you can.'

That was the year (1940) when a small brown bird with a sensuous larynx and an over-romantic disposition set up house in Berkeley Square, whilst up the road there were 'angels dining at the Ritz' and the nightingale supplied background music free of charge with a song that, against a backcloth of London under siege, and who knew what tomorrow would bring, was irresistible to lovers of all ages. On one occasion my lady and I raced through Highgate Woods as the bombs rained down, shrieking with happiness, tripping over tree-trunks and tumbling headlong, exhilarated by life and desire and the boundless vitality that the danger of imminent extinction excites in the young.

Being on leave and not quite twenty-one, it was a sweet time to be alive and, war or no war, I had begun to lean more and more towards a permanent arrangement with my young lady with the reserved occupation if she was agreeable, which I had some reason to believe she might be, when suddenly one evening she turned up out of the blue or, rather, *in* it: the light blue of the Women's Auxiliary Air Force.

I was thunderstruck.

'But – but whatever made you do a damfool thing like that?'

'You did, darling. Remember? You went on and on about my reserved occupation being indecent and how I ought to be making bombs or in one of the Services. Well, I thought about it and I decided you were right but I didn't fancy making bombs, I might have dropped one and blown us all up, so ... do you think it suits me?' She did a twirl in her uniform as though she was on some confounded catwalk.

In that outfit, with her figure, she looked more desirable than ever.

I didn't want her to disappear into the war, not now that I had made up my mind to – well, I was right on the brink of – and what's more, now I was transfixed with guilt, feeling that if anything terrible happened to her I would be responsible. When I told her so she said cheerfully, 'That's right.' Which did nothing to relieve my conscience. Dear heaven, why hadn't I kept my idiotic mouth shut? Happily, nothing terrible did happen, except that, as I feared, the war swallowed us both up. She became an officer in no time at all and was posted to the Far East and met 'the most terrific fighter pilot' whom she did not wed but she did eventually marry two other people (sequentially, not simultaneously) and now she has three attractive grown-up children and a nice husband and whenever I see her, which alas is only now and then, she still looks as delightful as ever and younger than all of them, at least in the eye of this permanently bewitched beholder.

It's August/September 1940 and there is a heatwave. There is also something else.

While we in navy-blue march and counter-march on land and learn about the mysteries of the wine-dark sea, high in the sky above the English Channel and the Sussex Downs a battle is being fought by another group of young men in a lighter blue uniform, and some older ones, a battle that is to be decisive.

Staring up at it from the hot pavements of the Hove Marina, we see what appears to be a delicate and spectacular ballet designed by a master choreographer and performed in total silence. So high up is it that not a sound can be heard below, where we stop our little earthbound manoeuvres and peer, fascinated, upwards at the delicate white traceries woven by the dancing, diving aircraft that stand out like toy machines against the backcloth of a peerless blue sky.

We do not know, we have no way of knowing that, miles above us in the seeming peace and beauty of those English end-of-summer days, not only our future but that of Europe and the whole free world is being decided in the battle that is named after the land the airmen saved, and is remembered each year on 15 September, and will surely be remembered, as those who fought and lived and died in it will be remembered, as long as that dear land continues to exist.

At the end of the eight-week course at Hove, we were told, we would be posted to our various ships. Which would be mine, I asked one of the Chief Petty Officers.

'Couldn't say, sir, even if I knew. Which I don't. Not to worry, sir. You'll be all right.'

Came the last few days and my spirits were high. Not that I hadn't enjoyed King Alfred. Once I had adjusted to the idea that tunes of glory in a swimming bath were likely to be limited, it had the appeal of novelty and Brighton's proximity to London was not to be sneezed at. Still, one couldn't help feeling that the time had come for a naval officer, however humble, to make some sort of contact with the seven seas (not all at once, of course, one at a time would be satisfactory).

When I received the standard Top Secret envelope within an envelope I withdrew to my boarding-house bedroom, locked the door and after making sure there was no one in the airing cupboard opened the envelope with trembling fingers. At last one was coming to grips with the war at sea.

'On behalf of Their Lordships... beg to remain... Sandwich Board or Sanitary Inspector.'

I was to report to HMS *Royal Arthur*... now that was more like it. Aircraft carrier, wasn't she? No, that was *Ark Royal*. No matter, *Royal Arthur* sounded impressive. Proud, romantic English name. Shades of Camelot. Knights in armour. Of *course*. Armour plating. That was it. Probably bristling with naval hardware. I examined my pass and rail ticket. Skegness? Well, plenty of sea there. Popular holiday resort. Bracing, wasn't that the word they used in the holiday brochures? 'Come to Jolly Bracing Skeggie.' By all means. Looking forward. Not that I knew anything about the place except – wait a minute, wasn't there a Butlin's Holiday Camp at Skegness?

There was indeed. Only now it was called HMS *Royal Arthur*...

En route to HMS Holiday Camp I had a night's leave and went home to the flat, breathing heavily. My mother, who had a week off from ENSA, took the news with a tremble of the lip that could not, by any stretch of the imagination, be attributed to fears for my safety. (I was hardly likely to be beaten up by a Redcoat, even assuming there were still some on the premises.) However, she saw the glint in my eye daring her to laugh and just managed not to. That evening we went to the theatre and saw Edith Evans in a Farjeon revue at Wyndham's and in a burst of extravagance sat in the stalls. The following morning I was on my way.

There was nothing wrong with His Majesty's Ship *Royal Arthur* except that it wasn't a ship. By now I was convinced that Blank-cartridge had indeed rumbled Paddy's good intentions and had seen to it that they backfired.

In addition to the main Butlin building which had been turned into bedrooms, sorry, cabins, for the officers and an officers' mess and bar and a billiard room, there was row after row of little chalets, plus huge dining halls which were also used for kitting out and giving basic training to the approximately one thousand potential sailors who arrived straight from home every ten days as the call-up got into full swing. They stayed a fortnight with us before being sent to sea. Oh yes, *they* went to sea. All except the brightest, who were attached to Signal and W/T units and stayed with us for a six-month course.

My fellow-officers were a cheerful bunch, many of them called back from retirement, and the pay-commander, RNR, turned out, to my delight, to be the Commander Leslie Millar whose connection with the Dardanelles might be tenuous but who was indeed my uncle (my father's brother) and a lovely man with a permanent twinkle. My job was to help train the regular intake of sailors-to-be in the rudiments of seamanship, a pleasantly Gilbertian touch since I had not myself been to sea. It was the CPO who had taken me under his wing and shown me the ropes who had the answer.

'Understand you were an actor, sir, in civvy street.'

'Briefly, yes, Chief.'

'Well, if I may make a suggestion, sir. Act. These blokes haven't even seen the sea, half of 'em. They won't know you don't know.'

I brushed up my seamanship from the official manual and they didn't. At least I hope they didn't.

'All right, sir?' asked the Chief whenever he saw me.

'More or less. But the thing's absurd, you know, Chief. I mean, sending me here to teach chaps things I haven't experienced myself, it's putting the cart before the ruddy horse.'

'Arse over tit, sir. Absolutely.'

'And another thing. We have shore leave and go ashore but we're ashore already. What do you make of that?'

'Never say die, sir,' said the Chief. 'We'll win this ruddy war just the same, sir, take my word for it.'

There was a part-time Entertainments Officer who actually knew nothing about entertainment and didn't much care for it anyway, so for light relief I knocked together a revue in which I donned bell-bottoms and vented my feelings by leading the 'ship's company' in my own heartfelt version of Fred Astaire's number from Irving Berlin's *Follow the Fleet*:

'We joined the Navy to win the war
And what did we do? We stayed ashore.
Instead of a hammock slung in a galley
Where do we sleep? We sleep in a chalet,
Sleep in a chalet's not what we joined the Navy for.'

One morning I was taking a parade of about half the sailors on the strength when a CPO with a particularly loud voice approached and saluted.

'Sub-lieutenant Millar, *sir!*'

I halted the proceedings. 'Yes, Chief, what is it?'

'Telephone call, *sir*!!' I backed away from the blast.

'I can't take it now, Chief. As you see, I'm right in the middle of – '

'Gentleman says matter of extreme urgency, *sir*!!!'

'What gentleman?'

'A Mr Ivor Novello, *SIR!*'

'What??'

'A MR IVOR NOVELLO, *SIR*!!' If I could have put him on a charge for shouting I would have. There was a rustle and a nudging from the assembled ranks. They may not have seen the sea but they'd heard of Ivor Novello. (Who hadn't?) I bit my lip, told the Chief to stand the men at ease and hurried to the Quarterdeck office.

'Hello,' I whispered.

'Ronnie. Thank God I've found you, you're my only hope. How are you, by the way?'

'Up to my eyes.'

'Speak up. I can't hear you.'

'Look, Ivor, I can't talk now.'

'I'm sorry but you must. You know Norman Rutherford?'

'No.'

'Yes, you do. He's the *Dancing Years* company manager and stage director.'

'Oh, *that* Norman Rutherford.'

'How many are there? Listen, something dreadful's happened. Norman's been called up.'

'Really? Well, every little helps.'

'Norman's help is out of the question, dear.'

'Is it? Why?'

'I'm on tour with *Dancing Years* and a huge cast and tons of scenery and he's my key man, that's why. Every theatre we play it's a major building operation. I can't possibly manage without Norman.'

'Ivor, why are you telling me all this?'

'Because he's coming to you, to your HMS whatever it is.'

'Oh. Well, I'll make a point of looking out for him when he arrives.'

'He's not going to arrive!'

'I think he'd better, otherwise he'll wind up in the brig.'

'No, no, no. It's all a ghastly mistake, he's in a deserved occupation or whatever you call it.'

'In that case I suggest you get on to the Admiralty. Have you got a pen handy? Here's the number.'

'There's no time for all that red-tape nonsense. He's supposed to leave for Scarborough or wherever it is – '

'Skegness.'

' – first thing tomorrow morning. Why do you think I'm calling you?'

'I can't imagine.'

'Because it's an emergency.'

'I'm terribly sorry but there's nothing I can do about it.'

'Well, that's a pretty thing. You're in charge there, aren't you?'

'No, of course I'm not in charge.'

'Well, who is?'

'A rear-admiral, retired.'

'If he's retired how can he be in charge?'

'He *was* retired. They've brought him back for the duration.'

'Put him on, dear.'

'I can't do that! He'll think you're mad – and me too.'

'Look, you can at least pull strings. Use your influence.'

'I don't have any. I'm just a wavy-navy sub-lieutenant. That's practically the bottom of the heap.'

'Nonsense. You're far too modest.'

'Ivor, I have to go now. I've got five hundred men out there on parade – '

'Then you won't miss Norman, will you? Please listen carefully. When he arrives just say "lovely to see you" and send him straight back on the next train. I'm counting on you.'

The next day, to my considerable surprise, a perfectly normal Norman who looked twice my age arrived with the usual intake and saluted smartly and called me 'sir' and I said 'at ease' and when I told him that Ivor seemed to think I was the First Sea Lord, Norman said, 'Not to worry, sir. My deputy will see him through. No one is indispensable.'

In fact, Norman *was* – to the *Royal Arthur*. He turned out to be a W/T trainee on the usual six-month course and was a notable addition to the ship's company (after the war he became a big wheel in BBC Television) and an excellent detective inspector in my production of Anthony Armstrong's *Ten-Minute Alibi*, in addition to practically building the scenery single-handed.

Bracing though it undoubtedly was, Skegness was not exactly the place I would have chosen to celebrate my twenty-first birthday but

Uncle Leslie and Aunt Eva, who had a rented house in the town, pushed the boat out and Dacre-Hill came up and they invited all my friends from the *Royal Arthur* and we had a splendid spree.

A different kind of party the following Saturday had an indirect consequence of some moment. My fellow officers were either on leave or on the town enjoying the wild salacity of nightlife at Skeggie when we got a 'yellow', a signal which meant that the balloon was about to go up and stand by for Hitler, and I found myself the senior officer on duty.

My cool, as I sauntered along the fortifications, which consisted solely of some barbed wire and a rifle apiece, most of them without ammunition, for our complement of approximately one thousand would-be sailors who, like their temporary Acting Officer Commanding, had yet to go to sea, astonished even myself.

As a youngish version of C. Aubrey Smith patrolling the Punjab I managed the lazy confident amble I felt was expected of an officer facing imminent attack against impossible odds. General Gordon, betrayed by Gladstone and about to be overrun by the Mahdi's screaming dervishes, was another image that gave an extra swagger to my saunter.

'The invader will be repelled' was the message my body language did its best to convey, along with the impression that this was just the sort of show I'd been longing for. I made encouraging noises, advising the men under my sole command to 'keep your eyes peeled and your pecker up' and other morale-boosting tips of this nature as we prepared to go down gloriously in the first major engagement on home soil of World War II, the Battle of Butlin's.

About two in the morning, however, the 'yellow' was suddenly cancelled. Apparently there'd been a cock-up. It had been a false alarm, and I surrendered my exalted position to the Captain, who had returned from high jinks in Skeggie, and much to my chagrin found myself an ordinary sub-lieutenant once more.

But my sangfroid in a crisis had not gone unnoticed. The following morning the Rear-Admiral Commanding sent for me and said, 'Good show, Millar. You did jolly well last night. Have a cigarette.' When I declined, he said 'In that case, carry on' and I said 'Thank you, sir', saluted and returned to chalet duty. However, word must have reached the Admiralty of my outstanding contribution to our island's defence, for a week later I was posted to the submarine base at Dunoon.

So this was it. I packed my kit in a state of mounting excitement. I was going to sea, or rather under it, at last.

But no.

Dunoon, it appeared, was where potential sea-going types were taught the complexities of the Asdic Course.

'Asdic' – which stood for 'Anti-Submarine-Detection-Control' (I think) – was how one learnt to detect and, hopefully, to sink the odd U-boat, should one be encountered. It sounded promising – a promise that was only partly marred by the discovery that one was taught this fascinating technique on land. After three weeks on a simulator, where the difference between a 'ping' denoting a school of fish, a wandering mermaid and a U-boat was drummed into me and my colleagues (as I am lucky enough to have 'perfect pitch' I was actually quite good at this) I was posted to Whale Island.

Again my spirits rose. This could hardly be a course in the use of whale blubber in wartime. (I really should have known, in view of my long line of naval ancestry, that Whale Island, Portsmouth, was the Navy's principal gunnery school.) On reflection the future seemed not without possibilities. After all, naval guns were mounted on ships, were they not, and ships went to sea, did they not, so presumably one would go to sea to be taught how to fire them, would one not?

No, one would not.

The course consisted of three weeks of gun elevations and trigonometry and learning the different types of guns at present in use in the wide variety of ships to which one might just conceivably one day, with luck and assuming that the war lasted roughly a hundred years, be posted.

The gunnery CPOs were the sergeant majors of the Royal Navy and boasted an equally colourful vocabulary. However, despite the fact that the guns on which we were eventually allowed to practise were on land and made one hell of a noise when fired which, wads of cotton wool notwithstanding, partially deafened me for a month, it was all rather enjoyable and one could nip up to town in time for the Blitz.

By now I was resigned to remaining on land for the duration and when time was up and the postings came through and I saw that my orders were to report to HMS *Montrose* I was certainly not going to waste time looking her up in *Jane's Fighting Ships*. Thrice bitten. What course was I off on now? Sunningdale Golf Course, I shouldn't wonder.

But what was this? HMS *Montrose* was 'an ageing destroyer'! Ageing? I didn't care if she was due for a pension, she was 'a sea-going vessel' at present completing a refit at – well, I suppose it's all right now to say Chatham Dockyard.

I was to report at 0800 hours on Thursday 25 April, 1941, to the Captain of this no doubt battered old hulk that had been called back to sea duty and was actually, three rousing cheers, afloat. Well, it hadn't been a bad guess. She was a World War I destroyer, pretty ancient but at least she wasn't a swimming bath or a holiday camp or a golf course.

The *Montrose* was tied up alongside a jetty when I arrived and there were sailors in seaboots adding licks of paint here and there along her gunwales. As I went up the gangway one of them turned and, seeing an officer, gave me a casual half-salute. I frowned and gave him an exceptionally smart one back. He pulled a face and grinned. Still, this was unmistakably a ship. Things were looking up. I found the Captain in his cabin, poring over a map which seemed to indicate we might be going somewhere some time. On a ledge beside his bunk was a coloured photograph of a pleasant country house and a garden full of flowers and in the foreground a pretty woman in early middle age and a young boy and girl and a labrador. I coughed.

'Er – excuse me, sir.'

He looked up. 'Hello. Who the blazes are you?'

I told him.

'Oh. Ah, yes, I seem to remember getting some sort of signal about you. Going to win the war at sea single-handed, are you?'

'Yes, sir. I mean, no, sir.'

'Well, I don't know what we're going to do with you but I dare say we can find something. Meanwhile, you'd better come along to the wardroom and have a piece of gin.'

We had a piece of gin. In fact we had several pieces. At the end of which, so far as I could recollect, he had made me Gunnery Officer, Asdic Officer, Paymaster and Captain's Secretary which meant, among other things, that I was responsible for all the top-secret code-books and other confidential literature. 'That do you to go on with, Sub?'

'Yes, sir. Absolutely, sir.'

'Better not lose any of them. Every blessed code in the whole blessed Navy has to be changed if you do and then you'll probably be court-martialled and shot.'

'Thank you, sir.' I wasn't worried. I felt more than a match for Conrad Veidt and Erich von Stroheim, either singly or in concert, if either or both should be foolish enough to try anything. 'One for the road, sir?'

'That's very decent of you, Sub. Now what shall I have? Do you know, I think I'll have a piece of gin.' It must have been our eighth or ninth.

The 'piece of gin' routine was to happen without fail every evening before dinner except when we were at sea.

91

The officers would assemble in the wardroom awaiting the Captain's arrival. Eventually, timing his entrance to a nicety, he would come down the gangway wearing his number ones, black tie, wing collar, the lot, and the following dialogue would ensue:

Officers: 'Good evening, sir.'

Captain: 'Evening, gentlemen.'

Number One: 'Will you have a drink, sir?'

Captain (taken aback by the sheer novelty of the offer): 'I say, that's very decent of you, Number One.'

Number One: 'What shall it be, sir?'

Captain: 'Well now, let me see. What shall I have?' (Concentrated pause for reflection.) 'Do you know, I think I'll have a piece of gin.'

Amazement all round at this bold and original choice.

The Captain was a lieutenant-commander, a retired two-and-a-half-striper who had been returned to the active list for the duration. Like quite a few naval officers who had failed to make the jump from lieutenant-commander to commander, he had a bit of a chip on his shoulder, but he and his kind were indispensable to the war effort and although he never stopped cursing the Admiralty for taking him away from his garden in Kent – 'Finest dam' hollyhocks in the county' – he was actually as pleased as punch to be back in the Senior Service and to have a command once more.

The refit completed, we went out on a series of exercises, working up the ship and the crew. I was actually at sea. I couldn't believe it.

The *Montrose* was well equipped with depth charges so it was no surprise on one of these exercises to find myself once more at Dunoon. No simulators this time. The idea was for us to play cat-and-mouse with a British submarine which would try to evade us, crisscrossing and turning this way and that underwater while I directed our course from the bridge of the destroyer through instructions to the seaman who was the Asdic operator. The Captain had to follow the course I gave, which was somehow strangely satisfying. I felt like John Wayne in charge of something rather more powerful than a horse.

As the exercise proceeded the Captain became gradually more and more apprehensive. 'Where the hell are you taking us, laddie?'

'Just following target, sir. Everything under control.'

I was never more calm as I barked, 'Port ten! Steady as she goes! Starboard twenty!'

The old ship swung this way and that at my behest like a carousel in charge of a madman but I was no madman. On second thoughts I wasn't John Wayne, either, I was Admiral Cunningham, that's who I was.

'Sub, do you have the foggiest what you're doing?'

'Absolutely, sir. Everything tickety-boo. I'm on her tail.'

'By God, you'd better be or I'll be on yours.'

I gave my ring-of-confidence smile. If this was a dress rehearsal I couldn't wait for my first U-boat. On we went, twisting and turning as our quarry twisted and turned. I had her measure. It was as though I could read her mind. This was tremendous stuff. Suddenly the Captain drew in his breath.

'Careful, man! You'll have us on the beach!'

'I think not, sir.'

We were heading straight for a tongue of land. This is truly glorious, I told myself. I gave the Captain the thumbs-up with a lazy cool worthy of Gable, Grant or Bogart, take your pick.

Finally the Captain, white as a seagull, said, 'I can't stand this. I'm taking over. Out of the way, laddie!'

I sighed. I was more relaxed than Robert Mitchum in *Heaven Knows, Mr Allison* and heaven knows, that's the ultimate cool. 'Whatever you say, sir.'

'Hard a-port!' the Captain yelled down the tube to the quartermaster.

'Hard a-port, sir.' The ship swung violently left.

'Er, excuse me, sir,' I ventured.

'Shut up, you idiot!'

'Quite so, sir. I just thought you might have missed the green flare, sir.'

'What green bloody flare?'

'Three o'clock, sir.' I pointed. 'About – let's see – say, ten yards off our starboard beam, sir.'

A green flare, signalling end of exercise, had indeed appeared to the right of us, followed almost at once by the submarine surfacing practically alongside. The Captain's face was quite interesting. 'Well, I'll be buggered!' It hardly seemed the moment and in any case the submarine's Aldis lamp was flashing.

'Excuse me, sir, may I borrow your binoculars?' He passed them over in total silence and I read aloud, ' "WELL – DONE – BLOODY – GOOD – SHOOTING". Thank you, sir.' I handed back the binoculars with a polite cough.

The Captain took one of his deep breaths and ordered the signalman, 'Acknowledge'. Then he turned slowly, very slowly, to me.

'You – cocky – little – bastard,' he growled as though signalling with an Aldis. 'When we get into port remind me to buy you a piece of gin.'

I was modesty itself. 'As they say in the RAF, sir, "Piece of cake".'

One didn't like to boast but one couldn't help feeling that if one were to last for a thousand years men would say this was one's finest hour.

It seems that whenever one thinks that life's a bowl of cherries, Hamlet's slings and arrows are standing by to balance the books.

Exercises concluded, the *Montrose* was assigned to what was known as E-boat Alley, escorting convoys up and down the east coast. The Norwegian coast, from which German E-boats had been operating successfully, was not that far off. So on convoy duty we zigzagged, strictly according to Hoyle, doing so many 'zigs' followed by so many 'zags' as laid down precisely in the naval manual. For safety, we sailed mostly at night, nursing the convoy south under cover of darkness.

One particularly dark night I was on the bridge at about 0300 hours. It was my watch and I felt strangely contented and more relaxed and at home in His Majesty's Navy than I had ever felt before. As we sailed quietly south at a steady fifteen knots covering the convoy, I lit a cigarette. I may not have had all that number of ancestors actually in the Service, I reflected, but there was no doubt that there was something in the blood of this island race to which I had the privilege to belong that responded to the sea. The tradition of Drake and Raleigh and Nelson and even that old devil Bligh was in the veins all right. Yes, come to think of it, I was a natural sailor and if I was still around when the war was over I might even sign on for a short-term Service commission.

'Sub-lieutenant Millar, sir!!' It was the duty signalman who suddenly interrupted my reverie, yelling and pointing to port and starboard and back again to port. I followed his hand, gaped and leapt for the intercom to the Captain's sea-cabin which was immediately below the bridge.

'Captain, sir!' A sleepy growl. 'Could you come up on the bridge, sir, right away, sir, please.'

'What is it, Sub?'

'I – er – I seem to have zigged when I should have zagged, sir.'

The comprehensive oath which had a couple of 'f''s and an 's' in it was followed by 'You bloody fool'. A moment later he staggered up, rubbing his eyes, blinking and adjusting his sight to the dark.

'My God, we're in the middle of the bloody convoy. *Stop both!*' The old destroyer shuddered to a halt.

'All right, I've got her.' He took over the ship and by a series of intricate, heart-stopping manoeuvres managed to extricate us without damage to ourselves or our charges. Then he took off his cap and mopped his brow. I passed him a mug of cocoa, which he drank in silence. Eventually: 'Sub.' His voice was gentle, almost tender, as one would address a child. 'This may seem a silly question but, tell me, *we* are escorting the *convoy*, are we not?'

'Yes, sir.'

'Quite sure?'

'Absolutely, sir.'

'Good. Good. You see, it occurred to me you might be under the impression the convoy was escorting *us*.'

'No, sir. No, I'm pretty clear about that, sir.' I'd finished my cocoa but I swallowed hard. 'Sorry, sir.'

'So I should bloody well think! Well, don't bloody do it again!' he roared and went back to bed.

No further reference was made to my watch-keeping activities, but one thing was clear. My Asdic triumph was a thing of the past. It was one-all.

My only problem with the war at sea was the sea itself. I was chronically seasick from start to finish (all those onions of Aunt Maggie McNichol's had done something antisocial to my stomach lining).

No one said anything, least of all the Captain, not even when, in the minute closet on the bridge in which I endeavoured to decode incoming signals, I regularly threw up all over his sea charts. I don't know if you have ever tried to decode anything while your stomach has temporarily left its moorings and is heaving about inside your skeleton like a packet of crisps in a hurricane. If not, take it from me it's not all that fun.

My involuntary upchuck reached its meridian in a notable little Scottish typhoon off the Kyle of Lochalsh, whither the *Montrose*, amongst others, had been despatched to welcome a batch of American World War I destroyers under the Anglo-American Lend-Lease Agreement.

This was the device by which President Roosevelt, on receiving Churchill's urgent request for more ships, cunningly circumvented Congress and came to the aid of the mother country without the United States actually declaring war on Germany. With waves rising ten feet high or more and my stomach following fast behind I can't say I recall too much about this storm-tossed meeting at what seemed like the edge of the world, except that it did a world of good to the lasting friendship between our two English-speaking peoples which has been reaffirmed time and time again since the war against Hitler.

My stomach only really returned to earth when, after escorting the American destroyers south, the *Montrose* was ordered to Chatham for certain 'urgent additional work' on the ship. The work in question was wrapped in mystery but when it turned out to be adding extra lagging to all the pipes on board against entry into icy waters and the onset of freezing weather we quickly put two and two together.

To ease the constant pressure from Stalin for a second front in Europe before the Allies were ready for it, regular convoys of arms and food were being sent to the Soviet Union for her northern armies and the port of arrival was Murmansk. The Murmansk convoy was not the most sought-after assignment in the war at sea. It was in fact fraught with danger. The merchant ships were escorted by cruisers which in turn were escorted by destroyers, like a lot of small dogs yapping round a big one, but for the latter part of the trip air cover was virtually nil. The convoy and their escorting warships were subject to submarine attack from the German bases in Norway and if a ship was holed the temperature of the water was sub-zero and the survival time for the human body was three minutes maximum. Not surprisingly, losses were up to forty per cent.

Well, if this was 'it', I pondered, it had been a short life but a sweet one, a very sweet and desirable one. Pity if this was the final curtain but, as Mrs Salmon had pointed out long ago, Normandale boys had to learn to stand on their own two feet. She might have added, 'Even if that meant getting them wet', as now seemed more than likely. I hoped that my mother wouldn't be too shattered when they told her and that the delightful-looking young lady, formerly of *Vogue* and now God knew where, would.

A week's special leave was granted and it was briefly back to the Blitz and the Ritz and the latest arrivals, the girls of the American and Canadian Armed Forces who were now flooding into wartime London, bringing with them their own distinctive and highly personal lend-lease, which was more than welcome.

My mother was still touring with ENSA but when she heard I was on leave came home for the weekend. I had never made reference to what the *Montrose* did when she went about her business in great waters, nor had she inquired, but you can't be as close as we were and not sense things and when I gave her a special hug before returning to Chatham she looked at me sharply and insisted on coming down all ninety-four stairs to the front door and when I looked back from the pavement and waved, for the first time her eyes were moist.

'No woman gives a son or husband to be killed,' cries Nora in O'Casey's masterpiece *The Plough and the Stars*. 'And if they say so, they're lying against God, nature and themselves.' Years before, my mother had played Nora in rep. I prayed the words hadn't stayed with her.

Triple-lagged and looking chic for an old lady, the *Montrose* sailed from Chatham to Scapa Flow, the Home Fleet base in the Second World War as it had been in the First (long ago, when I was innocent, I used to think that 'Scapa Flo' was a certain type of girl who served drinks to sailors behind a certain kind of bar, but that was before I met one Paddy Hadley and became sophisticated).

At Scapa where we joined the rest of the escort ships that were to accompany the convoy to Murmansk, a profusion of battleships and aircraft carriers and cruisers, surrounded by their support vessels and supply ships and a submarine flotilla, lay at anchor. It was a fine sight but, it seemed to me, a perfect target for a suicide attack from the air if one were to be attempted and got through the defences. Happily no such attack was launched in British home waters, though in the Pacific Pearl Harbor was but a few months away.

Shortly after our arrival we were out on an exercise pretending to be under hot pursuit from a German U-boat when the Captain overdid the realism and took the ship on the rocks, or rather, as he put it at the subsequent inquiry, a rock. With half the fleet looking on, the precise number of rocks involved seemed less important than our embarrassment. However, it's an ill wind... More significant than either was that at the eleventh hour Fate appeared to have intervened on our behalf.

Although the Captain's little divertissement might well have drowned us, in fact he probably saved our lives, for the *Montrose* could hardly make her way to Murmansk with a hole in her bottom and a repair job would take till who knew when, by which time a one-way ticket to Mother Russia might no longer be on the agenda.

Ever since he took us on the rocks at Scapa I have felt a lively sense of gratitude to my former sparring partner, the skipper of the old *Montrose*, for by his one mistake on the eve of our departure for the icy waters of the Russian North he almost certainly extended my allotted span on this unpredictable but on the whole beguiling planet.

He did something else for me. The Scapa episode had a psychological effect. As I guessed, Murmansk was a non-starter for us and after that last-minute reprieve it never again occurred to me that I might not survive the war. A constant reminder of man's mortality were the regular BBC news bulletins reporting 'one [or more] of our aircraft failed to return'. I did not say or even think 'but *I* will'. I just no longer believed that I wouldn't.

They patched us up at Scapa and we limped down the east coast to Chatham to acquire a brand-new keel. Soon after we arrived I wandered into the wardroom where the Captain was sipping his favourite noggin and staring out of an open porthole. We were at anchor and the sea was a millpond.

'Piece of gin, Sub?'

'Thank you, sir.'

The steward handed me a gin. 'Cheers, sir.'

Silence. The Captain seemed to have something on his mind.

'Sub, I was thinking,' he continued to stare out of the porthole. 'Whenever we're at sea and there's a bit of a swell you throw up like Vesuvius on a bad day. Am I right?'

'Er – well, sir – '

'Makes a hell of a mess of my charts. Not exactly Chanel No. 5, either.'

'No, sir. Sorry about that. The thing is I don't get much of a warning. One minute I'm fine and the next – well – it's heave-ho and up she rises.'

'Not your fault, my dear fellow. Something to do with the stuff behind the ears getting out of sync, I'm told. Nelson had the same trouble, you know.'

'So I believe, sir.'

'Unlike the Captain of the *Pinafore*.'

'Sir?'

'Never sick at sea.'

'What, never?'

'Hardly ever.'

We both knew our Gilbert and Sullivan. 'Look, while we're having our bottom scraped and a new one fitted why don't you toddle up to the Naval Hospital and see if the quacks can't fix you up with the odd pill and so forth.'

'I'll be all right, sir.'

'That's an order, Sub.'

'Aye, aye, sir.'

At the hospital I saw a wavy-navy doctor.

'Seasick, are we, sailor? Nelson had the same trouble, you know.'

Quite. But he had Lady Hamilton.

He prodded and prowled around my stomach and stuck things into and up various other improbable organs that go to make up the human anatomy. In between he frowned and looked at the floor rather more often than was comforting.

'I say, couldn't you just give me some pills?'

'Hm? I could, yes. Still, I think you'd better stay overnight and let us take a proper look at you.'

A series of undignified tests followed. Next morning the wavy-navy doctor reappeared with a surgeon-captain, RN.

'Morning, Millar. No, don't get up. I've just been looking at the lab report on your tests. Great glory, how long has this been going on?'

'Sir?'

'Look, young man, you just made it to us in time – I hope. Another week or so and – why the hell didn't you say something to your skipper?'

'I didn't want to be the first to – to bring it up, sir, if you'll pardon the expression. I mean, as he didn't say anything until yesterday, I thought if I did he'd think I was skiving.'

'Of course you realise you're a bloody fool?'

'Yes, sir.'

'Well, that's something.'

'What happens now, sir?'

'I come alongside your innards and take a closer look, that's what happens. Then you and I have a little chat.'

I was given a hefty local anaesthetic, made to swallow some perfectly disgusting mixture and wheeled into theatre (not the kind I was familiar with though it looked theatrical enough).

The eyes of a group of white-gowned nurses smiled a ghoulish greeting behind their masks. The Surgeon-Captain appeared in a white gown, a nurse plunged his hands into surgical gloves, various rubber tubes were stuck down my throat and I was promptly sick for the first time on land. Everyone was delighted.

'Now that we've cleared the upper deck,' said the surgeon with what seemed to me unnecessary relish, 'let's see what's going on in Davy Jones's locker.' The white-gowned harpies gathered close to watch Orpheus on his way down.

Every now and then the surgeon would murmur, 'Does that hurt?... Mmm... How about that?... Ah... Going up your backside now. Yell if you want to... ' By half-time it was clear they were intent on giving new meaning to the words 'no stomach for the fight'. Finally they were done and I was wheeled back to the ward. Presently the surgeon reappeared, once more in his number ones, and came and sat on my bed.

'So,' he began brightly. 'How are things down there in the vasty deep?'

I daresay Nelson would have gasped 'Never better' and headed straight for Trafalgar. The best I could do was belch. This seemed to please him. He smiled as though I had given him an Easter egg. So I produced another. He beamed approvingly. 'Bound to be a certain amount of wind in the bend of the lower bowel.' So I still had a lower bowel? No mention of the upper one, I noticed. Gone with the wind, no doubt.

'Look, old man,' he said in the soft voice doctors use when something serious is about to surface. 'Your guts are in a bit of a flap. I don't say they'll never be the same again. You're young and you should get over it, but it'll take at least a year or so. You've had this war. Don't worry. There'll be another one. There always is another one. Now do you want us to put you through the hoop here or would you rather have your own medico take over?'

A longish silence. Eventually: 'Can I sleep on it?'

'Yes, but don't mess about. The sooner you get cracking the better.'

I slept on it. I didn't want to leave the Navy. This wasn't false heroics, I'd made a lot of friends and I was just as likely to be blitzed in London if the Luftwaffe came back as I would at Chatham, which had had one pasting already.

When I woke the next morning I'd made up my mind. I put on my uniform for the last time, went down to the ship, collected my gear and told the Captain what had happened. He knew already.

'I'm bloody sorry, Sub. I should have said something sooner. I didn't know it was that bad.'

'Nor did I, sir. Not your fault.'

'Balls. My responsibility. Too early for a piece of gin?'

'No, sir, but I'm not allowed.'

'My God, that *is* serious. You'd better have a small one for the road.' I hesitated. 'That's an order, Sub. The last you'll receive from me.'

'In that case – aye, aye, sir.'

To my surprise he seemed genuinely upset at my going. Even more to my surprise, in fact to my utter amazement, when I was ready to leave he came up on deck and stood and saluted as he had me piped off the ship (a ceremonial exit to which I wasn't remotely entitled) and back into civvy street. Some time afterwards I heard that he'd been posted to a cruiser that was badly holed in the Channel – not by him, it wasn't his command, by enemy action – and half the ship's company went overboard.

I hope they fished him out. He was a good man, the skipper of the old *Montrose*, and I like to think that when the war was over he went home to the pretty wife and kids and the labrador and strolled round his Kentish garden in the early summer evenings with his piece of gin, content with his lot and marvelling at 'the finest dam' hollyhocks in the county'.

ACT II

1943–68

8

. . . .

Putting Words in People's Mouths

So I'm out of the war at sea and on my way home, jolting fitfully along from Chatham to Charing Cross, the carriage windows diagonally taped with sooty, partly torn brown paper to preserve the blackout, hemmed in by my fellow passengers and, as one does in wartime trains, contemplating an uncertain future.

I'm twenty-three, minus job, minus money, and nursing a set of intestines that by any stretch cannot be depended on but with luck and hopefully no following wind might, given time, settle.

Question: Should I return to King's? I have been assured, before coming down from Cambridge to assist in the demise of Schickelgruber that, assuming survival, when the war is over my place will be waiting for me. The game plan is that I should then get down to the rather more important business of acquiring a First in Classics that will, it has been politely stressed, be expected of a Greek Exhibitioner.

It was honourable and decent of the college to keep the door open and it had been my intention to return and resume my interrupted innings, but now the time had come the prospect of four years' classical study, once eagerly looked forward to, had lost its appeal. Ancient Greece and distant Rome, with their real and imaginary wars, seemed suddenly irrelevant in face of the urgent present with its daily fight for national survival. The truth was I had grown up in the war and, like most of us who were young at the start, was older now by more than the sum of the intervening years. Besides, I had something else in mind.

My mother guessed it at once but greeted my return, outwardly at least in one piece, with a relief that, had I decided to become a window-cleaner, she would have given it her unqualified blessing. But first things first and I was bundled off to the family physician for further interior reconnaissance.

Old Doctor Mayberry, a large Ulsterman with huge eyebrows, was despite his long life an optimist and after more tests of the usual obnoxious nature said 'You'll live' and gave me prescriptions for half-a-dozen different kinds of coloured pill and a diet-sheet of what not to eat, which wasn't too difficult since most of the items listed were either not available or strictly rationed.

'When can I go back to work?'

'Work? You won't be fit for work, boy, for at least a year.'

'But I don't have any money. There'll be bills to pay. Yours, for instance.'

'Well, of course, that's different. Come back again in a month.'

I was back in three weeks. More tests.

'Yes, well now, I've been thinking. As I say, you won't be a normal human being, if there is such an animal, for a twelve-month but you're the kind of bloke that's better working than brooding. Right?'

'Right.'

'So, provided you stick with the pills and it's a nice quiet desk job. Librarian, say?'

'Good idea.'

'No jumping about all over the shop.'

'Wouldn't dream of it.'

'Easy does it.'

'Absolutely.'

'There you go, then. Away with you.'

But I should have suppressed the Cheshire Cat grin until I was out of the door.

'By the bye, Mrs Mayberry prefers the dress circle to the stalls. When you get that nice quiet no-jumping-about job, you won't forget to send us a couple of complimentaries?' He was no fool, old Mayberry.

Instead of writing to the Provost I went up to King's to see him and after being embraced and blessed several times with customary fervour told him I wasn't coming back and why.

'I know it sounds awful but I'm afraid the classics have nothing to say to me in the present situation.'

He was genuinely shocked. 'But, dear boy, the classics have everything to say to you and me and the whole agonising universe in the present situation. The fight for a civilised world is ongoing and eternal and the immemorial poets are there to guide and instruct us and to put the present in perspective in a way that no other human in history, with the possible exception of Will of Avon, has ever come near. So don't be a juggins, bless your Simple Simon heart. Go on over to our glorious chapel and look about you at the beauty our forefathers built to the glory of God, and incidentally say a word of thanks to Him that, apart from a gastric disturbance that has left you thinner than you should be and intermittently in some pain, you're on land and on your feet. Come back to us, my dear, get your head down for a change and fill it with the wonders of the world of scholarship, from which you will emerge intellectually if not financially enriched, bless your myopic, addle-pated nut.'

But it was no good. I was in a fretful mood. Perhaps it was the war's fault, perhaps mine, but after the Navy the drowsy charm of academe seemed deactivated and remote from a young man on his uppers and restless to begin a theatrical career. 'Do not write on both sides of the paper.' I could not face all that again. After fifteen years of formal education I longed to turn the paper over and make a few untutored observations on the forbidden page.

The 'Q' Theatre, Kew Bridge, was run bravely on a knife-edge budget by Jack de Leon and his wife Beatie (the actress Beatrice Lewisohn). Salaries varied from seven pounds a week to ten to – well, all right – twelve if they wanted you badly enough or couldn't get anyone else for less. The plays, which were a mixed bag of established hits of the pre-war London theatre, classical revivals and the occasional new work, ran weekly.

The entire theatre was on one floor – box office, auditorium, stage and tiny dressing rooms, like a shrunken aircraft hangar with a low ceiling – and being within fifty minutes or so of Shaftesbury Avenue on the bus despite the blackout had the advantage of attracting stars who from time to time would come out to the 'Q' to try a new piece on the dog and if it barked enthusiastically transfer it to the West End. But these were exceptions. For the most part the 'Q' was a popular, respected repertory theatre with a faithful, local following.

When I turned up there a few days after my defection from university, confidence unbounded, if unfounded, and asked for a job, the de Leons gave me one immediately. This was due, not to any instant belief that Apollo had come down on a cloud to offer his services but to the dearth of young men, who had gone to war and were still engaged in bloody conflict.

Throughout the rest of 1942 and into '43 the de Leons continued to give me work and the 'Q' became an ideal drama school for an actor who had never been to one and had much to learn. The productions were workmanlike and sometimes more, and Beatie's solecisms, some of which were notional, kept us in high spirits. It is not true that, casting *Oedipus Rex* she said, 'Can't we get Harrison? He created the part,' but she did once offer an actor Tony Lumpkin in *She Stoops to Congreve* (I was that actor).

Due to the lack of competition I began to find myself playing leads at the 'Q', for most of which I was far too young and inexperienced, but the plays were good of their kind and time and acting in them, and occasionally directing, was a useful course in dramatic construction before the well-made play became unfashionable. (Bennett and Hare and Simon Gray have brought it back, lightly disguised, but that's another curtain call.) Among my tutors were A. A. Milne's *The Dover Road*, Coward's *Design for Living*, Lonsdale's *The Last of Mrs Cheyney*, Ronald Mackenzie's *Musical Chairs* and Emlyn Williams's *The Light of Heart* and *Night Must Fall*, in which I played Danny, the pageboy in a country hotel whose hobby it is to smother elderly ladies with cushions and a Welsh accent, decapitate them and carry their heads around in a hatbox. One might think that in wartime anything gruesome and macabre would be repugnant, but one would be wrong. *Night Must Fall* was an early lesson that theatrical taste is capricious and unpredictable.

Many actors, writers, directors and designers learnt the basics of their craft at the old 'Q' Theatre and are in its debt. I am proud to be one of them. The de Leons were tough and shrewd and if they could get you for fourpence they would because in order to survive such economies were necessary, but they loved their theatre to which I used regularly to return and will do so again in this narrative.

Among the things I learnt from *Night Must Fall* was that in the theatre villains are popular. They stand out, they're showy, and they either make audiences feel virtuous and superior or cause them to identify with the dreadful things happening up there on stage and would dearly love to do themselves if only they dared. This ancient piece of theatrical lore, well known to Shakespeare and his contemporaries, stood me in good stead in the spring of 1943 when I auditioned for a part in a singular dramatisation of Tolstoy's *War and Peace*. The *raison d'être* for this mammoth and unique production was supposedly its topicality, Moscow threatened by Napoleon's Grande Armée being held to correspond, give or take tanks for horses, with Moscow threatened by Hitler's Wehrmacht.

Studying the text for this dramatic resonance it seemed somewhat forced, especially in the remarkable opening scene. This took place in a Moscow dugout circa 1943 where a Soviet army sergeant, trying to raise the spirits of his men by reminding them how Bonaparte had got his comeuppance in the snows of yesteryear, finds them wholly ignorant of that historic Russian victory. The scene went something like this:

'What 'appened, Sarge?'

'What 'appened? WHAT 'APPENED?' the good sergeant explodes. 'We won, that's what bloody 'appened. You've read your Tolstoy, 'aven't you?' Well, no, as a matter of fact they 'aven't.

'Tell us about it, Sarge!' 'Yes, tell us about 'ow we licked Boney!' 'Go on, Sarge, be a sport!' cry the humble seekers after historical truth.

'This is no time for telling stories!' roars the sergeant (not, I thought, unreasonably). 'Don't you know there's a war on? Besides, even I don't remember word for word how old man Tolstoy – ' he breaks off, popeyed. He has sprung up from the Russian step (steppe) on which he has been sitting as though bitten by a snake and is gaping at the mighty tome he has produced from beneath his rump and which he now holds awestruck in his hands.

'Well, stone me!' he cries, heaving it aloft. 'Here am I trying to tell you ignorant bastards about *War and Peace* and all the time I'm sittin' on it! Now there's a funny thing!'

Well, yes, it was a funny thing. Indeed one might call it something of a coincidence. However, before you can cry 'flashback' the ignorant bastards cheer and cluster round their Sarge and he opens the great work and lo and behold a hundred years or more are but as yesterday.

And now at Blackpool on opening night the massive stage set revolves, the lighting changes, romantic music fills the air and in a trice we have been wafted back by the wonder and the mystery of theatre to a great Moscow ball where half Equity is dancing to Tchaikovsky's famous polonaise from *Eugene Onegin* (which had not yet been composed, Peter Ilyich not having been born at the time but who cares, it's a lovely tune).

And there on a balcony high above the myriad dancers is the dashing Prince Anatole Kuragin, hit by the hottest of amber spots and starting to sweat in a uniform heavily lined with fake fur from Nathans', the theatrical costumiers. Taking his cue from that seductive rhythm he holds Natasha, played by the delicious Paulette Preney straight from Paris, closer, ever closer, until finally, as the music reaches its climax, and murmuring libidinously in her ear through the body mike attached to his bosom, he ravishes her in mid-dance.

And who is it playing the priapic Prince, complete with home-grown Douglas Fairbanks Junior moustache? Quite so. Here I was, in of all places Blackpool, doing my British best to convey that a little light seduction after dinner was the done thing in Tsarist court circles and keeping up with Kuragin a challenge to every officer and gentleman in Moscow. En passant I may say that holding Paulette Preney's body in one's arms and being paid for it was a not unsatisfactory way of earning a living. After the audition I had been offered a choice of roles in a cast of over sixty but, although Kuragin died at the end of the first half, I thought him more fun than Andrei, less sententious than Pierre and, above all, a double-dyed villain. (The uniform in which, thanks to my diet-slim stomach I felt I cut a certain dash, was a further bonus.)

War and Peace was booked into the Grand Theatre, Blackpool, for a six-week summer season, to be followed by three weeks at the Opera House, Manchester, before arriving hopefully in triumph at the Phoenix Theatre, Charing Cross Road. That at least was the plan. Unfortunately it met with one or two setbacks along the way. For instance, on the first night at Blackpool half the audience left at the interval. This was mildly discouraging but the first half had run three hours, there were two more to come, the last bus left at ten-thirty and, with due respect to Tolstoy, a long walk home in the blackout found little favour. By the final curtain there was only a handful of theatre-goers out front and several of them were asleep.

Furious cuts were made to reduce the running time but the show was heavy-going for holidaymakers. Not surprisingly, buckets and spades were preferred to *War and Peace*, the matinées were a desert, and although the evening audience grew a little as the show contracted and an extra bus was laid on at eleven-fifteen for those determined to have their money's worth, we were not exactly the talk of the beaches except in a negative sense.

A minor incident took place at my digs, where a family of bedbugs flew in for the season and settled in my mattress. Since the RAF and attendant WAAFs were billeted all over town there wasn't another bed to be had in all Blackpool. Happily Peter Cushing and his wife Helen came to the rescue. Peter played several parts in *War and Peace* before going on to international acclaim as a splendid Sherlock Holmes ('The needle, Watson, the needle.' 'For God's sake, Holmes, not again!') and a user-friendly Frankenstein ('Lie still, old chap, and don't fiddle with your tubes, I'm trying to get your head on straight'). The Cushings offered me their bath to sleep in, which I accepted gratefully and found surprisingly snug with pillows and rugs from the Cushing collection, until one of the stagehands came up with a cast-iron sofa from the scene dock. For some reason which I can't define, this, my first experience of touring, was not only educational but hugely enjoyable.

It was during the Blackpool run of *War and Peace* that for the first time I began to scribble some words on paper that I had no intention of putting in anyone's mouth. More than thirty years later I was to return to that happy holiday resort and do it seriously in a rather different context. But in 1943 my scratchings were simply dialogue written at random for a nonexistent play, to help relieve the monotony of Kuragin's two-hour wait until the final curtain call after his 'death' at the end of Act One.

However, as I shared a dressing room with eight fellow actors who also found time hang heavy of an evening, my scribble was passed from hand to hand and examined with interest followed by rigorous questioning.

'So, what happens next?'

'I've no idea.'

'Come on, man.'

'No, really. It's just an exercise to see if I can write dialogue.'

'And can you?'

'Tell me.'

'Well, it's not all that bad. What's the storyline?'

'There isn't one.'

'You mean you're writing in a vacuum?'

'Look, it's just some characters in a house, or rather – '

'Yes?'

'A hotel.'

'Where?'

'On a cliff by the sea. Doesn't matter.'

'Blackpool?'

'God, no.'

'Where, then?'

'Facing the Channel. Dover, perhaps.'

'Dover. Okay. You're in a hotel in Dover. Carry on.'

But I had no desire to be in a hotel in Dover or anywhere else, I was just playing a game to keep myself from being bored by three and a half hours of Mother Russia eight times a week. However, egged on by my dressing-room companions. I wrote another chunk of dialogue, then another chunk, and by the time we got to Manchester one or two of my characters had become less shadowy and a kind of plot was taking shape. I even had a title: *Zero Hour*.

With a hotel for a setting I thought it might be amusing to stay in one and research some authentic detail, so during the Manchester run I blew my salary on a room at the Midland. For three weeks, when I wasn't seducing Natasha at the Opera House, I lay in bed, munching chicken sandwiches, swallowing pills, cross-questioning the staff and trying to write a play. I had finished a draft of the first act and was barely into the second when I got stuck. By now it was time to move to London and the Phoenix Theatre, concentrate on my delicately lecherous performance and control my first-night nerves, so *Zero Hour* found its way into a drawer and out of mind.

The London opening went better than I had expected but a show with a large cast needs good notices. Without them, or major star insurance, it can't be nursed and *War and Peace*, which despite its longueurs had its moments, folded in just three weeks.

However, although the critics were hard on the military side of the entertainment they apparently enjoyed Natasha's seduction and were sufficiently kind to me to trigger quite a flood of offers for a young and available actor.

The most immediately attractive was to take over the RAF Wing Commander in the Jack Hulbert/Cicely Courtneidge musical at the Palace, *Something in the Air*. Not only was it an established success and starred two of my favourite artists, the Wing Commander was the villain of the story, in so far as there ever was a story in a Hulbert/Courtneidge vehicle.

I was about to sign the contract when an offer came to join the cast of *Mr Bolfry*, a James Bridie comedy which was packing the Playhouse. There were just seven in the cast, the part of Cully was a good one, the play hilarious and serious in turn, and its management, director and star the most beguiling comedian of his day. The salary for the musical was double that of *Bolfry* but *Bolfry* had Alastair Sim and, after thinking about it for half a minute, the die was cast and so was I.

Mr Bolfry, set in a manse in the Scottish Highlands during the war, was a play on more than one level, but the central situation was a clash between a minister of the Free Kirk and the Devil. Sim, who played the minister, Mr Macrimmon, had never been able to make up his mind which was the better part, Macrimmon or Bolfry (the Devil), and when after a few months Raymond Lovell who played Bolfry left to go into a film, toyed with the idea of switching parts and playing Bolfry himself. However, after blowing hot and cold and communing with his soul, his wife and the box office, he finally decided to stay with the minister and engaged a solid, reliable character actor to take over Bolfry.

Having made his decision he was instantly consumed with the certainty that he'd made a ghastly mistake and thrown away a golden opportunity of playing the best part in the play. Not unnaturally Lovell's successor, whose performance, if uninspired, was perfectly sound, failed to endear himself to his director and co-star, who regarded him as a permanent reminder of what he, Sim, could have done with the part. One afternoon, between the matinée and evening performance, I came upon him pacing the corridor outside the dressing rooms, which at the Playhouse were fortunately under the stage, muttering and moaning and shaking his head, the embodiment of total despair. When he was in the mood no one could despair like Alastair Sim.

'What's wrong?' I asked.

'What isn't, dalling, what isn't, what isn't!' Everyone was 'dalling' to Alastair, even the stagehands.

'Anything I can do?'

'No, dalling. No, alas. There's nothing anyone can do. The archangel Gabriel would be at a loss.'

'Good Lord.'

'I doubt if even He could be of assistance.'

'Whatever's the problem?'

'That Fitz, dalling.' He spat the word. 'That Fitz – whatever – his – name – is. Oh, what a terrible actor. What a terrible, terrible, terrible actor! He has that – that *cracker* of a part! That superlative *gift* of a part! And what does he do with it? Murders it. Kills it stone dead, that's what he does with it, every night and *twice* on Wednesdays and *twice* on Saturdays. One can only spend Sundays on one's knees – on one's *knees*, I say – praying that he'll suffer some minor disaster, some quite harmless little infirmity such as lockjaw or trench fever that will keep him housebound for the rest of the run. Whatever came over me to engage such a fellow? I must have been out of my mind, dalling, out of my mind!'

'He's not that bad,' I murmured.

'Oh, isn't he? Isn't he? That is your considered opinion, is it, drawn from the well of your vast theatrical experience? I'll tell you what he is. He's the unforgivable thing in an actor. He's dull. *Dull, dull, dull* as ditchwater – and that is an insult to ditchwater. Well, Devil take the fellow, that's all I can say, for *he* can't take the Devil, not in a month of Sundays, no, not for toffee!'

'You're the director as well as the management, why not say something?'

'I've sent notes, I've sent notes. I've sent them by the dozen, dalling. I've sent them by the score. By the hundredweight.'

'And it makes no difference?'

'It does not. I might just as well get into bed and play the ukelele.'

'Are you sure it wouldn't be better to say what you feel face to face?'

'No, dalling. No, it would not be better. I *know* when I'm beaten, dalling.' His voice rose like an Orthodox priest's at a funeral. I felt he would have torn his hair if he had any. 'I *kno-ow* when I'm beaten, I *kno-ow* when I'm beaten, I *kno-ow, I kno-ow, I kno-ow!!*' and he stumbled into his dressing room, closed the door and sobbed.

One of the many pleasures of playing in *Bolfry* was that Dacre-Hill, after understudying and playing for practically every star in the business, followed by two years' hard touring with ENSA, was back in the West End, playing in Esther McCracken's *Living Room* at the Garrick Theatre. As the Garrick was only the other side of Trafalgar Square, five minutes' walk from the Playhouse or two in a taxi, I would pick her up with a cab on nights when she wasn't firewatching on the roof of the theatre, as had been the custom for West End actors since the start of the Blitz. She hadn't the first idea what to do with a stirrup pump, or even what it was, but the cast took it in turns to guard the building from air attack, so 'I go through the motions' she said, 'and behave as though I know exactly what I'm doing. In the blackout no one can see that I don't.' I'm relieved she didn't add to the fire of London. Fortunately no bombs landed in the vicinity when Dacre-Hill was on duty. Had they done so, would the Garrick Theatre, I wonder, still be with us?

My mother was not given to sentimentality but she was, I know, quietly pleased to be playing in the West End at the same time as her obdurate son. It was happy timing and with it went her last reservation about my chosen career.

Haddon Mason of Film Rights, her longtime agent, had now become mine and after the run of *Bolfry* sent me to Shepherd's Bush to meet Anthony Asquith, who was casting his new film *We Dive at Dawn*, with John Mills as skipper of a submarine and Eric Portman as a CPO, plus the usual officers and crew. Haddon suggested that if I turned up for the interview in my naval uniform it might give me an edge over the competition. It must have, because I became the gunnery officer at £10 a day. Bliss was it in that *Dawn* to get the part. It went right through the picture.

Simultaneously I had received an offer from 'Binkie' Beaumont of H. M. Tennent's, who ruled the West End at that time, to do a tour of forty weeks playing a small part in a new play and understudying the lead. How small was the part, I asked politely.

'Oh, it's not *that* small, my dear,' said Binkie with overwhelming charm. 'In fact it's – well, I'd say it was one of the best parts in the play, wouldn't you, John?' he inquired of John Perry, his friend and partner.

'No,' said John.

'Well, anyway,' snapped Binkie, 'the other characters never stop talking about you. What more do you want?' I smiled and took the Asquith film. I was on Tennent's blacklist for years.

In those days Binkie was royalty. Today, with the Royal National, the Royal Shakespeare and other alternatives competing for actors with the commercial West End, no one – not even my friend and colleague, the prolific producer and tireless enthusiast for all kinds of theatre, Duncan Weldon, who is Binkie's natural successor – is king of Shaftesbury Avenue. It's healthier that way.

We Dive at Dawn, my first contact with the movie industry, was a wartime film with well-drawn characters and plenty of plausible action under Asquith's expert direction. A gentle sympathetic person (known to all as 'Puffin' because he looked like one, though bird of prey he certainly wasn't), this exceptionally polite and much-respected film director, the youngest son of the former Liberal Prime Minister, would sit crosslegged beside the camera with a newspaper folded into a tricorn on his head, as though movie-making was a jolly game which he had been invited to take part in, and say 'Action!' or 'Cut!' every now and again as circumstances required. He scarcely directed me at all, evidently assuming I knew how a naval officer behaved. I did, though on the waves rather than under them, but apart from reminding me in certain scenes that the submarine was supposed to be short of oxygen and would I mind awfully breathing with difficulty he let me get on with it.

Between shots, among those of us who passed the time playing poker were Portman (an old friend of Dacre-Hill's), Jack Watling, a tall handsome young actor who played the Navigation Officer, and occasionally the playwright Terence Rattigan, a close friend of Asquith's who had also written wartime movies, though not this one, and appeared to be keeping a watching brief. When he mentioned during a game that his latest play *Flare Path* was shortly to go into rehearsal, 'Anything for me?' asked Portman who had several films lined up and wasn't available anyway.

'Afraid not,' said Rattigan, 'it's all cast apart from the juvenile.'

At this moment he caught my eye and stared at me thoughtfully. No more was said about the play until the tea break when he said casually, 'You're not by any chance free for dinner tonight?' I'd have said yes if it had meant cutting the Lord Mayor's Banquet. 'Fine,' he said. 'Eight-thirty all right for you?' and gave me his address. I turned up at the St James's Street flat at a carefully judged three minutes late. 'Don't seem too eager,' I had told myself, not even for a part in a Rattigan play. A manservant opened the door, took my coat and ushered me into the drawing room. A bottle on ice stood in a corner.

'Champagne, sir? Or would you prefer a martini?'

'Champagne would be fine, thanks.'

I was given a glass and took a sip. It was indeed fine. *French Without Tears* had made its author a fortune.

'Mr Rattigan won't be a moment, sir.'

Alone, I took in the discreetly lit, beautifully furnished room, the Rachmaninov Concerto no. 2 coming at me at just the right volume from the radiogram. On the coffee table, next to a photograph of my host in RAF uniform, was a typed script. I edged towards it, glanced round to make sure I wasn't observed and flicked open the title page: '*Flare Path* – a play by Terence Rattigan'. Before I could turn to the opening dialogue there were footsteps in the corridor. I moved quickly away and became engrossed in a painting of 'Bubbles' over the fireplace.

Terry came in (if I was going to work for him I felt Christian names were *comme il faut*) wearing a silk dressing gown over pyjamas. He greeted me like an old friend he hadn't met for months. 'Lovely to see you. Now what will you drink? Oh, you've got one, good.' He helped himself to champagne, refilled my glass and sat down on the Regency sofa, patting the seat beside him.

'Come and sit down over here.' For a moment my mind flew back to Peterborough and my first meeting with Novello. And this was St James's Street, Oscar territory. Oh God. As Ivor had, he read my mind and grinned.

'No, no. This is strictly business. Now then – '

The manservant appeared. Saved by the butler? I sat down quickly on the nearest chair.

'Excuse me, sir. New York on the line.'

'Damn.' Terry turned to me. 'My American agent. He's been trying to reach me all day.' He picked up the script of *Flare Path*. 'I wasn't going to get around to this till after dinner. However ... ' He opened the play at a scene in the second act. 'Read that, would you? Read it carefully. Especially the part of Teddy.' He switched off Rachmaninov and went out. So it *was* the part he wanted me for. What an unmitigated swine I was to think for one single second that it was my body.

The scene was the one where the young flying officer has just been told by his wife that she is going to leave him and suddenly he can't see her. The news and the stress of flying mission after mission coming together gets to him and he is suddenly blind. It was a superb scene, brilliantly written. Rattigan had been a rear-gunner and knew all about flying under stress. What a part. As I read on I couldn't believe my luck. Even Cully in *Bolfry* didn't come near Teddy in *Flare Path*.

The author came back, saw the look on my face and smiled. 'Well?'

'Terry, it's – it's tremendous.'

'You really like it?'

'It's a great scene.'

'And Teddy? What about Teddy?'

'He's – whoever plays Freddie is made.'

'Yes, well, that's what I wanted to ask you.' I tried to look no more than politely puzzled and failed. 'But first, you must promise me you'll keep what I'm going to say now under your hat.'

'Cross my heart.' I waited, breathless, for what I knew was coming. Terry leant forward. 'Right, then.' He looked me straight in the eyes.

'*Do you think Jack Watling can play Teddy?*' he asked deliberately and paused. 'Think carefully before you answer.'

But I didn't need to think carefully. I don't know how good I would have been as Teddy in *Flare Path* but I do know the scene where I learnt I wasn't going to play Teddy in *Flare Path* was the performance of my young life.

'Gosh, that's a great idea!' I was brimming over with schoolboy enthusiasm. 'Why, Jack would be perfect. I mean – Good Lord, you couldn't do better! He *is* Teddy!'

'That's what *I* think,' said a relieved Rattigan, 'but the author's not always the best judge, you know. I wanted an objective opinion and, well, you're working with Jack and you've given me one. Thanks, Ronnie. I had a feeling you'd make up my mind for me. Now – shall we eat?'

During the filming of *We Dive at Dawn* I had taken *Zero Hour* out of my bottom drawer and finished it. I showed it to Eric Portman. 'It has possibilities,' he said, 'but it needs work. For instance... ' He gave me some good advice. I took it, rewrote and gave him a revised version.

'Better,' he said, 'and I must say you're strong on dialogue. Who do you want for the male lead?' I hadn't got as far as casting. 'Well, how about me?' The Powell–Pressburger film *49th Parallel* had made Portman a major star. It hadn't occurred to me he would even consider it.

'Do you mean that?'

'I've got a film lined up but if you'll wait I'll try it out for you somewhere.'

I took the play to Jack de Leon at 'Q', who said, 'If Portman is solid, of course I'll do it.' We waited and by the spring of 1944 had gathered a fine cast: Eric, the American Hartley Power, Sheila Sim (Dickie Attenborough's wife) and some of the best character actors of the day (J. H. Roberts, Lloyd Pearson, Dennis Arundell, John Carol).

There was also a young stage-struck assistant stage manager with a hint of a cockney accent who looked after the props, made the coffee and had the walk-on part of a sentry, to whom I took an immediate liking. He would come out front at rehearsals when he should have been in the prompt corner and watch the play, eyes popping out of his head with excitement and enthusiasm. One day he shuffled across to me, looking nervous.

'Ron, could I say something?'

'Go ahead.'

'No, I mean on stage. I know the sentry's a non-speaking part but – well, I couldn't have a line, could I?'

I gave him a line: 'All A-I and tickety-boo?' Richard Pasco, now a highly regarded National Theatre and Royal Shakespeare Company player, always wires me the same good wishes on opening nights: 'Hope all A-I and tickety-boo.'

Zero Hour played to packed houses at the 'Q', then transferred in mid-June to the Lyric, Shaftesbury Avenue, thanks largely to a remarkably encouraging notice by James Agate in the *Sunday Times*. (I had no idea the doyen of the London critics had seen the play.)

Portman had a film commitment so Walter Fitzgerald took over the male lead and I played the juvenile. The first night was notable for two events: the warmth of the reception and the arrival of the first V-bomb to fall on London. As the V-bomb campaign on the civilian population mounted in ferocity the Government closed London's theatres. When they reopened they did so at a nominal rent of a shilling a week. With a certain exception.

The lessee of the Lyric was Jack Buchanan, the immensely popular and attractive star of many a British musical. The rent of the Lyric was £500 a week. Bombs or no bombs, £500 a week it remained. When I went with de Leon to protest Buchanan said, with that charming crack in the voice that was so professionally beguiling, 'Sorry, old lad. A contract's a contract.' When I suggested that a war was also a war he shrugged and offered me a sherry. We never reopened.

However, there were consolation prizes. The drama critic of the *Evening Standard* was the Conservative MP Sir Beverley Baxter. *Zero Hour* was a political thriller set in a Dover hotel on the eve of D-Day. Baxter wrote a generous review and invited me to lunch. During the meal he said, 'You're obviously interested in politics. Why don't you stand for the House? I'll see you get a safe seat.' (This kind of thing actually happened in those days.)

I hesitated. He asked me to think about it seriously. I thought about it fairly seriously for a whole week and then declined. 'Except as a theme for a play,' I said, 'I'm really not interested in politics.'

Another consolation prize was being asked to organise a charity matinée of *Zero Hour* in aid of war victims to be held at the Duke of York's Theatre in St Martin's Lane. I wondered if our scenery, which had been packed off to store, was still viable. With a lick of paint it was and we gave one final performance in the presence of King Haakon of Norway and General Smuts. When presented I tried to appear as though this sort of thing happened to me every day. I was just twenty-four. Dacre-Hill gave a smashing curtsey.

Next day I received a phone call from a theatrical agent, Gordon Harbord, a tall military-looking figure with a moustache who always carried a rolled umbrella, wore a brown bowler and made women's hats as a hobby. He said he'd seen me in *Zero Hour* on the first night.

'The only night.'

'I know. That Hitler. Bloody shame.'

It seemed he was casting a musical, *Jenny Jones*, for George Black, the head of Moss Empires who ran the Palladium and the London Hippodrome as well as a circuit of provincial theatres, and would I come and see G.B. 'You know him, of course.' No, I didn't know G.B.

'Growls like a bear. Absolute poppet. Shall we say tomorrow at ten? Cranbourn Mansions, next to the Hippo. One floor up but take the lift if you're bad in the mornings.'

G.B. turned out to be typecasting for an impresario: plumpish, outwardly jolly, shrewd as they come behind the horn-rims, and straight to the point.

Jenny Jones was to be the musical successor to *The Lisbon Story*, still running after two years at the lovely, gracious Hippodrome (later reshaped and rechristened Talk of the Town – not so lovely, not so gracious – and now plain Hippodrome). Same composer and lyricist (Harry Parr-Davis and Harold Purcell), libretto based on some stories by Ronald Gow, scene director Hugh Miller, musical numbers and choreographer Wendy Toye. Two singing leads, two straight leads. One of them, ambitious young Welsh composer, roughly based on Novello. Did I play the piano?

Yes. Well, sort of. Good. Interested?

'Well – er – could I read the script?'

'Isn't one. That is, not finished. But *J.J.* has everything. Have a prowl through that and see what you think.' I took the outline home and had a prowl through with growing astonishment.

It began: Show starts down coalmine in total blackout. (To make audience feel at home?) Chorus of miners singing hearts out. Next scene, dim lighting, home of chief miner, mother dead, fourteen kids, eldest Jenny Jones, grown-up mother-figure. Establish Jenny. Next scene: Penry Bowen, young impoverished composer (me, supposedly) reeking with ambition, teaches song (mine) to boy soprano. Establish Penry. He meets Jenny. Romance buds. Next: establish singing leads. More romance. They sing smash-hit number ('Not yet written' says outline). Comedy interlude. Jimmy James, popular music-hall comic with gormless stooge, does familiar patter with cigarette-swallowing routine. Sole plot link: Jimmy knows Jenny by name. Second smash ('Dummy lyric, tune to follow'). More numbers: solos, duets, chorus, one or two actually written. First-half finale: famous French ballet: 'Le Jongleur de Notre Dame'. (In Welsh mining village?) Never mind. Interval. (Audience stagger to bar?)

The show certainly had everything. Rather too much, one felt, but not my business. Its connection with Ronald Gow, author of that fine play *Love on the Dole*, was puzzling. However, the money was good, Wendy Toye an acclaimed director of musicals, and I had nothing else in view. Any mine in a storm.

Jenny Jones opened at the Hippodrome, Brighton, for a fortnight's run ('to smooth out any rough edges') prior to following *The Lisbon Story* into the London Hippodrome.

Actors always know when a show isn't working and at the interval on the Brighton opening it wasn't and it was clear it wouldn't be long before *I* wasn't. However, the second half was better. On paper. At the final curtain calls G.B., cigar in mouth, marched cheerfully up on stage, the full company lined up on either side of him, beamed at the audience, threw his arms wide and said, 'Ladies and gentlemen, I think I can safely say I've got another *Lisbon Story*!'

It seemed the ladies and gentlemen in the gallery didn't quite see it that way. 'Boo! Boo! Bloody awful!' they yelled. 'What a stinker!' 'Take it off!' 'You've had this one, Georgie Boy!' came hurtling at us from all sides. Even the stalls and dress circle threw in a marginally restrained boo or two.

G.B. just stood there smiling, like a man who had seen it all before which he probably had. The cast looked at each other and a few began edging towards the wings. 'Don't move!' hissed G.B. out of the corner of his mouth. We waited rock-like until at last the uproar subsided. 'Well,' said G.B. softly, 'we'll see,' and signalled for the safety curtain.

The next morning I was woken from a troubled sleep by the phone ringing in my hotel room. Where was I? Ah yes. Brighton. *Jenny Jones*. We'd got the thumbs-down. I lifted the receiver. I was to come at once to the theatre, said the company manager. 'What for?' G.B. wanted to see me right away. 'Why?' 'Right away.' The voice was grim. The phone went dead. Ah well, you can't win 'em all. But I wasn't responsible. Or was I? Evidently for some reason I was to carry the can. I pulled on some clothes, went out on to the front, hailed a passing cab and was whisked to the Hippodrome stage door. I tottered through to the auditorium, unshaven and without breakfast. G.B. and his entourage were sitting in the front of the stalls, holding what appeared to be a post mortem. They looked as though they'd been there all night. Harbord was sitting slightly apart, knitting a hat. No one so much as glanced at me except Wendy, who threw me a rueful sympathetic smile. I slunk into row K and tried to dematerialise.

G.B. turned and growled, 'Oh, there you are. Come down here beside me.' I went and sat down beside him but leant the other way for safety.

'See here, young man. You've been rewriting your part.' He gave me the look that had reputedly sacked an entire chorus line in its time.

'Well, I – a word or two here and there, perhaps. That is to say – I'm sorry, Mr Black, but you see, some of the dialogue – '

'Shut up and listen. How long would it take you to rewrite t'whole bloody show?'

I'm still not sure whether to be young and nerveless in a crisis is a wonderful thing or a short cut to the sack. There was a brief silence. Then I heard myself say calmly, 'Three weeks.'

'You can't have three weeks. We're booked into t'Hippodrome.'

(He always lapsed into his homely Yorkshire (Lancashire?) accent when up against it.) 'You can have ten days, lad – fortnight at a pinch.'

'Can't be done. Three weeks.'

'Out of question. Opening night's all set.'

'Postpone.' I marvelled at my brass, my cool, my sheer damned impertinence. He turned away, huddled with Wendy Toye and his staff, turned back, eyes like harpoons.

'Right. Three weeks. But by gum, it'd better be good. Well, don't just sit there, boy. Get cracking.'

I went out on to the front to think and found Ronnie Gow sitting on a bench staring out to sea. When I told him it was back to the drawing board he was quite splendid, wished me luck and offered all possible assistance with 'an impossible task'. The new scenes went in one, sometimes two, at each successive performance. (By some strange alchemy my part seemed to grow longer and better with the changes.) G.B. said not a word of criticism or encouragement until the London dress rehearsal when he came up to me and half-nodded. 'Mrs Black says it's better. Not good, mind, but better. Here, lad. Thanks.' And he thrust a cheque for £500 into my hand. 'By the way, your performance has gone to hell. Gabble, gabble, gabble. Can't hear a word you say.' He was right. For three weeks I'd been on automatic pilot.

One matinée during the five-month run of *J.J.* (hardly a smash but no disaster) the stage-door keeper rang through to my dressing room. 'There's a friend of yours here, sir.'

'Oh yes. Who?'

'He says to tell you it's Ismene.'

'Who?'

'Ismene from Cambridge.'

'Good Lord, yes!' Ismene was Antigone's sister. He'd gone into the army. 'Send him up, send him up.'

'Sorry, sir, but he says can you come down?'

I ran down two steps at a time. He was in a wheelchair. He smiled cheerfully and put out his hand. He had lost both legs. A gentle soul, bright, decent, twenty-three years old. And we who came through dare to grumble at our providential lives.

Early in 1945 I read a brief news item in the old *News Chronicle* about a British officer who had married a German girl in unusual circumstances. It was to change one or two lives, mine in particular. The headline 'Drama faces two young people' had caught my eye, especially the word 'drama'. I read the item through several times. It seemed to me that here was the nucleus of a play, powerful, topical, even perhaps important. The more I thought about it, the more convinced I was of its potential. Then the doubts began.

Had I the technical experience, invention, craft, to develop it and make it work on stage? Probably not. If I continued acting in other people's plays, *certainly* not. I decided to take time off from acting, gave myself three months to complete a first draft and told Haddon Mason no matter what acting offers turned up to decline them. Inevitably they poured in but I managed to stick it out.

One joyous event, and one less happy, broke my concentration. The second war with Germany ended, the lights came on all over Europe and on 8 May, V-E Day, I joined the jubilant crowds dancing round the Victoria monument outside the gates of Buckingham Palace and shouting for the King and Queen to come out on the balcony. They appeared several times with Churchill, cigar and V-sign in triumphant action. The relief that the war was over was unimaginable and the feeling that evil had been cast down by a country united at every level of society, as I had not known it in my lifetime, overwhelming. True, the war in the Far East was still to be won but now the full strength of the Armed Forces of the Allies could be concentrated on Japan. She must inevitably surrender within months.

Sure enough V-J Day followed on 15 August.

The breaking out of peace brought rapid change. The National Government was dissolved, a caretaker Cabinet formed with Churchill at its head, and a General Election called for 26 July.

Two nights before the poll I chanced to be in Sloane Square when a familiar figure wrapped in a dark blue overcoat although it was high summer and wearing his individual bowler came by, standing up in a jeep. The jeep drove slowly round the square. Cigar stump clenched defiantly between his teeth, scowling, not a flicker of a smile and giving his V-sign in a perfunctory manner as though his heart was not in it, Churchill looked glum and depressed.

For a second I thought, My God, he believes he's going to lose! Then I remembered that he had these bouts of depression for no particular reason. His 'black dog', he called it. It was of course inconceivable that the British Prime Minister should, in the hour of triumph, be rejected by the nation he had led to a great victory. The return of Churchill and with him a Conservative Government was surely a formality.

*

Election Day weather was dark and grey with solid rain hour after hour. I stood, dumb with astonishment and disbelief, in the entrance hall of the Hyde Park Hotel, where the lights were ablaze as it were night, while the nuts and bolts of a Labour landslide poured off the ticker tape. It was as though it had been waiting five years to happen, which perhaps it had. They said it was the Service vote that did it, calling the pre-war Conservatives to account for sending them into battle without the arms with which to fight. Whatever the reason, I was stunned by what I saw not as the birth of a brave new Britain but a national disaster. Looking back, older and fractionally wiser, I see now that Attlee's peaceful revolution, for all its drab and colourless exterior and inevitable failures, did plant the first seeds of a more equitable society. Unassuming and laconic, Attlee proved an admirable Prime Minister and the ideal counterweight to Churchill, if such was historically necessary.

However, at the time none of this so much as crossed the mind of someone wholly preoccupied with a play that he had just completed, about a young British air force officer who marries the German nurse who has helped him escape from the prison camp in which he was interned and brings her home with him to wartime England, to the dismay of his family and in defiance of a scandalised public to whom 'fraternisation' with the enemy (if one can 'fraternise' with one's wife) is akin to treason.

Although I had finished the play, which I called *Frieda* after its central character, in the three months I had given myself, I was far from sure whether the powerful drama I heard in my head had materialised on paper. I gave it to friends who seemed to think it had, but they wanted me to succeed and could just be being kind. I sent it to one or two managements who failed to return it. This could be seen as either a good sign or a bad: good if they were lying down after a profound emotional experience, not so good if they were upright and *Frieda* prone in the wastepaper basket.

Christmas and New Year 1946 came and went and the play began to trickle back with what I quickly learnt was the standard managerial negative, e.g. 'Thank you so much for sending me your play. I much enjoyed reading it but I'm afraid it is not quite what I am looking for just at the moment. However, do please let me read your next which I have every confidence will be blah and blah and also very possibly blah. Yours, etc.' (No rush, Miss Felixstowe.)

Suddenly the giant figure of Henry Sherek, impresario and buccaneer extraordinary, loomed in sight. I had no recollection of sending him the play but somehow he had got hold of a copy and said that if CEMA (Council for the Encouragement of Music and the Arts, forerunner of the Arts Council) would find half the production cost he would find the other half.

The money was found and the play submitted for licensing. The licence was refused. Stunned, but prepared for a fight to the death, Sherek and I set off for St James's Palace and the Lord Chamberlain's office.

Why this delightful army officer had medieval powers of censorship over the British theatre halfway through the twentieth century was one of those English oddities that fascinate foreigners and make those who have to live with them fit to be tied. The Chamberlain received us in a beautifully-cut lounge suit, gave us an excellent dry sherry, threw more logs on a blazing fire and asked what he could do for us.

'Well, sir,' I said. 'You've refused my play a licence. I take it you consider it either seditious or pornographic or possibly both.'

'Oh, m'dear feller!' cried the Chamberlain. 'Perish the thought. Play straight as die, clean as whistle. All but three words in second act. Cut words, curtain rises and Robert is your relative!'

But I couldn't cut the offending words. They were the crux of a vital scene in which Frieda, who is anti-fascist, confronts her brother Richard, an irredeemable Nazi (modern equivalent currently resurgent in German State). The following dialogue takes place:

Frieda (with passion): But he is dead, Ricky! Hitler is dead!

Richard (calmly): *So is Christ.*

'Y'see,' said the Chamberlain, 'equation of Hitler with Christ – putting them as it were on same spiritual plane – of course, m'dear chap, know it's not *meant* to be blasphemous but queer customers, audiences. Take offence at drop of hat. Next thing you know, Canterbury hot under cassock, Pope unmanned, ecumenicalism dead as dodo and whole mess down to you. Have another noggin.'

With the aid of a number of noggins I tried endless variations of 'So is Christ', all of which, according to the Chamberlain, were theologically unacceptable and likely to cause schism, if not rioting on the steps of St Paul's. The guardian of the nation's sensibilities tried hard to be helpful, even at one inspired moment wondering if I couldn't 'make do with John the Baptist'. But the Baptist was not the Christ. At length he glanced at his watch and rose. 'Frightfully sorry. Must fly. Audience with His Majesty.'

He was halfway through the door when in desperation I called out 'Christ also died?' which saved the point but softened the punch. 'Will that do?' The Chamberlain stopped, turned, gave a deep sigh. The Army had not trained him for ecclesiastical disputation. At length: 'Have to, I suppose,' he said. 'Can't keep Head of Established Church waiting,' and was gone.

Sherek and I drank to victory with the last of the amontillado but twenty-two more years were to pass before theatrical censorship was finally abolished in Britain.

With a clean bill and under the joint management of Sherek and CEMA, *Frieda* went on a thirteen-week tour. The excellent cast – Barbara Everest, Barbara Cooper, Valerie White, Jack Allen, Ursula Howells – was directed by Irene Hentschel, wife of Ivor Brown, dramatic critic of the *Observer*. There were no star names but this made for reality and the piece, which was considered emotionally and politically ahead of its time, was well received across the country.

Less well received, at least by me, was the tendency of the actress who was Frieda to give notes to the distinguished player who was her mother-in-law and, when they were ignored, to stand in the wings and throw chairs at her. The rest of the cast took sides and by the time the play reached London and its first night at the Westminster Theatre you could slice the air with a machete.

In my ignorance I tried to pour water on the flames. I should have poured petrol. The tension generated offstage was electric, the actors carried it on stage like ectoplasm and on the first night communicated it to audience and critics, whose reviews ranged from favourable to fulsome. At its off-the-beaten-track theatre the play ran to excellent business for six months. The *Times* critic said, 'The piece should thrive on its "strong" situations.' They were stronger than he knew. If Frieda hadn't made it up with her mother-in-law we might have had another *Mousetrap*. For me the play was a turning-point. After *Zero Hour* I had continued to think of myself as an actor. But now... I went through the postnatal period that afflicts most writers after a successful birth. Suppose I never had another idea. Suppose *Frieda* was a one-off. Suppose the discovery of a gift I did not know that I had died as quickly as it was born. What then? *Finita la commèedia*. A door had opened and I had tasted blood. But where did I go from here?

The answer came swiftly. Michael Relph, who had designed the set for the play and was an associate producer at Ealing Studios – chairman and managing director Michael Balcon – asked if he might show the script to Balcon. The possibility of a film sale hadn't seriously occurred to me but I waited in hope for a call from Ealing and a week later it came. We met in the chairman's office: Balcon, Relph and his partner, the director Basil Dearden. Ealing not only acquired the film rights but engaged me to write the screenplay. I came out of the office in a daze, delighted but alarmed at what I had let myself in for.

'You do realise I've never written a screenplay?' I said to Relph and Dearden.

'Good. You'll come fresh to it,' said Relph. 'You go to the pictures, don't you?'

'Yes, but I don't know the first thing about writing for them. All those cameras and camera angles, I've never owned so much as a Kodak.'

'Leave all that to us,' said Dearden. 'Just tell your story in master scenes.'

'Yes and open out the play,' said Relph. 'Take your people out of doors and into the village whenever it's natural. Motion pictures means pictures that move.'

'Think pictures,' said Dearden. 'It's simple once you get the hang of it.'

'Hm.' I tended to think dialogue. 'Will you be around?'

'We're on a job just now but there's always the telephone. Meanwhile Angus will hold your hand.'

Angus McPhail, Ealing's scenario editor, was a tall lanky Scot who kept sane among the movie-makers by dividing his time between the studios and the pub across the road and had been in the business since the early Hitchcock days. Angus became my guru, guide and mentor and whenever I stumbled picked me up and pointed me back along the trail to final fade-out. When Relph and Dearden joined us and a rough shooting script was approved, casting began. The key question: who was to play the German nurse?

The war was still an open wound and even if a German actress were to be granted a work permit, which was highly unlikely even by a Socialist government, we had seen no German artists on film since before the war. We tested several admirable English actresses with carefully coached German accents but finally it was agreed that Frieda must be played by a foreigner and Relph and Dearden flew to Stockholm to test a Swedish girl who had had a success in a cult film called *Frenzy*. When they returned there was some hesitation about the attractive enigmatic Swede they had tested but eventually the enthusiasts, myself among them, won the day and Mai Zetterling was signed.

When she arrived with her husband Tutte Lemkow, a ballet dancer, Balcon, Relph, Dearden and I took them to tea in the Ealing canteen which resembled a large workman's hut in the down-to-earth, functional Ealing style. It was a strange encounter. Mai didn't speak a word of English except 'yes' and 'no' in a whisper, Tutte, who spoke a little, kept saying, 'Mai miss bay-bee, Mai miss bay-bee' and Mai kept shaking her head and looking shy and weeping. I sat bemused,

125

wondering if it might not be better to make a silent movie with lots of helpful captions.

Despite efforts to dissuade him Tutte kept on about Mai missing bay-bee until bay-bee's mother suddenly rounded on (presumably) bay-bee's father and they had a violent row in Swedish. This seemed to make them both feel better and Mai smiled and, opening her handbag, produced some large slabs of Swedish chocolate and gave us each a bar.

This charming gesture was worth a month's sweet coupons and we all said, 'Thank you very very much indeed' and had a good bite. Perhaps after wartime snoek and Spam one's palate had atrophied but my bar tasted like a synthesis of cayenne pepper and bitter aloes topped up with a sprinkling of curry powder. As the others were munching away apparently with gusto I pretended to nibble mine until I remembered an urgent phone call I simply had to make, excused myself and disposed of my generous gift down the chairman's lavatory. In case you should come across this book, dear Frieda, the fault lay not in your condiment but in my colon.

9

. . . .

Ealing to Hollywood

While Swedish Mai was learning English in order to play a German girl, one Bob Goldstein flew in from Hollywood, Cal. This irrepressible American, at once likeable and slightly off the pavement, had a brief from Universal International Pictures Inc. to discover what, if any, movie talent the Brits had come up with during the war years and, where appropriate, to capture it for the home market.

I was introduced to him as an actor/playwright/screenwriter, which was pitching it high to say the least, but exaggeration was his business.

'I gotta natural!' he cried. 'I gotta natural!' and took my phone number. 'Call you tomorrow, kiddo.' Bob Goldstein talked Hollywood argot like no one else I ever met.

Before I had downed my first cup of morning tea he was on the line. 'Hi there, Triple Threat,' he began, which would be hard to take even after a full breakfast. 'Ever heard the name Hal Wallis?'

'Hal B. Wallis, Head of Production at Warner Brothers?'

'Was. He's at Paramount now with his own outfit. Listen, I do no service to Universal by alerting you but Hal's a pal and about to go with a script he needs checking for kosher English. Are you with me? It's set in your country and based on a Victorian thriller-diller by a little lady called – wait, I have it written down – Margery Abingham.'

'Allingham.'

'You know Margie?'

'No, but she writes Victorian melodramas.'

'Check. So – how does a little Anglicising grab you?'

'Well, if you'd like to send it round –'

127

'You misapprehend, friend. I don't have it, it's not our movie. You'd have to fly over, talk to Hal's New York rep and, if she gives you the nod, go on out to the Coast.'

'Which coast is that?'

'There's only one coast that matters, kiddo. The *West* Coast, Hollywood, Cal.'

'It's kind of you to think of me but I doubt if I could do that.' *Frieda* was due to start shooting as soon as Mai's English was up to snuff, which could be any day.

'Hey, Triple Threat, you're not directing too, are you?'

'No, of course I'm not directing. But I've never seen a movie being made and this one's very personal to me, so –'

'Man, it's only a fortnight's work at best. Maybe ten days. Maybe you won't even get the job. Look, I'm doing you a favour.'

'I know and please don't think I don't appreciate it but there would be other problems.'

'Such as?'

'Money. I'd be going on spec and we're only allowed to take a maximum of two hundred pounds out of the country.'

'We'll stake you. If you get the job we'll bill you. If not, the trip's on us, don't worry about it. You want to fly or take the Lizzie? She sails New Year's Eve.'

As it happened, I knew that. Ivor Novello was going over en route to California to stay with Gladys Cooper, taking with him his friend Bobby Andrews and his longtime secretary, Lloyd Williams. Also Bea Lillie, Dorothy Dickson and other celestial passengers were going along for the ride.

'Well? Yes or no?'

I wavered. A trip – my first – to the United States with the chance of two weeks' work when I got there and, if not, the cost covered; all this and a star-studded *Queen Elizabeth*.

'Won't the ship be fully booked?'

'Leave that to us,' said Robert Goldstein and rang off.

That afternoon a PR man from the Rank Organisation called and said, 'I have a ticket for you for the *Queen Elizabeth*. Where do I send it?'

I gave him my address and thanked him profusely. 'Oh. What time does she sail?'

'Eleven, New Year's Eve, on the dot.'

'I'll be there and thank you again.'

'My pleasure. Have a good trip.'

Dacre-Hill thought I was crazy. I thought I was crazy. I also thought, if you don't do something crazy when you're young you could miss the boat.

The day came and I lay in bed, idly flicking through the morning papers. I was packed and ready to leave for Southampton but as we were not sailing till eleven at night I had all day so there was no need to rise and shine. It was seven and a half minutes past 0900 hours precisely – I remember the time to the second – when, glancing down the social column of the *Daily Telegraph*, I came across a picture of Ivor with the caption 'Sailing this morning on the Queen Elizabeth'.

This morning? No, they had that wrong. The *QE* sailed New Year's Eve. Eve stood for *evening* ... Oh God. Oh dear God, no, it didn't! Not necessarily. New Year's Eve was *all day*. All twelve hours of the – 'HELP!!!' I shrieked and hurled myself out of bed.

Dacre-Hill (arriving at the double): 'What is it?'

R.M. (grabbing telephone directory and flicking feverishly through): 'Remember, when I was a child, teaching me Christmas Eve starts in the morning? Well, so does *New Year's* Eve. You omitted to mention that.'

D.H. (aghast): 'You've missed the ship!'

R.M. (in a gabble, dialling): 'Check, as they say in the United States which I will now almost certainly never see if I live to be – hello, Cunard? Good morning. Yes, isn't it a lovely day. Would you be so kind as to confirm what time the *Queen Elizabeth* sails today for the United States? Eleven hundred hours. Not by any chance twenty-three hundred? No, no problem. Just making sure I hadn't made a ba— hadn't got it wrong. And a Happy New Year to you, too.'

I threw the phone down. I was done for. My big break gone, my career in ruins before it had started. Unless – I dialled feverishly.

'Hello, Inquiries? Could you be absolutely wonderful and give me the number of Croydon Airport in five seconds flat, it's a matter of life and – *grazie. Grazie tante!*'

I dialled again.

D.H. (returning with glass of whisky): 'What are you doing?'

R.M. (gulping Scotch): 'Thousand-to-one shot.

'Croydon Airport? Good morning. I want a plane. An aeroplane, that's right. I'm not fussy. Anything with wings will do. To fly to Southampton. Now. This minute. I mean, I'm leaving Knightsbridge now by racing car. The name is Millar. M for mad, I for insane, L for lunatic. Come straight to Reception? I'm on my way.'

'I'm on my way too.' Dacre-Hill was pulling on her fur coat over her nightgown.

There was no time to argue. I trundled my suitcase down the ninety-four Pont Street stairs and into a cab. The driver broke records to the airport where we were rushed from Reception across the tarmac and into a tiny aircraft, fell in, the door slammed and we were airborne.

As we circled Southampton, suddenly there below us was the Cunarder. She was still alongside but her siren was giving the goodbye hoots that ships give when they are about to sail.

'There she is!' I yelled. 'Land, man, land!'

'Can't land on the deck, chum.'

'Then land on the dock!'

'No can do. This isn't a 'copter.'

We landed at the very edge of the airport. There was a taxi waiting. We leapt in and arrived on the jetty just as her tugs began to ease the great liner out into Southampton Water. Passengers and relatives were waving and screaming inaudible goodbyes at each other. The ship gave a final farewell hoot. I shot along the jetty dragging my suitcase.

'Wait!' gasped Dacre-Hill to the *Queen Elizabeth*. 'He's coming! Wait!!' as though even a giant's roar could possibly be heard above the din.

At this moment I spotted Cunard's managing director at the end of the jetty waving his charge safely on her way to America. He was a friend of Bea Lillie's and we had met on a couple of occasions. I rushed up to him and poured out my plight.

'Sorry, old chap. You've just missed her.'

'Can't you get her back?' said my dear mother, as though the *Queen Elizabeth* were a tricycle that you just reversed by pedalling backwards.

'I'm afraid that's not possible.' Cunard smiled tolerantly.

Suddenly I had a brilliant idea. 'Look! That's the pilot's boat, isn't it? He goes on board when she's in mid-water, right? Let me go with him.'

'I'm sorry, that's against the rules.'

'Surely you can stretch a point in a crisis?'

'They're not my rules. She's sealed by Customs. Nothing and no one bar the pilot goes on or off that ship until she docks at New York Harbour.'

Long before we were back at Pont Street I had made my mind up. I would take the night flight to La Guardia from London airport. That is, if there was a seat available. I telephoned. There wasn't. Were they sure?

'Absolutely, sir. I'm sorry but we're chock-a-block. It's New Year's Eve, you know.'

The sweet voice the other end didn't *sound* as if it were rubbing it in. Nevertheless I made a mental note to murder its owner if I ever came across her.

'Oh. Hold, sir. Are you still there?'

'Yes, I *am* still here. In all probability I shall be here until coal sprouts.' I gave it all the bitterness one feels when trapped by a folly of one's own making.

'Just one moment. Hold.' Sound of hand covering instrument. Blurred voices. I held for eternity. At last the voice again, doubtfully, 'Sir, I – I don't suppose this would appeal to you.'

'Try me.'

'Well, there is *another* plane, leaving for New York at nineteen hundred hours our time. That's seven o'clock this evening. It's not one of our scheduled flights, it's... rather unusual.'

'Does it have wings? When it goes up does it come down again and vice versa?'

'Oh yes, sir. There's nothing wrong with the aircraft. The thing is, it's a GI brides' special.'

'A what?'

'The wives of American servicemen who married over here, sir, during the war or just after. They're going to join their husbands.'

'Very right and proper of them.'

'*With* their babies, sir.' The voice had taken on what sounded like a warning note.

'I've nothing against babies. I was one myself a year or so ago.'

'There's just the single spare seat, sir. Apart from the crew you'll be the only man on board with fifty-two young ladies.'

'Really?' I began to warm to the idea.

'Then you'll take the seat?'

'Yes. I'll take it.'

The voice became formal. 'That's one seat for the BOAC Special for New York, La Guardia, leaving at 1930 hours. Your ticket will be at Reception. Please check in one hour before takeoff. Your aircraft will stop at Shannon for dinner and Newfoundland to refuel. Otherwise straight through. Have a nice flight.'

As soon as we were airborne I looked around me at my fellow passengers. They were cheerful, noisy, jolly girls, bubbling with excitement at being on their way to a land they knew all about from the movies, a land of silk stockings and shiny optimistic motor cars and whatever-you-want-we-have-it-and-isn't-life-just-wonderful-United-States. Some of them were pretty as paint (of which they were wearing rather more than a sufficiency), some less so – well, much wartime courting had taken place in a blackout – but all were clearly overjoyed to be swapping prefab ration-bound Britain for New York or Chicago or the corn belt of wealthy, warm-hearted middle America.

As one or two of the bolder brides began breast-feeding the outward and visible sign of the American occupation I decided the BOAC Special was going to be fun. The weather was good and the company original and unexpected. Some of the wives were exchanging pictures of the husbands whom they hadn't seen for two years. It reminded me of a wartime conversation between two Cockney girls on a London bus overheard by James Agate.

'What you doin' tonight, Doreen?'

'Goin' Yankin'. Comin'?'

Yes, indeed they were coming, a planeload of Doreens all heading westward where, as F.D.R. had pointed out to Churchill, lo, the land was bright. All agog to be goin' Yankin'. I too, when I came to think of it . . .

At unrationed Shannon the promised meal was waiting: lashings of fresh salmon and cucumber followed by double helpings of Irish lamb and beef, plate after plate of vegetables, choice of creamy sweets and cheeses, coffee, wines, liqueurs. Irish generosity was pressed down and running over and the young brides dug into the first good meal they'd had for years as though it were their last. As for me, with an Atlantic crossing ahead, and a stomach that remained a weak spot, I opted for the salmon, ignored the cucumber and left it cautiously at that.

Our last sight of land behind us, BOAC Special was swiftly into rough weather, gale-force winds tossing the DC-6 about as though it were a children's toy. First the babies, then their mothers began to bring up all that had gone down and to scatter it around with a fine abandon. The two stewardesses in their immaculate uniforms, under rapid fire from beef and lamb and Gorgonzola, dashed valiantly up and down the gangway distributing a variety of receptacles until the entire cabin was in every sense a sick-bay.

'Excuse me, sir, but could you possibly – ?' gasped one of them, trying desperately to hold on to an armful of three howling infants and remain on her feet in an aircraft lurching wildly from side to side. As the children were about to go sailing down the cabin I grabbed a couple, the stewardess yelled 'I'll be back' and, holding fast to the third child, vanished into the toilet.

Sitting in my single seat, benumbed and clutching my two charges, the thought occurred that somewhere far below was a nice warm bed in a nice warm cabin in a ship sailing peacefully towards the New World, a bed in which, had I not been chronologically illiterate, I would at that moment be happily tucked up and dreaming blissfully of Californian beaches beside the broad Pacific.

As the plane continued to heave, and its passengers with it, the intercom suddenly crackled. 'Good evening, ladies, and to you, sir, good evening. This is your captain speaking. On behalf of BOAC we apologise for the turbulence but we should be into a more peaceful airstream in about ten minutes. Right now the weather in New York is fine, so be of good cheer. Remember, you're pioneers like Columbus and he had it even worse.' With a babe on each knee taking it in turn to throw up over each other and me I doubted that.

But all things come to an end and gradually there was nothing further to egest, the wind dropped outside and inside the cabin, and as the peace of exhaustion descended my charges were returned to their mothers. (At least, each was returned to *a* mother. In the low purple lighting one couldn't be categorical about who got which.)

'Thank you so much for your help, sir.' My friend the stewardess had reappeared spick-and-span, not a blonde hair out of place.

'Any time,' I murmured, dabbing ineffectively at my best suit with my second handkerchief.

'Would you care for a cup of tea, sir?'

I considered the offer carefully. 'Er – yes. Yes, I think I could just about manage a cup of tea.'

It arrived in a large paper cup with a doughnut floating around inside it. I had a vague idea that Americans only dunked doughnuts in coffee. Never mind, life is a permanent education and I was probably wrong. In the semi-dark I fished around for the doughnut, plucked it out and took a healthy bite. As I brayed, choked, spluttered and screeched the thing in my hand split asunder, its contents shooting up my nose and down my throat and on to my already sodden suit.

I once read in *Reader's Digest*, 'From each of life's disasters there's a lesson to be learnt.' Well, all right. From BOAC Special, not to say Unique, to New York La Guardia, this traveller learnt that in the United States tea is more likely than not to be made from teabags.

On arrival at the airport a car the length of Bond Street with huge tail fins was waiting. Also a chauffeur with a note from Bob Goldstein: 'Welcome to the Big Apple. You're booked into the Savoy Plaza, check your gear and come straight to Lindy's. Chauffeur in limo will convey.'

'Ought I to know who Lindy is?' I asked chauffeur in limo. No doubt she was delightful but I really wasn't up to any more tonight.

'She's a restaurant, sir. Made famous by Mr Damon Runyon.'

A restaurant! Oh, *no*. No, please God, no more food. The thought alone was a terrible thing.

At Lindy's I found Bob at a table with the renowned writing team of Ben Hecht and Charles MacArthur (*The Front Page* and other celebrated works) and was given a welcome fit for the Wright brothers.

'Now – what'll you start with, kiddo?' Goldstein handed me a vast menu. I explained that my stomach was ahead of theirs, I had already eaten. This was brushed aside and a vast T-bone steak that overlapped the plate set in front of me. Urged on by Goldstein and the two eminent playwrights ('You Brits have a lot of chow-time to make up') I toyed with it and just managed a spoonful of the mountainous ice-cream sundae topped with maraschino cherry that followed, before being whisked away semiconscious in an even more extended limo to a New Year's Eve party somewhere off Central Park. There I became aware of a few vaguely familiar faces before being handed a huge bourbon on the rocks, finding an armchair in a corner, collapsing into it and falling instantly into a deep dream-laden sleep.

I dreamt I was at a noisy party somewhere in New York where I was introduced by Goldstein to Humphrey Bogart and Joan Crawford and Helen Hayes and Ethel Merman and Richard Rodgers and a host of other faces who all seemed to know me because they said, 'Glad to meet you, Triple Threat. How's little old England and welcome to New York City and a Happy, Snappy, Snap-Happy New Year!'

I don't know how long I was out but when I came to there were balloons and streamers all over everywhere and among those singing 'Happy Snappy New Year!' or whatever *were* Bogart and Crawford and Hayes and Merman, and the man at the piano playing 'Auld Lang Syne' *was* Richard Rodgers, and I *was* in New York and it *was* New Year's Day 1947. *ALL* day.

Next morning, as soon as my head began to clear, I called the Wallis office and made contact with the lady who was his New York proxy.

'Well, hell*o* there! Can't wait to meet you, Mr Mill*ar*. Good trip?

Well, that's just fine. Now, would you care to stop by around, say, noon or is that too early for your hangover?' Was she psychic or had the bad word spread?

'I'm fine. In excellent shape. I'll be there.'

She was brisk and charming and after a brief chat set my mind at rest with 'I'm sure you'll do a fine job for Hal. Now you'll want to draw breath before going out to the Coast. There's no wild rush and I guess you've had your fill of the joys of flying. Why don't I book you on the Superchief for Thursday, no, Friday. That'll give you time to look around and say hello to the greatest city in the world.'

It seemed the Superchief was famous: the train that went from New York to Los Angeles via Chicago, crossing the United States from east to west in two and a half days. 'I'll send your ticket round to the hotel. Now what shows would you like to see? You must catch *Okie*, it's a breakthrough, and *Caro* too, though you need a sweet tooth for the mushy ending. Why don't I get you seats for tonight for *Okie* and tomorrow night for *Caro*?' I had not heard of *Okie* and *Caro*, I assumed they were off-Broadway productions.

'That sounds wonderful but – ' I reached for my wallet. 'I'm afraid I only have a limited amount of – '

'Now just you put that away, honey. We'll take care of every little thing. Ask at the box office in your name and the house seats will be waiting for you. Mill*ar* with an "a". Right?' Whatever it was Tennessee Williams had Blanche DuBois say in *Streetcar* about the kindness of strangers, the US of A gets the Oscar. And whoever pretends that New York for the first time is not one of life's specials is either hopelessly jaded or a sourpuss without a soul.

Okie and *Caro* were, of course, *Oklahoma!* and *Carousel*. The two Rodgers and Hammerstein musicals, neither of which London had seen, were a revelation and for forty-eight hours I went around in my usual daze. Any thought I might have had of one day writing a musical had expired with the overtures. When the *Queen Elizabeth* arrived I went down to the dock to meet her and assumed a casual air as Novello and party and a bouncy Miss Lillie came down the gangway and gaped. 'Where did *you* spring from?' 'We looked all over!' 'How in the world did you beat us to it?' It was a mordant pleasure explaining, and a bonus to discover that they too were travelling west on the Superchief.

Ivor in New York, though it was far from new to him, was like an excited schoolboy and retained his wide-eyed wonder on the train heading west until, on the second day, suddenly everything changed. His friend and secretary, 'Lloydie' Williams, suffered a severe stroke. An odd thing about Ivor: he turned away from illness. Not through any lack of concern, too much of it perhaps, or the feeling that in his world of musical escape such things as strokes didn't happen or, if they did, should not be dwelt upon. This most considerate of creatures couldn't cope with sudden misadventure to one close to him. He just stared out of the window, smoking one cigarette after another, and left arrangements to others.

Frantic calls were made to friends in Hollywood to have an ambulance meet the train at the staging post for Beverly Hills, the small Pasadena station where we were to alight. As the great Superchief drew in it was evident that Hollywood tradition had been observed. I counted five ambulances: one each from Gladys Cooper, Fanny Brice and Constance Collier, who were all waiting on the platform, and two more from the Cedars of Lebanon and Pasadena hospitals respectively. Clearly, in Hollywood, if you are on your way to Abraham's Bosom you are expected to arrive in style. After considerable discussion as to which ambulance would take the patient where, Constance Collier's was chosen – on what grounds I cannot say, perhaps because she was the eldest – and sitting beside the driver she rode off in triumph, with Lloydie and a nurse who looked like Rita Hayworth in the back. Gladys swept Ivor and Bobby Andrews off in her open Chevvy and Bea Lillie asked Fanny Brice if her ambulance could drop her at the Beverly Hills Hotel.

'You're not going to no Beverly Hills Hotel,' said Brice. 'You're staying with Fanny.'

'Will that be cheaper?' asked Miss Lillie.

It had been arranged that on arrival I was to call the Wallis office who would have arranged accommodation. Bea would have none of it. 'Tell the hotel I'm not coming and you can have my room. Ask at Reception for Arthur. He'll take care of you.'

I took a cab to the Beverly Hills and asked for Arthur at Reception and gave the message. He looked with scarcely veiled contempt at my single, rather battered suitcase. 'Well, of course, if that's what Miss Lillie wants... ' he snapped his fingers. 'Boy, number fourteen for the gentleman.'

Number fourteen was not a room, it was a suite, from the look of it the presidential suite. The diminutive page deposited my suitcase and waited and in my nervousness I overtipped him from my rapidly dwindling store of dollars. When I called the Wallis office I was put through to a male voice. 'Is that Ron Mill*ar?* Hello there and welcome. Now we have a room for you at the – '

'It's very kind of you but actually I – er – I've checked in at the Beverly Hills.'

'Oh? *Very* scrumptious, I must say.' The voice sounded like Eric

Blore taken aback in one of those Astaire/Rogers movies. (Come to think of it, he was taken aback in all the Astaire/Rogers movies.) 'Well now – Mr Wallis wants that you should have the script ASAP, Ron, so we'll have it sent over by carrier pigeon to the BH at dawn. It's a great script, you're going to love it.' I said I was sure I was. 'It just needs tidging up a touch to check the English is spot-on, bullseye and what-have-you. Just as soon as you've read it we'll fix for you to come right over to Paramount for a chatteroo with Mr W. Great to have you with us, Ron. 'Bye now.'

I sleep luxuriously and long in the giant bed and wake up fresh as the orange juice that arrives with the *Los Angeles Times* without my ordering either. Eggs-over-easy, whatever that is, follow, and tea in a real live teapot. I'm wallowing in the huge bath when the house phone rings. I stumble dripping to the instrument.

'Mr Mill*ar*, this is Arthur. Your car is here, sir.'

'My what?'

'Your Buick. It's blocking the driveway, sir. Could you move it, please?'

'But I don't have a Buick.' It wasn't All Fools' Day, was it?

'What car *do* you have, sir?'

'I don't have a car at all. There must have been a cock-up.'

'Sir?'

'Someone has bungled.'

'You're Mr Mill*ar* from England. I recognise your voice, sir.'

'Nevertheless someone is in error, as the Christian Scientists have it.'

'Please come to Reception, sir. Your car is obstructing the traffic.' The phone goes dead.

I pull on slacks and a coloured shirt and rush to Reception. As I arrive a tall blond man walks into the hotel, sees me and waves. 'Hi there. Merry Christmas.' It was gone New Year. I wave back and wish him a happy Easter.

The man looks like Danny Kaye except that I don't know Danny Kaye.

'Morning, Mr Kaye,' says the diminutive page. It *is* Danny Kaye. I wonder who he thinks *I* am.

In the driveway car horns blare to wake the dead. Immediately outside the front entrance stands what looks like a brand-new Buick convertible. As I drift out, inwardly tense, outwardly cool, two men in white overalls close on me. 'Mr Mill*ar*? Sign here please, sir.' One of them thrusts a piece of paper at me. The horns from the growing

line of cars queuing for the hotel entrance go into prolonged fortissimo.
I wave, smile idiotically and mime 'Shan't be a tick.' This sets off
another infuriated fanfare.

'If you'd just sign here, sir. Ain't she a beauty?'

'Very pretty but I didn't order her. Please take her away at once.'

He shakes his head. 'From Universal Pictures, sir. She's all yours
while you're with us.'

R.M. (thinks): Yes, but who's paying for all this, if I don't get the
job?

More blasting of horns.

R.M. (decides): Must get job, come what may.

A huge commissionaire sashays up. He looks like a John Ford
Western cowboy, only taller and bigger. (I have yet to learn that in
Hollywood everyone looks like a movie actor waiting for the call to
glory.)

'I'm sorry, sir, but you can't wait here. You're blocking the – '

'Yes. Right. Thank you. Okay.' His physique is not one to argue
with. The piece of paper is from a car-hire company under instruction,
I suspect, from Goldstein. Well, at least I'm not *buying* the Buick. I
sign. White Overalls tosses some keys at me, urges me to have a nice
day, which I consider unlikely in the circumstances, and he and his
buddy jump into the van that is parked in front of the Buick and are
gone. Control of events, which from the start of this American venture
has been steadily slipping away from me, seems to be receding further.
I now have the best suite in the Beverly Hills Hotel, a brand-new
Buick convertible, the friendship of Danny Kaye, a dwindling of
dollars and no contract. Meanwhile the frustrated drivers are going
berserk.

'Excuse me, sir.' The gentle giant doorman/cowboy/movie actor
advances and I find myself wafted into the Buick behind the driving
wheel. The door is slammed. A final hysterical blare of horns signals
the hunters are going in for the kill. The ignition key is in its socket.
I turn it. The engine leaps to life. Alarmed but proud I press my foot
on the accelerator. The engine roars but 'Ain't she a beauty' stays
becalmed. I realise I've got the handbrake on, release it, forget I have
my right foot hard on the accelerator and we hurtle like a jack-in-
the-box down a short slope into the main road. There by a thousandth
of a second I miss a passing Cadillac whose petrified chauffeur yells
'YOU GODDAM CRAZY BUM!!'

He has a point. I take one hand off the wheel, give a wild apologetic
wave, plunge into a ditch and out again and slither down a side-
road. Finding myself at the rear of the hotel where the garage is
miraculously only half full, I drive or rather jerk in, head straight for

a concrete wall, find the footbrake just in time and judder to a halt. I switch off, jump out and, sweating with terror and the Californian heat, slip gasping through a side door into the hotel lobby.

'Ah, Mr Mill*ar*!' It's Arthur calling. I close my eyes. What have I done now? 'Just arrived, sir.' His voice has a new respect. I open my eyes and take the package he hands me. On the red cover are the words 'With the compliments of Paramount Pictures'. I suppress a yawn.

'Not another.'

'New script, sir?'

'I fear so. They keep coming. Still, I suppose I'd better take a dekko.' I nod and force myself to stroll slower than any tortoise down the corridor and into my suite.

The moment the door closes, I tear the wrapping off the package like a starving man coming suddenly across a Chateaubriand. *SO EVIL MY LOVE* reads the title page. *Screenplay by*: LEONARD SPIGELGASS. *From the Novel by* MARGERY ALLINGHAM. *Director*: LEWIS ALLEN. *Producer*: HAL B. WALLIS. A HAL B. WALLIS PRODUCTION.

I rip my clothes off, throw myself naked on the bed and start to read.

Two hours later I have read the screenplay three times and I have a problem. The problem is still with me that afternoon as I am ushered, fully clothed, into an elegant air-conditioned office in Paramount's executive building.

Dimly visible in the distance behind a desk at the far end of a thick pile carpet, seated underneath a half-open window, is a pleasant-looking middle-aged man of medium height in a well-cut light grey suit. I journey on foot across the vast expanse of carpet and finally arrive before him. He rises. 'Hello. I'm Hal Wallis' is quietly spoken, his smile as innocent as a baby's. I have read somewhere that such men are dangerous, which does nothing to help me with my problem.

At various points around the room stand four characters in dark suits who do not smile or say 'Hello' and are not introduced. Those who don't look like Edward G. Robinson look like George Raft, itching for a rerun of St Valentine's Day. I remember Hal Wallis turned out gangster movies by the score for the Warner Brothers and wonder if these are extras left over from Central Casting whom he now employs as minders. Seated in a corner apart from the others is a man of even more alarming aspect. He is, I guess, in his early forties. The senior hood.

Mr Wallis indicates to one of the minders, if that is what they are, to place a chair for Mr Mill*ar*. The chair is placed, not adjacent to the desk but in the centre of the room.

Mr Millar sits down, feeling isolated and a long way from home.

'So you're a friend of Bob Goldstein's?' murmurs Mr W.

'Er – well, not exactly a – '

'Great man, Bob. Always has something going on the griddle.'

'Yes, indeed.'

'Do anything for a friend.'

'Yes, indeed.'

'How are things back home? Is England getting back to normal?'

'Yes, indeed.' My needle seems to have stuck. I must be making a strong impression.

'Well now, you've read our script?' The voice is quietly confident.

'Yes, ind— Yes, I've read it.'

'You think you can do this little job for us?'

'Er – well, I – yes, I could do that all right.'

'Fine. How long do you need? A week? Ten days? Let's say two weeks. Victorian England is kind of an alien landscape to us, you understand. I want to make this a really authentic picture.'

I recognise the moment of truth is nigh but I'm still not sure how I'm going to handle it. 'Do you mean that, Mr Wallis?'

'You bet.'

'In that case – ' I hesitate. The prospect of being down and out in Beverly Hills, albeit with a Buick convertible on tick, is unattractive. On the other hand if my young and tender integrity goes down at its first Hollywood fence, I may have trouble facing my shaving mirror.

I hear myself say, 'Sir, what you want me to do – to fix the English for you where it's needed – that's money for old – I mean, I could do it in a day. The thing is – I don't think that's your problem.'

The producer stares at me. The producer's voice is very quiet. 'So... what is my problem, Mr Millar?'

'Well, it starts on page one, sir, and frankly – Look, I'm sorry, there's a fine scene with the housekeeper but apart from that and the one where the lady turns the tables on the killer – well, frankly I don't believe one word of it.'

Silence. Are the minders shifting their hands to their jacket pockets or is it my imagination? Eventually Mr Wallis says in an even quieter voice, 'Are you trying to tell me I shouldn't make this picture, Mr Millar?'

'Sir, I've only written one script in my life. You've been making movies since before I was house-trained. I mean, you're the expert. I'm probably up the creek without a paddle.'

'*No!*' The word comes zinging across the room like a fireball. 'No, you're not up the creek.' The 'senior hood' who has been sitting in a corner on his own is on his feet and coming my way. Beautiful he isn't. His hair is close-cropped, his nose prominent and there's something deeply sinister about him until he smiles, which now he does and is suddenly transformed.

'You're right. It's a lousy script, and I should know. I wrote it.' He holds out his hand. 'I'm Lennie Spigelgass. Welcome to Hollywood!'

Hal Wallis was generous. He hired me, at $750 a week, to write a new script with the man who had written the first one and who now invited me to be his house guest for the eight weeks it took us to deliver, at the end of which I was able to settle all the bills I duly received from Universal and still have a dime or two left for the journey home.

So Evil was made in England with Ann Todd and Ray Milland in the leads and, without winning any Oscars, earned its keep. Among other things, my first trip to Hollywood taught me it's best to say what you think even if you're wrong but that it's a lot easier to throw bricks than to make them. I also found that Lennie Spigelgass, who had written early Humphrey Bogart movies and knew the business like 'the hack from way back' that he wasn't, but chose to call himself, was an honest man and my most loyal benefactor in the United States.

Being away from home for two months instead of two weeks meant that the shooting of *Frieda* had been completed in my absence. Relph and Dearden showed me the rough cut. The film was wholly true to the theme of the play: 'You can't treat human beings as though they were less than human without becoming less than human yourself.' Mai Zetterling, Flora Robson, Glynis Johns and David Farrar were all excellent and Balcon gave me a two-year contract.

This meant working on anything that came up in the Ealing pipeline. *Saraband for Dead Lovers*, for which I did a little last-minute tinkering, was an expensive costume piece that looked pretty but was fairly dreadful. *Train of Events*, the story of a train crash and how it affected a cross-section of those on board, was mostly low lighting, wet cobblestones and smoky marshalling yards behind King's Cross Station. Accurate and very Ealing. In contrast, my contribution to this portmanteau movie was a sophisticated comedy piece starring John Clements and Valerie Hobson about the well-tailored conductor of a symphony orchestra with a roving eye for the ladies. When anyone suggested that I had Sir Malcolm Sargent in mind I said no one was further from it, a statement which somehow lacked conviction. This very un-Ealing episode was splendidly acted and directed and might have been extended to a full-length film if one had spotted its possibilities in time.

Meanwhile, the title *Frieda* conveying not a clue to what the film was about, concentrated thought was given as to how best to market it. Suddenly Monja Danichevsky, the head of the Ealing Press Department, came up with a brilliant gimmick. In a series of carefully chosen newspapers there appeared in bold lettering the simple question, WOULD *YOU* TAKE FRIEDA INTO *YOUR* HOME? That was it. No explanation. No reference to a film, book, play or any other form of entertainment. The theatre-going public apart, no one knew who this person was or why, before taking her into one's home, a measure of caution was advisable. But they *wanted* to know. That was the hook. It was the first of the mystery ads which have since become commonplace and by the opening night public curiosity was nicely whetted.

I was sitting in the original Berkeley Hotel in Piccadilly, having tea with L. Spigelgass who had arrived on a holiday excursion, when the phone rang in his living room. The conversation that took place was to change my life for the foreseeable future.

'Speaking. Who is that? Ken, you old son-of-a-bitch. Where are you? So what brings you to my favourite island? Sure I'm listening. Yes, I rather think I *can* help you. It so happens I have the guy you need right here in this room. Hang on, I'll ask him. Ron, did you ever see a wartime movie MGM made called *Mrs Miniver?*'

'Of course. Greer Garson, Walter Pidgeon. It won the Oscar. So did she. Churchill used to run it at Chequers over and over during the war.'

'He says he knows it by heart and Churchill ran it every night before he went to bed. Mill*ar*. Ron Mill*ar* with an "a". Never heard of him? He and I wrote *So Evil My Script*. Hold a minute.' (Covers mouthpiece, lowers voice. Rapidly) 'Listen carefully. On the line is Kenneth Mackenna, no less.'

'Should I know him?'

'He's only the scenario editor at MGM Culver City. Here to find writer for sequel to *Miniver*, same cast, same director. Went straight to N. Coward. Coward desperately sorry, up to eyes. Mackenna frantic, leaving tomorrow, ready to sign waiter, porter or upstairs maid. You want the job?'

'Lennie, calm down.'

'Ken doesn't know your work. Anything of yours showing in town right now?'

'Well, it just so happens ... '

What just so happened was that *Frieda* was opening that night at the Odeon, Leicester Square. (Fate or coincidence? Either way, put it in a play or novel, no one would believe it.) Mackenna said he would go right along and I said it was a celebrity premiere for charity, all seats sold but he could have mine, and he said he wouldn't want to deprive me and I said no problem, I knew the piece, and he said to come to supper at Claridge's afterwards and I said I had to be at the Dorchester for a celebrity dinner where the guest of honour was Hugh Gaitskell, the Labour Minister i/c the Arts, and Mackenna said how about a celebrity breakfast at Claridge's and would seven-thirty be too early and I said no, that's fine, I'm an early riser which was a wicked lie.

Over breakfast Mackenna, a former New York actor of distinction who had been seduced by the Californian sun, invited me to write a treatment for a *Miniver* sequel.

'Make a deal through our London office and send the treatment to Culver City. If we like it, come on over and work on the screenplay with Sidney Franklin, producer of the original and many another mighty movie. All right?'

I wasn't sure. A second Hollywood expedition so soon after the first was not in the ground plan of my career. Also I had a two-year contract with Ealing. I'd need to get a release from Balcon.

'Talk to him,' said Mackenna, 'and cable me the answer.'

When I saw Balcon he was reluctant to vary my contract. I didn't try to over-persuade him. *Frieda* was filling the Odeon and Ealing had treated me like one of the family. He said, 'Let me sleep on it,' which he did for a week, then sent for me.

'Listen. Do your treatment. It may or may not work out or the project may founder anyway. But if they decide to proceed to screenplay we'll release you. If not, come back to us. Meanwhile your contract stays on hold.' He was letting me have it both ways. It was exceptionally generous.

I wrote a story about the upper-middle-class Minivers and other characters from the original coming to terms, or not, with post-war Socialist Britain. It was a tougher, less romantic view of England than the original and even I, who regarded just about everything I did as potentially disastrous, rather liked it. MGM went along and a deal was struck for me to go over to Culver City and write the screenplay. And so for a second time I found myself en route to New York via BOAC and the Superchief to Hollywood, Cal.

On the train from Grand Central Station I shared a drawing room with a vivacious American matron who looked like an older version of Bette Davis, which was understandable since she turned out to be her mother. In her mid-sixties, I guessed, smart and still attractive, Mrs Davis was a fountain of Hollywood gossip, much of it indelicate and all of it unprintable, which I found alternately delightful and alarming. The weather in New York had been icy but as we sped west became progressively warmer until by the time we reached Albuquerque the temperature was in the nineties and I had the cold of a lifetime.

Mrs Davis, like the experienced American traveller she was, had come furnished with every conceivable prophylactic, cathartic, analgesic and medicinal herb (only a philosopher's stone was missing), most of which she insisted on my swallowing one after the other. Their effect was as dramatic as her daughter's performances: within the hour my cold had gone and I had an attack of tachycardia for which, of course, Mrs Davis had the instant antidote.

Being doctored by Bette Davis's mother was like riding the big dipper at the circus, the 'ups' being followed by the 'downs' being followed by more 'ups', until my metabolism had been battered into submission and was begging for mercy. But she was a nice, spry, companionable lady and the two-and-a-half-day journey in her company was a pleasant overture to my second trip on the Hollywood merry-go-round.

I had barely arrived at the Chateau Marmont, the apartment block above Sunset Boulevard where the Studio had rented me a flat, when the telephone jangled and a warm lilting voice said, 'Well, hello there, and welcome. *This* is Mrs Sidney Franklin. Call me Ruth, dear, and I'll call you Ronald and we'll get along just fine. Now then, tonight Sidney and I and Ruthie – that's my daughter by my first husband – we're going to the Hollywood Bowl – Sidney has one of those cute little box affairs – and we'd just love to have you come over for dinner and afterwards to the Bowl and the music. It's just so beautiful out there under heaven's canopy, dear. Unless it rains, of course, but this is summertime and the living is easy as the song says. We live on Maple, dear, 142 Maple, that's barely half a mile away from Chateau Marmont. Don't you just love the view of L.A. from Marmont, all the lights twinkling away below like electric candles on a birthday cake? Sidney is all agog to meet you, dear, and so am I and so is Ruthie. So you just put your feet up and take a little nap, and then mosey on over to Maple around sevenish. Black tie? Lordy no. This is California, not Covent Garden. Till seven, then. Oh, and Ronald,

144

don't oversleep, dear. We don't want to miss the overture to *Fleder-maus.'*

After that I didn't dare take any kind of a nap in case I went out like a light and caused everyone to miss the overture to *Fledermaus*. So I prowled around the apartment chewing Bette Davis's mother's buck-u-uppos until around seven when I moseyed on over to Maple.

Sidney Franklin, for years the number-one MGM producer and/or director – of *The Good Earth, The Yearling, Random Harvest, The Barretts of Wimpole Street* and *Mrs Miniver,* among other worldwide money-spinners – was a highly strung, quietly spoken little man, in love with what he believed to be England, who looked like a small edition of Walt Disney and had indeed worked with him on *Bambi*. Ruth was a larger Billie Burke, not so fluttery and with deeper tones but brimming over with American hospitality and goodwill. I'm still not clear whether she had been married to Conrad Nagel until he ran off with Nelson Eddy's wife or to Nelson Eddy until *he* ran off with Conrad Nagel's wife. Unless you're born there the Hollywood habit of 'change partners and dance with me' can be confusing. Whichever it was, Ruth wound up with Sidney Franklin and as daughter Ruthie, a dominant blonde, had Nagel's jutting chin and so far as I knew had never sung a note, I say *he* was her father, not Eddy, and if it was the other way round I apologise and wish I'd never raised the subject.

In the early fifties it was considered smart and sophisticated to regard the popular open-air concerts at the Hollywood Bowl as molasses for the masses. I can only report that, listening to Oscar Levant and the Carmen Dragon Orchestra play Strauss and Tchaikovsky and Gershwin under the stars on that cool Californian night, this Englishman abroad was, with apologies for the pun, bowled over.

The MGM Writers' Building, originally named the Irving Thalberg after the one genius the industry had produced, was one floor writers and producers, three floors lawyers (which makes a point about the values of the major studios). A handsome off-white building, it was led up to by some half-a-dozen wide steps of which Ziegfeld would strongly have approved.

The writers' rooms on the first floor, on either side of a long corridor, were white-walled and strictly functional: desk, not-too-easy chair, and divan with plain cover for occasional respite and meditation. On my desk were reams of typing paper, ready to be filled, plus blotter, pads, pens, pencils and a copy of the original *Miniver* screenplay with which MGM British had already furnished me and which in any case I knew down to the smallest detail.

On the blotter was a pencilled scribble: *'What would happen if Occam's razor were used to attack Schrödinger's cat?'* What could it mean? Perhaps the previous occupant of the room was a Yale intellectual striving to keep his mind from collapsing under the strain of writing endless Andy Hardy movies (Louis B. Mayer's favourites). Or was he worried about the next tenant going under without some sort of cerebral challenge? I tore the scribble off the blotter and taped it to the wall facing my desk as a friendly warning from the recent past.

On the yellow cover of the original *Miniver* script were the writers' credits: Screenplay by Claudine West, Arthur Wimperis, R. C. Sherriff and George Froeschel. Producer: Sidney Franklin. Director: William Wyler. There was also a small side-table on which, under a pile of dust, were a few ancient discards. Among them, unbelievably, was a Tarzan script: 'Screenplay by Ivor Novello'. Had there once been a plan to set the lord of the jungle to music? Well, why not, and if so who better?

Claudine West, now retired, had been Franklin's right hand through most of his career. Arthur Wimperis – lyricist of the famed Edwardian musical *The Arcadians* – was my predecessor as MGM's English writer on the block. R. C. Sherriff, author of *Journey's End*, had been engaged specifically for *Miniver* for which he had written the much-admired air-raid-shelter scene in which Greer Garson read *Alice in Wonderland* to her children to keep their minds off the bombs. Only George Froeschel, a refugee from Hitler's Germany and an old UFA man, was still on the lot.

On my first morning I had been asked to lunch in Franklin's office suite to discuss the screenplay. When, excited and eager to begin, I arrived at what looked like an elegant apartment at the Waldorf his secretary, Margaret Ursem, middle-aged with pebble glasses, a nice but nervous type, I felt, said she was real sorry but Mr Franklin had just called in that very minute to say he wasn't feeling too wonderful and wouldn't be in today and would I please excuse him.

'Yes, of course. I'm sorry to hear he's not well.' Miss Ursem gave a little humming sound. 'He seemed fine last night at the concert,' I said.

She hummed some more. Then: 'One minute he's dancing on air, the next it's all over bar the cremation. That's Mr Franklin, Mr Millar.'

'You must find it rather unsettling.' I was unsettled already.

'Been with him as long as I have, Mr Mill*ar*, you'd be accustomed.'
She gave another little hum and started to type.

'Well... so long as it's nothing serious.'

'Try again tomorrow.' Her tone was neither hopeful nor totally
pessimistic.

I tried again tomorrow and tomorrow and tomorrow, while Miss
Ursem gave little hums and shrugged and typed fatalistically on. Had
I come all the way from Knightsbridge for this? As the days went
by I began to wonder if my producer had died and no one dare tell
me.

'Miss Ursem, are you sure there's nothing seriously wrong with
Mr Franklin?'

'I didn't say that, did I?'

Ah. So there *was* a skeleton in the cupboard. I hoped it wasn't
infectious.

'Mr Mill*ar*, Mr F is a – well, he's a brilliant man, of course, but
he's an artist and out here they're – you know – kinda ...' she
tapped her forehead. 'Not all of 'em but most of 'em. Know what I
mean? He's also a hypo from way back.'

'A hypo?'

'Chondriac. He really works at it. Yes*sir*.'

She gave another tuneless little hum and went back to her typing.
When, after seven days, Franklin finally turned up, he looked cheerful
and healthy enough. 'Sorry to have kept you waiting,' he said as
though he were no more than twenty minutes late and ushered me
into the grand inner office. There he sat down in a deep armchair
and put his feet up on a footstool to which he added and subtracted
several cushions before he had the height to his liking. He then
adjusted his trouser-legs until they were exactly equidistant from his
socks. This took quite some time. He had, I noticed, delicate artistic
fingers, beautifully manicured, that would have looked good racing
up and down a Stradivarius. Satisfied at last, he swallowed a couple
of pills and washed them down with iced water.

'Well now,' he began, then stopped and frowned. 'Do you feel a
draught?'

'No. No, I'm fine.' A draught would have been welcome. We were
in the middle of a heatwave.

'Well, I feel a draught... Miss Ursem,' he whispered in a voice that
sounded as though he was dying. The door to the outer office was
closed, she couldn't possibly have heard him but she appeared at
once as though in response to some psychic communication. 'Yes,
Mr Franklin?'

'There's a draught. Close the windows and lower the shutters.'

Windows were closed and shutters lowered. I loosened my tie. 'Tilt the shades. The sunlight's hitting my left eye.'

The shades were tilted.

'Now you're hitting the other eye.'

Further adjustments were meticulously made. By now all light had vanished and the room was plunged in total darkness. It was very hot indeed. I removed my tie.

'All right, Mr Franklin?'

'I suppose so.'

There was a humming sound and the door clicked shut as pre-sumably Miss Ursem departed. The suite was now stifling as well as blacked out as for an air raid. It seemed only a matter of time before we suffocated.

'Well now,' said a faint voice, presumably that of the great motion-picture producer/director. 'Where were we?'

I knew where I was. I was sitting in the dark somewhere in space with an extra-terrestrial. 'Er – we hadn't actually begun, Mr Franklin – '

'Just a minute, Donald. Goddammit, there's still a draught. It must be coming from under the door.'

I wondered if I should lie across the door to keep out the last remaining source of oxygen. It would be an interesting way to go. Franklin sneezed.

'This place is a deathtrap. Well, never mind, one can only cross the Jordan once. Where were we? Oh yes. Storyline. What is our storyline? Why don't we kick it around a little and see what we come up with? We need something with a grip, that runs under every scene. What I call "the undertow". Too bad England isn't at war.' He sounded thoroughly depressed. 'You can kill off your characters in a war. Bullets – bombs – funerals – fear. Nothing grabs an audience like fear. We had a war in the first *Miniver*, you remember.'

Oh yes, I remembered the war. 'That was our running thread, our undertow. We don't have an undertow this time. No war. Just peace, peace, peace.' He sighed a sigh of deep regret at the prospect of everlasting non-aggression. 'We've got to come up with an undertow to take the place of the war. Otherwise we have no storyline and without a storyline we have no picture. Any ideas?'

I didn't know about undertows, I'd never heard the expression, but I thought we had a storyline. I seemed to remember writing it. It showed each member of the Miniver family adjusting in his or her way to a very different England to that in which they had been born and brought up and educated. For the first time the British middle class were living under a Socialist government with a huge majority. Had he perhaps not read my treatment?

'Socialism ... um ... yes, I thought that was what you were getting at.' Getting at? It was the nub of my narrative. 'I don't feel somehow that's quite what we're after.' Really? So what was I doing here? Why had he hired me?

'I liked your writing, Donald.'

'Ronald.'

'It has something. Quite what, I'm not sure but ... something. You're a sensitive. Like me.' *I* was like Mr Franklin? 'Yes, that's what I like about your stuff. There's sensitivity there ... Now what we need is our undertow.' He became nostalgic. 'We had four writers on *Miniver*. There's only one still here on the payroll.'

'George Froeschel.'

'You met George?'

'No.'

'Keep it that way. Steer clear of George. Sure as God made little apples he'll destroy you. Hates everything. You'd never get on with George. Wouldn't get to first base. Oh, he's a good plot man on his day. Knows about construction. UFA and so forth. Can't write English, of course. Nope, I wouldn't let George loose on you, you're a sensitive plant. He'd kill you dead, Donald.'

'Ronald.'

'Be a nervous wreck in five minutes flat.' There was a silence. 'Well, I guess that's enough for today' (he turned on a lamp) 'Rome wasn't built between Tuesday and Thursday with Wednesday off for coffee and buns. But we're on our way.' Were we? I hadn't noticed. 'Let's have a think and meet again in a week or so. We'll come up with something, never fear. And, Donald – '

I gave up. 'Yes, Mr Franklin?'

'Hang in there. You're going great guns.'

I was glad to hear that. From where I was sitting I hadn't come under starter's orders.

While Franklin stayed at home, wrestling with the problem of how to embroil the United Kingdom in some deadly conflict – World War III would do nicely – I came into the Studio each day and did little except read the *Hollywood Reporter* and have a solitary lunch in the MGM Commissary.

One day, when I was halfway through the chicken noodle soup which was L. B. Mayer's favourite (deservedly: it was nectar), a bald figure of medium height with little tufts of grey beside the protruding

ears and wearing a grey worsted suit limped up, the left shoulder
well above the right so that when he walked he looked as if he was
banking before coming in for a three-point landing.

'Sir, is it in order if I take this seat?' The voice was hesitant,
apologetic, with a slight German accent.

'Please. Help yourself.'

He sat down opposite me, ordered some sausages and a lager,
peered at me for a moment, seemed about to open a conversation,
apparently thought better of it and buried himself behind the *Los
Angeles Times*. When I ordered a lamb chop he lowered the paper and
peered at me again. In his early sixties, with ears that stuck out like
Clark Gable's or Dumbo's, he looked as though he might have stepped
out of a children's horror comic.

'Sir,' he asked tentatively. 'You are from England?'

'That's right.'

'Are you by any chance engaged in writing a sequel to *Mrs Miniver*
for Mr Sidney Franklin?'

'Well, that was the general idea. So far I've been here a month
and we've done damn all.'

'Ah yes, sir. That is – how do you say – father for the course with
Mr Franklin.'

Explaining that the par in question had nothing to do with fathers
was too complicated. I let it ride.

'Do you know Mr Franklin well?'

'I have worked for him, sir, on several pictures, including *Miniver
Mark One*.'

'You're George Froeschel.'

'I am, sir. Or Herr *Froe*schel, as your compatriot Miss Clemence
Dane chose for some reason to address me.'

Evidently Froeschel hadn't cared too much for Clemence Dane.
'What are you working on at the moment?'

'Nothing, sir.'

'Isn't that rather boring?'

'Yes.' He speared a sausage. 'Yes, it is boring. But I am Jewish
refugee. I am paid. Not a lot but enough. And I am alive. That is to
be grateful. I am one of the lucky ones. Not to be gassed is good.' He
said it as a statement of fact. He wasn't looking for sympathy. 'Sir, I
wish you luck with Mr Franklin.'

'Thank you.'

'He is unusual man.'

'Yes.'

'Neurotic and of course a little mad but gifted. Highly gifted. This
may not at once be plain.'

150

My mother. A lively,
loving and abiding soul.

My father. The ideal
partner, though I only
knew the photograph.

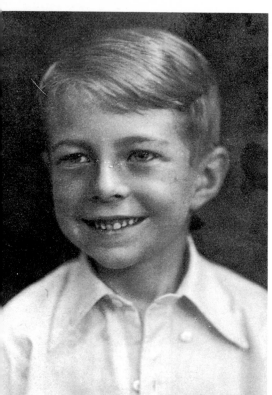

1928. Their joint production, rising nine.

A small man with a huge heart. My uncle, John Sell Cotman.

1940. Nevertheless we won.

1950. With my mother. Hollywood bound.

1954. Home again. St James's Theatre.

LEFT A very different kind of Dad. John Clements as Barrett with June Bronihill as Elizabeth in the musical *Robert and Elizabeth*. RIGHT 1964–7. *R and E* on the Avenue.

Some light writing and a little dark.

1961–3. Three from the book.

1970–2. *Abelard and Heloise.* Wyndham's Theatre with the delicious Miss D. Rigg.

A fruitful alliance. With C.P. Snow and his wife, Pamela Hansford-Johnson.

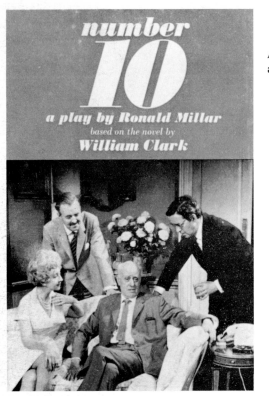

Alastair Sim, Michael Denison, Dulcie Gray
and John Gregson. Just pretending.

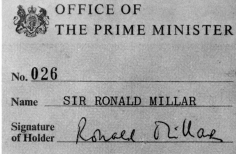

The real thing.

Edward Heath. Before it rained on his parade.

1990. The Political Office, the night the Lady said goodbye.

1992. A Major Tory triumph. The election team at Number 10.

The Theatre Royal, Haymarket. The Deputy Chairman peers into the future.

'No.'

'Sir, I give a toast. *Miniver* Mark Two!' He raised his lager.

'Cheers.'

If he looked sinister he didn't sound it. On the contrary I felt an immediate rapport with this odd fellow. I liked his directness, his way of taking circumstances as he found them without resentment or complaint, and when Franklin reappeared, still without his undertow, and I told him I had met George Froeschel and he hadn't killed me dead, on the contrary I liked him and we got along fine, he shrugged as if to say 'There's no accounting for taste' and invited George to join us on *Miniver* Two. Why this ageing refugee from Hitler's Germany and a typical product of pre-war public-school England should have taken to one another at once is curious but it was so. In years he could have been my father but there was nothing paternal about the relationship. If anything he deferred to me, at least in the early days of our collaboration. Cautious deference is perhaps the instinctive reflex of an exile and as Culver City was unknown territory to me too, being strangers abroad may have been the foundation of our friendship. Whether or no, we became good friends.

One hot and sunny Californian morning, with all the windows in the producer's office closed, George said dramatically to Franklin, 'Sir, I have it! I have the undertow!'

The producer, who was gargling at the time (there had been rumours of a flu epidemic in South Dakota), turned and looked balefully at Froeschel.

'I'm listening.'

'Sir, why don't we kill her off?' said Froeschel with a happy smile.

'Kill who off?'

'Mrs Miniver, sir.'

(George said 'sir' at the beginning, middle or end of virtually every sentence, sometimes all three. Not out of any singular respect, it was a kind of tic.)

'*Kill her off? KILL HER OFF??*' Franklin hurled his gargle into the washbasin. 'George, don't arse about. Just *don't*. You hear me? Mrs Miniver is a beloved character and making movies is a serious business.'

'Sir, I do not arse. I am serious man. Consider, sir.' And he began to elaborate in fractured English a theory that if the audience were made aware from the early reels that the enchanting Mrs Miniver (once more to be played by the delightful Greer Garson) had an incurable illness, a fact to be revealed only gradually to her husband

151

and the other characters in the film – it would 'put something *under* our story', as he described Sidney's 'undertow' theory, and the audience would be tearful and fearful throughout the picture. 'We make the grand weepy, sir,' said Froeschel with a flourish. 'A five-handkerchief block-breaker,' and to illustrate the point he waved his pocket handkerchief, wiped both eyes and heaved as though heartbroken.

I said tentatively, 'But, George, won't the audience for a sequel expect more of what they loved the first time? Up-to-date, of course, but basically a warm bath in familiar waters?'

'So we pull the plug and give the shock!' beamed the man from UFA. 'We lead them up the Friedrichstrasse and then – bang! We sock them in the solar – how do you say – ?'

'Plexus.'

'We sock the plexus and the world is weeping!'

There was a prolonged silence while Franklin digested the slaughter of the adored central character of a wartime movie that had raised civilian morale to the heavens, won the Oscar and even, according to those who find life without hyperbole intolerable, the war itself. Franklin took a couple of pills and lay down. At length he said faintly, 'No, George. No. If I were to murder Mrs Miniver the people of America would never forgive me. They'd string me up like that Miss Whatshername who couldn't make lunch on account of she was being lynched.'

'Miss Otis,' I murmured.

'Whatever. No. Forget it.'

'But, sir – '

'I said forget it, George. And now if you'll excuse me, gentlemen. I don't feel too wonderful,' and he rose, clutched his breast and walked mortally wounded from the room.

Several days later he returned carrying three boxes of tissues. Looking grave and deathly pale he handed one each to George and me without a word. Then he sat down with the third, a little man in a big armchair, and went through the cushions-on-the-footstool and equidistant-trouser-legs routine.

At last, 'Boys,' he said in funereal tones. 'Yesterday I told Mrs Franklin what you had in mind. She wept all night. All through the night she cried.' He took out a tissue and wiped his eyes. There was a pause. Then: 'I think maybe we got something,' said Sidney Franklin, and he grinned a great big box-office grin.

During the following weeks my treatment of post-war Britain under

socialism sank without trace. As for my delicate account of Mrs
Miniver's affair with an army officer, it was watered down to a hint
of a glimmer of a mere suggestion, and saving even that was a battle.

'But they don't actually *do* anything,' I argued.

'Maybe not, but they *think* about doing it – *and* in close-up,' said
Franklin. 'Kay Miniver would never think about doing a thing like
that in close-up.'

'So she thinks about doing it in *long shot!*' cried George triumphantly.

'You'll have the FBI on to me,' muttered the great producer/director.

We won that one but only because Franklin was in love with his
tragic undertow. One remarkable morning he was completely carried
away.

'Boys, I've got it!' he cried. 'Eat your heart out "Little Women"!'
He struck a dramatic pose. 'It's the middle of the night. We're in the
Miniver bedroom. Kay and Clem are in bed. He asleep, she wide
awake, staring at the ceiling. That day she's been to the doctor to
hear the result of – George, are you listening?'

'Sir, I am all ears,' said Froeschel, which was only a slight
exaggeration.

'Miss Ursem, you're getting this, are you?'

Disembodied sound from behind door: 'Yes, Mr Franklin.' (Repeats,
in voice flat as ironing board): 'Night. Miniver bedroom. Kay Clem in
bed. He asleep, she stare ceiling. That day been to – I'm sorry, I can't
quite read this – oh yes, been to the boxer.'

'The *what?*'

'Boxer?' she inquired hopefully.

'*Doctor*, woman, *doctor*! If you were dying, would you go to a *boxer*?
Would you say "Pardon me, but if you're not doing anything could
we go a few rounds?"'

'I thought it sounded a bit funny but you make me nervous, Mr
Franklin, really you do. I've told you before, I can't hear very well
behind this door and it's so dark, half the time I can't decipher my
shorthand.' She poked her head round the handle. 'Couldn't I just sit
in the room like a normal person?'

'No!' Whenever the great producer had an inspiration his secretary,
shorthand notebook at the ready, had to sit out of sight behind the
open door to the outer office.

'If I see her face it puts me off,' he told me when I inquired why
she had to be invisible. 'She looks like Zasu Pitts, that's why.'

'That day she's been to the *doctor*,' he glowered at the door behind
which Zasu Pitts was once more ensconced and then resumed with
growing emotion, 'to hear the result of the tests ... I see moonlight ...

Tender, delicate shafts of moonlight dipping through the window caress the walls. Camera pans to Kay. Poor love, she can't sleep. Careful not to disturb Clem, she slips out of bed in her nightie ... ' Franklin's voice became choked. 'She knows now ... Knows there's no hope ... She wants to tell her husband ... to share her secret with him ... At the same time she wants him spared the pain ... I see her ... Yes, I see her clearly ... Standing at the window ... ' He seemed to be going into a trance. 'There she is ... In the moonlight... Alone ... Camera closes on her ... God, she's beautiful ... Her eyelids flutter, she bites her lip. The eyes say it all... Suddenly two hands appear gently, so very, very gently on her shoulders. Without turning, slowly, very slowly ... her hands go up and touch, yes, that's what they do, they touch *male knuckles* ... CLOSE-UP KNUCKLES ... Close-up Kay ... She knows those knuckles ... They're Clem's knuckles ... Maybe she's got tears in her eyes and a lump in her throat... maybe he's got tears and a lump too ... ' Gathering speed, he ad-libs in a kind of hysterical ecstasy. 'As she turns to him, camera closes on Clem – cut to Kay! – cut to Clem! – back to Kay! – back to Clem! – wide-angle two-shot ... Suddenly thought strikes her. *Does he know? HAS HE GUESSED?* ... She sort of ... kind of ... has a hunch ... no, more than a hunch ... She KNOWS! ... Goddammit, SHE KNOWS THAT *HE* KNOWS!' His voice rose to a frenzy. 'AND WE KNOW SHE KNOWS HE KNOWS! ... Oh Clem, she says ... Clem ... ' Franklin was sobbing. 'Oh Kay, he comes back ... Kay, I, oh my dear, oh ... okay, Kay ... Clem, my darling – Kay – Clem – It's okay, Kay, it's okay ... ' Suddenly he shrieks, 'Got it, Miss Ursem? Miss Ursem, you gone to sleep?'

Zasu Pitts (unemotionally): 'No, Mr Franklin. I'm here.'

'Well, read back that last bit.'

'Where from, Mr Franklin?'

'From where we know she knows he knows.'

From behind the door there now came in a flood and a voice flatter than a pancake, without punctuation: 'Oh Clem Clem oh Kay he comes back Kay I oh my dear oh Kay it's okay Kay I – '

'WILL YOU STOP THAT?' roared the producer.

'That's what you said, Mr Franklin. I have it right here.' Miss Ursem appeared from her hideyhole, rattling off from her shorthand notebook. 'Oh my dear oh then another oh then Kay Kay it's okay Kay – sorry I think there were two okays first and then a third Kay after the – '

'KNOCK IT OFF! WILL YOU KNOCK IT OFF BEFORE I RIP YOUR HEAD FROM YOUR SHOULDER-PADS!'

'Mr Franklin, I swear you said – '

'I don't give a damn *what* I said! I didn't say it LIKE THAT!!!'
Franklin fell into his chair, his voice breaking. 'Here am I trying to
make a tender beautiful motion picture and you deliberately – '

'No!'

'Yes! *Deliberately* turn a great, heart-rending, harrowing scene into
a psychopathic farce! No tears – no pity – no soul – and not so
much as a goddam comma!'

Ursem (muttering): 'Just a secretary ... Not Greer Garson ... If I
were Garson be getting her salary ... '

Franklin: 'Will you stop that muttering under your breath? If
there's one thing I can't abide – '

Ursem (collecting herself with an effort): 'My, look at the time.
Now, Mr Franklin, what would you like for lunch? How about a nice
big liverwurst on rye?'

Franklin (with a terrible cry – Olivier as Oedipus): 'Lunch!
Liverwurst! I'm trying to make a lovable beautiful desperate movie
that'll tear your heart out and go down in history and what do I
get? Liverwurst! *Liverwurst on rye!* Someone get her out of here! Go!
Go and never come back!'

Ursem (erupting with a scream): 'All right! I will! I'll go! I've been
wanting to for years. I resign! I quit! I quit, quit, quit, quit, quit!'
(Bursts into tears.)

Franklin (suddenly tender as a calf): 'Did I say something? Did I,
Donald? What is it, love? Is it that sinus of yours again?' (to me): 'It's
her sinus.'

Ursem (sobbing): 'It's not my sinus! It's *you!* It's *you!*'

Franklin (to me): 'She's hallucinating, call Doc Freedman. Come
and lie down, dear. Lie down on this pretty brown sofa and close
your eyes. That's it. And have some nice cool eau de Cologne ...
There ... there ... ' (dabs her brow with eau de Cologne).

Ursem (overcome by his solicitude): 'Wonderful man ... so kind ...
wonderful ... oh ... oh ... eau de Cologne ... loving ... caring ...
wonderful ... saint ... '

Franklin (dabbing away): 'I am. I am. Everyone says so. Now you
just take it easy ... ' (to me): 'Poor soul ... so emotional ... least
little thing sets her off. Her sinus ... her mother's ovary trouble ...
How's that for faithful – ' (Suddenly becoming aware of Froeschel
asleep in armchair): 'George! Wake up, George!! Would you believe
it? He's slept through the scene of the century!' Froeschel, who has
indeed nodded off, wakes with a snort, having caught only the last
four words.

Froeschel: 'Sir, it *is* the scene of the century! A superb, a sensational
scene! Sir, you are genius! We go now and put it on paper. Come,

my English friend. To my room. We make a masterpiece!'

(Exeunt screenwriters: elderly Austrian limping, exalted. Youngish Limey dazed, dumbfounded.)

You think I exaggerate? That this sort of thing happens only in Hollywood movies about Hollywood movies? If anything I understate. My hysterical pen upon it.

After several more exotic interludes George and I finished the screen-play of *Miniver* Two according to Franklin's specific requirements. It was greeted by the panjandrums on the fourth floor with general rejoicing and cries of 'A weepy it may be, a winner it will be!' (Franklin: 'Great! Take that down, somebody.')

William Wyler, director of *Miniver* One, agreed to direct Two and Greer Garson invited me to dinner *à deux* in her fairytale home in ultra-fashionable Bel Air. (Her husband, a Texan oil tycoon, lived mostly in Houston where she joined him when she wasn't working.) The living room was like a movie set, exquisitely furnished, with a waterfall flowing behind glass panels, a grand piano with spotlit keyboard on which I presumed to play a few notes while waiting for the star to make her entrance down a staircase spotlit to hit her exactly halfway as she paused to say, 'Well, hello, Mr Millar' (a soothing English voice, no accent on either syllable, the relief). 'How nice of you to come and see me.'

Miss Garson was at the height of her loveliness and over dinner, the Oscar she had picked up for *Miniver* One prominent on a side-table, told me how much she was looking forward to making the sequel to what had been her favourite part in her favourite picture from the moment she had read the original script. She knew at once, she said, that *Mrs Miniver* would be a world-beater and she had thanked God for giving her such a wonderful role, and now, to have the opportunity to play it again – well, all she could say was, her cup was full.

She was utterly charming and it was an enchanted evening, only very slightly devalued by my infernal memory which kept reminding me of something Froeschel had told me about an incident at the on-set party on the final day's shooting of *Miniver* One. A small band had played light music for dancing and George, unabashed by his limp, had made bold to approach the leading lady and, bowing with old-world courtesy, requested the privilege of a waltz.

'But of course, my dear,' said Miss Garson, smiling radiantly. As they circled the floor she said, still with a radiant smile on her lips: 'Mr Froeschel, if you write me such a truly dreadful part ever again

I shall have you fired from the lot.' At the subsequent Oscar ceremony she was apparently so moved by her role that her speech of thanks overran by twenty-five minutes. I asked George how he felt when he heard it. He shrugged. 'Sir,' said philosopher Froeschel, 'that is – how do you say? – the business of the show.'

Two days before I was due to fly home George and I were playing poker in his room when the phone rang and I was invited by one of the 'Ogres', as the members of the board of MGM were politely known by the writers, to go upstairs for a chat. There had been heavy hints between hums from Miss Ursem that, at Franklin's behest, I was to be offered a long-term contract by the Studio as its resident English hack. George at once said excitedly, 'Sir, this is it!'

For a number of reasons I was less than thrilled at the prospect but was persuaded by Froeschel that it would be churlish and ill-mannered to refuse even to discuss such an offer. Reluctantly I agreed, provided he came with me as my adviser. He said he'd be thrown out, it wasn't his business.

I then telephoned a highly intelligent woman agent, Meta Reis (sister of Irving Reis, the director) whom I had met at a dinner party and who had said to me, 'Anytime you need an agent, honey, call me.' Honey called her. The blurred and incoherent mumble the other end indicated a heavy night on the town the previous evening. Honey hung up.

'Well, that does it. I'm not going into the lion's den on my own,' I said to George.

'Sir, are you crazy?' asked my Jewish friend. 'Will they eat your gut for the garter? Who wants who, sir?'

'I know, but these are the most powerful men in the movie business. They rule an empire.'

'You are Englishman. You too ruled the empire.'

'Not personally. Anyway, we're handing it back as fast as we can.'

'Sir, you are letting down the side. Where is the boy who stood on the burning roof?'

'Burnt to a cinder, I shouldn't wonder. I must have someone who knows the Ogres and how they operate.'

'Verrückt! Go on up, make your deal and save yourself ten per cent.'

He practically dragged me down the corridor, bundled me into the lift, pressed the button for the top floor, stepped out and, as the doors closed, shouted 'Rule, Britannia!' and gave the V-sign the wrong way round.

The Ogre was charming. Don't be fooled by charm, I told myself and, trembling inwardly, played hard to get, which isn't that hard when you don't mind losing. I said I really shouldn't be here without an agent. He said, 'I won't bite' and offered me a cigar and a seven-year contract at a generous salary, with a yearly rise.

I said, 'It's very kind of you but no.'

'How about five?'

I said, 'Three at the most. That is – '

'You did say four, didn't you?'

'Well, but four years doesn't really mean four years, does it? In writers' contracts there are options to break at the end of each year.'

'Okay. Scrub the options.'

I said that was very decent of him but I didn't want a fifty-two-weeks-a-year commitment. If I accepted I must have time off each year for a holiday, a short trip home, perhaps, whatever.

'How many weeks a year will you settle for?'

'Nine months. Nine out of twelve.'

'Done. Next?'

I said that it would mean my breaking off all my English connections, giving up my London flat, becoming a resident alien. Otherwise I'd be liable for double taxation.

'So? Become a resident. It's a beautiful country.'

I agreed it was beautiful but renting a house in California was a bad investment. I'd have to buy one and I didn't have that kind of money.

He said, 'We'll advance you the money and deduct so much a month from your salary. Next?'

I couldn't think of anything else. I had to admit he'd been more than handsome.

'So – do we have a deal?' he held his hand out. I found myself shaking it.

'About the contract. I'm flying home the day after tomorrow.'

'You'll have it by five p.m. today.' He saw me to the door and gave a wry grin. 'By the way, son. If you ever tire of the writing racket, become an agent. You did all right.'

I wasn't sure. I tottered out, part-thrilled, part-appalled at having committed myself to four years incarcerated in the Writers' Building at Culver City. Still, I told myself, I'm only thirty-one and I'll only be thirty-five when they are over and presumably England, my England (other people's England too, of course, but very much one's personal property when one is away from it), England will still be there at the end of the line and with luck the lights of London and the London theatre, bright and warm and welcoming. Anyway, for better or worse the deal was done. I wondered what Dacre-Hill would say.

*

When I told her in the cab from London airport that I had signed up for a four-year stretch at Culver City and I would take it kindly if she would come over and run the house I planned to buy with money I hadn't yet earned but hoped to borrow, she rolled her eyes and asked if I knew what I was doing.

'Probably not. Are you on?' She stared ahead, lips pursed. 'I must say you've got a nerve.' She lit a cigarette. Finally: 'When do we leave?' In my experience – and I have seen the Californian redwoods – women like that don't grow on trees.

I had asked for, and been given, a month to wind things up at home before returning to the Coast. It wasn't long. However, I hadn't been back ten days before Franklin rang with what turned out to be an unexpected reprieve. It seemed William Wyler had been taken ill and as film and cast were all set to roll at MGM's British studios at Borehamwood a new director, H. C. (Hank) Potter, had been hastily appointed. Franklin said that as Potter was unfamiliar with Miniver England and the kind of movie we, or rather Franklin, wanted – Potter's best-known film had been the Fred Astaire/Ginger Rogers musical *The Story of Vernon and Irene Castle* – the Studio would like me to be right there on the set with him throughout the three-month shooting schedule to cover 'anything that might be necessary'.

When I asked Franklin precisely what that Delphic utterance implied he said, 'Must go now. Not feeling too wonderful. Letter follows, but you know what I mean, Donald.' Donald had a pretty good idea and Donald wasn't too happy about it. Breathing into a director's ear in full view of cast and crew could undermine his authority even if one breathed in a whisper. However, it *would* use up part of my four-year contract and to say no to the first thing asked of me by my American employer might not be the height of wisdom.

Hank Potter turned out to be a tall, rangy, nervous, crewcut American. He knew his technical way about to a 't', but his qualification for this particular assignment appeared to be that in the Castle film Vernon Castle died at the end, as did Mrs Miniver in this one. The reasoning seemed simplistic but that was Hollywood. Hank was a thoroughly nice man who put me instantly at my ease, saying how grateful he was to have me around to 'keep him in the picture', a phrase which I guessed might have a double meaning. As for the original cast members – Greer Garson, Walter Pidgeon, Henry Wilcoxon, Henry Travers, Reginald Owen – they were what I had long regarded as that little corner of Culver City that is forever England and they knew their way about the identical replica of the original set as though they had never left it. When 'Letter follows'

159

arrived, I was appalled to find it was down to me to say which 'take' to print and, if I was not satisfied that what the script said was actually up there on film, to order further takes until it was. Unlike playwrights, screenwriters seldom have any control over what they have written once they have written it and I was still a novice. However, although the rushes that went nightly by air to Culver City seemed to satisfy Franklin and the Ogres, if H. C. Potter had not been a very considerable gentleman the arrangement could have been a disaster. As it was, shooting continued smoothly and no one was frosty to anyone. The only problem was that the season of mists and mellow fruitfulness gave way to a persistent fog that slid under the studio doors, invaded the set and smudged the cameras in a brown blur.

It was during this period that Garson, Pidgeon, Potter and I were invited after a day's shooting for dinner at Cliveden, the country seat and political hothouse of the Astor family. We drove over from Elstree through a dense fog bank, lost our way and arrived an hour and a half late, frozen, frantic for food and drink, especially drink. As we crawled up the drive towards the great house at a snail's pace, Pidgeon wrapped in scarves walking in front of the car to guide us clear of the flower-beds and occasionally succeeding, Nancy Astor, Lord Astor's American wife, a diminutive figure in gold lamé without so much as a cardigan on to keep out the freezing cold despite her age (she must have been in her seventies), appeared on the steps.

'So there you are. Drunk, I suppose,' declaimed the notorious Prohibitionist. 'Well, you won't get any booze here. Still, I suppose you'd better come in.' We went in, shivering, humbled and dripping apologies, to find bottles of whisky, gin and brandy waiting in front of a roaring fire. The dinner was superb, the wines even better and as for the cognac ... Nancy Astor was wonderful value, warm, dry and altogether a worthy mistress of the influential political incubator that was Cliveden before Christine Keeler. Today it's a luxury hotel.

Two days later and halfway through the picture, Greer's husband in Texas had a near-fatal heart attack. She said at once, 'I must go to him.' The Studio was sympathetic but, with only half a picture in the can and huge daily overheads to meet, did everything to dissuade her. 'He's in good hands ... if you go rushing over he'll fear the worst ... he knows you're making a movie, he'll understand.'

But Greer was adamant. 'It won't cost you, you're insured,' she said. 'Movies are always insured against acts of God.' MGM was indeed insured against tempest, plague, pestilence and earthquake, also if any of the stars themselves fell ill, but if something untoward happened to a spouse, aunt, or third cousin, divine intervention was

160

not recognised. 'I'm going anyway,' she said firmly. 'Back as soon as I can', and flew to Houston. As she was in virtually every shot the film came to a complete halt.

Ten weeks later she returned, having seen her husband out of danger and added more than two months to the shooting schedule. The Studio was privately less than pleased but said nothing publicly, she was one of their biggest stars. As for the rest of us – director, cast, crew and writer – we were on her side to a man and a woman. Only the worst kind of cynic would suggest that our being on full salary throughout the lay-off had anything to do with our total support.

Miniver Two was completed without further mishap, and a week later, having said goodbye to my home, my bank manager and the Inland Revenue with a descending graph of regret, I followed the luggage and Dacre-Hill into a taxi. She looked back at the flat and seemed to have tears in her eyes and a lump in her throat like Mrs Miniver by moonlight but it could have been just fumes from the traffic. For myself, my accidental life had entered yet another phase. By now I had learnt when these things happened not to fight them but to swim with the tide.

'Victoria Station,' I said to the cabby.

'Mainline, guv?'

'Right. Southampton boat train.'

'Lucky devil,' he muttered.

I wasn't so sure about that.

10

. . . .

'Hiya, Kid, Come for the Funeral?'

Go out and try your luck
you could be Donald Duck
Hooray for Hollywood!
Johnny Mercer

However, once the *Queen Elizabeth* had sailed even Dacre-Hill, who had regarded my second mission to Culver City with caution tinged with homesickness at the thought of leaving England and her friends, relaxed and by dinner on the first evening decided that the liner was bonny, California could be fun, and I had done the right thing to secure my financial future for another four years of the high-risk profession into which I appeared to have stumbled.

The following morning I was woken by the scratching sound of the ship's newspaper being pushed energetically under my cabin door. I got up and peered through the porthole. Land had vanished and the sun shone on a smooth-as-silk Atlantic through which the great ship was cutting at what felt like eighteen knots. I collected the paper, climbed back into bed, ordered breakfast and glanced at the headline. If earth had been visible I would have been brought down to it with a bump. TRUMAN RAISES TAXES BY 11% was the Korean War headline. I had certainly chosen a piquant moment for becoming an American taxpayer.

After an aggressively British breakfast – eggs and bacon, tea, toast (none of your crumbling croissants) and Oxford marmalade – I shaved, dressed and went up on the sundeck, to come face to face with Noël Coward, spruce in blazer and slacks, cigarette in holder. I did not know him as I knew Novello but we had met at theatrical parties.

The face of a benign and understanding senior devil crinkled into

162

a familiar grin. 'What precisely are you doing here or is it a state secret?' The unique, clipped diction was crisp as ever.

'I'm on my way to the Coast.'

'Paramount or the Brothers Warner?'

'MGM.'

'So. A long sentence or just a quick sprint in and out?'

I told him I had signed up with the Studio for a four-year stretch. There was a silence.

'Shall we stroll a little?'

As we strolled he told me he had recently seen *Frieda* at the Liverpool rep.

'Was it a good production?'

'No. But the play came through.'

There was hardly anyone about. He stopped and leant over the ship's rail, smoking his cigarette and staring in silence at the empty ocean. Eventually he tossed his cigarette overboard and turned to me. 'I'm going to tell you a trite little tale that in the circumstances you will find irksome in the extreme. Many years ago *I* was offered a long-term contract by Metro-Goldwyn-Mayer' (he pronounced it 'Maia'). 'The money was a small fortune and I was on the brink of accepting when I had the idea for a play. I took a deep breath and turned them down. Now ask me what play I had in mind.'

'What play was it?'

'*Bitter Sweet*. It made rather a large fortune. But that's not the point of this irritating little saga, which is this.' And he wagged the forefinger of his right hand at my upper lip. 'The man who wrote *Frieda* shouldn't be playing footsie with the movie mafia. He should be writing plays for the theatre, with which I suspect you have been in love from the moment they severed your umbilical cord. Am I right?'

'More or less.'

'Very well, then. Starve if necessary but stick with the live audience which will sometimes kick you in the crotch but at others lift you up, take you to its heart and make you glow with all the brightness of a shooting star. End of finger-wagging lecture. Is your lovely mother on board?' I nodded. 'Embrace her for me and as soon as we dock, don't forget. First plane home.' He wagged a final finger, gave a mock wave and disappeared below.

Behind the ultra-sophisticated personality which he had so brilliantly invented and behind which he sheltered, Mr Coward was a practical, wise and kindly man, a fact which he took some care to conceal.

I have found this to be the case with others who have been

163

particularly fortunate in life. Whilst they genuinely want to help those who need it up the ladder they themselves have climbed, and frequently take considerable pains to do so, they take even more pains to camouflage their kindness. Strange.

We stayed two nights in New York (*Annie Get Your Gun* – Merman a great Annie – and the whimsy *Brigadoon*. Left at interval. Scotland for ever but oh dear, whisky, yes, whimsy, no). We flew on to Los Angeles and the Chateau Marmont, which was to be our base for house-hunting. The elderly telephone operator from the Bronx who had acquired a cockney accent years before from besotted visits to the film of Coward's *Cavalcade* greeted me like an old friend. 'Wotcher, me old cock-sparrer. Bin followin' the van, 'ave yer?'

Ruth Franklin was through in a flash. 'Why, de-ar, I he-ar that "MOTHER'S HERE!"' she practically sang in inverted commas. 'Now, de-ar, why don't you bring "Mother" over Saturday evening for a nice quiet little dinner. There'll be just the four of us. Would you do that, de-ar, and afterwards Sidney is going to run *Bambi* if that won't be too tiring for "Mother".'

'I think she thinks you're some sort of aged crone,' I reported to the relative.

'I shall lean heavily on a stick and put on a funny voice like Sybil Thorndike in *Peer Gynt*,' said "Mother".

'Not unless you want to be sent flying by your son, you won't.'

We moseyed on over around eight and the Franklins were kindness itself, though Ruth looked bewildered when "Mother" skipped through the hall like a twelve-year-old at her first dance. She became even more so when at dinner, as a compliment to her hosts, "Mother" enthused about President Truman.

'He's very popular in England,' she said. 'I imagine he's safe for a second term?'

'God forbid,' said Franklin.

'Oh,' said Dacre-Hill. 'Why do you say that, I wonder?'

Ruth moved in swiftly with a worried hostess smile. 'Truman's a Democrat. We're Republicans, dear.'

'Ah,' said the sophisticated politician "Mother" had suddenly become. 'You'd rather have Ike.'

'Ike?' said Franklin, looking startled.

'I beg your pardon, General Eisenhower.'

'*That Commie??*' cried Franklin and let out a yelp of agony. In aiming what I thought was a swift kick at Dacre-Hill's ankle I had caught the producer on the shin-bone. Franklin rounded on his wife.

'Don't *do* that, Ruth!'

'Do what, dear? I didn't do anything.'

"Mother" decided to come to the rescue with what she took to be a safe question.

'Who would you really like as President if you could choose?'

'MacArthur of course!' cried my producer and his wife as one.

'MacArthy?' Dacre-Hill looked totally flummoxed.

'*Thur – Thur!*' I hissed. 'General MacAr*thur!*'

'Oh. I see. I thought for a moment –' I knew exactly what she thought for a moment: that what our hosts really wanted for President was Charlie Macarthy, ventriloquist Edgar Bergen's dummy. Well, perhaps they did. Hollywood producers were so far Right in those days anything was possible. After dessert which we had reached safely by steering clear of political debate, Ruth rose with a tight smile.

'Well now, why don't we have our coffee in the drawing room and then Sidney will run *Bambi* for us. Have you seen *Bambi*, dear?'

'Several times,' said Dacre-Hill heavily. I was preparing for another ankle job when she added swiftly, 'But of course one can't see that dear little faun too often.'

'That's what *I* think, dear,' said Ruth happily. 'Come along, Sidney.'

But Sidney wasn't feeling too wonderful. 'If you'll excuse me, I'll just mosey on up and soak my leg in Listerol for an hour or so.' He gave my mother a little bow. 'Do come again soon, won't you?' and limped away up the broad staircase.

'But, Sidney!' cried Ruth, clinging to the wreckage of her nice quiet little dinner. 'What about *Bambi*?'

He turned and leant over the balustrade. 'Bugger *Bambi*,' said Mr Franklin and went his way.

Ruth gave a wild laugh. 'Such a shame, and he'd oiled his projector and everything.'

She said it as one would of a difficult child who had got his toy train out to show the visitors and suddenly thrown a tantrum.

This episode strengthened my conviction that politics is a subject best avoided in someone else's country, even if you do have a special relationship.

At the Spigelgass party two nights later the guests were Hollywood with a strong British bias, presumably in our honour. Among them were Cary Grant (Archie Leach from Bristol, former acrobat), Kirk Douglas whose wife Diana was English, Ray Milland born British, Peggy Cummins from Ireland (the best natural dancer I ever circled a floor with), wartime Colonel David Niven and his ravishing wife, C. Aubrey Smith who once captained England at cricket and Constance

Collier, elderly doyenne of the British colony with rasping voice and heart of gold who had in tow – it couldn't be, could it? Yes, it was – Charlie Chaplin, short, thickset, beaming, extrovert. Among those with no British connection was Billy Wilder, the German director and screenwriter who had taken to the American scene in both capacities with a wit and brilliance that would have been remarkable in his own language. In a foreign tongue it was unique. When I was introduced as 'a fresh arrival from the UK' he said, 'Hiya, kid, come for the funeral?'

In fact, Wilder's greeting anticipated the future, but only just. The days of the Hollywood mass product were numbered. The major studios – 20th Century, Warner Brothers, Paramount, MGM – which for years had been turning out almost a film a week (some brilliant, some average, some trash) to distribute to the world's cinemas were about to be superseded by television (some brilliant, some average, some trash). The box in the living room had already begun to provide in the home what the cinema had meant going out in all weathers and queuing up for. The public would still stand in line for a spectacular movie but there would soon no longer be a call for the contract artist. Or the contract writer.

However, it wasn't quite time for the funeral bakemeats. The writers, players, orchestrators and technicians who had made the MGM musicals the best in the business were to go out in a blaze of glory with a stream of memorable movies – *Meet Me in St Louis, Easter Parade, Seven Brides for Seven Brothers, Gigi, An American in Paris* and others that have not to date been equalled. If the end was nigh it was to be quite a passing.

After a month of house-hunting I bought 709 Beverly Drive from Joe Pasternak, the producer of the Deanna Durbin musicals who had moved to Metro from Universal. I paid $50,000 which I borrowed from the Studio who deducted $2000 a month from my salary ($2000 a week).

709, a charming house in the centre of Beverly Hills, was everything your moviegoer would expect of a Hollywood home. Large dining room and drawing room from which a graceful staircase swept up to the bedrooms. One could imagine Astaire and Rogers dancing down it to Berlin or Porter or, best of all, Kern. There was a built-on study complex, adjoining the house but separate from it, where one could write or ponder the meaning of life undisturbed. Also a two-car garage, and a large swimming pool in the garden, blue water surrounded by avocado trees whose fruit I gave away until I came

166

to relish it. The kitchen had every conceivable gadget a cook could desire and the small bar off the terrace was neat, friendly and well equipped.

The house being only partly furnished, Dacre-Hill had the time of her life at a series of auctions buying sofas and chairs, a piano, paintings, bedroom furniture, cushions, cutlery, TV sets, everything except carpets and curtains (drapes in the States) which went with the house and were part of the price. In short, it was a small (by Hollywood standards) luxury home, if you happened to like that sort of thing. Coming from post-war Britain – rationing had ended, but only just, and the work of rebuilding was still in its early stages – I had no doubt. I liked.

In one respect – one only – the village of Beverly Hills was like the town of Reading, Berks: there was nothing to do in the evenings, except go to other people's movies or to parties where you would meet again the people you'd met at the one the night before.

Nobody walked after dark. If you tried it you were liable to be stopped and questioned by the armed police patrolling the palm-lined streets in their police buggies or on motorcycles. The nice guys would ask politely if you were lost, sir, and could they help you, while the tough guys would ask just where you thought you were goin', mister. Whether the movie cops copied the real ones or the real ones the movie cops I was never quite clear. Either way, to walk was to invite suspicion, so I borrowed some more studio dollars and acquired a Buick convertible which was virtually a replica of 'Ain't she a beauty' except this time I didn't hire, I bought.

Being now a resident alien with appropriate passport, this meant taking a driving test, which is tough in California – compulsory written paper as well as evidence of ability to manoeuvre machine. I wish to place on record that to general astonishment, especially mine, I passed at my first attempt.

'Want to drive on the left, sir? Sure? Okay, just checking you out. You're from England, right?' And then later: 'Well, you'll do, here's your certificate. Drive carefully now, none of that trick stuff you see in the movies – though if by any chance you should hear of someone wanting a double for the here-I-come-over-barrels-watch-this, I'm available. Have a safe day.'

I had learnt never to be surprised by anything that eccentric master of the movies' middle period, Sidney Franklin, did or did not do. Nevertheless, having signed a long-term contract with MGM largely because he had asked for me, I was not prepared for his apparent

167

inability to find a subject sufficiently enticing to go to work on. He can't not have been feeling too wonderful for the whole four years of my contract. The fact is, in all that time we never made a picture together. He came into the Studio once in a while and put his feet up and adjusted his trouser-legs and lowered the shutters, then raised them again and talked in general terms of vague possibilities, but for some reason the spark of inspiration wouldn't fire. Either that or he couldn't find enough stories that won his wife's approval.

Ruth Franklin was a major influence in his choice of subject and her prerequisite for a motion picture was that it should be about 'nice people'.

'Yes, but they're not nice people, dear,' she would say, which effectively ruled out half the world's literature, but Ruth was a dedicated Christian Scientist and keeping the screen clean was how she saw her duty. (Exposed to today's diet of sexual sadism dear Ruth would have been permanently hospitalised.)

Whatever the reason for Sidney's silence, the Studio took his behaviour in its stride. I suppose they were used to odd ducks who were talented and Franklin had made them several fortunes in his time.

But that didn't apply to me. I was on the payroll and felt my weekly cheque had to be justified. Also, unless you are a child or an OAP, to be idle in Hollywood is a short cut to the padded cell. It was Froeschel who came to the rescue. He had got wind of a possible remake of Rafael Sabatini's *Scaramouche* of which Metro had made a silent film and still had the rights.

'Sir, why don't we go for it?'

Ever since *The Lion's Skin* I had thought of Sabatini as a soul mate. We ran the silent movie in one of the basement projection rooms. I was tempted but thought the story, even on its chosen mock-heroic level, didn't really add up.

'Okay, sir. We keep the title and rework the story.'

We did just that, gave it a tongue-in-cheek slant, took our outline upstairs to Kenneth Mackenna who sold it to the top floor and we went to work. Directed by George Sidney, the result was a fast, colourful swashbuckler, full of dashing swordplay and romantic nonsense in the France of the near Revolution, with a long climactic duel in the final reel that is still considered one of the best, if not *the* best since Rudolph Rassendyl v. Rupert of Hentzau. With Stewart Granger as the hero (his best performance), Mel Ferrer the villain, Janet Leigh the romantic interest and a strong cast of Culver City regulars, the film was well liked and still stands up on television.

Thanks to *Scaramouche* Froeschel and I were now considered a reliable team and were sent by the Story Department a variety of novels, plays and ideas for the wide screen, which we would consistently turn down until we sensed that 'upstairs' was becoming restive, when we would discover quite remarkable qualities in the next property offered to us. With intervals for chess and a little light poker we wrote *Never Let Me Go* (Clark Gable rescuing ballerina Gene Tierney from Communist Russia), *The Unknown Man* (small-scale American thriller with Walter Pidgeon), and – although we fought hard against it, it was our turn to say yes – a remake of *Rose Marie* (Howard Keel, Ann Blyth, Fernando Lamas). The Studio had last made *Rose Marie* in 1936. A tuneful but tiresome operetta with the popular team of Jeanette MacDonald and Nelson Eddy in fine voice, it had earned the Studio a heap of dollars.

But that was sixteen years ago. Rudolph Friml's original score for *Rose Marie* had only three hit numbers – 'The Indian Love Call', 'The Song of the Mounties' and the title song. That wouldn't suffice for a 1950s movie and so Friml, an elderly but spirited old gentleman who lived in Japan, was sent for.

When he arrived at Culver City with two young handmaidens who looked like geisha girls in professional costume, he appeared physically and emotionally exhausted. In view of his age and their youth it was understandable and probably worth it. His little companions seemed quite happy, buzzing around him like devoted flies, bowing and giggling and showing every sign of pleasure given and pleasure rewarded.

Friml was treated like a lord and allowed three months to produce some additions to the score. 'Leave it to Rudi,' he said. 'Rudi already has a great new melody in his heart,' and with that he shut himself away with his inamoratas in the bungalow provided by the Studio, insisting that he should not be interrupted until time was up. Occasionally there was a rustle of kimono and the top of a Japanese headdress was glimpsed as one or other of his light-o'-loves opened or closed a window, but apart from chords being struck and phrases gone over the great man remained incommunicado with his small companions and his grand piano. Three months to the day he and his lively little ladies emerged, glowing with accomplishment.

'I have it! I have it!' he cried. 'What did I tell you? Rudi has the great new smash!'

'Sir, I congratulate you,' said George, bowing, I thought, unnecessarily low to Japan. (George tended to be overwhelmed by women, especially his wife Elsa who laughed at him with love and whom he adored.)

Excitement was intense as we assembled in the Music Department

169

to hear the new masterpiece – the Ogres, the technical staff assigned to the picture, Friml and partners, the lyricist Paul Francis Webster, Froeschel and I.

The great man sat at the concert grand, which had been wheeled in and specially tuned, flexing his fingers as though at Carnegie Hall. A hush descended. He looked mistily into the middle distance and closed his eyes. Then the old veined hands descended on the keys and the first few bars of a sweet, lush melody filled the air. He played gently on to the final frail fortissimo. Then he turned triumphantly and waited for the applause. There was a mystified silence, followed by a faint clap of palm on palm. Friml inclined his head in acknowledgement. The Mikado girls, glowing with pride, inclined theirs.

While the Ogres left in silence and a body, the rest of us patted Rudi on the back and said the melody he had in his heart was, as he had promised, 'great' and 'a smash'. Which indeed it was. It always had been. The new smash was the old smash, the title song: 'Oh Rose Marie I love you, I'm always thinking of you', phrase for phrase, bar for bar, note for note. What the composer and his beloveds had been up to for three whole months no one, to the best of my knowledge, lacked the grace to inquire. Well, it *is* a marvellous tune. Noblesse oblige.

Throughout my four years at Culver City George and I managed a film a year, by which I mean films that were actually made, which is not as routine as it sounds. Your screenplay had to find a producer, a director, at least one and hopefully two genuine stars who made music at the box office, and get financial approval from New York head office, all areas in which the writer had no say and was seldom invited to offer an opinion.

We were paid – and well paid – to write and, having writ, to shut up and leave the rest to others. If the result was frequently nothing to put out extra flags for, and sometimes badly miscast, the mass-production movies of the fifties were designed for a broad cross-section of the public, not merely the more intemperate and inflammatory young as in the years that followed. When they crop up on television, they seem to me a rather pleasant change from the over-the-top violence and horror that are today's staple ingredients. But then I'm probably prejudiced. I hope.

The last film George and I wrote together was *Betrayed*, a wartime spy thriller, set in Holland, again with Gable, partnered this time by Lana Turner and Victor Mature. The producer and director was Gottfried Reinhardt, son of the great Max, and that one too crops up

170

from time to time. Offscreen Gable, Turner and Mature bore no resemblance to the provocative personalities put out by the Publicity Department. All three were friendly, hard-working professionals without an air or pretension between them. Gable especially was a quiet man, a decent, unaffected human being who just happened to be a world star. He invariably played himself because that was what the public wanted, but he was a fine actor. Rhett Butler proved that for all time. Reinhardt, a witty civilised European in the Lubitsch tradition, who knew exactly how to handle his artists, had other projects in mind to follow *Betrayed* and invited me to stay on and work with him on them. I thought about it but I had been away from home a long time and suddenly one more movie seemed a film too far.

I sold my much-loved house to a plump, cigar-chomping business-man who owned a world-famous liquor company. He and his equally plump bejewelled wife called each other 'lover' whenever they addressed one another during their tour of inspection. I shuddered at the thought of 709 going to them but since they offered $50,000, which was precisely what I had paid for it, I calculated that I had lived free for four years (I had forgotten inflation) and within two days we exchanged contracts.

Shortly afterwards the price of Californian property went through the roof and if the house existed today – it has vanished under a road-widening scheme – it would be worth at least two million dollars, probably more. Had I known this at the time, would I have waited for a better offer? To be truthful, probably not. After four years, I longed for England, for the lights of London and the London theatre, for those live audiences that Coward was so right about, and, as Dacre-Hill did, for the friends we had left behind.

'And so,' as the James A. FitzPatrick travelogue used to intone, 'we say goodbye to sunny California, land of the warm sand and the waving palm.' On 22 March, my mother's birthday, with expensively over-weight luggage filled with the bric-à-brac that time had garnered, we flew to New York and, after a few hours' rest, straight on to London airport, where the weather was cold and raw and wet and wonderful. The cabby who, spotting American labels on the luggage, had grossly overcharged for the journey into town, was so astonished to receive the further bonus of a healthy tip that he tried to give it back.

'No, guv. Fair's fair. I've done you already.'

'I know. Nevertheless it's yours.'

Nothing was going to dilute the euphoria that seemed to be saying, in Goldstein argot crossed with London cockney, 'Okay, kiddo. That's your lot. You're home.'

171

11

. . . .

Proscenium Arches

During my last year at MGM I had come across a novel by Nigel Balchin, *A Way Through the Wood*. Like nearly all Balchin's books it was a psychological study – in this case of a young married woman living in England's stockbroker belt – as well as a rattling good yarn about who, directly or indirectly, was responsible for a car crash that caused a death. I thought at once it could make a gripping play and contacted Balchin's London agent, who gave me six months to come up with a draft.

As soon as I arrived back in England my first appointment was lunch with Balchin. He whisked through the draft, gave it his blessing and the play, which I called *Waiting for Gillian*, was acquired for production by the Laurence Olivier/Vivien Leigh management who had taken a lease of the historic St James's Theatre, soon to be torn down and replaced by a dim and graceless office block. (Is this the way the world is going?) I had written the leading part of the young wife for Glynis Johns. Glynis, who had become a close friend since the film of *Frieda*, had the ideal quality of seeming innocence which was her trademark and, combined with that delightfully husky Welsh croak, had made her a star. Gillian, cunning and endearing child-wife, was tailor-made for Glynis and she leapt at it. A contract was signed with the Olivier management, a rehearsal date set and, within a week of my return, I was back where I had always felt most at home, behind the proscenium arches of London's theatreland. I could scarcely believe my good fortune. This was just as well as it contrived to evaporate almost overnight.

Glynis was much in demand for plays, films and television and, wanting in her singular fashion to keep everyone happy, had a way of promising to accept all three engagements simultaneously, sometimes in three different countries, and was genuinely nonplussed when this turned out to be difficult. So it was on this occasion and, as usual, contractual chaos followed.

Not knowing what to do or where to turn, Miss Johns withdrew to the London Clinic where she threatened to sue the nurses unless they gave her an instant enema. How this was supposed to be helpful wasn't clear to me but Olivier had the answer. 'Something had to give,' he said.

At that time Olivier was appearing with his wife Vivien Leigh in Rattigan's *The Sleeping Prince* at the Phoenix Theatre in Charing Cross Road (brief home of the inimitable *War and Peace*). It was arranged that I should pick him up after the evening performance and take him to supper at the Ivy to discuss the casting crisis.

In the dressing room he said, 'Come and say hello to Vivien' and took me next door. I don't think I have ever seen such a beautiful creature. She was glowing with happiness and exuded the kind of pure and stylish sexuality that drives cardinals to distraction. She had recently suffered a nervous breakdown and as we walked up the road to the Ivy restaurant I said to Olivier that it was wonderful to see Vivien restored to health and strength. He stopped dead. 'Oh no,' he said grimly. 'No, dear boy. I wish to God she were.' Looking back, here was tragedy in the making.

The Ivy, for years the most famous theatrical restaurant in town, welcomed Sir Laurence with appropriate ceremony. I was determined to do him proud and as there was an 'r' in the month suggested oysters and champagne, followed perhaps by *filet mignon* and *crême brulée* with or without strawberries, the whole washed down with a bottle of Saint-Emilion '49.

Olivier said, 'It's very sweet of you but would you mind if I just had sausage and mash? *Burnt* sausage, burnt really *black*, okay? Oh, and a glass of cold water, if I may,' he added. 'I'm not a fancy eater.' (Nearly four decades later I was to know a down-to-earth Prime Minister with an equally undemanding appetite.)

During the meal – feeling anything else would be ostentatious I had settled for bacon and eggs and coffee – I asked Olivier what we were to do about Glynis.

'Let her go, old love,' he said, tucking in to burnt sausage with every sign of enjoyment.

'But isn't she being incredibly wicked?'

'Yes, of course she is and we could sue for breach of contract but she doesn't mean it, she just gets in a muddle. Besides, we'd be on a hiding to nothing. Doctors' certificates by the dozen. Wish her luck as we wave her goodbye and recast. I say, these sausages are the cat's whiskers.'

Luckily the splendidly reliable Googie Withers was free and after a week at the Opera House, Manchester, *Waiting for Gillian* opened at the red plush and gold St James's (where Wilde's *The Importance* had first seen the light and drawn the town) with Googie, her husband John McCallum and Frank Lawton co-starring. They were a strong team and the story gripped as I'd hoped it would. Later a French production did well in Paris and *Gillian* won a *Daily Mail* award for the year's best television drama, with Googie and John repeating their roles and Michael Denison in the Lawton part.

During the London run of *Gillian* I had written a light comedy called *The Bride and the Bachelor*: one set, eight characters, nonconformist St John's Wood family. Its plot combined the supernatural with the matrimonial, its tone pitched halfway between Coward's *Blithe Spirit* and Esther McCracken's *Quiet Wedding*.

The play had three star parts but the quirky, sportive materfamilias, slightly off the pavement but keeping her head above water in strange and extremely trying circumstances, had to carry the show. I sent the script to Edith Evans, a genius with offbeat characters, stressing that I had no higher purpose in mind than to cheer people up and ring box-office telephones and I hoped this would not put her off. She returned it with a detailed and unselfish letter which said, in effect, 'I think this would make a splendid near-farce if you stepped up the pace here – and here – and also here, but in that case of course it would not be for me.' I thought it sound advice and sent the play in revised form to Peter Saunders, whom I knew as a shrewd commercial manager. He read it at once and returned it as quickly with a letter that reflected his natural courtesy. It could not have been more charming – or more negative. Not for him, this one, but great fun to read, wouldn't know how to cast it, love to do one of my plays, don't forget him next time, all good wishes and sure it will be a huge success in the right hands. (English producers of the old school said 'Wouldn't touch it with a bargepole' in the nicest possible way.)

Despite the comparative success of *Gillian*, *The Bride* went the rounds for about a year without finding a management. Finally I turned to Jack de Leon at the 'Q'. This meant staking everything on a try-out at my old stamping ground which, despite my faith in the piece, I had wanted to avoid. If it failed at the 'Q' that would be the end of it, and I wasn't sure that the 'Q' would attract a 'name' cast as it had with *Zero Hour*. I told Jack my fears and to my surprise and delight he said, 'Let's go straight for the West End.' His impatience to launch the play without testing reaction on his home patch was surprising but I put it down to enthusiasm. The weeks ticked by and Saunders' remark about the difficulty of casting, which I had thought to be no more than a polite excuse, was being amply confirmed.

Then, as with *Frieda*, a news item caught my eye. It was a three-line paragraph in the London *Evening News* reporting that a new musical, starring the husband-and-wife team of Jack Hulbert and Cicely Courtneidge, which had been touring prior to London, was unexpectedly not coming into town and that Hulbert was to join the cast of William Douglas-Home's *The Reluctant Debutante* that was running at the Cambridge Theatre. My mind raced. This must mean Courtneidge would be free. Could she play the mother of my St John's Wood family? The part called for an expert comedienne and there was none better. But her life had been spent in musicals. How would she feel about going 'straight'? The actor Thorley Walters, a mutual friend, gave me her phone number and I called her at the Hulberts' house in South Audley Street, wangled an invitation to tea and told her the plot of the piece while she bustled about gulping Earl Grey and blowing imaginary dust off the antique furniture ('I'm listening, I'm listening'). When I had done she said, 'When do we start? Have another bun.'

'No thanks, really.'

'Go on, be a sport. They're perfectly foul and I want to get rid of them.' I felt an instant rapport with this twinkling dynamo.

There were two other star parts – the father of the family and the bachelor of the title. We were having no luck with either but at least we had a leading lady whom I had worshipped from half-a-dozen galleries and who took life at a galloping pace with a vitality that was seemingly inexhaustible. Things were looking up at last. Then, Sunday evening, telephone.

'Good evening,' the voice was a rich, beautifully modulated baritone that was almost but not quite Jack de Leon's. 'I'm Jack's brother, Herbert,' said the voice. 'We met some years ago at the "Q".'

'Ah yes, I remember it well.' I had no recollection.

'Mr Millar, I have both some bad and, I hope, some good news for you. My brother Jack is not at all well. His doctors say he needs a rest. A long rest. Otherwise . . . I believe he was hoping to present a play of yours.'

'*Was* hoping?'

'Still is.'

'In that case, why – '

'He mustn't. If he does your play it could kill him.'

'Oh, come. It's not a bad little comedy.'

'I'm serious. We want you to take it away from him without giving the real reason.'

'That's an extraordinary request. We've been working on it for months. If I don't give a reason he'll think I've betrayed him or gone mad or – '

'Just do as I ask and the family will take it from there. *Please.*'

'But listen, I have a management, a contract, hopefully a major star in Cicely Courtneidge. It's taken me a year to get this far. You're asking me to throw it all away.'

'I have reason to believe,' said the voice, 'that another management would be interested in presenting your play.'

'And who would that be?'

'Peter Saunders.'

I laughed. 'My dear man – '

'I have reason to believe – '

'Just one moment. Mr Saunders read *The Bride* some months ago. He was the first management I approached. He turned it down.'

'I have reason to believe – '

'And I have his letter. I assure you you're quite mistaken.'

'If he rings you as soon as I put the phone down, will you believe me?'

Saunders rang within minutes. Next day I went to see him in his office at the corner of Whitehall and Trafalgar Square. Neither of us mentioned his previous rejection of the play. If he remembered it, he had changed his mind. The reason was obvious: Cicely Courtneidge. We had quite a jolly chat, out of which came Saunders' inspired idea of casting Robertson Hare as her husband.

When she heard this Miss Courtneidge said, 'Oh, *no*! Not dear little Bunny! I love Bunny and he makes me laugh but not as my husband. Oh, calamity! I wouldn't be seen dead with that darling little man.'

But actors, like authors and other curious creatures, don't always know what's best for them. Cis Courtneidge came around and she and Bunny Hare made a brilliant comedy team. With Naunton Wayne as the Bachelor and Jill Raymond (Clement Freud's wife) as the Bride suddenly everything fell into place.

Just before Christmas, after a successful tour, *The Bride and the Bachelor* opened at the Duchess Theatre in the Strand to the worst first-night audience I have ever known. The weather? Exhausted Christmas shoppers? They were the only excuses I could think of and they didn't even convince me. Whatever the reason, for the first time the laughter that had greeted the play at every performance did not so much die on that dreadful night, it was stillborn. Cis was in tears, the press was predictably dire and immediately after Christmas – usually a good time for theatre business – the house was only half-full, which is a polite way of saying it was half-empty.

On New Year's Eve I wandered into the foyer where I found Saunders standing with a long face. He handed me the box-office return. 'I'm afraid we've had it,' he said.

There's no arguing with figures. Short of a visit by the entire Royal Family on successive nights I could think of no reason why the tide should turn. However, never, but *never*, give up the ship. In those days BBC Television's Drama Department was strongly supportive of the stage (it drew on it for actors and writers) and with a little arm-twisting a forty-minute television excerpt, introduced by a young Ludovic Kennedy direct from the theatre, was arranged. The effect was magical. Within minutes we had lift-off. The box-office telephones at the Duchess were jammed, *The Bride and the Bachelor* went into orbit and stayed there for 590 performances.

What makes normally rational people gamble their livelihood on the big dipper that's the living theatre? Money? Fame? A child's love of 'let's pretend'? All those things. But most of all, I think, it's because there's no thrill like the thrill of the hundred-to-one-shot that's trailing the pack, then suddenly, against all the odds, comes from behind and wins the Derby.

'Hello – ello – ello! Everything under control? Jolly fine, jolly fine.' At parties held to celebrate *The Bride's* various anniversaries Jack Hulbert would turn up and, after a couple of drinks, would say to me, 'Of course, you know what's wrong with this show of yours, don't you? There's no part for a tall man with a large chin and a smile that stretches from Land's End to John o'Groats. Well, Gateshead, anyway. If only you'd had a chap like that in the cast you might have had a decent run. As it is – well, better luck next time.'

Cis said, 'You know what he's after, don't you?'

'No.'

'A sequel with a part for him in it.'

'A sequel?'

'Yes, but not till I've put my feet up for half an hour.'

'If I did write a sequel – which of course I won't – '

'Certainly not. You'd be crazy.'

'Can't go through all that again, can we?'

'Be out of our minds, that's what we'd be. You were saying?'

'If I did, I suppose you'd want Jack to play your husband.'

'Good Lord, no. Must have Bunny as my husband. Won't do it without Bunny as my husband. Not that you're going to do it, of course. Jack can be the butler.'

In the words of the mighty Alastair Sim, 'I know when I'm beaten, dalling', so I wrote *The Bride Comes Back* for Cis, Jack and Bunny Hare. It ran merrily at the Vaudeville for eight months following a pre-London tour.

During that tour Cis had phoned from Leeds. 'Good morning. Are you lying comfortably?'

'Why? What's wrong?'

'Third-act trouble.'

'I'm on my way.'

It was before InterCity took over from InterMinable, so at Euston bookstall I bought a novel to while away the journey. The word 'Cambridge' on the cover had caught my eye. At Leeds I went straight to the Grand Theatre, saw the show, took notes, went back to the Queen's Hotel with the Hulberts, had supper and sat up till 4.00 a.m. having one of those post mortems for which they were famous. When at last I crawled into bed exhausted I glanced at the book I had bought and decided to read for ten minutes to help me unwind. I was still reading when my alarm call rang at seven.

The revised third act went in two nights later with Cis and Jack reading new dialogue that was pinned on to cushions, behind curtains and on the backs of chairs. I was terrified but they seemed to enjoy the danger, it gave their performance an extra spice.

They were tremendous professionals, the Hulberts, much-loved by their public and by me. Cis, being hot-tempered, took comedy at a cracking pace and switched moods and wigs with equal speed. Jack, deliberately slower on the draw, was the perfect comedy foil, huge chin stuck out, smile a mile wide, waiting for the penny to drop. As Donald Sinden said at Jack's memorial service, even his feet were funny. But behind the light comedian's façade was a well-honed theatrical instinct. His, as she constantly acknowledged, was the brain behind his wife's musical comedy successes, most of which he directed. Individually and collectively the Hulberts could drive you out of your mind at times. 'Never again!' one would promise oneself. But one always came back for more. I miss them greatly.

In the train going home from Leeds I finished the Cambridge book and thought no more about it until the weekend. Then, lying in bed that Sunday morning, it suddenly came home to me that despite a journey to Leeds, a visit to the theatre, a Hulbert post mortem till

4.00 a.m. and a new third act to write, I had sat up reading until breakfast-time. That novel must have had something...

'Good evening. Could I speak to Sir Charles Snow, please?' I had looked him up in the phone book, expecting to find him ex-directory.

'Speaking. Harrumph.' It was a deep neutral voice, followed by a grunt.

'My name is Millar. You won't have heard of me but I write the odd play from time to time.'

'Millar with an "a", isn't it?'

It was a promising start. I told C. P. Snow how I had come upon his book at Euston Station and couldn't put it down. A second grunt with an upward inflection came from the phone which indicated pleasure or minor wince, I wasn't sure which. I asked if it had occurred to its author that there could be a play in his novel. No, it hadn't occurred. Harrumph. Well, could we perhaps meet and discuss the possibility if the rights were free?

A third grunt, a pause, and then he said that someone called Sydney Box, whom he'd never heard of but who was apparently in the film industry, had taken an option on the novel with a view to making it into a film. Had I ever heard of Sydney Box? Oh yes, he was quite well-known. Well, anyway, he, Snow, was off to the South of France but if Box didn't pick up his option he would let me know and we could possibly take it from there. I wasn't too happy with that 'possibly' but I had received a civilised reception and the ball was at least in play.

Nothing happened for a couple of months. Then the dramatic critic John Barber, who was now with the literary agents Curtis Brown, telephoned.

'I'm sending you our one-page contract, is that all right?' I had no idea what he was talking about. 'You want to dramatise Snow's *The Affair*, don't you, or have you gone cold on the idea?' I began the play that afternoon.

Snow and I did not meet until I had finished a draft. Then he came to my Knightsbridge flat one evening around six, as I thought to pick up the script and take it away with him. But after a few preliminary exchanges and a harrumph or two he sat on the sofa in my study, the great bald dome of a head gleaming in the firelight (one had the feeling the head was that size when it emerged from the womb) and started to read. I put a bottle of Black & White and a jug of iced water beside him and left him to it.

Forty minutes later I returned. Two-thirds of the Scotch had gone, the iced water had barely been touched, he was stone-cold sober and smiling over his horn-rims. He tossed the script aside and refilled his glass.

'Don't you want to finish it?'

'I just did.'

'That was fast. What do you think?'

'Fine. Harrumph. What happens now?'

What happened was that Donald Albery (son of Sir Bronson, father of Ian) took an option to present the play at one of his West End theatres. After five and a half months and no sign of activity I went round to see his general manager, Ann Jenkins, formerly of the Royal Court, and a friend.

'Any news?'

'I'm afraid not. Look, don't quote me but I don't think he's going to do your play. Why don't you take it away from him?'

This was the second time I had been invited to remove my work from a prospective management. If this went on there wouldn't be a producer left in London with whom I was persona grata. However...
The script in an envelope with my handwriting on it lay on her desk. I picked it up, hailed a taxi and went straight to Arlington Street where Henry Sherek had a flat over the Caprice restaurant. I handed the porter the envelope and asked him to see that Mr Sherek got it.

'He's just gone in, sir,' he said, indicating the restaurant. I retrieved the script and followed. Huge Henry and his wife Pamela were sitting at the first table to the left of the door. Sherek's eyes missed nothing.

'Ah!' he cried, diving at the script under my arm before I'd said a word. 'What's it about?'

'Cambridge.'

'Call you tonight,' said Sherek. I thought I'd hear from him in a week if I was lucky but when he rang about nine that evening both he and Pamela had read *The Affair*. Henry said he liked it and Pamela loved it and he planned to present the play as soon as he could get it financed.

Not a word for a month, then a phone call to say all his backers had turned it down on the grounds that no one wanted to see a lot of old dons wandering about in black gowns knifing each other in the back. If this was a wild travesty of Snow's plot it was also, I suspected, not the real reason.

The year was 1961 and for more than five years the theatre had been going through something like a civil war. The London stage had been transformed by the coming of the 'kitchen sink' plays to the Royal Court Theatre with John Osborne's *Look Back in Anger* firing the first salvo.

180

In his play Osborne raged against society and the status quo, which was no doubt ripe for being raged against, but, unlike Shaw's and Priestley's similar attacks, Osborne's offensive lacked humanity or compassion. The play has a niche in the history of modern drama as the first to combine the class war with the sex war. Also, for those who delight in malevolence at second hand, a command of acerbity and venom that to me was unprecedented. However, state-of-the-art spleen hardly makes for a balanced work. The definitive and infinitely superior play of that era, one that had feeling as well as fury, was in my view Arnold Wesker's *Roots*, in which the young Joan Plowright made a joyous debut.

It was a strange time in the British theatre. Coward and Rattigan were written off as old hat and finished (happily not true in either case) and 'the well-made play' was out. *The Affair*, which had a strong storyline, sets that were more than halfway elegant and language that wasn't perpetually hitting the f-word until it bored rather than shocked, fell solidly into the 'well-made' category. It was clearly out of sync with the current fashion and critical mood and I came to the conclusion that the wise course was to put it on ice until the pendulum swung back and lifted us out of the equally class-conscious kitchen. Then, as is the way of things, the decision was taken out of my hands.

Pamela Sherek's brother had died in South Africa and, finding herself his principal beneficiary, she decided to back *The Affair* with her own money, or rather his. This was brave but probably foolish. I told Snow that in my opinion and the present climate the most we could hope for, if we were lucky, was a limited run at a medium-sized theatre like the Apollo or the Comedy, where Forster's *A Passage to India* had only had a moderate success. Horses for courses.

In the event the only available theatre was the large 1000-seater Strand. I apologised to Snow, saying that at such a time it was far too big a theatre to fill with a play like *The Affair* but we had no choice, it was the Strand or nothing.

With John Clements and Alan Dobie leading a large and carefully chosen cast of character actors, *The Affair* opened at the Strand Theatre on 21 September 1961. Unlike the first night of *The Bride* the audience was with the play from curtain up. It ran for almost a year. The pendulum had swung without our knowing it. There was life after *Look Back* after all.

During the run of *The Affair* I had dramatised an earlier novel of Snow's, *The New Men*, which fascinated me. It dealt with the making of the first atom bomb, of which Snow as a scientist had special knowledge, having been partly responsible for gathering the British

181

end of the team of Anglo-American scientists who made it. The play followed *The Affair* at the Strand with several of the same cast. My old friend Richard Pasco, the coffee boy from *Zero Hour* at the 'Q', was outstanding as the leading scientist, Luke.

After a week at Brighton *The New Men* opened on 6 September 1962. It made a ripple but not the splash I had hoped for. The notices were respectful but scarcely box office (except for Ken Tynan who gave it an excellent review in the *Observer*). I learnt from talking to theatre-goers as they came out that, though the piece had its devotees, the subject kept them from recommending it to maiden aunts or honeymoon couples. This was hardly surprising. People lived in the shadow of the bomb and on the whole their idea of a night out at the theatre did not include two-and-a-half hours of the birth pangs of nuclear fission. I should, of course, have thought of that. Snow said it was his fault for not having provided a central narrative. It wasn't. It was mine. The play ran for 79 performances. *The Affair* had clocked up exactly 300 more.

The third play of the Snow trilogy was *The Masters*, which Charles had been nudging me gently towards for some time but its setting and several of its characters were the same as in *The Affair* and I had resisted it. Even so it stayed with me, nagging away like an unfinished crossword. Charles tells the story of how it finally came about in his preface to the published edition of the plays:

'I was having a glum time that autumn (1962) with eye operations. [He had a detached retina.] R.M. came into the hospital [Moorfields in the City] to cheer me up. He brought the first two acts of *The Masters*. As my eyes were still covered, he read the acts to me... I wasn't feeling well or cheerful, but I thought, *This is all right*, in fact I thought then, and still think, that *The Masters* is by a very long way the best play of the three. I also thought... that it would draw an audience. But with the failure of *The New Men* we had gone back to the beginning. No one would want to see a play about Cambridge dons. It took the combined strength of John Clements, R.M. and a new producer, Martin Landau, to get the play on the stage at all...

'The first performance took place at the Golders Green Hippodrome, and this was the most pleasurable night I have spent in the theatre... it was a joy to feel the play being communicated to an enormous, happy, friendly audience, and to feel the communication flowing back... it was the kind of experience, I suppose, which ties people to the stage. For two and a half hours I knew how playwrights and actors feel. From that night, all was smooth. The play [first at the Savoy Theatre and then at the Piccadilly] found its audience at once, and ran for 257 performances.' In fact, until the assassination of America's President Kennedy, when the country went virtually into mourning. On the night of his death, in London's theatreland the American national anthem was played instead of 'God Save the Queen'.

For Martin Landau, like George Froeschel a refugee from Nazi Germany, the success of *The Masters*, which he had co-produced with Clements, was his first West End hit as a producer. Fired by its success he told me that he planned half-a-dozen productions a year ('I think that's about right, don't you?'). So when he invited me to meet him in the bar of the Savoy Grill opposite the theatre to discuss a project he had in mind, I was agog. What could it be? With Landau, who loved the theatre and pretty women, not necessarily in that order, anything was possible.

After the drinks had arrived and the vagaries of English weather discussed and deplored, he asked casually, 'Did you ever see Besier's play *The Barretts of Wimpole Street?*'

'Before my time. I saw the film.' Like the play, the romance of Elizabeth Barrett and Robert Browning in the teeth of her despotic father's overwhelming opposition, had been an international success.

'Might it make a musical, do you think?'

I didn't think anything one way or the other. Landau reached under his chair and came up with a manuscript of biblical proportions.

'This is a first stab at it.'

'Really? By whom?'

'An American judge. An amateur.'

'An amateur judge?'

'No, no. He used to be a baritone on the *Lucky Strike Show*.'

Curiouser and curiouser. Landau dumped the tome in my lap. I nearly dropped it. 'I take it this is the book, lyrics and musical score?'

'No. Just the book and a few lyrics.'

I turned to the end. 'Five hundred pages of libretto?'

'Yes, well, it needs cutting, reconstructing, rewriting by a professional dramatist. Naturally I thought of you.'

'Kind. Kind. Nevertheless – '

'Take it home. See what you think.'

'I'd rather not if you don't mind.'

'It won't kill you to read it, will it?'

I weighed the work in my hands. 'It might.'

Two days later I returned it. 'I'm sorry, Martin, but it's bargepole time.'

183

'Better things had worse beginnings.'

'It won't do, really it won't.'

'Answer me this. Does the tale lend itself to music? One of the world's great love stories? Sentiment without sentimentality?' I hesitated. The tome was back in my lap. 'Go on, have a go.'

'My dear man, I wouldn't know where to begin. The book needs a complete rewrite.'

'When can you start?'

'And then there's the score.'

'That too.'

'I've never done a musical.'

'Neither have I.'

'Even if I were mad enough to take a crack at it, I wouldn't move without a director.'

'Wendy Toye's free.'

This was cunning. All who had gone through *Jenny Jones* together were friends for life.

'Well?'

I was tempted. I had loved music from birth and probably before. (Dacre-Hill had played and sung throughout her pregnancy to take her mind off the matter in hand.)

'What about the judge?'

'Leave that to me. He'll be handsomely rewarded for starting the ball rolling.'

While Landau negotiated contracts with the judge and the Besier Estate Wendy Toye weighed in with her usual enthusiastic expertise. An immediate priority was a professional composer. She suggested a man named Grainer. The name meant nothing to me. What had he done?

'Ron's with the BBC's Radiophonic Workshop. He also writes musical jingles for television. *Doctor Who, Steptoe and Son, That Was the Week That Was.* You know the sort of thing.'

Jingles and radiophonic workshops? But surely what was required was the score for a full-scale musical. Had Miss Toye stepped briefly off the pavement?

'He did the music for a film I directed. *The King's Breakfast.*'

'Oh yes?' I'd never heard of it.

'He's Australian,' she said, as if that made all the difference.

'And he has a flat at Roehampton,' said Landau, contributing his own non sequitur. The conversation was becoming bizarre.

On a soaking wet summer night I found myself in the middle of a Roehampton housing estate, drenched to the skin and ringing a doorbell that nobody answered, cursing the Barretts and Wimpole

Street and musicals in general and my folly in getting even remotely involved with a project without a future. No matter. I had signed no contract. I would withdraw first thing in the morning.

When the door was at last opened a sandy-haired man with a shy crinkly expression stood there.

'Ron Grainer?'

'Er, yeah – well – ' He seemed none too sure but there was a hint of an Australian accent.

'I'm the other Ron.'

'Ah.' We stared at one another. 'Well – you'd better come in.' I followed him into a room almost bare of furniture. An old upright piano leant against a wall. Sheets of music manuscript were scattered over bare floorboards.

'Like a Coke?'

I hated Cokes but I'd had no dinner. I nodded. My overcoat was dripping rain. I took it off. There didn't seem to be anywhere to hang it. Grainer took it absent-mindedly and half dropped it on to a battered armchair. It slithered down and joined the music on the floor. Beyond caring, I left it there. There was a silence.

'This Barrett business,' said my host at length. 'How d'you reckon it starts?'

'Well, I suppose in Wimpole Street. The Barretts lived on the corner of Wimpole Street. Wimpole Street and Cavendish Square.'

Grainer slid on to the piano stool and tinkered with a few notes. I sipped my Coke. Ugh. Presently: 'Bit of luck, that.'

'Really? What was it?'

'Tune to your lyric.'

'What lyric?' I hadn't written a lyric, I'd merely described a location.

He played the sequence of notes again, this time accompanying them in a voice to frighten horses.

'Here on the corner of Wimpole Street ... Wimpole Street and Cavendish Square... ' It was a catchy little tune. He began to develop it. He had the period precisely. I sat down ...

Next day: 'I hear you got along fine,' said Landau.

'Well, yes. Except that he thinks that I'm writing the lyrics as well as the book.'

'Good idea,' said Miss Toye.

'Oh no.' We'd been having trouble finding a lyric writer.

'You can do it,' she said firmly as though I were one of the *Jenny Jones* children.

'Thanks but no thanks.'

'Didn't you write lyrics at Cambridge?' said Landau.

'The Footlights is a step or two from Shaftesbury Avenue.'

185

But I was outnumbered and they were confidence-builders. In the end I said I would try, on the explicit understanding that if, after a month, I hated the result, even if they were happy, they would hire someone else. I insisted on a special clause in my contract to that effect and to make assurance double sure I drafted it myself.

But writing lyrics is a fascinating business and within days of working with the brilliantly gifted Grainer I began to realise that if the same person wrote the lyrics as wrote the libretto, the chances were that dialogue might segue into song and out again more smoothly than if another lyricist did the job. I became so intrigued by this technique that if, after the month was up, Landau and Toye had turned elsewhere I would have taken umbrage on a sizeable scale.

Grainer and I were a most unlikely couple but we never had a cross word. The man was a joy to work with. He never argued, constantly asking my opinion on the style of composition and even the detail of the music, which was a boost to my own feelings of inadequacy. The mutual understanding that developed was uncanny. Some numbers were written in twenty minutes. I've no doubt this happens to other collaborators but to me it was a unique experience.

We had decided to stay musically and lyrically as close to 1845 as possible, but not pedantically so, and Grainer's score moved effortlessly via music hall to sweeping ballad to operetta to the fringes of opera. Jingles? The man had genius.

As soon as a rough musical outline was ready Prince Littler, the chairman of Moss Empires who controlled more than half the theatres in the West End, came to my flat with his assistant Toby Rowland to hear our first tentative score. They were captivated and Littler promised Landau Her Majesty's Theatre, which would shortly be available.

Excited by this reaction we plunged into casting. We wanted John Clements for Barrett, Keith Michell for Browning and June Bronhill for Elizabeth. Instantly we ran into problems. Michell, an Australian, was bewitched by a play he had written about an Aborigine. It took eight months and a fortune in telephone calls to Sydney to persuade him to postpone his oeuvre and come with us.

Clements, although it was a non-singing role, wasn't sure he wanted to play Barrett. We had had two hits together and the part was powerful. I couldn't understand his resistance until one day I referred casually to Barrett as 'the man the audience loves to hate'. The word 'loves' did the trick. John hadn't wanted just to play a villain but if he could be on terms with the audience, if his villainy could be relished, if one could ultimately even perhaps feel sorry for him ... ? Ah, actors, dear actors.

Finally June Bronhill, like Keith Australian by birth, couldn't come to England yet without running into double taxation. Her singing was matchless but the score was demanding and, being trained for opera, she had never played eight performances a week in an open-ended run. Also, Elizabeth was an acting as well as a singing role and up against Clements and Michell she could be outclassed. Wendy Toye who had worked with Bronhill had no doubts ('She's a great big zonking star'). At length it was arranged that Landau, Grainer and I should fly to Paris, meet June and set all minds at rest – or not. We were to rendezvous at the Théâtre des Champs-Elysées where she would test the range of her principal numbers and hopefully feel at ease with them and we with her.

The Kirov Ballet was dancing Prokofiev's *Cinderella* at the Champs-Elysées at night but the stage was free in the afternoons. However, on arrival we learnt that the Soviet Cinderella had been taken ill with mushroom-poisoning and the stage was required for her understudy to rehearse. 'Regrets. So sorry. Das veedanya,' said the Russian impresario and turned dismissively away.

Das veedanya be damned, we had hired the hall and stuck to our guns. The Russians claimed prior rights and stuck to theirs, national pride was at stake and a diplomatic incident in the making, which, who knows, might have led to crisis at the United Nations but for the British genius for compromise.

And so it came to pass that Cinderella's understudy whirled valiantly about the stage hearing Prokofiev in her head while the musical version of *The Barretts of Wimpole Street*, played by Grainer and sung by Bronhill in glorious voice, soared up over the orchestra pit and filled both stage and auditorium. In the history of international give-and-take it was a notable first.

The following day June read Elizabeth's dialogue scenes to our complete satisfaction and we flew happily home, where preparations now moved into top gear. A six-week prior-to-London tour was booked: three weeks at Leeds, three at Manchester, then straight into the West End. Malcolm Pride was engaged to design a production that would fill the large stage of Her Majesty's Theatre and our musical director, Alexander (Sandy) Faris, set about hand-picking a twenty-four-piece orchestra that would make the full rich sound required for Beerbohm Tree's lovely theatre. Equally tailored to Her Majesty's capacity was the number of singers and dancers.

Meanwhile Clements made regular checks with my libretto and lyrics to make sure that the audience 'loved' to hate him, June

Bronhill arrived from Paris with the blessing of the Inland Revenue and engaged a nanny named Norma to look after her small daughter while Mummy was working. Finally Michell checked in from Australia and, having got the play about the Aborigine out of his system at Guildford, embraced Browning with both arms.

Then, virtually overnight, all hell broke loose. The production currently running at Her Majesty's, a play called *The Right Honourable Gentleman*, was presented by Emile Littler, brother of Prince. Business had dropped and was hanging on by its fingernails but was still just above the figure at which the landlord, Prince, could give notice. (Shades of *Abelard* waiting for Wyndham's.)

One might think that, being brothers, there would be no problem coming to terms. One would be wrong. The brothers were not only business rivals, they detested one another, especially Emile who dug in his heels. Not only did he refuse to vacate Her Majesty's, he let it be known that he was looking forward to an indefinite run and, when two of his stars left, he promptly replaced them. The brothers sued each other in the lawcourts and Emile won.

On hearing the news, Landau went gunmetal grey and Wendy wept. Prince Littler offered any of his other theatres as soon as one was free but the size of the entire production – scenery, chorus, dancers, orchestra – had been geared to Her Majesty's. The show teetered on the brink of collapse but eventually it was agreed, with the utmost reluctance, that if the scenery could be modified to fit the smaller Lyric Theatre in Shaftesbury Avenue without completely ruining the design, and provided the orchestra could be reduced in size from twenty-four to eighteen players, the production could proceed. Once again spirits rose, scenery was cut, reshaped and adjusted to the Lyric, and the two touring dates – Leeds and Manchester – were confirmed.

But Landau had reckoned without the Musicians' Union. One of the most powerful in the land, it refused to reduce the size of the orchestra. Twenty-four musicians had been promised, twenty-four it must be. Landau was ashen. No show at the Lyric, with a cast of fifty, even at capacity, could sustain an orchestra of that size and make a profit, let alone recoup the cost of production. In addition, to accommodate the twenty-four-piece orchestra one row of stalls would have to be removed and two boxes taken out of circulation to house the timpanist and harpist, thereby reducing the possible box-office takings by more than £300 a week. But it was too late to turn back.

As soon as *The Barretts and Mr Browning* opened at Leeds Grand Theatre it was clear that, as Snow said of *The Masters* when he first heard it, 'this was all right'. The show was, of course, too long –

musicals are always too long to start with – but cuts were no problem. We changed two numbers for stronger ones, tightened here and trimmed there, and after three weeks of capacity audiences moved on to Manchester, confidence sky high.

Business at the Opera House was reasonable but a long way from capacity. We told ourselves it was the size of the theatre, which is huge, that the reception was as good as ever, which it was. We gave June an additional number – 'Woman and Man' – which used her top register to the full and worked beautifully. Still the box office was not under siege.

One night the doorman at the Midland Hotel said, 'Lovely show, sir, pity about the business. They ought to be queuing around the block. 'Course, you know the trouble, don't you?'

'No. Tell me.'

'That title. *Barretts and Mr Browning?*' He yawned. 'Sounds like a temperance lecture, don't it?'

Before the doorman knew what was happening I had seized him by the hand and hauled him through the main lobby into the Grill Room where Clements, his wife (Kay Hammond), June, Keith, Wendy and Landau were having supper.

'Tell them, Harry, what you told me. Tell them about the title.'

He told them. What I really meant was 'Tell John Clements', who had insisted on having the word 'Barretts' in the title to remind people of the famous play on which the show was based. Everyone agreed with the doorman but John remained obdurate.

'Anyway, dear boy,' he said, 'you don't have an alternative, do you?'

I didn't, but halfway through that night, suddenly I did, and when Fred Carter, Littler's man, came up to see the show, I tried it on him. He snapped his fingers. 'That's it! You've got it!'

On 20 October 1964 *Robert and Elizabeth* opened at the Lyric Theatre, Shaftesbury Avenue. It was an immediate success and subsequently won the Ivor Novello Award for the year's best musical (which I like to think would have given Ivor as much pleasure as it gave me). It was still running merrily two years later.

As soon as it went into its third year, with winter under way, Landau again approached the Musicians' Union. The twenty-four-piece orchestra originally booked for Her Majesty's had enjoyed two years at the smaller Lyric at full strength, most of the original players had gone and their places taken by deputies to whom there had been no commitment. Would the Union now agree to a reduction more in keeping with the size of the theatre in which they were playing?

Again the answer was an emphatic 'No', and with threats of an all-out strike of all London's musicals if Landau persisted he bowed to the inevitable and, with business still nudging two-thirds capacity, the notice went up.

I was content. The musical had given a lot of pleasure to a lot of people at home and abroad and, according to Chappell's royalty sheets, continues to do so. John Gale presented an excellent revival at Chichester in 1987. Certainly, of all the shows with which I have been associated, *R and E* was the happiest. I have a great affection for it.

Finally, as Browning sang, 'A twist in the wrist of the story'. June's nanny was a pretty young woman named Norma Johnson. Soon after the run of *Robert and Elizabeth* she met and married a Lambeth councillor with a future. She is now an even prettier Norma Major.

'Never be seen coming out of the same hole twice.'
Noël Coward

Having by great good fortune struck oil with our first musical, Grainer and I looked around for a second, as far removed as possible from the style, songs and setting of mid-Victorian romance. A vague half-glimpsed picture of a young light-hearted show in tune with the mood and sounds of the sixties floated in and out of my mind – so-called Swinging London with the possibilities of pastiche was all around us – but where, oh where, was the kernel of a plot to hang it on?

Then I came across an article in one of the Sunday papers about a scandal that had hit Paris involving the higher echelons of French society. Hundreds of pupils, several of them children of members of the French Government, had been caught cheating in the baccalaureate examination. Transposed to London where offspring and parents alike were suffering from A- and O-level neuroses, here was surely the ideal nucleus of the musical we were looking for.

I telephoned my friend and partner and told him to drop everything and go out and buy the *Sunday Telegraph*. Ron Grainer called me back within the hour and said, 'Ready when you are.' I phoned Martin Landau and Wendy Toye who were equally fired up. All I had was an idea and a title – 'On the Level' – but everything smelt right. We went to work.

The first draft of the show came quickly. We were after a fast singing-and-dancing musical, up to the minute and uncluttered, with plenty of space, so I kept the plot simple. Grainer moved fluently into the modern idiom with which he was wholly familiar and the words and music flew in on the wind.

'Love Gets Younger Every Year', 'My Girl at the Dance', 'Let's Make the Most of Now', 'Strangely Attractive', 'Nostalgia' and the title song 'On the Level' – we had become so used to each other's way of working that the numbers poured out. Wendy collected a superlative team of young dancers: even after *Hair* happened (and it hadn't yet) I am not alone in thinking they were the best of their kind in town.

The scenic design was unique. Wendy had seen a Czech production, *Lanterna Magica*, which consisted of mirrors, projections of coloured slides, and illusions of scenery that moved and blended with the action. Fascinated, Landau flew to Prague and with help from Miloš Forman, whose show it was, came back with examples of how it worked.

A brilliant jazz orchestra of eighteen – no mistake this time, just eighteen, no more, no less – was engaged under Ed Coleman's direction. Ed was the most flamboyant MD I ever saw in action in a theatre. Convinced that those on stage were supporting him and his band, rather than the reverse, he would literally hurl himself into the air to whip his musicians into ever wilder, louder and more exotic rhythms. Apoplexy seemed only a matter of time.

A six-week prior-to-London tour was booked – three weeks at Liverpool and three at Southampton – before coming into the Saville Theatre, Shaftesbury Avenue (now, alas, a cinema). It's an open question whether the first Liverpool dress rehearsal which went on until three in the morning, followed by the second which lasted until 7.30 a.m., was more or less disastrous than the Liverpool opening when everything that could go wrong did. The scenic complexities needed a lot more time to perfect and the audience should have been not the Liverpool burghers but their children and grandchildren. It wasn't that.

On the Level had no centrepiece, and so no star, or stars, to carry it. The young dancers and singers were the star, but the shows that were to make that clear – *Hair* and *Grease* and their like, where youth was the key audience – were still to come. The Liverpool reviews were cataclysmic.

Coming out of the stage door the following morning, wearing the totally relaxed air I had learnt to adopt in time of theatrical mayhem, I ran into Jules Benjamin and his wife Audrey, backers from *Robert and Elizabeth* who also had money in *On the Level*, which they were about to lose. Audrey smiled enigmatically – she always smiles enigmatically before somehow finding food for actors where there is none – and Jules was cheerful, if resigned. He was also curious.

'What's the name of that girl in the chorus with the blonde

pigtails?' There was more than one with pigtails. 'The one with personality plus.'

'Ah. You mean Sheila White.'

He tapped me on the chest. 'She's the spirit of the show,' he said. 'Good luck,' and headed for the London train. I wished I could have gone with him.

I thought no more about his remark until a few days later when Grainer and I were back in town, brooding on what to do to rescue the show or at least improve it. I suddenly realised Benjamin had hit the nail. The kid with the pigtails *was* the spirit of the show. Grainer agreed and in about ten minutes we wrote a dotty little number for her called 'Bleep-Bleep'.

Back in Liverpool Wendy disliked it heartily but agreed to set it for Sheila with a dance to go with it, on one condition: no one was to come near rehearsals until she was ready. A week later she said glumly, 'Well, I suppose you can look at it now if you can bear to.' Miss Toye is a very remarkable lady. Despite her distaste for 'Bleep' she had done a brilliant job with Sheila White who responded like the star in the making she was. The number went in that evening and promptly stopped the show, as it did in every subsequent performance throughout the run, including matinées. One swallow doesn't make a smash but that crazy little number and the way Wendy had choreographed it lifted morale, the cast's hopes began to rise and as other new numbers followed, first at Liverpool, then at Southampton, even I began to think there was an outside chance we might pull it off.

The Saville opening went well but in a large theatre without stars, mixed reviews are not enough and we needed two-thirds capacity to break even. However, there were bright spots along the way. *On the Level* became a cult show for the young generation, its supporters coming night after night to clap and cheer, one even began to recognise them individually.

'What, here again?'

'Great, man, great! See you tomorrow!'

Brian Epstein, the Beatles manager, bought the film rights for rather more than a reasonable sum which was soothing, but a musical calls for more than a cult audience, it needs across-the-board appeal to survive. *On the Level* was the greatest fun to do and was ahead of its time, but after five months of switchback business it was clear that its time was up.

With my venture into musical theatre showing one smash, one crash, it was time to draw breath, review the position, and even – something not in my nature – take a holiday. Happily this last resort was avoided.

Since the three Snow plays, friends, acquaintances and total strangers had out of the kindness of their hearts taken to sending me books, magazines and articles with little notes suggesting 'This would make the most marvellous play' or 'Here's a fortune waiting to be made' or 'I expect you're writing this one for the stage already. If not, what are you waiting for?'

It's not as simple as that, would that it were, but one day out of the blue came a copy of a novel by William Clark called *Number Ten*. Clark had been Anthony Eden's Press Secretary until he felt honour bound to resign over the Suez fiasco. The plot of the book – the story of an African crisis as seen from Downing Street – was fiction, but credible fiction, and the atmosphere of Number Ten and the clash of Cabinet opinion, described by an insider, was vivid and had the ring of authenticity.

I went to see Clark in his apartment in Albany, found him shrewd, likeable and a keen theatre-goer, and received his blessing to proceed with a play. The young impresario Peter Bridge liked the piece, decided to present it and gave me virtually a free hand with the casting. For the leading part there was one choice and one only: Alastair Sim. I sent him the script, waited a week, then bearded him in his Hampstead den.

'Cully dalling!' (Cully being my part in *Mr Bolfry*) 'How *are* you, dalling! Comeincomeincomein. Well now, do you really want me for this play of yours? Are you serious? Well, this is a turn-up for the book! So I'm to play a Prime Minister, am I? An out-of-the-ordinary Prime Minister. But then they are all a bit out of the ordinary, wouldn't you say, they must be or they wouldn't do it. Well, dalling, if you mean it, if you really and truly mean it and you're not pulling my leg and you won't take no for an answer, I'll have a go. I will, I'll have a definite go! What fun! Who else are you having? Who's supporting me, dalling? Or who am I supporting? Do I have right of approval? I suppose I don't, do I? I must remember I'm not in management this time. I'll make a note. Look, I'm writing it down. "Must behave. Cully says so." There.'

I told him with any luck the other three principals would be Michael Denison, Dulcie Gray and John Gregson.

'Love them, dalling. Love every bone in their bodies. Oh, I can see we shall be one big happy family, indeed we will. Even if we die of boredom. I'm the easiest man in the world to get on with. You know that, dalling. Oh, it's all going to be splendid. There won't be a cross word between the lot of us. Dear me, how dull.'

There were three sets: the Cabinet Room and Blue Drawing Room at Number Ten and the Cabinet Room at the House of Commons. For authenticity William Clark had arranged with the current Press Secretary, Henry James, that the designer, J. Hutchinson Scott, and I would be smuggled into Downing Street for a quick look on a hush-hush basis, in the temporary absence of the Prime Minister, Harold Wilson. We were to stand by for a call.

It came almost at once. 'Can you and your colleague be here in ten minutes flat?' I grabbed Jay and we took a taxi to Number Ten. It was not the last time I was to step through the door of that building but no soothsayer was on hand to tell me so.

In the Cabinet Room Jay made hurried sketches and took notes. I asked Henry James how long we had. 'It depends whether Harold has cake or not,' he replied. Apparently the Prime Minister was at a garden party at the Palace. When we left with profuse thanks to Henry he put a hand to his lips and said, 'What for? We haven't even met.'

We hastened across to the Commons and the Prime Minister's office where his amanuensis in excelsis, Marcia Williams (Lady Falkender to be), was expecting us. A tall, charming, gracious woman, she was quite unlike her public image of an *éminence grise*, but perhaps Richelieu too showed his innocent side to strangers.

She took us into the Cabinet Room and said Jay could make notes of anything and everything. She could not have been more helpful. 'Feel free,' she said.

Also present was Wilson's Parliamentary Private Secretary, a genial little man sitting on a horsehair sofa and smiling a welcome with all his flies undone. Torn between giving a whispered word of warning and rising hysteria I took deep breaths and tried with all my strength to concentrate on the geography of the room.

Our prior-to-London tour, which opened at Glasgow where Alastair was practically a totem pole, went splendidly, though his promise of good behaviour fell rather by the wayside, and by the time we reached London and the Strand Theatre he was not on speaking terms with his affectionate, dutiful wife, played with her usual skill and charm by Dulcie Gray. Denison and Gregson, indeed the whole cast, were excellent and Alastair made an outstanding PM, his occasional wickedness being the price one frequently pays for comic genius.

Number Ten was successful without setting the town on fire and when the run ended I had no immediate project in mind. I was coming up to my half-century and felt that a pause for reflection on the meaning of life beyond the proscenium arch was perhaps in order. Just for once I was content to sit back, listen to music and wait for whatever the future had in store. I had not the ghost of an inkling what it would be, although the marquee over the Strand Theatre, proclaiming the title of the play in lights, had for months been giving a broad hint that real life was about to take its cue from fiction.

Interval

. . . .

My colleague and friend Ron Grainer, the composer of Robert and
Elizabeth, *died of cancer in 1981. He was fifty-nine. Here are three of
the lyrics which his music made memorable.*

SOLILOQUY
(Elizabeth)

Tied to a sofa in an airless room
Like Andromeda chained to a rock
While the seasons fly and the days drift
  by
To the aimless tick of the clock
And the doctors call and puzzle and
  frown
And strike a professional pose
One says this and the other says that
As they dither and differ and diagnose
But for all their chatter
The truth of the matter
Is no one really knows
What's wrong
Nobody really knows
What's wrong with me?
In ten years you may be well, they say
What's wrong with me?
Ten years? That's almost a century
What's wrong with me?
Why do my arms and legs and feet
  decline to do
What every fibre of my being begs them
  to
Even a dog can move at will
Even a child of three can stand
Must I be like this
Alone in all the land?
Is it so very much to ask?
Such an extravagant demand?
Why am I helpless?
Without a helping hand?
I wasn't always like this. When I was
Small I was lithe and strong and rather
Wild. A tomboy, in fact, I doubt
You'd have known me
Like a boy I took to the trees

Like a boy I rode and I ran
And tumbled and fought
And the family thought
She'll grow up to be a man
Quicksilver swift was I
And as boisterous as they came
And you'd never have thought
I'd a thought in my head
Or a poem to my name
Black and blue from the fights I had
With the neighbours and friends next
  door
If anyone said
It was time for bed
I'd protest 'Just one fight more!'
Not a care in the world had I
Nor an introspective fear
I was supple and strong
As the days were long
Until Edward died
And then something inside –
Well, nothing was quite the same since
  Edward
No, nothing was quite the same
And now I'm a woman of parts
With a talent to rhyme and scan
And now I can do what few can do
But not what everyone can
For a long time it didn't seem to matter
Not really
Until you came, Robert
When you came
Another air blew through the room
A blazing light lit up the gloom
And filled the sky
My heart was high
And hope was new

197

The wildest dream I dreamed came true
The day you came
With your help
I found the strength to leave my cell
I felt so certain I was well
And, oh, my dear
Just for the moment it was true
Just for the moment love I knew

For you were there
Want to be well
I want it so
This much I know
Don't ask me how
It will be never
Or I vow, it shall be
Now!

WHAT THE WORLD
CALLS LOVE
(Barrett)

What the world calls love
Is a purely passing passion
An irrational infection of the brain
What the world calls love
Is pain
What the world calls love
Is a momentary gladness
Then the madness and the agony begin
What the world calls love
Is sin
Love they beg
Until they're hoarse
Love is degradation and remorse
What the world calls love
Isn't sweetness, isn't kindness
But a blindness that the simple see too
   late
What the world calls love
I hate
I tell you
Love's a game for fools to trust
Love is just another name for lust
What the world calls love
Is a torment and a folly
And this melancholy, miserable state
That the sinful, wilful
World calls love
I abominate

ESCAPE ME NEVER
(Browning)

Escape me never, beloved
While I am I and you are you
So long as earth contains us two
While one eludes must the other pursue
Forever, beloved, forever
Escape me never, beloved
While you are you and I am I
While there is ocean, while there is sky
Though it be not 'til the day we die
We'll be together
Escape me never, forever and aye
Escape me never
Beloved
The earth divides. Beyond the hill
The land is frozen, the seas are still
But hope lives on and eternally will
We'll be together
Escape me never, forever and aye

ACT III

1969–92

12

. . . .

Dinner at Drayton Gardens

Those who believe there's a logical sequence to life maintain that man's random, haphazard existence is nothing of the kind. Everything's planned, they say, as though God were a socialist. On the whole I doubt it. However, it may be so. In which case I must record that the events chronicled in the third part of this narrative were set in train by a small dog named Percy.

Percy was a Jack Russell terrier who belonged to and was much loved by Helen, Lady Runcorn, whose husband had been MP for that fine Cheshire town before proceeding to Their Lordships' House. He (Percy, not His Lordship) was also doted on by a neighbour of Helen's, one Elizabeth Cobham, whose elder sister Lena Palmer (wife of Reginald Palmer of Huntley & Palmer's, the biscuit people) had been my mother's bridesmaid. When, thanks to Percy, Helen and Elizabeth became friends, Fate had made what Don Juans and ball players call a forward pass.

Not quite half a century before these events Elizabeth (known as Bett) had pushed my pram and me round Reading without doing more than superficial damage to either and had recently determined to give me one more push, not in a pram but a political direction. A right-wing Conservative, Bett was good value when she wasn't driven to hysteria by watching Harold Wilson on television (that early snap of young Harold, aged seven-and-three-quarters, standing on the steps of Number Ten ready to take over, had seriously affected her nervous system and she was never quite the same again). Bett had decided, from the moment he actually entered the building as Labour Prime Minister some few years later, that Harold must go. Fur-

201

thermore she had come to the conclusion that, whilst writing plays and films was all very well, Fate had selected me as the instrument of his going and that when the bugle blew to come to the aid of the nation, never mind the Party, it was one's duty to answer the call.

Not having heard so much as a whisper, let alone a call, I didn't take all this too seriously. True, Bett and I had had various discussions and arguments of a political nature (she worked hard for the Chelsea Conservatives and considered me a left-wing Tory who needed educating) but I pointed out that the theatre was a full-time occupation and that if I'd really wanted to climb on to the political bandwagon I would have done so long ago, when Beverley Baxter had offered to find me a safe seat. But Bett was a Cobham and Cobhams, being of yeoman stock, having once put their hands to the plough don't give up till the field has been well and truly furrowed.

Accordingly she spoke to her friend Helen who as wife, now widow, of a former MP and subsequent peer had political contacts throughout Whitehall and Westminster. Helen, like Bett, was also a redoubtable character and a JP to boot. And so it transpired that on 1 December 1969 I was under orders to report for dinner at the Runcorn house in Drayton Gardens, SW10 9RH, seven-thirty for eight. The meal – egg mousse, veal ratatat, orange and apricot cream – was excellent. As were the wines. As was the company. There were eight of us round the table, four of each sex, including the hostess.

Now although I was clear that everyone present had political ties of one kind or another I was by no means clear what kind, or how close, that tie was. Nor, being British and therefore bad at names, had I taken in those of my fellow guests, the customary smiling and mumbling having taken place when we were introduced. ('You know X, don't you? Come and say hello to Y, oh, and have you met Z?') No, I hadn't actually, but it wouldn't have conveyed a great deal if I had, as their world was not mine. No doubt this would emerge – a good Conservative word – during the course of the evening. Meanwhile it was enough that they were congenial, civilised folk whom it was pleasant to be with and by the time the ladies had withdrawn I seemed to find them increasingly civilised and congenial the more the port went round. When the talk turned to the General Election that was due the following year I was therefore not entirely surprised to hear myself say casually that I presumed the Tories had chosen to lose in 1970 in order to win by a landslide next time round. This observation was greeted by the three other male guests with a certain wonder and by none more so than the slightly tubby, amiable-looking man who was sitting opposite me.

'That's most interesting,' he said when he'd recovered his breath. 'Do tell us, why do you say that?'

'Well, it's axiomatic, isn't it?'

'Is it?' He adjusted his glasses and peered at me.

'Absolutely.' And I proceeded to hold forth at length on the cunning of the Conservative Party in taking the long view and going flat out for 1974 or '75 since it was beyond the realms of probability that they could win in '70 as they hadn't got their act together or their message across. Mind you, the Party had never been Top of the Pops at communicating, we all knew that, didn't we, presentational skills sub-Olympic, and as for their Party Political Broadcasts, good Lord above, obviously the game plan was to hand it to Labour on a plate this time, knowing that once in power Wilson would make a hash of it and the Tories would romp back without even trying.

The port continued to circulate and I was just beginning to hit my stride when Helen put her head round the door and asked if we were here for the night. We moved into the drawing room and I had several cups of black coffee rather quickly before the party broke up. As we were getting our coats the gentleman who had sat opposite me, who wasn't all that tubby when he stood up and whose eyes were alarmingly shrewd, said, 'I wonder, would you come and see me in a day or two and have a chat? I'll ask my secretary to ring yours, shall I?'

'I don't have a secretary.'

'Be that as it may, will you come?'

'Forgive me – why?'

'I just thought you might like to carry your political theories a stage further. You see, everything you've been taking pot shots at I'm responsible for.'

'It must have been the port. I'm most terribly sorry. If only you'd told me I wouldn't have said what I did. It's probably all nonsense anyway.'

'Never mind. I wanted to hear it. By the way, I'm Geoffrey Tucker, Director of Communications at Central Office. Shall we say Tuesday about three?' Had I known that this was the beginning of an open-ended twenty-one years at the heart of the political spider's web I would almost certainly have excused myself, in which case I would have missed the experience of quite a large part of a lifetime.

I went over to Central Office on the Tuesday and we had a warm, friendly meeting in that cold clinical building. This time I was on my guard and said nothing provocative or even mildly interesting until, disarmed and encouraged by Tucker's invitation to speak freely, I said it seemed to me that political radio and television was deeply boring, that politicians of all parties had for the most part not grasped that a really effective Party Political Broadcast on the box or steam radio was worth more than half-a-dozen rallies around the country. It could reach a much larger audience provided it overcame the urge of listener or viewer to switch off the moment he realised that he was in for a political lecture, so the opening minute was crucial. If that could grab and hold, there was a good chance of crossing the boredom threshold and provided the rest of the broadcast was lively, intimate, original and packed a punch at the end, the PPBs could earn their keep in extra votes and possibly even swing an election.

Tucker listened to all this with exemplary patience and refrained from pointing out that in experience, if not in years, I was teaching my grandfather to suck eggs.

'Right,' he said. 'Ted Heath's doing a radio PPB next week. It's only five minutes. There's the first draft. Go and have a chat with him and see if you can do better.'

These were deep waters. I began to wonder what I was getting into. 'Oh, I don't know about that. Besides, I wouldn't know where to find him.'

'In Albany, Piccadilly. He has a flat there.' I said, 'What you're saying is put up or shut up.' Tucker grinned. 'He won't eat you. John Lindsay will go with you and hold your hand.' Lindsay, who made all the arrangements for the PPBs, was sent for: a short, genial man with a moustache who looked like the secretary of a local golf club. I took to him at once.

Before leaving I was introduced to someone else whom Fate had decided to include in my CV. Sir Michael Fraser, a Scot who hailed from Kilmorack, was Deputy Chairman of the Party and responsible for the day-to-day running of Central Office. A tall, slim, military figure with a permanent smile, spectacles and a ready laugh who had served the Party for years and had been a close friend of both Rab Butler and Harold Macmillan (which wasn't unique but slightly unusual), Fraser had been in his last year at King's when I was a Freshman, though we hadn't met. He said he'd heard about me from Helen Runcorn (the Frasers lived next door) and why didn't I come and have a bite the following evening?

At this second dinner in Drayton Gardens – there were no other guests, just Michael and his wife Chloë – I found myself getting more and more involved in the political slipstream, which I wasn't at all sure was the best idea in the world. Dear Bett Cobham notwithstanding, I knew just enough about politics to know that it was time-consuming and, if it got under one's skin, life-consuming. I think Fraser sensed my hesitation because he changed the subject and we moved on to more important matters like music and opera and the voice of the divine Anneliese Rothenberger whom we both worshipped from afar. By the time he'd played several of her recordings and we'd had a brandy or two it was 3.00 a.m.

As he poured me into a taxi he said, '1970 isn't going to be easy, you know. Always remember, the Labour Party has "bottom".' I said that didn't seem sufficient reason why they should come out on top. This appeared to satisfy him because he said, 'Good to have you on board.' I hadn't said that I was on board and all but told him so but Fraser was a charmer and Anneliese had been totally beguiling so I let it go. 'Goodnight, my boy. Let me know how you get on with Ted.'

13

· · · · · · · · · · ·

Ted – Then Suddenly Margaret

T he following afternoon Lindsay and I were shown in by Edward Heath's housekeeper to a pleasantly furnished sitting room. (A previous tenant had been one Terence Rattigan.) There was a Bechstein by the window, a model of a sailing ship (a schooner) in a prominent position and large signed photographs everywhere of the present Leader's predecessors. 'He won't be long,' said the housekeeper. We sat down side by side on a sofa and waited.

Half an hour later we were still sitting side by side on a sofa and waiting. As time ticked by I felt a growing urge to go and play chopsticks very loud on the piano to make something, anything, happen.

Finally Mr Heath appeared, went straight to the opposite sofa and sat down. No hands were shaken, no smiles exchanged. He barely glanced at me though we had never met. He seemed to lack the usual courtesies but, as I got to know him better, I realised he was not rude but shy. I had learnt on the grapevine that he played the organ and the piano, loved sailing and the sea and conducted Christmas carols in Bexleyheath, his constituency, and his home town of Broadstairs with panache and a warmth that for the rest of the year tended to elude him. That afternoon I wasn't entirely sure we were on the same planet.

'Right,' he said. 'Care and compassion today, isn't it?' It was as though there were a specific date and a special compartment labelled 'Care and Compassion' that one pressed a button to release and out they popped, like sweets in a Christmas cracker, all shiny and ready for distribution. I felt like asking, 'What about care and compassion *tomorrow?'* Later I wondered was *this* what was wrong with the Tory Party? For a few minutes we discussed the weather and one or two other matters of no consequence, until finally he said, 'Well, do you think you can do this thing?' The thing in question was presumably the broadcast, for which he seemed to have a healthy distaste.

'I'm not sure. I'll try, sir.'

He nodded. At which the housekeeper reappeared and announced that the American Ambassador had arrived. I wondered if she always did this when an audience was over – perhaps there was a secret button under the sofa which her master pressed to give her the cue to come in and say 'The American Ambassador has arrived' or 'The Soviet Chargé d'Affaires is with us' by way of a change – but then I saw a large man in the corridor and Heath leapt up and went into the hall to greet him, face wreathed in smiles, hand outstretched as though here at last was someone worthy of his undivided attention. While the Ambassador was receiving this heartiest of welcomes Lindsay and I, rather less than the dust beneath the Leader's chariot wheel, crept silently away. As we walked down Bond Street I decided that Edward Heath was a man of substance and well worth knowing but by no means easy to know, an opinion that the passage of time has so far only partially revised.

The recording studio at the back of Central Office, as like a BBC studio as the designer could make it, is fully equipped with cameras, microphones and all the technical equipment necessary to rehearse and record radio and television broadcasts. Here politicians practise the art of communication and, as few are natural communicators, it's worth every penny it costs to run.

Present are Fraser, Tucker, Lindsay, a radio technician and myself. We assemble behind a glass panel. Heath arrives, nods and goes straight into the studio. I follow. He shows me 'a few additions' that he has made to the script I have sent him. These additions are written all round the sides of the typed text. I start to read them – there are quite a number – but he glances at his watch and says: 'Right, shall we go?' The technician asks him to test for voice-level. Heath relates how Mary had a little lamb, her fleece was white as – 'Thanks. That's fine.' I remind him it's a four-and-a-half-minute script, leaving half a minute for 'topping and tailing'.

'What does that mean?'

'The BBC announcement at either end, sir. You know, "You have been listening to a Party Political Broadcast by, et cetera".' He grins. 'They'll know that by the time I've finished,' and the big shoulders heave. He seems in a good mood and I have the feeling we're on the same planet after all.

I go back behind the panel. The red light comes on. Mr Heath records. When he's finished the rest of us look at one another in stunned silence. 'Who's going to tell him?' We all look at Tucker who says, 'No. It's Ronnie's script.' He turns to me. I realise I should never have got involved in politics but it's too late now. I go back into the studio.

'All right?'

'Er – no, sir. Not quite. You overran a bit.'

'Oh. I'll go faster, shall I?'

'Er – I don't think that's quite the answer. You see, these additions have added ten minutes thirty-four seconds to the recording time. That makes a total of fifteen minutes four seconds. We're only allowed four and a half.'

I discover later that Mr Heath is a master of the prolonged silence. We have one now. Eventually: 'What do you suggest?' I retrieve the script, take my pen in my right hand and my courage in both and go all round the sides of the A4 sheet deleting the 'additions'. I return the script. He looks at my handiwork, then at me, and grins. 'Shall I go again?'

'If you wouldn't mind.'

I go back behind the glass panel. He does it again. This time it's four minutes twenty-nine seconds. I look at Lindsay and the others. Lindsay beams as though a club member has just done a hole in one and Tucker signals 'fine' with his right thumb raised. I go back into the studio.

'Well?'

'Spot on, sir.'

He gives a broad grin. 'I thought I was very moving,' and he shakes with silent laughter. 'You knew how long it would take. How did you know that?'

'I read it aloud several times, timing it with this thing.' I show him my stopwatch.

'That's useful. Where did you get it?'

'I bought it when I was in the Navy.'

'Navy? I sail. I've got a boat. Have you got a boat?'

'No. It was in the war. It wasn't my ship.'

'I was a gunner. It wasn't my gun.' He grins for the third time and once more the shoulders heave. This is promising. Have I misjudged this man? I mean, with luck and a fair wind human contact seems a distinct possibility. The group behind the panel come in.

'How was it?' asks Heath.

'Excellent,' says Fraser.

'Not bad,' says Tucker. 'Should do better next term.' He and Heath obviously understand one another. There's a rapport. Heath gives a broad smile and goes.

'Well done,' says Tucker. 'But don't call him "sir".'

'What should I call him?'

'Ted. Everyone else does.'

During the next few months I attended occasional meetings at Central Office with the Chairman of the Party, Peter Thomas, Willie Whitelaw who was Chief Whip, Fraser, Tucker and once in a while the Leader himself. I said little or nothing, I was on a learning curve, drinking everything in. A General Election was expected in the summer so it was something of a crash course but I began to get the feel of politics at the highest level, which seemed to me fascinating and more than a little mysterious. It was about this time I suddenly realised that, without making a conscious decision, I had acquired an additional career. I was coming up to my half-century but I didn't feel tired or stale, rather stimulated by the extra freight I had taken on board. If this was to be the way of my world I had no complaints. On the contrary, another window appeared to have opened. My two careers, theatrical and political, had come together and were currently running in tandem.

I had written a play about the twelfth-century lovers, Abelard and Heloise. Haddon Mason having retired, Herbert de Leon was now my agent and the idea of Abelard had originated with his wife and secretary, Hazel. Herbert, who had become a close if occasionally eccentric friend, had omitted to mention it to me for three-and-a-half years in the belief that Abelard was a Greek sailor from Cyprus and why would I want to write a play about a nautical Cypriot, however famous? Once I had sorted this out and written the piece the impresario John Gale took an option and was hoping to present it with a gifted young director, Robin Phillips, provided we could cast the two principal parts. Both the artists we wanted were at that time in the United States.

Diana Rigg, the unanimous choice for Heloise, after several years at Stratford had been out of the theatre working in television, playing a character, Emma Peel, as unlike Heloise as could be imagined but which had made her a star and in great demand. She was due back from the States in ten days but we were anxious to make her an offer before anyone else did, so a script was sent to her by courier through her agent John Redway.

When she landed at Heathrow she went straight to the telephone and rang him. After welcoming her home Redway asked if she'd read the script. She said, 'Of course. That's why I'm calling. I love it. I'll do it.' Redway was taken aback. Stars didn't behave like this. Playing hard to get was part of the game. It increased your salary, helped with your billing and generally gave you leverage.

'We haven't discussed a deal,' Redway protested.

'Whatever you say I'll go along with. Tell them I'll do it.'

'Look, Diana darling, at least read it again over the weekend.'

'All right, John darling, but it won't make any difference.' She read it again and it didn't. Even so, when Redway called me he was cautious. 'I think it's all right but she'd like to meet you and talk about the part.' It was arranged that we should meet in the American Bar at the Savoy at six that evening.

I arrived ten minutes early but she was there already, wrapped in a fluffy three-quarter-length fur coat. She looked stunning but I was impressed quite as much by the fact that she was there first as by her beauty. Most stars – and all starlets – arrive late for such meetings. Keeping the other party waiting makes clear who wants whom and that one may, or may not, be available and needs to be wooed and wheedled before committing oneself, one has other offers, you see, there's a possible film and talk of a TV series, maybe one could squeeze in a play though of course one would want a three-months get-out clause, didn't one's agent mention that?

Miss Rigg comes from a different stable. 'Listen,' she said almost before I'd sat down. 'I love the play and I'm going to do it. I know I shouldn't say this before we've talked contract and you're not to tell John Redway but I don't mess about when I've made up my mind and Heloise is lovely, she's for me. Just one thing. About the billing.'

Ah, I thought, now it comes. Oh well, no one's perfect.

'Who have you got for Abelard?'

'We'd rather thought of Keith Michell.'

'Fine. About the billing. I don't give a damn whose name comes first. Again this is *entre nous*. I just wanted you to know.'

The woman was pure gold. I called the waiter and ordered a magnum of champagne. To this day I have never met another artist, let alone a star, with as little pretentiousness as the delicious no-nonsense, down-to-earth and, appropriately, straight-as-a-die Di Rigg.

Knowing that Michell was an old friend from *Robert and Elizabeth*, Gale asked me to call him in New York and offer him Abelard. As

Keith had taken all of eight months before committing himself to play Robert Browning I steeled myself for delaying tactics. To my astonishment he merely asked, 'Who's playing Heloise?' and when I told him said, 'When do rehearsals start?'

'March the second.'

'I'll be there. Oh, send me a script, will you? I suppose I'd better read it.'

Later, when I asked him why he'd been such a bore about Browning and trusted me instantly over Abelard he grinned and said, 'I knew you better by then.'

Abelard and Heloise opened at the Northcott Theatre, Exeter. In that delightful little university theatre with its open stage the play worked beautifully. But we had an eight-week tour ahead of us, in large theatres with a proscenium arch, beginning with one of the largest, the Royal Court, Liverpool, and I wondered what would happen then. However, all was well. Everything – management, casting, direction, design – had gone so smoothly I kept touching wood but wherever we went the tour continued happily and the company was not only first-class but actually liked one another, which in the theatre makes hard work a holiday. Then it happened.

All the London theatres were occupied, almost all were doing well and the tour was coming to an end. Our only hope of a West End home was Wyndham's where the current attraction had fallen below the 'break' figure for a single week. If it fell below for a second consecutive week then the Wyndham's management, under the terms of the contract, could give notice.

They wanted *Abelard*, which they had seen at Exeter, but everything hung on Wyndham's becoming available. There were no more touring dates booked and both the stars were in demand. You can't keep a show hanging around without paying the company and that's wildly expensive, even if they were to agree. Most actors don't come into the theatre just for a living, what they want is to be up there acting. So it was now or never.

At around ten o'clock on the second Saturday night I was at home, biting my fingernails and watching television, trying to work up some interest in a not very good film called *Bedtime for Bonzo* which starred a chimpanzee and President Reagan of the Screen Actors' Guild. (He notched up another presidency later.) Suddenly the phone rang. It was Gale. 'I thought you'd like to know,' he said, 'the notice has just gone up at Wyndham's. They're below the figure. We have our London home.' I suddenly realised that *Bonzo* was a marvellous movie.

Abelard and Heloise opened at Wyndham's Theatre on 19 May

211

1970. Wyndham's, in Charing Cross Road next door to Leicester Square underground station, is the best passing-trade theatre in London. The play was an immediate success, the film rights were bought by Romulus Films and my bank manager told me delightedly that he couldn't get seats. I too was delighted and bought him a box.

A week later Harold Wilson called a General Election for 18 June. Central Office went into top gear and I was asked to join a Communications Group preparing Ted's speeches for major rallies, radio and television. This was becoming quite a year. While the Conservative challenger travelled the country in his campaign bus I found myself working with other writers in the Leader's office in the House of Commons till all hours of the morning. With just a week to go, the *Times* MORI poll had Labour twelve points ahead. When I discovered that, despite the Tories trailing badly, Central Office had decided to give the final ten-minute radio broadcast as a consolation prize to some unnamed member of the Shadow Cabinet who had recorded an election broadcast for television that was unsatisfactory and had to be jettisoned, I stormed into Lindsay's office.

'Labour twelve points ahead and you're handing out consolation prizes to a non-communicator? Good Lord, John, rather than waste ten precious minutes I'd do the thing myself!' Lindsay stared at me for what seemed like half an hour. Finally: 'Do you mean that?' I didn't know if I meant it or not but I said I did. Lindsay fondled his moustache. 'I don't have to offer consolation until six o'clock,' he said deliberately and looked at his watch. 'I make it twenty to four. What do you make it?'

'Right!' I said and tore down the stairs, grabbed a taxi, rushed home, wrote like fury, grabbed another cab, dashed back to Central Office, ran up two flights of stairs and tossed the script on Lindsay's desk. The time, as they say, was 5.45 precisely.

'John, it's no masterpiece but at least it's better than letting the broadcast go for ducks.'

He read it in silence. Then: 'Let's go down to the studio and see how it sounds.' I recorded it on tape. It ran nine and a half minutes by my sturdy stopwatch. Lindsay picked up the phone and called Willie Whitelaw who, as Chief Whip, was in overall charge of radio and television broadcasts. He came across from the Commons wearing an open-necked shirt, a pair of slacks and sandals. It was a heatwave summer and he was sweating. So was I but more from nervous anxiety than the heat.

Lindsay ran the tape again. Willie listened in silence, rose abruptly, said 'Put it out' and left without a word. I assumed he didn't really like it. Later he sent me a note saying 'I didn't mean to be rude, it was just that your ending choked me up and I couldn't say anything.' Willie has several things in common with Winston Churchill. One of them is that when he's moved he weeps easily and is rightly unashamed of it.

The broadcast went out at prime time the following evening: six o'clock on the Home Service. When Lady Pamela Berry, wife of the then proprietor of the *Daily Telegraph*, heard it on her car radio on the way home she stopped the car at the nearest telephone booth, rang the editor and said, 'I've just heard a Conservative broadcast on the radio. Now listen . . . '

Next morning I found my script splashed across the back page of the *Telegraph*. This caused a stir at Central Office. Various Conservative candidates (among them the four-minute-miler, Chris Chataway) phoned and asked if they could use chunks of the broadcast in their campaign. To Bett Cobham's delight the broadcast ended with an attack on the Prime Minister.

Harold Wilson in perpetuity? Is that what we want? Government by gimmick for as far as the eye can stretch? Forget for a moment which Party you normally vote for. What's best for the country? Whose hand on the helm? Mr Wilson, say the professionals, matches the mood of the nation: he's complacent. And so they say are we.

Are we? I don't believe this country, so proud of its past, is asleep in the sun. I don't believe that it's careless of its future, and about to let it go by default. And I don't believe that it wants a Prime Minister who has such a trick with words that, as *The Times* says, 'The ball is through and scattering the bails without anyone noticing that it was doctored and bowled from halfway up the pitch.'

Yes, much has been devalued these last few years besides the currency. But one thing has *not* been devalued – yet. The *vote* in your pocket.

There are five days left. Come in, England, out of the sun. Come in – and have a long, cool think.

Many years later I met Harold Wilson at a Theatres Trust council meeting on which we both sat. By then he was an old man, not very well, no longer the manipulator of anything, just a rather nice old gentleman for whom one could feel nothing but sympathy.

A final note on that broadcast of 12 June. By gently twisting Lindsay's arm I discovered whose television PEB had been jettisoned because it wasn't up to snuff and whose consolation prize I had nipped in the bud. It was Margaret Thatcher.

By Thursday evening, 18 June 1970, Edward Heath knew he was to be Prime Minister. When he appeared at Central Office there was the usual crush of Party workers and supporters waving and cheering and clapping, arc lights blazing, cameras jostling and whirring, passers-by stopping and cheering they knew not what, as a scene which was to become increasingly familiar to me reached fever pitch.

Standing halfway up the staircase Ted waved and beamed away while the cameras turned and flashbulbs popped. Here at last was a really happy man. I had never seen him like that before. It was rather pleasant. Later, upstairs in Central Office the Communications Group gathered and he signed autographs for all of us – on newspapers, napkins, notepads, posters with Ted's face on them, anything that took ink and would mark the date, which he also signed on everything pushed in front of him.

Jim Garrett, whose advertising agency organised and advised on Ted's television broadcasts, announced that he was marking the victory by ordering a hundred and twenty ice-creams for the boys of his son's prep school. I hoped they wouldn't melt before they got there. I also found myself hoping that the Heath Government, for which we had all fought so hard and had such aspirations, would not melt in the face of harsh political reality.

The final figures were:

Conservatives	330 seats
Labour	287
Liberals	6
Others	7

CONSERVATIVE OVERALL MAJORITY 30

The immediate aftermath of victory at the polls – the honeymoon period which all governments are accorded even by the Opposition – gave life a predictable glow. On 25 June, a midsummer night which wasn't a dream but felt like one to this political tenderfoot, the new Prime Minister gave a reception for all those who had contributed to his arrival in Downing Street. Apart from my clandestine visit to the Cabinet Room three years earlier, wearing my playwright's hat, this was my introduction to Number Ten.

The Bechstein had been transferred from Albany to what at the time was the Yellow Stateroom on the first floor where Ted played host, though not the piano. He seemed genuinely pleased to see us.

For the son of a boat-builder from Broadstairs in Kent to have reached the top of the political pole it must have been a time of deep satisfaction and I found his obvious happiness touching and infectious.

Among the guests was Iain Macleod, the new and, for those days, comparatively young (he was still in his forties) Chancellor of the Exchequer. For years he had suffered from acute arthritis and walked with hunched shoulders and a pronounced stoop, leaning on a stick. But if his body was not in the best of shape, his mind was razor sharp.

Macleod had graduated to the Commons by way of that forcing house of Tory talent, the Research Department. He had been appointed Minister of Health by Churchill straight from the backbenches, and already had a brilliant political career behind him, having served as Minister of Labour, Colonial Secretary, Leader of the House under Macmillan, Conservative Party Chairman (when he had attacked the so-called 'magic circle' method of choosing a leader which had chosen Lord Home as Macmillan's successor, for which he was in turn attacked by the Marquess of Salisbury as 'too clever by half'). He was now Heath's next-door neighbour at Number Eleven.

His sudden death on 10 July, less than a month after the election, was a shattering blow to the new administration from which, in one respect, it never fully recovered. For Macleod, in addition to his many other qualities of mind (he was a first-class bridge player) was the Trumpeter of the Tory Party, its finest orator who wrote his own speeches, delivered them superbly and was widely regarded as its next leader and a future Prime Minister. Had he lived, Margaret Thatcher might never have succeeded to the premiership and the history of this nation would have taken a very different course.

As it was, she was now a member of the Cabinet and on her way up as Secretary of State for Education. It's said that Heath had seated her at one end of the Cabinet table on the same side as himself, so that she couldn't readily catch his eye and embark on one of her more protracted expositions. It may have been a coincidence but from then on Ted and Margaret seldom did see eye to eye.

Without its Trumpeter the Heath Government lacked natural communicators. Heath himself had courage, integrity and a vision of a 'quiet revolution', a precursor of what came to be known as Thatcherism, that called for political reform, but his natural reticence and reserve were not best suited to conveying that vision to others. After becoming Prime Minister he became increasingly mandarin-orientated and corporate-minded and in the process lost the ways and means of communicating with ordinary people that he had begun to develop in Opposition.

215

In his excellent book *An End to Promises*, published in 1979, Douglas Hurd, Heath's Political Secretary throughout his premiership, recalls those years. 'The other main failing was in communication... having moved into ever-more complicated fields of government action, they (governments) have failed to find simple and accurate words to describe those actions.' Yes, indeed.

Macleod was succeeded as Chancellor by Anthony Barber and that year, among other events of passing interest, a national dock strike paralysed the ports and made a mess of the balance of payments, the power workers declared a work-to-rule over pay, causing a series of blackouts throughout the nation, and Diana Rigg and Keith Michell left the London cast of *Abelard* after six months to join the American company and were succeeded by Daniel Massey and Ciaran Madden. It was feared by some that changing the leads would wreck the business. Happily it made little or no difference and the play ran steadily on and into the following year.

In 1971 decimal currency was introduced, Rolls-Royce went bust and had to be rescued by the Government and ninety Russian diplomats were expelled from Britain for spying.

Some of these lively goings-on I only learnt about from a distance, as early in January John Gale rang me in the middle of the night from Los Angeles, where *Abelard* was shortly to open a prior-to-Broadway six-week run at the huge Ahmundsen Theatre, and said, 'If you want to rescue your play you'd better hop on a plane and get over here fast.' When I asked what was wrong he said, 'Come and see for yourself,' and hung up.

I flew out within hours and found on arrival that some of the American cast were less than authentic but, above all, that the brilliant and intimate set design of the original production had been discarded in favour of a huge monolithic structure more suited to a pageant, which indeed the play seemed to have become, rather than the intimate tragic love-story I had written. Since the director was Robin Phillips, who had directed the original production and with Daphne Dare designed the London set, I asked him why he had been persuaded to agree to it. He said he hadn't been persuaded, it was his idea, and when I asked why he said, 'Oh, I'd have been bored simply repeating myself.'

We were halfway through some judicious recasting when I was jolted awake just after six o'clock one morning in my room at the Beverly Wilshire Hotel by shouts of alarm, the sound of falling masonry and the crash of bricks and mortar coming from outside and inside the building. On investigation I discovered my bathroom ceiling lying on the floor. Moving with some speed into the corridor where other guests had emerged in various states of undress I was able to establish, via a gentleman who was clutching a transistor radio with one hand and his pyjama trousers with the other, that Los Angeles had been struck by an earthquake which had, it was feared, killed more than sixty people downtown.

Digesting this horror it suddenly came to me that downtown was where the Ahmundsen building was located so I thought I'd better put some clothes on, grab a yellow cab if the roads were still passable and go and see if our theatre was still there.

The roads were evidently cracked in places since the cab kept skidding across the surface but my cheerfully brave Irish driver said, 'Them's not cracks, man, it's the after-tremors you're after feelin'.' I certainly was after feeling them and was still after feeling them after several days.

At the theatre the night security guard let me in through the stage door which had been blown loose, but not quite off, by the blast. The building was still standing but the huge chandelier that hung above the auditorium was swinging crazily to and fro and from time to time the after-tremors rocked the theatre. Suddenly hope dawned that maybe the new monster set had been demolished and creeping up on stage I peered like a burglar behind the safety curtain. Alas, it was still intact. I gave it the hardest shove I could muster but the damn thing was 'quake-proof. 'She'll be okay, buddy, not to worry,' said the security guard. I said I'd try not to.

As the chandelier continued to sway, my instinct was to get the hell out of the City of Angels while the going was good but I realised the company had to stay on and where they were I should be, so while the season continued, assuming a cool I didn't feel, I remained until the tremors gradually subsided. I flew back with the company to New York, where I saw the play open successfully at the Brooks Atkinson Theatre at the beginning of March 1971 before flying home. On 19 May the London company celebrated a year's run at Wyndham's where it continued to play for a further eight months until the end of January 1972.

Meanwhile the Heath Government was running into every kind of trouble with incomes policies, 'U-turns' and a six-week miners' strike which was settled by the notorious Wilberforce Report that put the cat among the industrial pigeons with a more than generous recommendation of an increase of twenty-one per cent.

217

In January 1973 Prime Minister Heath secured his place in history by signing Britain into the European Economic Community (as it was before they dropped the 'Economic'), an event which was marked by a grand firework display and a gala at Covent Garden. I became infected by the general enthusiasm and wrote a broadcast for Ted for the occasion. But this year saw the beginning of the end of the road for the Heath administration.

In October the Middle East erupted with the Yom Kippur War. The Israelis won but the consequences for the West, and for Britain in particular, were grave. The Arabs quadrupled the price of oil and this, with coal at a premium, encouraged the British miners to go for a further payrise.

On 12 November (my birthday, forsooth) the miners' union led by Joe Gormley started an overtime ban, a month later the train drivers joined in with a work-to-rule, cutting the amount of coal that could be moved by rail, and next day the Government announced a three-day week for industry and the National Grid introduced power cuts to save electricity.

It was during one of these power cuts that I first met the Rt. Hon. Mrs Margaret Thatcher, Privy Councillor, Secretary of State for Education and Member of Parliament for Finchley.

During the Heath administration, the Conservative Communications Group – Sir Michael Fraser, Geoffrey Tucker, James Garrett, Barry Day (speechwriter to Mr Heath) and myself, with occasional visits from Tony Newton of the Research Department – had held regular dinners in the Disraeli Room at the Carlton Club. It was felt the group had been effective in Opposition and should be kept together informally to maintain contact with what had become the Government. On these occasions, which were jointly hosted by Fraser and Tucker, each senior member of the Cabinet in turn was invited to be guest of honour and to speak freely and confidentially on communication problems affecting their department or anything else they cared to discuss.

Because of the power cuts, when Margaret Thatcher's turn came the dinner took place in candlelight. This was during the 'Thatcher, Milk Snatcher' campaign. Her decision to discontinue free milk to state schools had made her extremely unpopular and she wore 'the little black dress with pearls' that was currently being widely mocked by the media.

She sat at the centre of the long table in the flickering light of tall candles standing in gleaming candelabra, with Disraeli and other former Ministers of the Crown gazing down on her from the walls. She looked radiant and ridiculously young.

In due course the conversation turned to the attacks on the little black dress and the pearls and what should be done about them. The obvious solution was for her to avoid the dress except for funerals and not to wear the pearls in public. I remember thinking it a pity, especially about the pearls, which set off the rather imperious neck to perfection.

A suggestion was put to her to save the pearls for private occasions. She fingered them for a moment while she considered this, then suddenly blazed, '*No!* I'm damned if I will! They were a wedding present from my husband and if I want to wear them I'm going to!' Her voice was rather high-pitched and her fair hair bobbed furiously but there was no mistaking her contempt for such personal attacks or her resolve not to bow to them.

In the silence that followed this revealing outburst I leant forward from my end of the table. We had scarcely said more than 'Good evening' and I don't think she had the smallest idea of my name or why I was there. I said, 'Mrs Thatcher, if you went on television and said that to the voters exactly the way you've just said it to us, you'd have every woman in the land at your feet.'

She turned towards me and smiled vaguely – the remark had obviously made no impression or perhaps she thought I was joking. Then she turned away and began to discuss unit labour costs in the mining industry.

At that time she clearly had little idea of the impact of television on public opinion and in her occasional appearances to date had tended to come over as stilted and self-conscious, with a tendency to over-elocute. She had much to learn, but by the time she became Prime Minister she was a practised performer prepared to take on all comers.

It's interesting to note that, although Douglas Hurd, as Heath's Political Secretary, attended the dinners from time to time to report to him on the table-talk, Heath himself never came until he was out of office. By that time whatever advice we might have tendered was too late and the dinner was in the nature of a post mortem.

My first meeting with Mrs Thatcher was followed early in the new year by my first visit to Chequers. Heath had been holding detailed talks with various officials and advisers as to whether he should go to the country on the theme 'Who runs Britain – the Government or the Miners?' The Communications Group – what Douglas Hurd called 'the outside help' – was the final group to be consulted.

As my car was being serviced it was arranged that I should drive down with Michael Fraser and Michael Wolff, who was Heath's man at Central Office and one of his speechwriters, in Wolff's car.

12 January 1974. It's a pouring wet night but despite the weather I'm excited and eager to see this famous grace-and-favour house, since the 1920s every Prime Minister's second home. We are passed through the guardhouse, up an avenue of sodden beeches (a gift from Churchill) to the front door, where we are welcomed by a WRAF sergeant. We find Jim Garrett, Geoffrey Tucker, and Barry Day in the Hawtrey Room. The Prime Minister, wearing slacks, a blue cardigan and house slippers sits on a sofa working on his red boxes. Michael Wolff joins Douglas Hurd who is perched on a window-seat, looking tall and elegant and diplomatic, the epitome of an English gentleman. Ted looks up briefly. 'Dick Clement here?'

Fraser: 'No, it's a filthy night, but he's coming. He shouldn't be long.'

Ted grunts and returns to his boxes. The WRAF girls ply us with alcohol. The Hawtrey Room – bleached oak, cream pile carpet, comfortable country-style luxury – has apparently been redecorated at the Prime Minister's request and looks chintzy and charming. Outside the rain pours down. The PM works on as though we do not exist. We talk softly to each other in a desultory fashion. Finally diplomatic Douglas, evidently feeling his lord and master should pay some attention to his guests, goes over and, with the ease and delicacy of a conjuror completing a trick he has done a thousand times, gently removes the red boxes. The PM looks round the room.

'Dick Clement here, is he?'

Fraser: 'Not yet. Any minute now. It's a terrible night.'

Whereupon the PM picks up a magazine entitled *Sailing Today* which is on the sofa beside him and buries himself behind it. This is typical Ted but by now one has learnt to take this sort of thing in one's stride. He means no offence, it's just the way he is when the mood takes him and it seems to take him rather frequently.

We are all given yet another drink. The rain hurls itself against the mullioned windows. I half-expect Jane Eyre to float through, Mr Rochester in hot pursuit. I think, If Dick doesn't make it soon I shall be drunk. Finally he breezes in. Clement has directed most of Ted's television appearances and they get on well. At once Ted is transformed. He stands up, beams, 'Ah. There you are, Dick' which is undeniably the case, and becomes the perfect host. 'Let's go straight in to dinner, shall we?'

Thank God, I think, leaving my fourth whisky untouched. We move into the dining room. I'm relieved to find I'm steady on my feet.

'Now – Michael, you sit there. Dick next to me, Geoffrey over there, Ronnie next to Geoffrey' and so on.

Our host is bright, witty, cheerful and relaxed, putting everyone at their ease. The shoulders heave with merry quip and blithe banter. This is all very confusing. Has Dr Jekyll banished Mr Hyde for the night or have I gone a Scotch too far?

The meal is excellent, the kipper pâté even better than Elizabeth Jane Howard's and better than that you can't get. The wines are equally first class.

The story runs that the Defence Secretary Lord Carrington, dining at Chequers soon after Heath became PM, said, 'Sorry, Ted, but this food really won't do,' and borrowed a chef from Fortnum & Mason and sent him to Chequers. I can't swear to this story but it sounds exactly like Peter Carrington, a man guaranteed to lighten the darkness of any administration.

After dinner we adjourn to the Long Gallery on the first floor for coffee, brandy and cigars. We are certainly getting the full treatment. It's all very agreeable and the Long Gallery, which is a library full of the most priceless books and memorabilia including Napoleon's instructions to his marshals in his own handwriting, is quite superb. I feel I could happily spend a month here.

We then get down to the purpose of the meeting. Each of us in turn is asked his opinion of the crisis with the miners' union. None of us has discussed it with anyone else and Ted listens in silence as we each give the same advice independently. 'Yes. Go to the country. But go immediately or not at all. If to go now isn't possible, then forget it and make the best deal you can.'

Ted gives no sign of his reaction but he's an excellent listener and the feeling is that he has had similar advice from the other groups he has consulted and his instinct is not to negotiate with the miners further but to put the elected Government to the non-elected union hazard.

The business settled, we drive in a cavalcade of cars down to the local pub which we are told the Prime Minister likes to visit on Saturday nights when he is at Chequers. The country pub is crowded, there is plenty of noise and laughter and a pop group plays and sings. As a regular, Ted is treated like a local and unbothered by autograph-hunters. No one pays him any special attention, which is how he likes it. It's all very natural and English and reassuring and Ted is at his relaxed best. I have clearly misjudged this man. We have a couple of beers and then drive back to London through the never-ending rain. No one has said as much but it's understood the decision has been taken. The election is on and will be announced by Downing Street on Monday.

Noon on Monday. Telephone. 'Ronnie. Michael Fraser. Just to let you know it's off.'

'No election?'

'Right.'

'What happens now?'

'We continue to negotiate.'

Almost at once everything began to go wrong. The miners' 'washing-time' became central to the argument on pay and the Campbell Adamson letter, which was highly critical of the Government, was leaked.

On 5 February the miners called an all-out strike. Two days later the Prime Minister asked the Queen for a dissolution and called a General Election for 28 February.

A single-issue election, like a 'khaki' election, is always hazardous and although the Conservative campaign was efficiently managed the mood of the country was very different from that of June 1970. Either that, or I was becoming politically more sophisticated. I kept reminding myself that our cause was just but February is not an inspiring month and the people seemed to feel that the Government, which still had fifteen months to go before its term of office expired, was running away from its responsibilities and should have seen the miners' strike through to a sensible solution. Even so the result was close.

The final figures were:

Labour	301 seats
Conservatives	297
Liberals	14
Ulster Unionists	11
Scottish National Party	7
Plaid Cymru	2
Others	3

With a Labour majority over Conservative of only four, and no overall majority, Heath tried to negotiate a pact with the Liberals but failed. On 4 March he resigned, becoming once more Leader of the Opposition, and Harold Wilson was again Prime Minister. Two days later the Employment Secretary, Michael Foot, who had boasted that he could settle the miners' strike in a week, did so by the simple method of giving them even more than they had demanded. I have never quite understood why this was regarded as a triumph of negotiating skill worthy of Talleyrand, if not Lord Goodman.

Not having an overall majority Wilson went to the country again on 10 October and this time he got one, but by a mere three votes, and was only able to govern by standing on their head many of the policies on which he had been elected.

No one held this particular result against Ted Heath. However, he had lost three elections out of four and a challenge to his leadership of the Party was now distinctly on the cards. It was intended that Keith Joseph would stand against him but a speech that Joseph gave at Edgbaston about rates of crime among what he called 'classes C and D', and a reference to what was taken to be a hint at compulsory contraception, had received a critical reaction from the press. The language seemed to indicate a lack of popular touch and this brilliant academic and most honourable politician decided the leadership was not for him and stood down.

At this Margaret Thatcher said, 'Well, *someone* must stand against Ted' and when Airey Neave, a prominent backbencher whom she had known since they were in the same chambers in the Inner Temple, approached her she agreed at once. She had recently made a strong impression at the dispatch box with a speech on taxes (a former tax barrister, she was a mistress of detail and adept at mastering a brief) but she had no special support in the Party or in the House and was putting her political career on the line. It was a brave, even reckless thing to do, but Margaret Thatcher has never lacked courage. Airey Neave's original motive was not so much to elect Thatcher as to get rid of Heath, largely on the grounds that he was a three-time loser, but he quickly became Thatcher's staunchest supporter and eventually her campaign manager in her challenge for the leadership in 1975.

It was customary for the Prime Minister and the Leader of the Opposition to give a brief New Year's Eve broadcast to the nation. In December '74 I was asked to write Ted's broadcast and to meet him and a secretary at noon on the Sunday before New Year's Eve, at his

London home in Wilton Street, to finalise the text. I duly turned up at five to twelve to find the secretary ready and waiting but no sign of Ted. No sign of so much as a biscuit either, though as hour followed hour without a message his embarrassed housekeeper plied us with canteens of coffee. At three-thirty Ted turned up.

'All done?' was his only comment beyond the information that he had been lunching at the Savoy with two ladies. We agreed the final text of the broadcast within minutes and he then asked me to meet him at Broadcasting House at seven-thirty that evening where the speech was to be recorded in case there were any technical problems. Not wanting to start the new year in a negative frame of mind I agreed.

He was on time and we were greeted by a senior BBC official and offered a drink in the VIP room. Ted declined. 'No, no, let's get it over with. I want to get away.' He was clearly not in a seasonal mood. After the recording, the offer of a drink was repeated and this time, with apparent reluctance, he said, 'Well, just one perhaps.' He had three whiskies and so did I. But he remained glum and apparently filled with something akin to foreboding.

As we left I asked him about the leadership challenge. Was he going to be all right? He spread his hands wide, gave an indeterminate shrug of those huge shoulders and climbed into his car.

I thought him unduly pessimistic. I doubted that the Party would vote a woman into the leadership. It never had and I was unaware that the Conservative Party had any feminist tendencies, politically speaking. Besides, whatever the dubious attractions of novelty, Heath had the experience of being Prime Minister for nearly four years under his belt and had taken Britain into Europe, which for good or ill was a formidable achievement. When it came to the crunch, what had Margaret Thatcher to set against that? Both came from what Tories of the old school regard as the wrong side of the tracks but Ted would surely be chosen again, if only on the basis of 'the devil you know'.

It was February and I was in rehearsal for my play *The Case in Question*, suggested by C. P. Snow's novel *In Their Wisdom*, which was due to open at the Haymarket on 10 March.

We were in one of those large, depressing, rather dirty rooms in Earls Court in which plays with elegant settings tend to rehearse. It was coming up to five o'clock in the afternoon when I suddenly remembered that the result of the first ballot for the leadership was due to be announced. I ran out to the car and turned on the radio.

The result – Thatcher 130, Heath 119 – both astonished and disturbed me. My reaction was partly chauvinistic and partly, to my surprise, a sort of residual loyalty to the strange man with whom I had worked intermittently for some four years, shared good times and bad, found hard to talk to and difficult to admire yet who had some intangible quality buried deep that compelled respect, if not affection.

Others threw their hats in the ring in the second ballot but by now the tide was flowing the challenger's way and she proved unstoppable. So that was it. Ted was gone and this comparatively unknown, albeit attractive, woman was Leader in his place. What the devil was the Conservative Party up to?

Margaret Thatcher was elected Leader on 11 February 1975 but stubborn loyalty to her predecessor was still with me when, six days later, I was summoned to meet her in the House of Commons. She had done her best to give the Opposition Leader's cheerless office a feminine touch with vases of spring flowers dotted about at judicious intervals but in stage terms the set was still dowdy and ill-favoured.

At this first meeting – she had no recollection of the candlelit dinner at the Carlton Club during the power cuts (when I referred to it she smiled vaguely) – her attitude to me was guarded, as was mine to her. I had the feeling she was thinking: What sort of writer is this who worked for Ted? Not one of us, that's for sure. I was thinking: she must have something special or they wouldn't have made a woman Party Leader, but I wasn't clear what it was and in any case not at all sure that I wanted to be further involved politically.

I had heard that she was intent on change and fine, I thought, change is not only inevitable, it's desirable, but let's not wipe out yesterday like a wet sponge cleaning a blackboard. No one had said she intended this but the word was that she was a force to be reckoned with, a woman with all the determination of a man and therefore, in all probability, up to no good. However, seeing her in daylight for the first time, and suppressing one of those cliché assessments that were to dog her throughout her political life, there was a kind of senior girl-scout freshness about her that was rather appealing, as though she had stepped straight out of *The Sound of Music*, though I doubt if soft woollen mittens and whiskers on kittens were ever her favourite things.

She offered me a chair and a coffee and said she had inherited a five-minute Party Political that was to have been given by Mr Heath and she understood that I helped with these broadcasts, was that right? 'Helped' was an understatement but I nodded. Well now, would I consider doing this one for her? I explained that my play was opening in a few days' time and I was completely taken up with final rehearsals. She said she understood that but the broadcast only required a five-minute text. Couldn't I find the time to squeeze it in?

I pointed out that a five-minute text took rather more than five minutes to write and in any case I'd no idea what she wanted to say. 'Just set out my stall in general terms. There won't be time for more than that. My politics aren't quite the same as Mr Heath's, you know.' Yes, I did know that. I also knew that as well as strong views she had a sense of mission and people with missions could be difficult to work with.

'Well?'

Assuming I could find the time, exactly when did she want it?

Could I manage a draft by tomorrow morning – say, about eleven? This really was rather tiresome. Reluctantly I said I would see what I could do.

'Thank you. Till tomorrow, then.' A polite smile, which I returned. There had been no instant meeting of minds, rather on my part a feeling of irritation at being diverted from something more important to me, if not to the charismatic new Leader of the Conservative Party. I too could be stubborn on occasion, I really shouldn't have agreed so easily.

I hurried away from the Palace of Westminster and sat at the back of the stalls in the Haymarket, my eyes on the stage and the actors and my mind concentrated nine-tenths on the play. During the lunch break I scribbled a few thoughts in my Ryman's notebook but couldn't think of an ending. 'If stuck, go for a quote' is a cliché but it's not a bad fall-back position. I didn't have my *Oxford Dictionary of Quotations* with me but managed to remember some lines from a speech attributed to Abraham Lincoln, his most memorable after Gettysburg, which I had learnt once for an audition.

When the company returned from lunch I asked one of the ASMs if she'd type it for me. She was a bright jolly girl, bursting with unexploded energy. 'How many copies? One for each of the cast as usual plus director, management, stage management and under-studies?'

'No!!' I yelled. She reared up as though I'd lassoed her. 'Look, love,' I went on softly, 'just type it, there's a dear, and for God's sake don't give copies to half SWET and the Council of Equity, they'll think we've both stepped off the pavement.' She threw me a peculiar look but did as I asked and gave me the typed script and an even more peculiar look at the tea break.

Next morning at eleven I returned to the new Leader's office. 'May I have it?' she held out her hand. On a sudden impulse I said, 'May I read it to you?' She seemed surprised but indicated a chair some way from her across the room. Then she sat down and half covered her eyes with her left hand. Was the light troubling her or did she fear the worst? 'It helps me concentrate,' she said. 'Go ahead. I'm listening.'

When I had done there was a total silence. I thought, well, that went down like a sack of potatoes. I'm off the hook. Glory hallelujah! But then she took her hand from her eyes and reached into one of those large holdalls in which nowadays women carry everything but the microwave. From this receptacle she produced a handbag. Out of the handbag came a wallet and from the wallet a piece of yellowing newsprint. All this was done very slowly and methodically without a word being uttered. Finally she got up and came across the room to me and handed me the piece of newsprint. 'It goes wherever I go,' she said. It was the Lincoln quotation.

There are moments in life when something goes 'click' in what one assumes to be the brain and you find yourself without warning on the same wavelength with a total stranger. This appeared to be just such a moment. I started to explain that I'd turned to Lincoln because I hadn't really had time for a peroration, my mind had been up there on stage with my actors. She said, 'If that's what you can do when you're not really trying, what will it be like when you are?' and this time the smile was more than polite. It was a dazzler.

The BBC transcript of the radio broadcast, reproduced in full, was preceded by the following warning:

BECAUSE OF THE RISK OF MISHEARING AND THE DIFFICULTY IN SOME CASES OF IDENTIFYING INDIVIDUAL VOICES THE BBC CANNOT VOUCH FOR ITS COMPLETE ACCURACY.

It was accurate all right and in time the BBC, in common with the nation, learnt to identify the voice without too much difficulty.

The first of quite a number of words I was to write for Margaret Thatcher over the next sixteen years or so were written in haste and in no way remarkable but they did, I think, obey the first rule of speechwriting. They were tailored to suit the speaker: in this case, it seemed to me, a crisp, direct, immediate personality, without time for decorative frills and furbelows (decoration and variety could come later, if there was a later).

I see the Socialists have been celebrating twelve months in office. I wonder why. What exactly is it that this Government feels so proud of? The year that has seen the greatest acceleration of wage and price inflation in modern British history hardly seems an excuse for dancing in the streets. Can the cause of their rejoicing be the bigotry of Mr Benn, the foolishness of Mr Foot, presided over by the wiliness of Mr Wilson putting Party before country in the name of Labour unity?

Labour united? I hardly think so. Only last Saturday we were treated to the spectacle of one of the most senior members of the Government publicly accusing another senior member of economic illiteracy. And in the same speech Michael Foot informed the nation, 'I want to move towards a Socialist society as fast as I can.' Well, Mr Foot, I don't.

What I want to do is to lead the people of this country *away from* the quicksands of socialism. I don't think they want a Socialist society as fast as they can. Or even as slow as they can. I don't think they want a Socialist society at all.

Certainly a majority has never voted for it. Least of all for the particular brand of Marxist socialism peddled so assiduously by Mr Foot and Mr Benn and their friends.

To stop the drift towards their kind of government and all that it implies won't be easy. It will call for hard, dedicated and united work by all those who do not want this country taken over root and branch by a carefully organised and highly articulate minority of the Socialist Party, itself of course a minority. But if the danger is recognised in time it can be stopped in its tracks. Tracks that are daily becoming more clearly defined. Indeed it must be stopped if we're going to restore the standards on which this nation was greatly built, on which it greatly thrived and from which in recent years it has greatly fallen away.

So I say now to all our people, and particularly those in the Midlands and the North and to my friends in Scotland who may have felt in the past that there was not all that difference between the parties, that it didn't really matter who was in office – I say to you, come back into the fight. *There's all the difference in the world.* Join hands with us in the Conservative Party and help us rid the nation of this Socialist albatross.

But wishing won't make it so. It has to be worked for and that, as the new Leader of the Conservative Party, I pledge myself to do with all my heart and strength.

To those who have been tempted to turn Left, let me say this – in words attributed to Abraham Lincoln:

You cannot strengthen the weak by weakening the strong.
You cannot bring about prosperity by discouraging thrift.
You cannot help the wage-earner by pulling down the wage-payer.
You cannot further the brotherhood of man by encouraging class hatred.
You cannot help the poor by destroying the rich.
You cannot keep out of trouble by spending more than you earn.
You cannot build character and courage by taking away man's initiative and independence.
You cannot help men permanently by doing for them what they could and should do for themselves.

It's been said that all that the politicians are doing now is rearranging the deckchairs on the *Titanic*. Well, here is one who isn't.

I come fresh to this job with fresh ideas. Help me to help you.

As I was leaving she asked me about my Haymarket play. I said, 'Come and see it as my guest when you have a free evening.'

'How about Saturday week and may I bring the family?'

She brought her husband and her son and daughter. A buzz went through the theatre as the audience saw who it was. She was surprised – it was her first private engagement since becoming Leader – but smiled away happily. She was news.

After the play they invited me to go with them to Annabel's, in Berkeley Square, for a drink. We sat and chatted in the bar. After a time Mrs Thatcher said to no one in particular, 'Isn't the music rather loud?' but was persuaded to stay for dinner. 'I expect it's quieter in the restaurant.' It wasn't. In the crowded, low-lit room the 'music' was even louder.

M.T.: 'Really, I can't hear myself speak, let alone anyone else!'

Daughter Carol: 'Oh, *Mum!*'

I agreed with 'Mum', but then I suppose not everyone tries to talk politics in a disco.

I dropped them off at their Flood Street house. Driving home I thought, it's been a pleasant and successful evening, but what exactly am I getting into? I mean, who *is* this woman? Or rather, to be frank – who is this *woman*...?

During the eight-month run of *The Case in Question* at the Haymarket there was almost as much drama offstage as on. The Theatre Royal, which is Crown Property, is to straight plays what Drury Lane is to musicals and it had long been my ambition to have one of mine produced at that lovely playhouse. *The Case* was presented by Duncan Weldon and Louis Michaels, on behalf of their company Triumph, for which Duncan found the plays and the cast and Louis the money.

Louis Michaels, a man of much charm and occasional rages, who had made a fortune out of shops and property, was in love with the theatre in general and the Haymarket in particular. Once *The Case* had settled in, he asked Sylva Stuart Watson, the redoubtable old lady who was the Haymarket's current chairman, if she would grant him a ten-year sub-lease.

Mrs Watson had inherited control of the theatre from her late husband and for many years maintained the artistic standards expected of the Haymarket, under the guiding hand of Binkie Beaumont of Tennent's, the premier management of the day. But after Beaumont's death the building, which like all old buildings requires constant expenditure on maintenance, had begun to deteriorate. Louis promised, if she gave him a sub-lease, to help restore the theatre to its former glory.

The old lady led him a high old dance. In the words of the song 'she didn't say yes, she didn't say no, she didn't say stay, she didn't say go', and finally Louis lost patience, and said to me, 'You seem to get on with her, see what you can do.'

To have a management guarantee product for ten years and also help with the cost of repairing the bricks and mortar was clearly in the best interests of a theatre that is famous worldwide. I enlisted the help of Anthony Peek who had been the Haymarket's general manager for many years, but we were no more successful than Louis. She didn't say yes, she didn't say no.

Then one evening when, champagne in hand, she was sitting in her favourite chair reminiscing, she made a reference to her 'beneficiaries'.

'Who are they?' I asked.

'My shareholders, dear. They don't come to my Annual General Meetings. I always have sandwiches ready but hardly any turn up.'

'Why is that?'

'They trust me, that's why. They know that their shares in my hands are doing nicely.'

How nicely, I wondered.

'Let's find out,' said Louis. We traced the shareholders through the Registrar of Companies. There were eighteen of them. Their dividends had been virtually static for quite some time and had seldom kept pace with inflation. They were far from happy. Through his solicitors Louis made a generous offer to each in turn and quickly obtained a majority holding. He then approached Mrs Watson, who had the largest holding herself. With some prodding from me he made her an even more attractive offer for her shares.

Once more she havered but after extracting a further promise of weekly hampers of food and wine from Fortnum & Mason the tough old lady accepted. Louis Michaels became the Haymarket's chairman and managing director, Duncan Weldon joined the board and I was given a box of After Eight mints and made deputy chairman for life.

Another building, with which I was to have regular contact over the years, came unforgettably into my life that autumn. On Friday 10 October, 1975, in that hub of the universe, the Winter Gardens,

Blackpool, where every other autumn the Party politicos strut their stuff and bring the rest of us up-to-date on the meaning of life, Margaret Thatcher was due to give her first speech to the Conservative Party Conference as Leader. As it was also her first major speech since deposing Ted Heath, both the speech and her performance were on the line.

The Party faithful – the delegates from the constituencies who come annually to Conference to debate and be comforted and reassured and finally sent home confused but in good heart to fight on the doorsteps – had not offloaded Heath and elected Thatcher; it was the Tory backbenchers in the House of Commons who had done the deed. She therefore had to face a grassroots audience whose goodwill could by no means be taken for granted. Their affection, which still belonged to the fallen Leader, had to be won, and transferred to herself in a single speech that was seen by most, including the lady, as a 'make or break' occasion.

Since that first brief broadcast at the end of February I had worked on some minor speeches for Mrs Thatcher but it was understood that the crucial Party Conference speech she would write herself and that, to my relief, any 'i's to be dotted or 't's to be crossed would be in the experienced hands of the director of the Research Department, Chris Patten, and an able colleague, Adam Ridley.

Two mornings before the speech, on Wednesday 8 October at nine o'clock precisely, I was asleep in bed, nursing a mild hangover, when the intercom buzzer rang in my flat. I struggled up, hobbled down the corridor and barked into the receiver 'Yes?'

'Can I come up?' It was a female voice.

'Who is it?'

'Me. Caroline.' Caroline Stephens was Thatcher's senior secretary as she had been Heath's, and my good friend.

'Good Lord. Er – yes, I should think so.' I pushed the release button, grabbed a dressing gown and looked in the mirror. As I feared, not a pretty sight. Being a theatre man I'm not a morning person at the best of times and this was not one of them. I half-opened my eyes and my flat door and waited for the lift but, disdaining such mechanical aids, Caroline came bounding up the stairs in a fearful display of energy for that hour of the day, one hand clutching a typewriter, the other a wodge of something white.

'Hello and good morning. Have you read this?' She thrust the wodge at me. It turned out to be a number of thick typed pages, stapled together.

My glasses were on my bedside table. 'What is it?'

'The Leader's speech.'

'No.'

'Read it, please. Where's your kitchen?'

'Down the corridor, first right. Why?'

'I'm going to make coffee. Lots and lots of coffee. You're going to need it. We're both going to need it.' She set off for the kitchen.

'Caroline! Wait! You won't be able to find anything.'

'Yes, I will. Time is of the essence. Read.'

She was, and is, an attractive, masterful girl who tears about all over London on a bicycle (if I were a bus I'd be terrified of her). What's more, her father, Sir David Stephens, had been a notable Clerk to the House of Lords. One doesn't argue with girls like that.

There were sixty-six pages of closely-typed manuscript. I fetched my glasses and sat down on the settee in the hall and started to read. Steaming coffee appeared in huge mugs I didn't know I possessed. I clutched one automatically, gulping coffee while Miss Stephens moved into the dining room with the second mug, set herself and typewriter down at the centre of the table and helped herself to an apple from the fruit bowl. She said not a word until I'd finished reading.

'Well?'

'Who wrote this?'

'Who do you think?'

'I see your problem.'

'I didn't say I had a problem.'

'Then what's your typewriter doing here?'

'Oh, I often cart that around. Just in case.' She smiled conspiratorially. 'Right. I'm ready when you are.'

This is madness, I thought, starting to walk up and down, at first in silence, then ad-libbing a syllable here, a paragraph there, an occasional half-page whenever I felt a brief swirl of wind in my sails. Caroline's hands flew over the keys like a Liszt of the mechanical age. After a while I stopped suddenly in mid-sentence.

'I say, whose idea was this, coming here?'

'Mine. It's all right. I haven't told anyone but Alison.'

'Do you mean nobody knows what we're doing?'

'That's right.'

'But, Good Lord, girl, when they find out there'll be hell to pay!'

'No, there won't, not if it's any good. Press on.' I felt I was in a Whitehall farce.

By lunch my head was splitting. We went into the kitchen and I swallowed a couple of Disprin while Caroline cooked some liver and bacon she'd found in the fridge. We ate at the kitchen table. The girl could cook, I'd say that for her. After the meal she telephoned the front line and spoke to one of the secretaries in the Blackpool bunker. Alison Ward was a friend of both of us.

'How are things? ... Hm ... Listen, there's something happening down here ... What I mentioned last night, yes ... Too soon to say, keep in touch.' She turned to me. 'Mind if I give Alison your number?'

'She has it.'

'Really? I mean, of course.'

The afternoon wore on, I continued to free-associate and Caroline to type, between phone calls to the Imperial Hotel for spot checks on progress. This cloak-and-dagger stuff wasn't my style but the girls seemed to know what they were up to.

By six o'clock I'd run out of steam. Caroline checked again with Blackpool. It seemed the famous illuminations had come on all along the front but so far the Leader's speech had failed to spark.

'Ask Mrs T if she'd like R.M. to come up.'

The word came back, 'Thank him very much but we can talk on the phone if there's anything we need.'

'Carry on,' said Caroline to me.

'No. No more tonight. We've earned a drink.'

We were in the kitchen making inroads into a bottle of Chardonnay when the telephone rang. Caroline took the call and was back in a couple of minutes. 'They want you to come at once.'

'Sorry,' I said. By this time I was bushed. 'But I'll be on the first train in the morning if that's any good.'

She was gone and back again. 'Agreed. Meanwhile I'm to send what we've got by Red Star from Euston tonight and one of the girls will collect it off the train. Oh – and they're sorry, there's no bed for you in the hotel but Alison says you're welcome to hers.'

I decided not to analyse this interesting statement until later, fell into mine and was instantly asleep.

The following morning I woke early, refreshed if not fully restored, and caught the seven twenty-eight from Euston.

I have always liked writing on trains. There's something about the rhythm of wheels in motion that stimulates the creative process. Michael Stewart, author of the musical *Bye Bye Birdie* (he also wrote *Hello, Dolly*), could *only* work on a train, which meant that whenever the producer wanted rewrites he had to spend days, and sometimes nights, with his librettist going to and fro on the New York subway.

I don't go that far, but the steady clatter of train on track can be both restful and a stimulus, and one or two passages that survived all editions of the Leader's Conference speech of 1975 ('I sometimes think the Labour Party is like a pub where the mild is running out. If someone doesn't do something soon all that's left will be bitter, and all that's bitter will be Left') were written roaring down the track from Euston Station to Blackpool North.

A taxi took me through the town to the seafront, passing the Grand Theatre where I had seduced Natasha six nights a week and twice on matinée days during that memorable summer of 1943.

On arrival at the Imperial Hotel I went straight to the Leader's suite, where I found Patten and Ridley contemplating the carpet, which was a labyrinthine maze of typed foolscap.

I started to apologise for my, or rather, Caroline's unsolicited intervention, at which Chris looked up, said glumly, 'You're very welcome', Adam offered 'Mad – but welcome' and they both went back to their reverie.

It was now high noon by the clock and in the sense immortalised on film by Mr Gary Cooper. It was still high noon at midnight. Plates of sandwiches had come and gone, Mrs Thatcher had come in and out in a series of remarkable costume changes as she worked her way round the social engagements that are a maddening but essential part of Conference jollies for those who are there not to work but to meet old friends, raise a glass and have a good time.

As for the three of us, we had not left the sitting room except for the bathroom while we tried to weave a combination of the Leader's original, Chris's and Adam's rewrites and my random suggestions into some sort of coherent text.

During a lull I had noticed, in a corner leaning against a wall, a pair of shotguns. I wondered idly if these were a modern version of the pearl-handled revolver, to be handed to speechwriters (or 'wordsmiths' or 'helpers' as the Leader preferred to call us) with a request, when the last draft had failed to jell, to go down to the beach and do the decent thing, but apparently they belonged to Adam. He had brought them with him to go pheasant-shooting when, if ever, the speech was finished and delivered and the more civilised (except from the birds' point of view) pursuits of country life resumed.

Around two-thirty in the morning Angus Maude, chairman of the Research Department, MP for Stratford-upon-Avon and distinguished journalist, whose voice had a nasal asperity that was oddly reassuring, wove in. Angus, a unique character who did not mince words and whose blunt ways I came to admire, was wearing a dinner jacket and appeared to have had a convivial evening.

'How's the weather with you boys?'

'Fair to stormy,' said Patten, soup plates of exhaustion beginning to form under both eyes. 'We have a beginning and a possible end. What we don't have is a middle.'

'Hm. How long is what you've got?'

234

'I don't know. We haven't done a word count.'

'Rough idea?'

'Thirty-five, forty minutes' worth.'

'Perfect. Look, forget the middle. Take what you've got and make a join. Ted used to go on and on. An hour, sometimes an hour and a quarter. You can't hold five thousand people for an hour and a quarter unless you're Winston or Macleod or Cicero. Forty minutes, that's your speech. Don't let her go over. Nighty-night.' And he wove out.

And that's how it was. Thirty-eight-and-a-half-minutes, to be precise. It set a precedent. In sixteen Party Conference speeches she never went over fifty. But I'm jumping the gun. When the Leader returned from her final engagement, the Conference Ball, she changed out of her gown into a simple shift, metaphorically rolled up her sleeves and said, 'Now – where are we?'

Wherever we were we went back to the beginning and I continued my self-appointed task of putting each syllable under the microscope. Finally, limp but game, we were into the home stretch. We thought that our peroration, if not a masterpiece, was better than routine. But: 'Oh *no*! No, that won't do at all,' said the Leader.

'Sorry. What's wrong with it?'

'It's just not me, dear.'

It was the first time I heard that phrase which was to be a marker buoy for the next sixteen years.

We tried again. And again. And again. I wondered if Mrs Thatcher was cursing the day she had moved the start of the annual Conference a day earlier so that the Leader's speech fell on a Friday rather than a Saturday. Another twenty-four hours on the final five minutes, I reflected savagely, would no doubt save the speech from total disaster. By Lord knows what hour it felt as though we'd written several dozen perorations. I sat bemused, humming *The Mikado* in an undertone and scribbling sleepily on the back of a throwaway for the Blackpool Tower Circus (and wondering if I was a part of it):

'A wand'ring wordsmith, I,
A thing of shredd-ed speeches
Of seaside towns and beaches
And when are we going to bed?'

It was Denis Thatcher, who had been sitting silent on a windowsill in black tie and dinner jacket who came, as he was to come so often in the future, to the rescue.

'That's the one,' he said softly as I read out our umpteenth finish. The Leader looked up sharply.

'Do you think so, dear?'

He nodded. He had been a rugby referee and knew when to blow the whistle indoors as well as out.

There was a pause. 'Right. That's it,' said the Leader and gave one of those all-time dazzlers that almost made you disappointed not to be starting again from the top.

'Well, we'd better get some sleep.'

'Bit late for sleep,' yawned D.T. 'Only make you feel worse.'

'Why? What time is it?'

'Ten past five.'

'What??'

'In the morning,' and to prove it he opened the curtains. If the dawn had come up like thunder 'cross the bay none of us had heard it. But then none of us would have noticed.

I fell into Alison's bath and lay and soaked till the dining room opened, when I ate a huge breakfast which I normally never do (but what's normal about the Conference experience?). Then I went back upstairs to check the final draft for the press release which Caroline, Alison and two girls from Central Office had been typing and retyping as change followed change throughout the night.

I was still in the sitting room making 'final' adjustments – it was ten past eleven and the speech was scheduled for 11.30 a.m. – when the Leader came out of her bedroom, looking as though she'd come straight from a health farm. She was wearing a Conservative-blue dress with a wide skirt that was very becoming and her hair had been set by someone who actually knew about these things. She was three days short of fifty but she looked young and vulnerable and pretty and scared. I felt suddenly protective. 'Here. Come and sit down.'

'I can't. It'll crease my dress. What are you up to?'

'Nothing. Just last-minute fussing.'

'Show me.' She knelt beside the chair.

'I just stuck an "and" in there and a "stop" there – and don't forget to pause before letting rip there. I put some dots in to remind you. All right?'

'Got it.' Somewhere a telephone rang. She moistened her lips, reached for a glass of iced water. 'I wish it was over.'

'Piece of cake.'

'Good heavens, not now.'

I let it go. Alison appeared.

'That was the Winter Gardens. They're running late with the

236

financial appeal. Could you hang on here for another ten minutes?'

'*No!*' The tension snapped suddenly. 'No! I'll wait as long as they like when I get there but I'm not staying in this damned room another minute!'

This was reassuring. Rage is fine, you can't be furious and nervous simultaneously. She was like a star on a first night. She not only looked it now, she sounded like it and that was what mattered.

'Right. Let's go.'

Chris and Adam had gone on ahead. I took one last quick look round that room, I can see it now, and followed her out and down to the waiting cars.

As she came on to the platform and took her place at the centre, surrounded on either side by her Shadow Cabinet colleagues, all men, most of them older and senior to her, the applause was more than polite, but not a lot more. She gave the audience her soft look, then her hard look, then her 'Don't rush me, I'm weighing you up' look. Suddenly a plump woman in the front row handed her up a large blue feather duster. This brought a laugh from the five thousand filling every inch of the hall below the platform and the surrounding boxes on the floor above.

She reviewed the duster, turning it this way and that as though wondering what it was for and then suddenly dusted the Chairman, Peter Thomas. This piece of business caused a roar. Was it rehearsed or a last-minute inspiration? Impromptus can be dangerous. Still, this one had worked. It broke the ice.

Peter introduced 'Our new Leader, Margaret Thatcher' and sat down.

Through the watchful applause she moved to the microphone and looked round the hall. I crossed my fingers. These were Conservatives with a small 'c' as well as a large one. There were few in that audience who thought it a case of 'cometh the hour, cometh the woman'. That had yet to be proved.

She began quietly, slowly, feeling her way...

The first Conservative Party Conference I ever attended was in 1946
and I came to it as an undergraduate representing Oxford Conservative
Association.

The voice was steady, if a fraction high.

That Conference was held in this very hall and the platform then seemed
a long way away and I had no thought [she looked up briefly from the

237

> typed script] none whatever, I assure you [and down again] of joining
> the lofty and distinguished people sitting up there...

'None whatever, I assure you' was not in the text. She was ad-
libbing. If this was tension it could be disaster. On the other hand, if
it meant she was starting to relax it could be a sign of premature
confidence.

> During my lifetime all the Leaders of the Conservative Party have gone
> on to serve as Prime Minister...

'Gone on to serve' was another ad-lib. 'Have served' we had written,
but dammit, 'gone on to serve' was an improvement. Extraordinary
woman.

> I hope the habit will continue...

Laughter. Applause. The voice was coming down. There was a touch
of authority.

> Our Leaders have been different men with different qualities and different
> styles, but they all had one thing in common: each met the challenge of
> his time...

She spoke of the great challenges of *our* time – the moral and political
challenge, and the economic challenge.

> We have to master them. What are our chances of success? It depends
> on what kind of people we are. What kind of people are we?

She answered herself.

> We are a people who have received more Nobel prizes than any other
> nation except America...
>   We are also the people who among other things, invented the
> computer, the refrigerator, the electric motor, the stethoscope, rayon,
> the steam turbine, stainless steel, the tank, television, penicillin, radar,
> the jet engine, hovercraft, float glass and carbon fibres – and the best
> half of Concorde...

Each invention was greeted with a varying degree of remembered
pride and applause. She went on to speak of the kind of life we
wanted for our country and our children.

> Let me give you my vision: A man's right to work as he will, to spend
> what he earns, to own property, to have the State as servant and not
> as master – these are the British inheritance. They are the essence of a
> free country and on that freedom all our other freedoms depend...

> Some Socialists seem to believe that people should be numbers in a
> State computer. We believe they should be individuals. We are all
> unequal. No one, thank heavens, is quite like anyone else, however
> much the Socialists may pretend otherwise...

They were very still in the hall. It was the stillness of total
absorption. Without realising it I had uncrossed my fingers. I looked
across at Chris and wondered if he too was thinking of Eliza Doolittle
and the rain in Spain. 'By George, old man, she's got it ... ' or,
rather, them...

> Our capitalist system produces a far higher standard of prosperity and
> happiness [than the Communist system] because it believes in incentives
> and opportunity, and because it is founded on human dignity and
> freedom. Even the Russians have to go to a capitalist country – America –
> to buy enough wheat to feed their own people... [This was 1975. *Plus
> ça change...*]

She spoke of education and agriculture, of unemployment and
penal taxation and empty promises... The tour d'horizon went on,
wide-ranging but crisp and taut and cohesive. There was the ring of
overwhelming conviction. Finally she drew all the strands together.

> I have spoken of the challenges which face us here in Britain – the
> challenge to recover economically and the challenge to recover our
> belief in ourselves – and I have shown our potential for recovery. I have
> dealt with some aspects of our strength and approach and I have tried
> to tell you something of my personal vision...

She had reached the peroration (the ninth, or was it the twenty-
ninth? I no longer cared. She was irresistible).

> I believe we are coming to yet another turning-point in our long history.
> We can go on as we have been going and continue down, or we can
> stop and, with a decisive act of will, say 'Enough'.
>   Let all of us here today, and others far beyond this hall who believe
> in our cause, make that act of will.
>   Let us proclaim our faith in a new and better future for our Party and
> our people: let us resolve to heal the wounds of a divided nation, and let
> that act of healing be the prelude to a lasting victory.

I scarcely heard the cheers, the shouts, the foot-stamping. Emotion,
the theatricality of the occasion and twenty-four hours without sleep
had finally got to me and I turned away and stumbled out into the
street, tears coursing idiotically down my cheeks. I was something of
a political innocent in those days.

*

For once it wasn't raining in Blackpool. I strolled gently back along the front to the hotel, letting the sea breeze do its work and bring me back to normal. When I arrived the large dining room was full but there was one seat at a table for three. As I sat down I recognised the two men occupying the other seats, though I had never met Robert Carvel, political editor of the London *Evening Standard* or John Dickinson, who fulfilled the same function for the London *Evening News*.

The praise of these two hardened political journalists for the performance in the Winter Gardens was generous and unstinted.

'Were you there?' asked Carvel.

'Er – yes, I did drop in.'

'Exceptional,' said Dickinson.

'A promising start,' I murmured.

'Promising? My friend, let me tell you something. That little lady struck oil this morning.'

As this was an independent assessment and they didn't know who was tuned in to their every word I skipped the apple pie and took the lift to the Leader's suite. She was sitting with Denis on the sofa, pecking dispiritedly at a Dover sole. The morning star of the platform, sparkling, confident and shining bright, had vanished. Here was a nervous schoolgirl awaiting her examination results. She had changed out of the blue dress into the plain shift of the night before.

'Sorry to disturb you but I wanted you to know that you're going to get a cracker of a press.'

She looked wan and flat and not even pretty. The adrenalin was way, way down.

She sighed. 'Let's hope so, dear.'

'I promise you. I have it on the authority of the horse's mouth.' And I told her with whom I'd been lunching and what they'd said.

She thought about this. 'Well, if they're right, what *are* we going to do next year? Brighton could be the most dreadful anticlimax.'

This was too much for Denis. 'My God, woman, you've just had a bloody great triumph and here you are worrying yourself sick about next year! I'll get the others, shall I? Then you can settle down for another all-night session. I mean, obviously there's no time to be lost ... ' I slipped away. So long as she had this man around she was going to be all right.

Adam Ridley and his guns had gone off to reduce the pheasant population. Chris and I headed for the London train. When we reached Euston the 'Evenings' were out. They were everything one could hope for – and more.

So began sixteen years of Party Conference speeches which were

240

to take me each October to hotels in Blackpool, Brighton or Bourne-mouth for a week of working days and sleepless nights and excitement and exhaustion and disbelief and indescribable standing ovations. Let me be clear. The portrait of an elemental human being, seen at close quarters over a period of sixteen years, is as objective as I can make it and, as it would be with the rest of us, the picture that emerges does not always flatter, but to the faithful she could do no wrong.

These extraordinary Roman triumphs of Margaret Thatcher's beside the seaside set the seal on her total command of her Party activists and their unwavering loyalty and devotion which were to endure to the end of her political supremacy and indeed beyond, into the twilight time of her farewells. They were exceptional, unique, and so, on these occasions that were hers and hers alone, was she.

On 16 March 1976, five months after the new Leader had been acclaimed by her Party Conference, Harold Wilson suddenly resigned as Prime Minister, a totally unexpected move that has never been adequately explained. Margaret Thatcher, for the Opposition, promptly demanded a General Election which was as promptly refused by the Government, and Foreign Secretary James Callaghan took over the leadership of the Labour Party and the premiership.

Callaghan, outwardly a big, lovable 'Uncle Jim' character, was a very different man from the wily Wilson. A smooth operator, less waspish than Wilson but every bit as skilled and devious a politician behind the bonhomie, he was an equally formidable opponent for the Tory Leader to face. However, almost at once he ran into a load of trouble. The economy was in serious difficulties (when is it not?), Labour lost its majority in the Commons and when he and his Chancellor, Denis Healey, gave the unions, whose spokesman Callaghan had been for many years, a four per cent rise the pound plummeted to an all-time low, the bottom of the barrel was being scraped. On 28 September, when Healey arrived at Heathrow and received the latest figures from the Treasury, he literally did a U-turn, drove straight back to his office and called in the International Monetary Fund.

It was against this background that we began preparing for Brighton and Margaret's second Party Conference speech since becoming Conservative Leader. After the Blackpool experience she no longer attempted to write her major speeches without help. She would think about them, discuss what she wanted to say with her 'wordsmiths' and we would write a draft and she would rewrite parts of it and each of us would rewrite those parts of her rewrites that the others couldn't reach and so on back and forth and to and fro until suddenly it was time for the caravan to up sticks and descend on whichever watering-place – Blackpool or Brighton alternately in those days – was that year's happy hunting ground for the annual Conservative *conversazione*.

On the eve of the speech Patten, Ridley and I were about to have dinner in the hotel dining room – the soup had just arrived – when the immensely tall figure of John Stanley, one of Mrs Thatcher's two PPSs (Adam Butler, son of Rab, was the other) loomed alongside. 'Sorry, boys. Up you go.'

'What's wrong?'

'Need you ask? Right away, please.'

Our arrival at the Leader's suite was greeted with 'Listen, this won't do at all.' She waved the latest edition of our joint work.

'But I thought you'd agreed – ' began Patten.

'No, no, no. You must have misunderstood me, people are always doing it. Now there's only one thing to be done when you're in a crisis. Spread it all out on a table and see what you've got and what you haven't and take it from there. Help me, somebody.'

She began dragging a long table with a tray of glasses on it that was set against a wall into the centre of the room. The glasses rattled and were saved just in time from smashing to the floor by Ridley whose reaction was trigger-swift (all that pheasant-shooting) while Stanley, Chris and I heaved the table under the chandelier. 'That's it. Now then.' She started tearing the pages one by one from the stapled text with a fine abandon. I shuddered. We were in for what was known, at least by me, as 'table hopscotch'.

It meant setting out each separate page of typed script side by side, in order, down the spine of the table and staring at it. Then, when staring-time was up, you played 'switch the sequence'. For example: 'Let's try swapping agriculture – pages 12 to 15 with 43 to 49, the NHS. Then if we transfer 57 to 63 – the unions – and bring them right up front where you've got – let's see – pages 4 to 7 – inflation – how does that look? You don't like it? Well now, if you don't care for that how about switching NATO, that's 29 to 33 – no, wait a minute – '

'Margaret – '

'Wait, Ronnie dear, I think I've got it – yes! Education – that's what's wanted – 58 to 61! There!'

This kind of political pass-the-parcel could continue for anything from twenty minutes to an hour and a half when one might, if one was very daring, suggest going back to the original order and changing the punctuation and if you'd started after breakfast, with any luck it would be time for lunch.

During lunch someone who wasn't hungry, or pretended not to be, would do a quick rewrite of pages 8 to 11, go back to square one with the rest and suddenly where all had been black as Egypt's night the darkness lifted, the sun came out and we were back in business.

On this occasion, however, there was no meal break. 'You've had dinner. Good. Now let's get on.' Mercifully sandwiches arrived at midnight and by 2.00 a.m. we were still passing the parcel when the Leader suddenly threw herself on the *chaise-longue*, kicked off her shoes and went into orbit. Bea Lillie was right. It's better with your shoes off. Firing on all cylinders the words poured out of her – good ones, brilliant ones, startling ones, the adrenalin was flowing like the Mississippi in flood.

'There, you see, what did I tell you? It's my table method, it's the only way to get you going!'

The next day Chris and I had a prearranged lunch with Heath's Political Secretary, William Waldegrave. Ted had taken the loss of the leadership to Margaret Thatcher as though it was a personal insult. Several attempts had been made by those who admired and had worked with both (Willie Whitelaw, Peter Carrington, Tony Barber among others) to heal the rift between them that was entirely of Ted's making. The Brighton lunch was yet another effort at a make-and-mend job by the three of us. It was agreed that what was needed was a quid pro quo. If Margaret would make a friendly public reference to Ted in the Leader's speech on Friday (which Chris and I boldly guaranteed) he would reciprocate, acknowledging her words with a broad grin from the platform or a couple of nods of that massive head, or possibly both. He might even, if the force was with him, make an amiable reference to her afterwards to the media. These were minimum requirements but at last it seemed we were getting somewhere.

Came the Friday and Margaret duly delivered, in a reference to the approaching visit of the bailiffs of the IMF to the Labour Government, before the Conference speech was five minutes old.

As Ted Heath said with such force on Wednesday, Britain is at the end of the road. As we all know, he is a man who never sold the truth to save the hour. I am indeed grateful for what he said. Let us all have his courage.

That was the 'quid'. We awaited the 'quo'. There was no 'quo'. Despite Waldegrave's best efforts Ted sat, impassive, at one end of the platform, no smile, no acknowledgement, no response. Had he forgotten or could he simply not come to terms with his defeat by his successor, brought about by a vote of the Parliamentary Party in obedience to rules that he himself had helped to fashion?

The Brighton Conference speech went down as well as had the first at Blackpool. The faithful were hers now, root and branch, and this time we had no problem with the peroration.

> I am deeply conscious of the challenge to our party and of the responsibility I face as its Leader, but I believe we shall be sustained by millions who are hoping and praying today that we shall rise to the level of events. As I look to our great history and then to our dismal present, I draw strength from the great and brave things this nation has achieved.
>
> I seem to see clearly, as a bright new day, the future that we can and must win back. As was said before another famous battle: 'It is true that we are in great danger: the greater therefore should our courage be.'

By Christmas of that year inflation had risen to 17 per cent and before 1977 was three months old Labour had lost a couple of by-elections and, shortly afterwards, control of the Greater London Council, the IMF continued to hold the purse strings and things looked grim for government and country.

Labour, without an overall majority, was constantly in danger, not least from its own backbenchers, of losing a vote of confidence which would mean an immediate General Election, but Callaghan hung on, thanks to a marriage of convenience with the Liberals who, with only tenuous support in the country according to the opinion polls, also wished at all costs to avoid an election.

While these manoeuvres were taking place Margaret Thatcher was quietly learning the job of leading the Conservative Party in Opposition and planning in detail for a future Conservative government, which surely could be only a matter of time.

In October '77 we were once again back at the Imperial, Blackpool, for the Party Conference. That was the Conference when, as we were coming up to a final draft of the Leader's speech, Margaret asked Patten, 'How is it coming?' and Chris replied, 'All right, but it needs Ronnification.' The word was the cross I had had to bear since Blackpool (1). I'm not sure who invented the noun or the verb that went with it but it was shorthand for the style or imprint that

244

gradually came to typify my contribution to the Conference speeches and others she delivered at home and abroad in which I subsequently became involved.

Chris turned to me. 'Will you go through it and "Ronnify" it and then take a crack at the peroration?'

R.M.: 'How long have I got?'

C.P.: 'Half an hour.'

R.M.: 'I can't do both in the time. Which matters most?'

C.P.: 'Peroration.'

I withdrew to my bedroom which faced a back alley into which the rain – it always rained at Blackpool during Conference week – pounded ceaselessly. It was a lowering sight for a writer seeking inspiration. Not surprisingly none came. I rifled through my briefcase in growing panic and among a mishmash of random thoughts and notes came across an old peroration I had written some months before for an open-air speech that Margaret gave at Blenheim, the ancestral country home of the Churchills. She hadn't liked the peroration so I had done another and by chance I had the original, which I had always preferred, with me. Would she remember it? Hopefully not.

I was back in the suite in ten minutes. The room had filled up. In addition to the Leader there were John Stanley, Angus Maude, David Wolfson and Alfred Sherman, director of the Centre for Policy Studies, created by Margaret Thatcher and Keith Joseph to 'think the unthinkable'.

'That was quick,' said Patten.

'A bit too quick,' said Margaret. 'Is it any good?'

I looked round the room and cursed my foolhardiness. The last thing I wanted was an audience, and a critical one at that. Too late now, though. 'May I read it to you?'

'Yes, all right.' She covered her eyes as usual. A hush fell. It was an emotional piece and I was giving it the full treatment when I became aware of a strange snorting sound coming from – it *couldn't* be from behind the Leader's hands, no, it wasn't she.

I ignored it and was in full flood when out of the corner of an eye I became aware of John Stanley, the tallest man in the Commons, prone on the floor and crawling like a giant caterpillar across to where Sherman was snoring to beat the band. On arrival he struck Sherman's left knee at the joint where the doctor tests your reflex with such power I wouldn't have been surprised if the limb had come off. Alfred jerked awake with a final violent snort and looked about him, bewildered, wondering where the devil he was. The caterpillar returned to base. I finished in a rush, cursing myself, Sherman,

Blenheim, Blackpool and perorations in general. Margaret took her hands from her face. There was a silence.

Eventually: 'I'm not sure I can say this,' she said in a flat voice. So she'd remembered. No matter. It was worth a try.

Angus Maude (with that marvellous nasal twang of his): 'I think that's pretty good.'

M.T.: 'Good? Good?? It's so powerful I don't think I can do it. I'd weep.'

She did it – and beautifully. The moral of this story is: If you're a writer, never throw anything away. You never know ...

It's 1978 and Callaghan and the unions are blowing hot and cold.

On 1 January he sets a pay limit target of 5 per cent.

On 21 January a special assembly of the Liberal Party endorses the Lib-Lab Pact.

On 23 May it is announced that the Lib-Lab Pact will shortly be terminated.

So this pointless exercise, in which the Liberals had simply been used by Labour to sustain them in office, was about to be over, but eighteen months had been lost, while the country drifted politically and economically under a government with a single policy, the urge to survive.

That autumn, with Labour pactless and without an overall majority, the country plunged into industrial chaos. Strike followed strike: the lorry drivers, the dustmen, the gravediggers, the nursing unions, NUPE, COHSE, the ambulancemen, all exercised their right to withdraw their labour. Hospitals closed, or turned away patients, the London Underground ceased to run, and a bitter winter rent Britain from end to end.

On 10 January 1979 Prime Minister Callaghan returned from the warmth of a Summit meeting in Guadeloupe and, contrary to legend, did *not* say to the press at the airport, 'Crisis? What crisis?' What he actually said was, 'I don't think other people in the world would share the view that there is mounting chaos.' Whatever other people in the world might say, that was what Britain was experiencing and by 1 February Callaghan himself was denouncing 'Free collective vandalism' in the National Health Service. Three weeks later civil servants began a series of one-day strikes. It was then, as chance would have it, that Margaret Thatcher was due to make a Party Political Broadcast on television. The broadcast had been prepared by the advertising agency Saatchi & Saatchi, under the guidance of its managing director, Tim Bell, and filmed on the windswept roof of a building in Tottenham Court Road. When it was shown to Chris Patten and to me we were dismayed.

It had no theme, no passion, above all no relation to a country in turmoil. It simply ignored the temper of the times: people dying of cancer in hospital for lack of oil to heat the wards, families burying their dead because of the gravediggers' strike, the danger to health of plastic bags filled with rubbish scattered all over London due to the refuse collectors' refusal to work.

Patten and I decided at once to write a new broadcast, unsolicited, in which in effect Margaret Thatcher would say to Callaghan: 'We can't go on like this. Let's put the party political battle on hold. This is a national emergency. Let's get together and jointly call a halt.'

When we told her what we had in mind she said, to my intense surprise, 'No. You don't join hands with a government you're trying to overthrow except in wartime. Ceasing to be an Opposition and becoming the Government oneself is the solution to what's happening to this country. Nothing is more important than that. When at last that happens there won't *be* these intolerable strikes.'

Taking the long view she was right, but emotions were riding high and we were convinced that, quite apart from dramatising the urgent need for action and thus doubling the pressure on those on strike, an emotional appeal would take advantage of her being a woman, and her natural feminine sympathies could, if we found the words, have a powerful effect on the people. Above all, by offering to unite the country it would present her for the first time as a national, as distinct from a Party, leader.

Without informing anyone we went ahead and wrote the broadcast. When we showed it to Bell, far from taking offence he changed his mind and came with us, but before making a final approach to the Leader we all three felt we needed support from the hierarchy, so Peter Thorneycroft, the Party Chairman and former Chancellor, whom Margaret had persuaded to return from retirement, was invited to come over from Central Office to the Shadow Cabinet Room where he was shown the film of the original broadcast.

He sat and watched in silence, a tall man with a fixed smile on a florid, cherubic face which concealed a keen political mind.

'Well,' he said at length in his inimitable aristocratic cockney, 'I'd never vote for the woman on the roof of that building, not in a thousand years.'

'Will you say so?'

'You bet I will. We can't have this.'

It was in her study in the Commons that the four of us – the Chairman, Patten, Bell and I – saw Margaret and faced her with the new text. She read it carefully. Then: 'You know what you're doing, don't you? You're asking me to let Callaghan off the hook.'

'No,' said Thorneycroft gently. 'We're asking you to put country before Party.'

He had touched the patriotic nerve. She agreed to do it. But on two conditions. First, the broadcast must be filmed right there in her study at the House. She had no time for trips to rooftops or television studios.

'But TV cameras have never been allowed inside the Commons,' Bell protested.

'Leave that to me,' said Thorneycroft.

Second, she insisted, the room must be filled with spring flowers.

Spring flowers? This struck me as a bizarre request and once more out of tune with the mood of austerity we hoped to project. To my surprise Bell instantly agreed and when I turned and glanced at him whispered, 'Don't worry,' and winked.

At ten o'clock the following morning we crowded into the study where cameras, cables and crew were jammed tight. Into this came the Leader with a set face and sat in her high-backed armchair which had been moved to the centre of the room. She looked far too well-dressed for austerity. A roll-necked sweater and an old raincoat would have been my choice for her wardrobe, with her hair blown by the wind, but as ever she was immaculately turned out. Last-minute make-up and powdering made the best cheek bones in the business appear even more flawless. Never mind, too late to argue.

It was then that I noticed the flowers. They were positioned all round the room. Crocuses, daffodils, roses, tulips, from every nook and cranny all the canopy of spring assaulted the senses. I couldn't believe my eyes. The lady of the manor in her exotic greenhouse, way above the sordid reality of the city streets, negated the entire purpose of the new script and the mood of national crisis we had set out to reflect.

I hissed at Bell, 'What's this, the Chelsea Flower Show?' Out of the corner of his mouth he whispered, 'Look at the camera angle.' I looked. It was pointing straight down at Margaret in the tightest of tight close-ups. There was not so much as a buttercup in sight of the lens. But suppose she noticed that the flora and fauna were out of shot? Happily she didn't, and although she remained unconvinced by our strategy she did the broadcast like the professional she had become and it went out that night.

Next morning my telephone rang incessantly, friends saying: 'Last

248

night for the first time she sounded like a national leader.' So she did. There are those who believe that particular broadcast, in what became known as the Winter of Discontent, was a turning-point, that it did more to swing the country in her favour than any subsequent speech before or during her first election campaign. It certainly helped. It wasn't so much the words, it was the gesture of holding out the hand to the political enemy that grabbed the country. People who had no love for the Conservative Party warmed to its leader.

Certainly Callaghan understood and appreciated, not without a touch of envy, what Margaret had done. Next day, coming out of Westminster Abbey with her after a memorial service, she told me he had said, looking straight ahead and marching slowly step by symbolic step beside her: 'That was a damned good broadcast you did last night.'

I asked her what she had replied. 'I just said coolly "Oh. Do you think so?"'

She hadn't yet realised that it had been a breakthrough for her, that she had struck exactly the right note of unity and leadership. But Callaghan knew. '"I wish I'd said it," he murmured. "Well done."'

'What did you say to that?'

'Nothing.'

'Weren't you pleased?'

'No. He was patronising me.'

The female psyche is different from the male. Not better or worse. Just different.

14

. . . .

'Wave! It's a Marginal!'

It's March and still Callaghan clings on, but time is running out for Labour. Devolution for Wales, to which the Government is committed, is rejected in a referendum by 4 to 1. The result of a similar referendum on devolution for Scotland, another government commitment, is not clear-cut. Parliament has insisted on a 40 per cent majority. It doesn't quite make the required figure. Callaghan, masterly equivocator, ducks and weaves and suggests further talks between the parties.

Margaret Thatcher rises in the House. She says the people have made their decision, the referendum has failed to hit the target and the Government is simply buying time. 'I don't think that's the way to consider matters as important as the government of Scotland and Wales and indeed the United Kingdom,' she says and for the third time since becoming Leader of the Opposition puts down a motion of no confidence, demanding that Parliament seeks a fresh mandate from the people. Motions of no confidence claim priority over all other business. At 10.00 p.m. on 28 March the crunch comes.

After a gripping debate the House divides. In the division lobbies no one dares predict the result. It's nip and tuck. The Members return nervously to their seats. Finally the two tellers, one Labour, one Conservative, bringing the results of the vote, make their way across the floor of the House to stand before Mr Speaker. Willie Whitelaw puts a fatherly arm round Margaret's shoulders, whispers 'Third time lucky.'

There is just one vote in it. The BBC man on the spot gets the winner wrong (wishful thinking?) and has to make a hasty correction.

250

The Labour Government has been *defeated* on a motion of no confidence by a single vote: 311 votes to 310. The roar of Conservative cheers and waving of order papers signals to the country, to Prime Minister Callaghan and his erstwhile allies of the ill-fated Lib-Lab Pact that no further shifts, stratagems or ploys are possible. Parliament will be prorogued and a General Election will follow.

Two days later, just before three o'clock in the afternoon, Chris Patten and I were working in the Leader's office on a draft speech for the coming campaign when there was a sudden bang. Chris looked up and said, 'That sounds like a bomb.' 'Just a car backfiring,' I said. The noise had indeed come from a car but it was no backfire.

There was the sound of running feet. We went to the window and stared down from the office which overlooked the ramp coming up from the Commons car park. On the ramp was the smoking wreck of an automobile on which police were rapidly converging. Chris said 'Get back from the window' and closed the curtains. The police were everywhere and Parliament was cordoned off. The reaction of those in the Leader's office was a mixture of calm and restrained horror, an emotion I was to feel again five years later in the middle of the night at the Grand Hotel, Brighton. At first no one knew whose car it was or who had been driving. Then the registration plates were checked. The car was Airey Neave's and he had been at the wheel when it exploded. Mrs Thatcher, who was opening a children's fete in her Finchley constituency, couldn't be contacted immediately (the Opposition Leader's car did not then have a car telephone) but she was due shortly at the BBC who were asked to notify her the moment she arrived.

Some forty minutes later she turned up. I happened to be standing just by the door as she walked in. She looked pale and stricken but controlled. 'Thank God one doesn't know when one wakes up in the morning what will happen before one goes to bed at night,' she murmured.

Shortly afterwards news came that Airey, who had been rushed to Westminster Hospital, had died on the operating table. The Commons staff, the secretaries and various members of the Shadow Cabinet stood around, shaken, helpless. I thought of the irony that a man who had survived the war, been taken prisoner, interned at Colditz, escaped and won the MC, DSO and OBE for his exploits, should lose his life to an INLA bomber who had crept into a civilian car park and planted a delayed-action bomb.

Indeed there was a double irony. In recognition of his work as campaign manager in her fight for the leadership, Margaret Thatcher had made Airey Neave Shadow Secretary for Northern Ireland. It was the Irish connection that cost him his life.

There is naught for comfort to be said on such occasions. Feeling useless I just said, 'I'll leave you now.'

'You can't, dear,' said Margaret. 'The police say no one can leave the building. Anyway I have to write a statement for the press and I want you to go over it.' She disappeared into her study with her constituency secretary, Alison Ward.

Ten minutes later Alison came out. 'She says will you go in.'

She was sitting behind her desk with her glasses on. Taking them off she passed me a handwritten note on which she had scribbled the press release. She said, 'See what you can do with that.' It was half a page of controlled emotion written under acute stress. It could not have been better done.

I said, 'There's not a word I would add or subtract. Well, perhaps just one.'

'What's that?'

'"Hero". I don't think anyone who has been a soldier would think of himself as a hero.' She deleted the word and said, 'Ask them to phone that through to the Press Association.'

Parliament was to be dissolved on 7 April and a General Election called for 3 May. All she had to do was win it. Meanwhile, until the campaign proper got under way, there was nothing to do but wait. Doing nothing is something Margaret Thatcher has always been extremely bad at. In this case everything had been thought through in four and a half years of Opposition for the first session of the new Parliament in the event of a Conservative victory. She fretted restlessly, finding work for idle hands, dictating letters that were not necessary, inventing problems that didn't exist and generally driving her devoted secretaries to distraction. It was like waiting for D-day.

'Can't you get her mind off it somehow?' begged Caroline Stephens.

'What do you suggest?'

'How about taking her out to dinner?'

'A dinner dance,' urged Alison, getting into the swing of the thing.

'You're joking, of course.'

'Take her to the theatre,' said gentle Tessa who had recently joined the secretarial inner circle.

Next day I said casually to the candidate, 'Did you see the Two Ronnies on TV last night?'

'Oh, I love the Two Ronnies.'

'Three, I hope.'

'I didn't know there were three. Oh, ha ha. Yes, well, you're different.'

I told her they were playing to capacity at the Palladium and would she like to see them on stage? She was thrilled, but how would we get seats? I said Harold Fielding, the producer, was a friend of mine and the following evening I collected her and Denis in my car from Flood Street.

The house manager met us at the top of the Palladium steps and we were conducted like royalty to the retiring room behind the Royal Box where champagne and smoked salmon sandwiches were laid out. While we ate and drank she went on talking easily to the manager for five, ten minutes, a quarter of an hour.

Through the half-open door of the box I could see Michael Reed, the brilliant young musical director, baton at the ready, glancing anxiously at his watch and then up at the box. The orchestra was fidgeting, the house full and starting to cough. Finally the manager said, 'Mrs Thatcher, I think perhaps – '

'Oh, are they ready? Good. I wondered what was keeping them,' and we went through into the Royal Box, which is just above the stage on the right of the auditorium at dress-circle level. A relieved Reed started the overture.

Margaret sat in the downstage corner seat by the draped curtain, beaming with anticipation, and fixed her eyes on the stage. The audience fixed their eyes on Margaret. I sat next to her, Denis on my right.

The curtain rose on a colourful opening number à la Ziegfeld with some dozen or more gorgeous girls parading up and down a staircase in glittering sequined gowns and headdresses high with feathers. Margaret looked happily on. 'I love this sort of thing,' she whispered in my ear. 'So pretty' and leaning forward in the box as the scene ended clapped vigorously.

Then came the first sketch. It was set in a men's lavatory, with Ronnie Barker standing in line, clutching his crotch and becoming more and more desperate as he waited his turn. The audience roared. The language suited the setting. As the show progressed other sketches continued in the same broad vein. I watched Margaret covertly and so did the audience. The smile had become fixed. I glanced at Denis. He was loving every minute.

At the interval we returned to the retiring room for more champagne. The manager glowed with pride. 'Great show, isn't it?'

M.T.: 'Er – yes. Very jolly. I must say they're rather more blue than they are on TV.'

R.M.: 'Well, it's a good Conservative colour.'

One was not amused.

At the end we were escorted backstage to the star dressing rooms where the Two Ronnies and still more champagne were waiting for us. Margaret sipped hers politely and to the question 'Did you enjoy the show?' lied like a trouper and said, 'Every single minute.' Well, manners are manners and votes are votes. It was election year.

As we returned through the pass door the chorus girls were lined up in the wings. They clapped heartily. Margaret waved and smiled and stopped in front of one or two for a gracious word like HRH the Duchess of Kent chatting up the ballboys at Wimbledon on Finals Day.

The manager asked if Mrs Thatcher would like to see the theatre from the stage. 'It's quite a sight,' he said. There's something melancholy about an empty theatre but Margaret surveyed the huge auditorium with a politician's professional eye.

'Ideal for a Party rally,' she said crisply.

'Never misses a trick,' murmured Denis. (As he did a few months later when we waited outside the local church near Chequers while Margaret chatted to the choirboys and girls, who had no vote but would one day.) I doubt if the great Frank Matcham had a Party rally in mind when he designed the Palladium but then if one wants to be Prime Minister one has virtually to eat, drink and sleep politics. I have never felt the urge but Margaret Thatcher had not the smallest difficulty.

Outside the front entrance in Argyll Street, where my car was drawn up, a crowd of about two hundred had gathered. As we came out and down the steps they clapped and cheered. Margaret started to get in the car, stopped suddenly, turned back to the crowd and pointed to the vehicle.

'It's not mine!' she cried reassuringly. 'It's not mine!'

The car was a Rolls. Not very clean and not very new. Nevertheless a Rolls. She wasn't going to lose a couple of hundred votes by being taken for the Nobs' candidate.

'Never misses a trick,' I said to Denis before he could say it to me.

'She loved her evening,' said Caroline. 'You're saving our lives.'

'Winning the election single-handed,' said Alison. 'When's your next little outing?'

I took Margaret to the Tim Rice/Andrew Lloyd Webber musical *Evita* at the Prince Edward. She thought the direction by Prince Hal was terrific. Hal Prince would have been doubly flattered.

In her bread-and-butter letter to me she wrote, 'I was thinking, if a woman like that [Eva Peron] can get to the top without any morals, how high could someone get who has one or two?'

It was a question to which she was about to give a comprehensive answer.

Our final excursion before the election came under starter's orders was to the other big musical hit, *Annie*, at the Victoria Palace – a sophisticated but sentimental story of a gang of kids in an orphanage in the lower reaches of New York under the domination of a wicked matron-figure played by Sheila Hancock. This being an American musical the eponymous 'Annie', all of twelve years old, gets to meet the President at the White House, solves half a dozen of his problems before breakfast à la Shirley Temple ('Why, *thank* you, Annie.' 'Kids' stuff, Mister President. Nothin' to it'), leads the youngsters to a triumphant victory over the wicked matron and is rewarded with the hit number 'Tomorrow' ('Tomorrow, tomorrow, I love you tomorrow, you're only a day away') which I thought was politically apposite, though I don't think Margaret took the point.

After the show I led her up on to the stage, as promised, to meet the cast, who were all gathered in the final set. They gave her a rousing reception, all but the sturdy little girl who had played Annie, who took one look at the candidate for Downing Street, turned her back and burst into tears.

There were no votes in it but show Margaret anyone in distress, let alone a child, and she's all theirs. She went straight to Annie, enveloped her in a motherly embrace and said, 'My dear, whatever's the matter?' Inconsolable, Annie sobbed on. It was explained to Margaret that, because they were under-age for an adult contract, there were several 'Annies' who worked on a rota system and were changed every three months as the law stipulated, and for the time being it was this one's last night.

'My dear, you mustn't take on so, you'll be back again before you can say Jack Robinson,' said Margaret (as she may, or may not, have said to Leon Brittan a few years later when he resigned from the Cabinet after the Westland Affair). 'Time will fly, it always does. Meanwhile, you know what you must do?' Not having a clue what she must do Annie howled some more. The candidate hadn't brought up twins for nothing. Rising above the weeping and wailing she said firmly, 'You must write a diary, that's what you must do.' The child was so stunned by this mysterious advice she stopped crying instantly and Margaret was hailed as a miracle-worker by the entire company.

255

While I was wondering whether this general precept for the young could become a vote-winner for the adult population I noticed that Margaret was looking around for someone. 'Where is that clever Miss Hitchcock?' she inquired.

An awkward silence followed. Apparently Sheila Hancock, a long-time Socialist, at the mere prospect of meeting the Conservative candidate had withdrawn to her dressing room, nose in air. When this was delicately explained to Margaret she said, 'Well, never mind, if she won't come to me, I'll go to her,' and promptly marched up to Hancock's dressing room and knocked on the door. Taken aback, Sheila gave a studiedly cool reception to the potential Prime Minister, but Margaret's technique in the face of rebuff, refined on many a constituency doorstep, worked as well, if not better, in a theatrical dressing room. An entertaining little encounter took place which, if manners also maketh woman, Margaret won on points.

It's April and we're off at last, destination Downing Street.

No illusions. From the beginning she has said 'When the time comes I will only have one chance', meaning that if she fails to lead them to victory the Conservative Party, with its customary ruthlessness, will choose another Leader. (In due course she has three chances. She wins all three. The Conservative Party still chooses another Leader. But let us stay sequential.)

. The road we're travelling is a radical road. She seeks a mandate to roll back the frontiers of the State, to rescue government from the union stranglehold, to turn the country round politically and economically, to open up free markets, to denationalise and return to private ownership, to encourage individual enterprise, to restore Britain's reputation in the world and to see off socialism. And that's just for starters. She has had four and a half years to prepare and she is ready. The future is right there in her handbag. It's time for a change. The time is now. Right, let's go...

ON THE CAMPAIGN TRAIL: A TYPICAL TWENTY-FOUR HOURS

8.00 a.m.   Central Office. Meeting with Tory high command followed by regular morning press conference.

9.15 a.m.   Campaign bus to Victoria Station. Swiftly through concourse to train. Leader sets cracking pace. Security, I suppose. Keep up, keep up. Party consists: Thatcher, Janet Young (statutory female support), David Howell (MP and fellow speechwriter), Caroline Stephens, John

Stanley or Adam Butler (PPSs), self, Roger Bowden, plus Central Office organising staff. Train to Gatwick. Writing, rewriting in carriage.

Arrive Gatwick. Coffee and buns in VIP lounge. Private plane to Cardiff. Writing, rewriting on flight. Caroline typing press release of speech at twenty thousand feet before speech written. Decide politics even nuttier than theatre but discover not quite as Lewis Carroll as sounds. Speech due delivery 8.00 p.m. Too late for first editions, therefore précis better than nothing. Not exactly par for course for normal people but who's normal at election-time? (Will someone tell me why they do it?)

Arrive Cardiff Airport. Swept by cavalcade of cars, police outriders, to hotel. Final additions and subtractions. Photocopier go, go, go. Brief dinner with local bigwigs. Cavalcade to town hall. Speech thirty-five, forty minutes. Reception rapturous. (Now I know why they do it.) Plane home. Cars to Flood Street, Thatcher domicile, small, neat, spotless. Supper in kitchen. Candidate lays table, gets smoked salmon, lemon, cheese, fruit from fridge. Wine, beer, coffee.

M.T.: 'Come on, everybody, get stuck in, we've got work to do. (Eh??) You all right, dear?'

R.M. (reeling): 'Never better.'

Into small downstairs lounge. Work on speech for tomorrow night. No one has told me this is typical Thatcher timetable. Should have guessed. Sustained, high-pitched whistle from somewhere upstairs. Without looking up she says, 'It's the television. Go and turn it off, somebody, and wake D.T. He falls asleep in front of the box.' Eventually rumpled, shirtsleeved, sleep-racked Denis appears.

M.T. (absorbed): 'Hello, dear. All well? Goodnight, then.' (To writers): 'I don't like that "You may not agree". It sounds defeatist. They'll agree all right if we persuade them.'

D.T.: 'My God, you're not on another flaming speech. Do you know what time it is?'

M.T. (immersed): 'And, Ronnie dear, can we lose that "perhaps"? I'm a conviction politician. I'm not in the "perhaps" business.'

R.M. (for the hell of it): 'You wouldn't go for "maybe", "possibly", "just conceivably"?'

M.T.: 'No, I wouldn't. And while we're at it, that "well now", it's not me, dear.'

R.M.: 'It's gone.'

257

D.T.: 'Good Lord, you're not writing the ruddy Bible, for Christ's sake!'

M.T.: 'Go to bed, darling.'

D.T.: 'Look who's talking!'

But he goes, shaking his head in disbelief. We work on till three, three-thirty, maybe, possibly, just conceivably, four...

A letter has been received from the Director-General of the BBC, Ian Trethowan, suggesting a television debate between James Callaghan and Margaret Thatcher on the lines of the famous Nixon–Kennedy duel. Callaghan has tentatively agreed. What should Margaret do? As this is a communications matter, Chris Patten, Gordon Reece and I are summoned to Flood Street.

Chris is in favour, Gordon against. I'm undecided. Chris feels that since our Winter of Discontent broadcast showed Margaret in a favourable light as a national leader and potential Prime Minister this should be followed up. A TV contest would again put her on equal terms with Callaghan before the nation.

Gordon is against, fearing that Callaghan's 'Uncle Jim' image and greater experience on TV would be a winner and in such a situation Margaret is still inevitably an unknown quantity. No one denies the impact of her winter broadcast but a scripted text is one thing, a free-ranging debate something else again.

I begin to come down in favour of taking a chance. To me, she has started to *look* like a winner and she's the challenger, the underdog. People, like fortune, favour the brave. Besides, she's prettier than 'Uncle Jim'.

But Gordon is firm. The debate would be live. The BBC's not interested in a pre-recording, and you never knew what could happen on live television. Look at Nixon and his famous five-o'clock shadow. People say it cost him the presidency first time round. Why risk it?

Margaret, who has listened to all this in silence, asks 'What five-o'clock shadow?' Gordon explains that Nixon's dark, sallow skin made him look sinister even at breakfast and by five o'clock he needed a second shave if he wasn't to come on like the Demon King in the pantomime. His people only realised the importance of the second shave during the first debate and then it was too late to send for a razor.

'Well, I don't have a five-o'clock shadow,' says Margaret firmly. 'All this talk about shaving and shadows is too ridiculous.' She gives Gordon a glare and clicks her tongue.

I feel we're heading into Marx Brothers territory and hurriedly throw my weight behind Gordon. It's two-to-one against now but of course the decision is Margaret's.

She hesitates. Chris tries one last throw, pointing out that if she doesn't do it the BBC will be unhappy.

'Really? How unhappy?'

'Very.'

Her eyes light up. She positively twinkles. 'In that case,' she says, 'the answer is definitely no,' and as Gordon is there we all have a glass of champagne to celebrate the BBC's discomfiture.

I was working on the final TV broadcast in the Chairman's (Angus Maude's) office in the Research Department when Angus suddenly appeared and said urgently, 'Listen. We've got this election sewn up. It's in the bag. All that's needed is to keep it cool and not trouble the waters. The problem is Margaret's all keyed-up and tense. It's understandable but it shows.'

'How?'

'She's in a fury with the BBC political editor who's got up her nose and all set to plunge into a public row with him if we're not careful. She says she'll never give him another interview, never have him to Chequers if she gets there, going to pen a stinker to his head of department, et cetera, et cetera.' I wondered what all this had to do with me.

'You're a theatre man not a politician. You can talk to her on different terms than the rest of us. Will you try and calm her down? It's urgent. If she blows up at this stage it could blow the election. It's as simple as that.'

I chewed this over. I said, 'I'll do what I can but I think you overrate my influence.'

'Just do it, will you?' said Angus and was gone.

That evening I went round to Flood Street. Angus was right. She was undoubtedly on edge.

I circled the subject for a while until she said, 'You wanted to see me about something?'

'Yes. Look, I think we're in good shape to pull this thing off. But you know how people get when it's coming up to a first night.'

'No, I don't. I keep telling you I'm not an actress.'

'Well, jumpy. Nerves, like spurs, go jingle-jangle-jingle.'

'There's nothing wrong with my nerves.'

'Of course not. *You're* fine. But not everyone around you is. I had a thought we might use. A message for the troops on the eve of battle.'

She looked surprised. 'What is this message?'

'Keep cool, calm – and elected. You know. The sort of thing you stick on your shaving mirror.'

'I don't have a shaving mirror. I don't need one. And I don't have a five-o'clock shadow either. All this shaving nonsense.'

'Absolutely. And anyway *you* couldn't be cooler or calmer. It's the others I'm thinking of.'

'You didn't make that clear... Cool, calm – and elected.' She tried it out, repeating it several times. 'Yes, all right.' She was getting more relaxed by the second. 'People do get excited, don't they? Calm – and elected. Yes, I like that.'

I don't know whether it changed her mind about the man from the BBC, probably not, but from then on if she seethed she seethed in private.

We were into the final week of the campaign and I had begun to feel that the tide was starting to flow our way. So, according to the press, did Callaghan, but this could be a deliberate bluff to encourage over-confidence engineered by Labour HQ which was trying to sell the electorate a bill about Margaret being an extremist, using the 'Iron Lady' tag as evidence. We countered with a passage from Blackpool (2):

> Let me tell you about my extremism. I am *extremely* careful never to be extreme. I am *extremely* determined to turn back the tide [of socialism] before it destroys everything we hold dear. I am *extremely* disinclined to be deceived by the mask of moderation that Labour adopts whenever an election is in the offing.

If the pace was feverish the candidate was tireless, her sense of mission sweeping her along and her aides and wordsmiths with her. To put her beliefs across, the need for words, words and yet more words was never-ending, although at times we were able to do a scissors-and-paste job, cutting up previous speeches and repeating certain passages in different positions, forever racing against the clock. (D.T. had become an expert at this particular exercise.)

It was in the Glasgow hotel where we were staying overnight after a successful rally that Margaret, in high good humour, asked at dinner in the private suite, 'What's this "Hello, Maggie" song I keep hearing? I can never catch the words. Where did that come from?'

'Me, I'm afraid,' I said. I had thought the Conservatives could do with a campaign song and had asked Jerry Herman, the composer of

Hello, Dolly and many another top American musical, if I could put
local lyrics to his title song. He had agreed at once and it was
recorded by Vince Hill and distributed by Central Office to the Tory
constituencies for use at rallies. I had a tape with me and she made
me play it.

It went:

Hel*lo*, Maggie,
Well, hel*lo*, Maggie,
Now you're really on the road to Number Ten.
You're going strong, Maggie,
Won't be long, Maggie,
Till you turn that key
Then, Mrs T,
You'll see Big Ben
All wreathed in smiles, Maggie,
In the aisles, Maggie,
There'll be dancing on that very special day,
So here's to you, Maggie,
Give 'em the old one-two, Maggie,
Maggie, we're right behind you all the way!

This received a ribald reception from others round the table – Denis,
Carol Thatcher, Janet Young, David Howell and David Wolfson – and
Margaret's spirits rose another notch, but something bothered her.
She wanted to know, 'What does "give 'em the old one-two"
mean? What's an "old one-two"?' Daughter Carol let out her usual
affectionate but exasperated 'Oh, *Mum!*' and I explained that it was
a boxing term for a knockout. Strange, I thought, she who knows
what most people don't doesn't know what everyone does. We were
halfway through our second chorus of 'Maggie' when the hotel
manager came in to say there was a phone call for Mrs Thatcher.
She asked Janet Young to take the call. The dinner was becoming a
party. When Janet returned after twenty minutes or so she seemed
embarrassed.

M.T. (happily): 'Who was it, dear?'

J.Y.: 'Er – Central Office.'

M.T.: 'What do they want?'

J.Y.: 'They were wondering – that is, the Chairman wanted to
know if you would be agreeable for Ted to appear on the same
platform with you and share Monday morning's final press conference.'

M.T. (all good humour vanished): 'What??'

J.Y.: 'Yes, I know but – they seem to think it might be helpful.'

Margaret exploded in a mixture of fury and supreme contempt. 'Scared rabbits! They're running scared, that's what's the matter with them! The very idea! How *dare* they!' 'Cool, calm – and elected, cool, calm – and elected' raced through my mind but this wasn't the moment.

Next morning as we were leaving I met Denis at the lift.

D.T.: 'My God, old boy, what a night I've had!'

R.M.: 'What's wrong?' As if I didn't know.

D.T.: 'This business of Ted appearing on the same platform with the Boss. She hasn't slept a wink all night. I've never seen her in such a state.'

When we got back to Flood Street there was a conference with the hierarchy at which she refused point-blank to appear with Ted. After all the flak she had taken from him since she had replaced him as Leader she wasn't going to have him come in at the last minute, kiss and make up, and claim he'd won the election for her.

Apparently the suggestion had been triggered by a National Opinion Poll that had Labour one point ahead of the Conservatives. When David Wolfson broke it to her she considered it for about a minute in total silence. At length she said with impressive certainty, 'I don't think I believe this,' and got on with preparing the evening meal as though nothing had happened.

The final speech of the campaign is at Bolton, Lancs. It's the first week in May and it's snowing. (Is this an augury and, if so, what is its nature?) We're in the manager's suite at a small hotel, The Crest, just outside the town. The usual aides: David Howell (soon to be Secretary of State for Energy), David Wolfson (soon to be Chief of Staff at Number Ten), Janet Young (later to be Leader of the Lords), Michael Dobbs from Saatchi & Saatchi, coffee boy and poll watcher (later still to be Norman Tebbit's Chief of Staff at Central Office for the 1987 election and, even later, author of *House of Cards*, a political novel and then television play that was a considerable success), and self (deputy chairman, Theatre Royal, Haymarket, the one official post to which I said 'yes, oh yes!', but then the Theatre Royal, Haymarket, is very special).

We bus to the hall. Outside there's a fair-sized crowd.

'Wave!' cries Margaret. 'It's a marginal!' Wolfson and I, who know not Bolton, wave furiously, as though Lancastrian born and bred, miming eternal friendship.

In the packed hall comedian Ken Dodd, dedicated Tory, is doing the warm-up. He's supposed to do five or six minutes, finds the audience receptive, drops the gags and goes political, carrying on for over half an hour.

M.T. (waiting patiently in a side room): 'I should have done the warm-up and let him do the speech.' (And they say she has no humour.)

At last she gets on, ad-libs 'That's a hard act to follow' and does splendidly as usual. D.T. and I lead the applause on key lines. As we always know when these are coming, this has been a feature of the campaign. I spot a woman reporter from the *Daily Express* watching me and taking notes. I have a feeling she's cottoned on to it and edge behind a pillar. Wild cheers and cries of 'Good luck, Maggie!' 'Give 'em hell, Maggie!' bring the campaign to a grand finale. Flying home, I'm confident the two Bolton seats are in the bag. Two days later we lose both.

On the plane Margaret walks down the aisle, stops beside me on her way to chat up the press who are in the rear section, curtained off. 'The media want to know our final message. Something short and snappy. What shall it be?' 'The same as the first. "Time for a change."' She nods and goes on through the curtain to face the press. There's a good relationship between candidate and camp-followers most of the time, and always when flying together. (Possibility of crash when airborne makes for fellow-feeling?)

The last crucial PEB was recorded by the Leader on Monday 30 April and went out on all TV channels on the evening of 1 May. Chris Patten had decided to try for the Commons and was fighting Bath, a marginal Liberal seat, for the Tories so I was once more flying solo.

The same director and camera crew as recorded the now famous 'Winter of Discontent' broadcast, with Tim Bell again in overall charge, had been assigned to the job so Margaret was at ease and all went smoothly on the top floor of the bleak, bare building in Tottenham Court Road.

After three 'takes' the broadcast was in the can and speaker and writer were shunted into a side room where a pot of tea and some plain biscuits were set out. The campaign had taken its toll and neither of us could think of anything to say. There was nothing to be done now but wait for Thursday 3 May.

At length tentatively, almost shyly, between sips of tea Margaret asked if – sip – I had by any chance – sip – thought of a few words for her to – sip – say on the steps of Number Ten, as was of course – sip – traditional, should the result of the – sip – election find her in the position of requiring them. 'If' – sip – 'you follow me.'

'I follow you. And yes, I've thought of something.'

She put her cup down and went into her familiar eye-covering routine. 'Go ahead.'

'Oh, good heavens, no, I'm not going to tell you now. That would almost certainly be fatal.'

She uncovered her eyes. 'You're superstitious.'

'Of course. I'm a theatre man. Also a Scorpio.'

'Are all Scorpios superstitious?'

'This one is.'

'All right. But whatever it is you have in mind I hope it's something people will remember. If, that is, the occasion should arise.'

'I think they might. If, as you say, it comes to that.'

'It may not.'

'Who can tell?'

'Not I.'

'Margaret . . . '

'Yes?'

'Good luck.'

And we clinked teacups in that cold, stark room and toasted whatever Thursday might have in store, if it ever came . . .

When Polling Day finally arrived a thousand years later it was warm and sunny. Wet weather is supposed to be bad for Labour, they have trouble getting out the vote, so presumably a fine day was fine for them. Well, there was nothing to be done about it except pray for a steady downpour and I thought God would probably regard that as cheating. I would in His shoes. Unable to settle to anything all morning I took myself off after lunch to the little cinema in Notting Hill Gate where there was a revival of MGM's *Scaramouche* (screenplay by R.M. and George Froeschel). It struck me as not a bad movie but, as with anything I have ever written, I found scenes that I felt I could have done better. However it's a long film, and it fulfilled its primary function of occupying my mind until nearly six o'clock, when I walked home just in time for the evening news bulletin.

As I thought, the fine weather had brought out the vote and polling, which had been fairly heavy all day, was now expected to reach a climax with the traditional Labour hard core dropping their 'X' in the ballot box on their way home from work.

Sunk in gloom, I had a bath and a chicken sandwich, switched on the television and promptly switched it off again, finding *Top of the Pops* an insufficiently peaceful distraction from wondering what conclusion thirty to forty million democrats had come to, deciding

264

the governance of their country for the next five years, and whether they realised the responsibility that was theirs. Probably not. People don't stop and analyse the way those with a taste for the dramatic do, they just get on with normal life and a good thing too, I reflected sleepily. After all, salt of the earth, as they say, the Brits, proud to *be* one, Land of Hope and Glory, Mother of the Free, God who made thee something pretty marvellous or other, make thee even more phantasmagorical, not sure I can spell phantasma ... phanta ... phan ...

I woke with a start. The daylight had gone. Where was I? I fumbled for the light switch, found it, came to, looked at my watch. 9.45 p.m. I must have slept for over two hours. Exhaustion plus tension, I supposed. But things would be starting to happen the moment the polls closed at ten.

My God, I'd miss it if I wasn't careful. I raced down to the car and reached Central Office just as Big Ben down the road was striking the hour. A crowd had already gathered outside the main entrance and the TV lights were on, flooding the building. I made my way through and into the hall where Gordon Reece, cigar going well, greeted me with a broad grin and the news that the ITN Exit Poll predicted an overall Conservative majority of 63. The Scot in me thought this wildly optimistic but they couldn't be *completely* wrong, could they? I mean, if they were 62 seats out, even then one would be enough, as Churchill said on whatever occasion it was that he said it...

Within twenty minutes the trend was confirmed and it was clear that Margaret Thatcher was to be the next Prime Minister. By midnight Central Office was bursting at the seams and just after three o'clock in the morning, when Margaret and her family arrived from Finchley which she had held with an increased majority, the noise of champagne corks popping was drowned in roar after roar of victory cheers.

Even without alcohol such moments are intoxicating. I had, of course, known one before with Ted Heath. Had anyone suggested then that there would be three to come with Margaret Thatcher I would have dismissed the idea as sheer fantasy. Soon after 4.00 a.m. she detached herself from the mob in her office who were glued to the television and beckoned me into the corridor.

'I think it's going to be all right, dear.'

'It's been all right for several hours, dear.'

'So... outside Number Ten tomorrow. Today, rather. *Now* will you tell me?'

'Well,' I said. 'I thought perhaps you might say...' and I quoted some words attributed to St Francis of Assisi:

'Where there is discord may we bring harmony, where there is error may we bring truth, where there is doubt may we bring faith, and where there is despair may we bring hope.'

(St Francis said 'I' but 'we' seemed more modest for Margaret.)

The lady rarely shows her deep feelings but this, on a night of high tension and the constant switchback of emotion, proved too much. Her eyes swam. She blew her nose.

'I'll need to learn it,' she said at length. 'Let's find Alison and get her to type it.' Alison was found and the three of us went into one of the cubbyholes that passed for offices at Conservative HQ. No sooner had I begun to dictate than Alison started to weep. It struck me that if anyone came in and found me with two attractive women in floods of tears at four in the morning there could be a problem.

It was five-thirty before I left with a request to be back at Central Office, please, by noon. I drove slowly back to Kensington through the early dawn, parked my car and strolled gently home to Sheffield Terrace.

I shall not forget that walk or the feeling of sheer undiluted happiness that went with it. It was a classical May morning, no one about, blue sky, birds singing, and we'd done it, we'd done it, we'd actually been and gone and pulled it off! I found myself singing *Oklahoma!*'s 'O What a Beautiful Morning'. Sentimental and theatrically over the top but there are moments in life when it's permissible to be self-indulgent. If this was to be just once in a lifetime, well, so be it. A lot of emotional hardware had been invested in the result of this election and now at last, praise be, all had been worthwhile.

I let myself into my flat. My mother was asleep but her nurse, Rosamund, a friend of mine who had given up acting to take up nursing, was awake. I had a long luxurious bath, a large breakfast, tried but failed to sleep, gave up and sat and watched television as the Conservatives continued to clock up gains around the country. As I had guessed, the Exit Poll had been over-optimistic, but good to note that in Bath, after a tough fight, Chris Patten was home and dry. (Not perhaps the adjective Margaret would have chosen to describe Christopher but nobody is right about everybody.)

At noon, tired but living on adrenalin and ready to go another twenty-four hours if necessary, I was back at Central Office. It was still fairly full though quieter in the light of day. There were empty coffee cups and dirty glasses and cigarette butts in profusion. As soon as she saw me Margaret, looking fresh and rested (which was constitutionally impossible), called me into her office and closed the door. Dropping her voice, she said a couple of her advisers were not sure about St Francis. What was my opinion? I said I thought he was a pretty good man and history would probably go along with that assessment.

'Yes, I know, dear, but they seem to feel there's a problem.'

'You mean he's strictly for the birds?'

'They're not sure I should quote him outside Number Ten.'

'Why in the world not?'

'They seem to feel he – how shall I put it? – he set a pretty high standard.'

'And they're not sure your government can live up to it?'

'They're afraid it could be a hostage to fortune. What do *you* think?'

I said, 'I think someone should explain to whoever it is that what the Saint said – if he said it – is a prayer, an aspiration. You're not promising heaven on earth. All you're doing is expressing a hope in some words that have come down to us through the centuries, that have a certain nobility and seem to me to be not entirely inappropriate to the occasion.'

'You don't think they're controversial?'

'More than possibly. What's wrong with that?' She obviously wanted to say them but needed maximum reassurance. Not for the first time I called in aid Winston Churchill, a name that usually worked with Margaret. 'Churchill spent half his life being controversial and much of what he said is remembered whether people agreed with it at the time or not.'

She brightened visibly. 'What shall I tell the boys?'

'Tell them it's too soon to get cold feet before you've kissed hands.'

Gradually the building emptied as everyone went home to their television sets to watch Margaret Thatcher leave for the Palace and return as the country's first woman Prime Minister.

By lunchtime there was only a sprinkling left.

Margaret, Denis, Carol and Mark were in her office. I poked my head round the door and said, 'I'll leave you with the family. Good luck.'

'No, don't go, dear. There's a cold lunch coming.' Some extremely depressing cold lamb was brought down from upstairs. We toyed with it. If it had been caviar we wouldn't have noticed.

267

By now the secretaries had left for Number Ten, bearing files and typewriters, all but Caroline Stephens who was manning the phones in the outer office. Otherwise the building was deserted and silent, a total contrast to the previous night's triumphant hilarity.

Denis, in morning suit, lay stretched out in an armchair, dozing. Carol and Mark hovered. Margaret, on an upright chair, sat quite still. It seemed to me that this was a private, personal time for the family and I again suggested I should leave them. But again she said, 'No, don't go unless you have to.' I leant against a wall and thought, this is history. That's why she's letting me stay. She wants me to feel a part of it, to remember. How many people would think of someone else at such a moment?

The clock ticks. The only sound. We wait. Irreverent thoughts flit through my mind. The traditional wording is that the Leader of the Party that has won the election is 'invited' by the monarch to form a government. There's something very English about the formula 'invited'. It sounds as if the Queen has just thought of the idea. ('Brilliant, Ma'am.') Also, not being a royal command, it leaves it open for the victor to say, 'Oh, hell, I can't be bothered,' without committing lese-majesty and winding up in the Tower.

Suddenly the phone rings in the outer office. We all jump. Denis jerks awake. Caroline appears in the doorway. 'It's Mr Heath. He would like to offer you his congratulations.' Margaret considers this for a moment. Then, quietly: 'Thank him very much.' Caroline disappears. Well, it was courteous of him. I wonder what he is really thinking.

The clock again. I glance at my watch. Eight minutes past three. Callaghan has left for the Palace to hand in his Seals of Office half an hour ago. Again the telephone. Again we go on red alert. Everyone stiffens. Again Caroline in the doorway.

'You're not going to believe this,' she says, 'wrong number.'

Margaret sits down once more in the upright chair. Presently she kicks off her shoes and flexes her toes; they play nervously with her high-heeled court footwear. Denis wonders aloud if she has the Palace confused with a Hindu temple. She cuts him short with a look but steps back into her shoes.

A thought strikes her. She breaks another silence. 'I hope the two cars don't pass. It would be embarrassing. I wouldn't want him to think I'm rubbing it in.' She means Callaghan's car on its way out of the Palace and hers on its way in.

Denis yawns. 'Buck House has been doing this for years,' he says. 'I imagine they know the form by now,' and lies back and shuts his eyes again.

'Wave! It's a Marginal!'

My mouth is dry. I long for a beer or whisky but don't like to ask. The telephone a third time. Who's this, I wonder? The Moderator of the Church of Scotland? The Dalai Lama? Ken Dodd?

Caroline in the doorway, the excitement showing. 'Sir Philip Moore from the Palace.' Sir Philip is the Queen's Private Secretary.

So this is it.

Margaret stands up, pats her hair as though coiffeurs are visible down a telephone line and walks unhurried into the outer office. Through the half-open door I hear her say calmly, 'Good afternoon, Sir Philip. This is Margaret Thatcher speaking.' As I lean forward, ready to monitor every syllable – solely in the interests of historical record, of course – a foot comes round the corner of the door and pulls it gently to. It clicks shut. History and I are frustrated.

Two minutes later she reappears in her most businesslike manner. 'Right. We're off,' she says briskly. 'Prime Minister,' says her son. 'Not yet, dear.' 'No,' from Denis, 'the car might break down.' 'In that case,' says Mrs Thatcher firmly, 'I shall walk' and, followed by her family, goes out through the door and down the stairs to the car. I open the window and lean out. An escort of motorised police in their yellow jackets and white helmets is waiting, engines running. I wave and shout 'Good luck' but the roar of the engines drowns the words. The lady is on her way.

I look round the empty room and feel suddenly deflated. It's like a first night when the performance is over and the audience have left and there's nothing more you can do except wait for the notices.

Downstairs Central Office was silent, not a soul about. As I was about to dash home in time to see the rest of the afternoon's history on television Gordon Reece suddenly materialised.

'If you go now and get stuck in traffic you'll miss it. Come on up to the office, we'll watch from there.'

We went back up to the second floor and he opened the fridge which he had installed for the election, took out a bottle of champagne, uncorked it with the expertise one would expect from a bon viveur, filled our glasses, passed me a cigar, lit his fourth or fifth or sixth of the day and switched on the television. Margaret's car was just disappearing through the Palace gates.

Twenty-three minutes later the cameras picked up the car as it swung out of the Palace, circled the Victoria monument, turned right and then left down Birdcage Walk and headed for Downing Street.

Passing the Cenotaph it swung left again out of Whitehall and up to the door of Number Ten. As she stepped out, the crowd surged

269

through the crush barriers and St Francis was all but drowned in the rush of reporters and cameramen surrounding the new Prime Minister, but she just managed to say her piece above the uproar and it went round the world. Finally, as tradition demands, she stood on the steps of Number Ten with Denis while the flashbulbs popped, before turning away and disappearing inside to take over the government of the country.

As the front door closed Gordon said, 'Well, my dear, we seem to have had a minor role in quite an interesting little production. Let's hope it runs. What do you say?'

I had nothing to say. I was remembering how I'd got caught up in politics by saying rather too much at a dinner party almost exactly ten years ago.

The final results were:

Conservatives	339 seats
Labour	269
Liberals	11
Others	16
Conservative overall majority	43

Among the new Conservative intake was a former Lambeth councillor and now MP for Huntingdon, John Major.

Two days later, I received a letter:

10 DOWNING STREET

5 May 1979

Dear Ronnie,

I could not have done without you. There is no better wordsmith in politics than Ronnie. But more than that, you have always been on hand as a friend to cheer Denis and I up the moment things were not going well. That is when you need friends and we could not have a closer one than you. We are both very fond of you and owe you a great debt of gratitude.

I hope that we shall be seeing plenty of you at No. 10. You are part of the family so please just ring the office and tell them when you are coming in. I mean that.

Oh yes – I almost forgot, can you please continue to help? I hope so. After all, we have only just begun.

> The final Party Political was superb. It had inspiration
> and feeling. I'm sure it made a lot of difference.
> Yours ever
> Margaret

Every major speech in which I was involved produced a letter not unlike the above, usually within forty-eight hours.

A few days after she took office Richard Ryder, who was her first Political Secretary at Number Ten, telephoned. She had to give the address at Airey Neave's memorial service at St Martin-in-the-Fields at which there would be five former Prime Ministers present. Would I write it? He said the Prime Minister apologised for asking this so soon after the election and was sending me round Airey's autobiography.

The book had a preface by Rebecca West which was impressive. After reading the story of Airey's life I wrote the address in the simplest possible words I could think of. There was no need to heighten the emotion, it would be there in the church and the occasion itself would be dramatic enough in that understated British way that expresses so much by what it does *not* say. I went to the service. St Martin's was packed. There wasn't an empty seat. In the front row, immediately below the pulpit, were Harold Macmillan, Harold Wilson, Edward Heath, James Callaghan and Alec Douglas-Home, seated together. On the aisle seat, a little apart, sat Margaret, looking lonely, frail and beautiful in black.

When she spoke from the pulpit her voice was quiet but clear and natural. She did not elocute. (I have always believed that playing 'against the line' is the most effective way of holding an audience.) It was a unique gathering, the first woman Prime Minister with five of her male predecessors seated side by side, silent, looking up at her. The service was simple and moving. This country is no longer first in many ways where we used to lead the field, but we probably still do this sort of thing better than anyone else in the world.

As we filed out into the sunlight Douglas Hurd and Adam Butler came over to me and asked if I had 'anything to do with that?' I nodded and said the only thing that had worried me was the length, how long it should be. That kind, warm Douglas said, 'It was just right.'

On the second Saturday after the election victory Bell, Reece, Alastair McAlpine (the Party Treasurer) and I were invited to Chequers for

271

dinner. I had not been back to that most English of country houses since my first visit for Ted's symposium on the miners' strike five years before. This would be a triumphant evening, a celebration to mark an historic event, but when we arrived Margaret seemed strangely subdued. Wearing the little black dress or its successor, she was curled up on a large stool in front of a log fire in the Great Hall, though the night was quite warm.

Striking what I felt was a light note to set the victory ball rolling I said, 'Sitting there like that you look as though you belong to Chequers and it belongs to you.'

'But it doesn't,' she said in a tone of detached melancholy. She seemed depressed. I wondered what had happened. Just reaction? Or had she seen the books and now knew the size of the task Labour had left her?

She suddenly mentioned two strongly worded letters she had received, one from Sir Ian Gilmour and the other from Chris Patten, protesting at the proposed sale of the Old Queen Street building which had for so long been the home of the much admired and respected Research Department. Apparently the lease was about to run out and, to obtain a new one, restructuring and redecoration was essential and after the election the money to do this simply wasn't there. The result had been a decision to sell and to transfer to Central Office most of the team of free-wheeling young politicians, many of them potential high-flyers carefully built up by Patten over a period of years and who were now to be placed under Central Office control. Chris was naturally upset at the breaking-up of what had been his department and his 'boys'. Furthermore he had not been consulted about its future or theirs but presented with a fait accompli.

I understood his feeling. I too had much affection for the old Research Department where I had found friendship and instruction and the opening out of a whole new world.

This unfortunate business of the letters cast a certain gloom over the evening, which was only slightly relieved by D.T. getting his 'a's and 'e's confused and fulminating against 'that man Peyton', apparently under the impression that it was John *Peyt*on, a former Conservative Minister of Transport, rather than Christopher *Patt*en, the new MP for Bath, whose 'confounded letter' had upset his wife.

I've always believed that Chris's political advancement was not helped by that letter, written as it was in the understandable heat of the moment, and it took Gordon Reece and me nearly six years to bring him and Margaret together again.

It finally happened at the delightful anniversary dinner in 1985 given by the McAlpines in Romilly McAlpine's large office over a butcher's shop in Mount Street for all those who had been with Mrs Thatcher in the ten years since she became Party Leader.

When I saw her sitting side by side with Chris on a sofa, deep in amicable and inevitably political conversation, I felt that at last all was well. I looked across the room for confirmation to Gordon who gave a 'thumbs-up'. I suppose the political lesson is, whatever your feelings, say them aloud if you must but before putting them in writing, sleep on it.

I can neither confirm nor deny the tale that Chris wrote a second letter along the same lines as the first, only more so, which his wife Lavender, attacked by a sudden bout of amnesia, omitted to post. I would like to believe that it's true, if only because it illustrates that Westminster wives are indispensable creatures, without whom the political ice-rink would be even more treacherous than it actually is.

A different kind of letter plopped through my letter-box that December which resulted in my going to the Palace to receive a knighthood from Her Majesty the Queen. As Chris would say, I was gobsmacked and whoever pretends they would not be is merely performing.

By now, Dacre-Hill was eighty-seven. She was to live until almost ninety but was not quite as aware of the passing show as she had been. Although they had never met, I learnt later that Margaret had moved swiftly to recommend me for that signal honour while my mother was still hopefully able to understand and enjoy it. Kindness of that order is not to be forgotten.

15

. . . .

All the World's a Speech

'Speak the speech I pray you as I pronounced it to you,
trippingly on the tongue . . . '   Hamlet, Act III, sc. ii

'I'm a politician, dear, not an actress.'
Mrs Margaret Thatcher

'So how do you like school?' they asked the five-year-old. She gave the matter her full attention. Finally: 'School can be boring-snoring,' she observed.

Likewise political speeches: 'boring-snoring', unless you learn the trick of it. Not everyone has the gift of tongues but without the basics of communication it's hard sledding trying to capture public interest in a political statement. Ranting and raving is unlikely to get you where you want to go. Equally, sincerity without sweep, substance without style can be a yawn, however pronounced the underlying truth. If these things are blazingly apparent they are also frequently ignored by those whose task it is to speak to us of many things and carry with them those who listen hopefully. In an age of instant boring-snoring and the trigger-happy turn-off, to have and to hold a large audience demands skill and expertise and effort.

When Debussy was asked to define music he said, 'It can't be poured into a mould. It's all sorts of colours and rhythms.' The music of a speech is the most difficult element to force into a text where facts are forever pressing their claim and eating up space. Ted Heath, Margaret Thatcher and John Major are very much of their time and less inclined to employ words and images that give tone and colour to their thoughts than the great speakers of the past, even the comparatively recent past, such as Churchill, Macmillan, Macleod. It's said that our age responds best to a more prosaic, down-to-earth approach. I would still go for the colour and the music whenever possible.

For me speechwriting grew naturally out of playwriting and when

274

I first began working for Mrs Thatcher on a regular basis one of the first things I put to her was: 'Politics is a form of theatre.' (I was fascinated to come across the same thought in Peggy Noonan's brilliant book about her time as speechwriter in the Reagan White House.)

As with a theatrical performance, the need is to grip, entertain, persuade and, when necessary, move a body of people who receive and react to what they are hearing *collectively*. Listening to a speech with others, like listening to a play, is not the same as reading a book in bed on your own (or not, as the case may be).

'If it doesn't work at the point of delivery,' I would say, 'it won't work anywhere, not on television, not on radio, not in the columns of a newspaper. It has to be performed.'

'But I'm not a performer, dear.'

'Not yet.'

Although she began by insisting that she was not an actress Mrs Thatcher came gradually to accept the analogy with theatre. She also went along with Gordon Reece's view that for speechmaking purposes her voice – a kind of high-pitched alto in the early days – was not her greatest asset and readily agreed to help from a coach from the National Theatre. Once convinced it was necessary, she submitted herself to instruction like a beginner and by the time she was Prime Minister her public voice had come down nearly half an octave and she had become a most powerful advocate of all she believed in. As the years went by, her range extended still further until, if she felt inclined, she could produce an impressive baritone, which if you weren't expecting it could be quite alarming.

The birth of a Thatcher speech was a complex and mysterious process that all but defies analysis. It sort of 'emerged', like the old Conservative Party method of electing a leader. Its origin was part design, part accident and part a host of disconnected and related factors, none of which was more important than mutual trust among those whose task it was to help create it. In all the years that I was involved in working for Margaret Thatcher – four and a half in Opposition, eleven and a half in Government – I don't remember any occasion when this was not implicitly understood by all of us. No one pushed their contribution just to be part of the process. Giving the lady our best shot was what mattered.

When there were differences of opinion, they were the result of genuine disagreement, not self-importance. Writers came and writers went – to try for a seat in the House, to become special advisers to Ministers, to go to the City and make serious money, to go to New York and edit the *National Review* – but whoever I worked with was a member of a team. We were there to help the lady. We helped her and we helped each other. If we knew her strengths and weaknesses, we knew our own. Working as a speechwriter was not a competition to establish who was top banana. There was no one-upmanship in Downing Street.

As with Ted Heath, my position was informal. I had no regular hours, no defined duties, no office. I worked on early drafts at home. When a date was set for a speech session, I would go to Number Ten and work with the PM and the other writers in her study or the flat or one of the dining rooms or the Cabinet Room. Policy was not the writer's concern but if he is to do it justice a speechwriter needs to believe in what he is helping to promote. Writing to order, in disbelief, is something I could never have learnt to hack.

As writers, we had areas of special interest. One of mine was economy of words. It seemed to me that politicians talked too much. Not necessarily too often, though that too at times, but in too many sentences, with too many paragraphs and sub-paragraphs and subsidiary clauses that may read well but do not speak well when you are addressing the nation or the Commons or the Party Conference. Once you're into a speech there are no intervals.

In earlier centuries rolling periods with plenty of flourish occasionally produced a rhetorical masterpiece. Not so today. Write it tight and taut, I told myself. Go for short sentences with plenty of full stops. It's a woman you're writing for so give her time to breathe. Also, when possible accentuate the positive. People don't want to be talked into a depression, they may be living one.

A major political speech, whether at home or abroad, is what cabaret artists call 'special material'. In Mrs Thatcher's case it was as custom-built as her wardrobe. As I saw it, she needed to be as feminine as possible, but with a commanding presence. Where Ted, once he became Prime Minister, forgot most of what he had learnt about communication, Margaret steadily improved. The strength and power of her delivery developed as her personality developed, with time and an unrivalled experience of the political scene worldwide.

But of all the requirements of a speechwriter or a playwright, what has always mattered most to me was to hear the voice of the person I was writing for in my head. The words must sound as though they sprang from that person's lips via that person's brain, not someone else's. I don't know how it is with others but the only way I can find the shape and music of a speech is to hear the lilt and rhythm of the speaker's voice down to the last nuance of each spoken syllable. Whenever I wrote for Mrs Thatcher I would listen for the echo in my head, and when the resonance was there it worked.

But these are personal humours. There is only one rule about speechwriting: as with playwriting, there *are* no rules. However there are pockets of experience that one absorbs along the way. For instance, a person can ad-lib or speak from a text. One or the other. It's extremely difficult to do both in the same speech for more than half a sentence unless the speaker is exceptional. Anyone else is liable to get lost in the syntactical wood and be unable to find their way out. Nothing can derail a speech faster than a sudden shift from the textual to the improvised. In my hearing Mrs Thatcher tried it only once, at a Welsh Party Conference. It was not tried again on a major occasion.

Pomposity is an instant turn-off. Also arrogance. A touch of modesty never hurt a speaker or damaged a cause. A hint that, however cherished your belief and resolute your will, you might conceivably be wrong can persuade an audience as nothing else can that you may just possibly be right. It's exceedingly difficult to get a politician to admit to error from a public platform. Ministers of the Crown tend to believe they should at least *appear* to be infallible, even if privately they are by no means convinced of it. I think they are wrong about this. Confession is not only good for the soul, it's a sympathy card and that's good for applause, applause.

At which point a personal confession. There comes a time when a speechwriter should stop chopping and changing, refining and polishing and, for better or worse, let what he's written go to press. You've done it. Time's run out. It'll only get worse if you pick it.

Straining after effect is never effective, but simple, everyday words arranged in a certain sequence can be magical:

'Never in the field of human conflict was so much owed by so many to so few.'

'... we shall fight on the beaches ... we shall fight in the hills ... we shall never surrender.'

'This is not the end. It is not even the beginning of the end. But it is, perhaps, the end of the beginning.'

Here was the English tongue deployed with genius, as one incomparable man held the spirit of the people in his hand and lifted them up by the brilliantly exact use of words, many of them monosyllables, to a glory of which they did not know that they were capable. We are minnows who write in the shadow of Winston Churchill. Never, indeed, was so much owed.

*

277

As well as the regular inside team at Number Ten a free-ranging contribution from certain political journalists and others favourably disposed to the Thatcher Government would periodically arrive. This provided an independent outside view. If it seldom survived the final draft verbatim, it nevertheless on a number of occasions triggered a line of thought. Even when the language was not the language of the lady – 'It's fine, dear, but it's just not me' – it could often be made over until it *was* she, provided it was politically on side.

In addition to all this material there was Mrs Thatcher's Aladdin's cave of cuttings, snippets, thumbnail sketches, quotations and random thoughts, anything which she had hoarded and put by over the years for possible use at some future date. Her memory was remarkable and somehow she always knew where to find what she was looking for. What was missing and had to be distilled from all this was a unifying style and that was down to whichever writers were assigned to the speech.

The lady had become a perfectionist and like most such people under pressure could let fly, so although there were good days, there were also bad days, not to mention nights, when all seemed lost and disaster threatened. So it is in the theatre when rehearsals are going seriously wrong, the first night looms inexorably and temperament takes over.

On one memorable occasion she shouted down the telephone in the next room to a Cabinet colleague who happened to be in Ulster that a contribution to a speech that she had asked of him had turned out to be a couple of paragraphs clearly dashed off by an underling. She made such a hullaballoo there was really no need for Alexander Graham Bell's little invention. All this was most enjoyable, though less so, I imagine, if one was on the receiving end.

There were other agreeable diversions. Before the speech was a 'wrap' it would go to whatever Department of State was relevant, sometimes several, for checking and final comment. Back it would come with 'I'm afraid you can't say that, Prime Minister, it's not strictly accurate' or 'The Secretary of State is worried about your slant on X which could be seen as out of line with his speech last Thursday' or 'what he plans to say on Monday'.

At this point Mrs Thatcher would either reluctantly modify or overrule with relish. 'Well, if it's really going to keep him awake all night I suppose we'd better... ' or, more often, 'Isn't that just typical of Y! I always said the man's a pedant!'

'So what shall we do, Prime Minister?'

'Nothing. Leave it exactly as it is!'

*

In the early days of her premiership, speechwriting sessions would take place in the small dining room or the State dining room on the first floor, where there was plenty of space for reference books and table hopscotch. Later we moved to the PM's study which had a drinks cabinet (closed during a session but always open at the end of it) and a view of the park that was pleasant if you sat facing it, as I usually did. The study was feminine and businesslike and informal and tense, according to the varying moods of the woman who worked there.

In due course we came to use the Cabinet Room, with Sir Horace Walpole, the first occupant of Number Ten, looking enigmatically down from the wall above the clock on the mantelpiece as though to say, 'Easy, gentlemen. I've heard it all before.' I never entered that room without being conscious of the generations of history that had flowed through it and its predecessor and the changing faces that had sat beneath that roof and decided the destiny of this and other nations.

For these gatherings of assorted 'helpers' the Prime Minister sat, where all Prime Ministers sit in Cabinet, at the centre of the table on the left as you go in, which made it all the more an official occasion although she never treated it as such. These were for me the happiest times. I always felt that in the Cabinet Room I worked faster and better and was less unsure that decisions about speeches in which I was involved were the right ones. Imagination, no doubt, but then I'm one-third down-to-earth Scot, two-thirds romantic.

Living over the shop, as modern Prime Ministers do, has many advantages. With Mrs Thatcher, if it was an all-day session there was lunch and often dinner in the flat for the speechwriters. This invariably consisted of coronation chicken or shepherd's pie, coronation chicken or lasagne, coronation chicken or boeuf stroganoff. (There were moments when I thought, One more coronation chicken and I'll turn Republican.)

There was white or red wine, sweet or cheese or both, coffee and mints and elaborate boxes of chocolates from Mrs Thatcher's admirers. Chocolates were her only visible weakness which she battled against like the warrior she was. It was almost the only substantive fight she lost, apart from the last.

Amazingly there is no resident cook in the Prime Minister's official home (State dinners are supplied by outside caterers) so meals were prepared and served with skill and despatch by one or two of the secretaries (Joy Robilliard, her constituency secretary who worked in

279

the flat, was frequently co-opted). The Prime Minister bustled about, making sure that everyone was properly fed, urging second helpings, clearing one course to make way for another and if necessary helping to wash up afterwards. The informality of it all was a constant astonishment. It was Flood Street revisited or as I imagined Grantham. The lady's own appetite was small. I could only assume this was due to the chocolates or that she had some internal machine which manufactured calories automatically.

Living over the shop had an additional advantage. It was an ideal arrangement for a woman who was a workaholic and frequently required by the demands of the diary to be a quick-change artist as well. Mrs Thatcher would work with us up to the last possible moment before racing upstairs to the flat, slipping out of one dress and into another, sailing down to the front hall to receive a foreign dignitary in full fig, pose for the press, spend twenty minutes or half an hour with him (or her) as if there was all the time in the world ('Oh, must you leave?') and then change back into her original outfit before returning to the speech with a breathless 'I thought he'd never go. Now – where were we?'

It was Oscar Wilde who said that Britain and the United States were two countries divided by a common language. Had he been able to be with us, another subject worthy of his study might have been the difference between the way Thatcher's Number Ten and Reagan's White House approached the speech-making process.

Having broadly indicated the subject matter, the President would distance himself from his major speeches until the final draft surfaced. His way was to have someone like Peggy Noonan (if there is anyone in the speechwriting class like La Noonan) prepare a draft, then for a team of officials (what Noonan calls 'the mice') to get their teeth into it, passing various versions to and fro and up and down and round about, putting the text through all the varied styles and idioms of the political meat-grinder until something approaching a final text, frequently unrecognisable from the original, which he had not seen, landed on the President's desk shortly before it was due for delivery, at which late hour he would add to, modify or delete. That is, assuming the diverse groups involved, with their special interests and opposing views, had fought their way to some sort of compromise or, if not, an edict had come down from a senior assistant to the President and done it for them. This was known as 'the staffing process' and from time to time the convoluted torture of it would all but drive La Noonan out of her poetic mind.

At Number Ten there was no 'staffing process'. The Thatcher method was to be involved personally in all major speeches from the beginning at virtually every stage of their development. She was there with the writers in the study or the dining room or round the Cabinet table so there was no backstage editing. Objections were voiced in the open and accepted or rejected on the spot. The result was she had a firm grip on the theme from the outset and could steer it in such a way that differences of opinion could be ironed out in her presence as soon as they surfaced.

In the Reagan–Thatcher era, where the two Leaders' political beliefs were close, their speeches came about by very different routes. In my experience, a Thatcher speech was more often than not enhanced by the additions, subtractions, insertions, deletions, cuts, rewrites and rewrites of rewrites to which it was subjected. The reason, I'm sure, was that, taking place in her presence, one could either fight them at once before they took root or surrender gracefully to someone else's inspiration. Despite the diversity of input the final draft, delivered by a single voice, really did sound in the end as though it was the product of a single mind. Take my word for it.

This was remarkable, considering the widely varied audiences Mrs Thatcher had to address in addition to the twice-weekly rigour of Prime Minister's Questions in the Commons and the regular demands of a set-piece debate or one which might suddenly surface. No Prime Minister, with hundreds of speeches of varying length and importance to get through in the course of a year, could possibly compose them all unaided. 'I'm not a writer, I'm a teacher,' the lady would say. Nevertheless many of her shorter homilies were ad-libbed from a handful of notes on the back of an envelope. These were some of the most effective. However, on the big occasion where every word would be scrutinised by the media not only in this country but worldwide, help was essential.

Her Foreign Affairs Adviser, Charles Powell's description of 'useful techniques' for anyone involved in a Thatcher speech can't be bettered. 'Never put anything worthwhile in the first draft, it will be rejected,' wrote Charles. 'Keep the structure for the second draft, the first will inevitably be condemned as not having one. Have the collected works of Rudyard Kipling to hand. Don't even try to draft a peroration until you are right up against the time-limit, because they are always revised right down to the line. Be ready to stay up till six in the morning on the day of delivery if necessary.' Ah yes, I remember it well.

For politicians of the past, speechmaking was easier. The Burkes and Pitts, the Disraelis and Gladstones did not, as their modern counterparts, have to learn, in addition to the technique of the Commons speech, a whole range of modern methods of communication plus the ability frequently to switch from one to the other in the course of a few hours: the nationwide Party Political, the radio and television one-to-one or one-to-group interview, the unexpected street appearance of roving microphone and intrusive camera recording the smallest whisper or grimace, making the chance of a public gaffe an ever-present danger, the Downing Street television camera waiting to record every entrance and exit. The flip side of these potential minefields is of course publicity, the beloved oxygen that was not available in such massive dosage to previous generations of communicators before TV shrank the world.

The Conference speech – the highlight and hazard of the political year – was unique. Whenever I was asked how it got written I would say, 'I don't know. In fact I am in a constant state of amazement that the Conference speech ever does get written.' I also have to say I don't know how the final draft of the Conference speech, the result of several Long Days' Journeys into Night, was ever said to be the final draft.

Mrs Thatcher's decision, unlike her predecessors, to attend virtually all the important speeches to Conference by her Ministers placed an additional strain on the speechwriting process. Although we worked away while she was in the conference hall listening to her colleagues, nothing could be decided until she returned, and that was usually late in the afternoon, often with the news that a Minister had innocently majored in his speech on what the PM had planned to major in hers. This meant pages 35 to 47 were out and there was a whole new section to be written. It also meant goodbye to the evening meal, the PM cancelling her scheduled appearance at the Conference Ball and sending Denis to deputise. He would groan but put on his penguin suit and go and do his duty. The next morning he would be hailed in the tabloids as Lord of the Dance, apparently having a whale of a jive with some young Conservative popsy who was in her glory and would never forget it.

The pressure of time, as the week sped by, governed everything. In the end, nothing dramatic occurred to signal victory. No white smoke went up to the waiting hacks or an astonished world to announce that, every sane prediction to the contrary, the Leader of the Conservative Party and, since 1979, Prime Minister of the United Kingdom *had* a speech and indeed to prove this remarkable thing that had happened against all the odds would actually deliver it at precisely 2.30 p.m. on the final day. It just sort of... debouched. We, the writers, also sort of debouched, usually just before lunch on THE

DAY, some of us haggard and ghostly pale, some of us in need of a bath and a shave, all more or less semiconscious, semi-triumphant and a little wiser or a little less.

That said, anyone who participated in Mrs Thatcher's annual Party Conference speech, which was a killer, was hooked for life or what remained of it. There was something compulsive about the agony, the despair and lack of sleep, the sheer impossibility that a coherent sequence of words and thoughts and images and policies could ever emerge, the excitement when a faint glimmer of hope appeared on the horizon, and finally the lady's inevitable triumph.

A special medal for all concerned – Prime Minister, Prime Minister's husband, writers, civil servants, secretarial staff, Special Branch, police patrols, drivers, hotel manager, domestics – should be struck and worn, like lesser battle-honours, such as Agincourt, on St Crispin's Day. Lesser? Agincourt? Yes, for Agincourt only happened once. We wordsmiths fought the same battle year in, year out, armed only with a well-chewed Biro. But let me be clear. The lady was the driving force behind the speech, its coronary artery was hers. Her views, her opinions, her kind of language and her guidance were behind every contentious syllable.

In the final twenty-four hours it became my self-imposed task to check for audience reaction, making sure we had the order right, the light and shade in balance, creating a deliberate piece of theatre, carefully paced with a powerful climax. By the time we reached the autocue rehearsal – the device of the twin glass reflectors, to which she had been introduced by President Reagan, enables the speaker to address the audience from side to side of a large hall with the head up, rather than down and clinging to the text, but it requires practice – she would ask me to read this or that passage aloud. 'Let me hear it as *you* would say it.' I would point out that only bad or bold directors gave inflexions to the star, that she was now sufficiently experienced to trust her own intonations, but she would insist, so, begging her not to copy me, I would do as she asked.

Margaret was not a natural orator, but growing skill in timing and sheer authority of manner made her a speaker who could command a huge audience seemingly without effort. In fact she did it, like all true professionals, by taking enormous pains. Whatever the mood of Conference, in her keynote address on the final afternoon she would lift the party with a bravura display that roused the faithful to fever pitch and sent them home, refreshed and reinvigorated, to carry the fight to the constituency doorsteps.

There was no high-flown rhetoric or sudden revelation, just a passionate belief in her personal vision that had the combined effect of 'Land of Hope and Glory', the National Anthem and 'Jerusalem' rolled into one. She knew this audience, they were her people. She spoke their language as no one else and year after year she gave them the reassurance they craved.

John Grigg comments: 'Her speeches may have been written by others, but her style was all her own and it was a memorable style.' Once a style had been found and established, that is true. She was, throughout those unique October annuals beside the seaside, meticulous and troublesome and pernickety and splendid and the whole extraordinary process never ceased to fascinate and infuriate and I wouldn't have missed the privilege of being a part of it for half-a-dozen smash hits.

If the rewrites of her speeches were nonstop, so was the work of the senior secretaries in the Political Office: the Carolines and Alisons, the Tessas and Amandas who succeeded one another as each got married but returned for a spell after the honeymoon and went again to have the baby, sometimes running the birth right up to the bumpers so that there were moments when one felt a talent for midwifery might be more important than a passable vocabulary. Caroline Stephens (now Ryder), Alison Ward (now Wakeham), Tessa Jardine-Patterson (now Gaisman), Amanda Colvin (now Ponsonby) not only knew more secrets than most Cabinet Ministers, they also knew when to keep their mouth shut and also to whom they could safely open it.

These lovely, loyal girls, and their more recent successors, were the crème de la crème of the secretarial staff, who understood the mysteries of the word processor, who could type rewrites faster than one could draft them, whose patience was forever and who, by some magical process which has to do with a warm heart, a natural cool and being a woman, made the annual stress and trauma of the five days and nights of the Party Conference speech at Blackpool, Brighton or Bournemouth not only bearable but a kind of blessing-by-the-sea.

Among other singularities of a Thatcher speech was her decision not to mention religion in a *political* address. She thought it was not a fair weapon. She would not even allow the word 'God' because, she said, perfectly honest decent people were atheists or agnostics and she thought it wasn't fair to call Him in aid. I'm not sure that I felt these reservations strictly necessary but I admired her scrupulous sensibility, not a quality with which she was always credited, though she frequently deserved to be.

There was also the question of her jokes. It was said that she never read a newspaper, relying for general information on the daily précis from Bernard Ingham, but I always found her remarkably well informed about the media.

M.T. (pretending to be miffed): 'Whenever I make a joke in a speech the press always say it's you.'

R.M.: 'I don't say it's me.'

M.T.: 'I know you don't, but they always think I can't be funny.'

R.M.: 'They always think I can't be serious.'

M.T.: 'I don't say that.'

R.M.: 'I know you don't.'

M.T.: 'Then I can't think why you raised the subject. Do let's get on. You're wasting time.'

Writing speeches wasn't always heavy artillery. There were little sly pleasures along the way.

Not having an exclusive commitment, once in a while I would write for someone other than the Prime Minister. On one occasion I was asked if I could help the Lord Mayor of London Elect with his speech for the Lord Mayor's Banquet at the Guildhall, which falls on the day he assumes office in November and to which the Prime Minister of the day traditionally replies. It happened from time to time that I was involved in this reply and it was so on this occasion.

As a courtesy the two speeches are exchanged between the Mansion House and Number Ten so that each has advance warning of the other's remarks and can, if necessary, refer to them without having to do so off-the-cuff.

It tickled my deplorable sense of humour to think that this time, without either party knowing, I might have a hand in both speeches which would then be swapped as usual, while I had copies of each in my briefcase. This duly happened. Over lunch Mrs Thatcher mentioned she had received the Lord Mayor's speech.

'All right?' I inquired, casually.

'Yes,' she replied. 'Oddly enough it's not unlike your style.'

'Fancy,' I said.

Well, such things can cheer one up on a dull day.

Another diverting interlude was the unveiling of the statue to Earl Mountbatten on Horseguards Parade at which Monarch and Premier were to speak for the first time from the same platform. When I was asked to help the PM with her short speech – apparently the first draft wasn't 'her' – it was clear that a little discreet one-upmanship was involved on both sides.

Despite rumours to the contrary the relationship between the two most important ladies in the land, whilst remaining formal, was never unfriendly. It was of course the first time that the Queen had dealt with a Prime Minister of her own sex, but she was far too experienced to allow this to influence her attitude to the first Minister of the Crown. There was, however, a certain professional rivalry of which on this occasion, and to my considerable amusement, I became aware.

To avoid duplication, speeches were to be exchanged between the Palace and Downing Street and the Queen's speech had already arrived at Number Ten. As Mountbatten was the Queen's cousin her speech referred to him informally, not once but several times, as 'Uncle Dickie', whilst in the first draft prepared for the Prime Minister he was referred to as 'The Earl Mountbatten of Burma'. After the fourth or fifth 'Earl Mountbatten of Burma' I felt that this mouthful was overdoing the formality to the point of indigestion and, incidentally, handing the laurel wreath to Her Majesty on a plate.

I racked my brains for a counter-ploy. One might perhaps begin, by way of apology for presuming to co-star with one's sovereign, by quoting Lobengula, Chief of the Matabele tribe, who once addressed Queen Victoria: 'We who are but the lice on the edge of Your Majesty's blanket.' No, on second thoughts, perhaps not.

Suddenly, I remembered that in the war Mountbatten, who was nothing if not a populist, liked to be known to forces and civilians alike as plain 'Lord Louis' (if a lord can ever be said to be plain).

And so it came to pass that in the draft of the Prime Minister's speech Mrs Thatcher referred casually to 'Lord Louis, as everyone came to know him', and thereafter it was 'Lord Louis' here, 'Lord Louis' there, 'Lord Louis' all the way. By the time she came to the fifth 'Lord Louis' you felt that Mountbatten and Thatcher had been bosom pals and would have danced many a night away at Ciro's in the twenties if only Margaret had been around at the time and liked dancing.

All this, whilst not the most momentous affair of state in which I was privileged to carry a spear, added briefly to the gaiety of the nation and after the two ladies had spoken I was gratified to note that the result was held to be a draw.

Not only public speech had its special refinements. From the beginning

I had called her 'Margaret' or 'dear' or even, on occasion, 'love'. I meant no disrespect but not being on the strength and having worked with her for more than four years before she became PM I felt that our relationship, like the one with the United States, if less seismic, was also special and except when the Great and the Good were present I was determined not to be formal merely because she had changed her address.

When I asked her Diary Secretary, the unflappable Caroline, what she called her employer she said, 'It depends. If she's being good I call her Prime Minister. When she annoys me it's Mrs Thatcher.'

It was in John Hoskyns' office at Number Ten, when he was head of the Policy Unit, that TLNFT first surfaced.

Seated on opposite sides of his desk we were playing around with sections of the Brighton '80 Conference speech. I scribbled it on a scrap of paper to see how it looked before pushing it across to him. We had been discussing the need for something that might fit a headline space. Not too short, not too long, crisp and easily remembered for maybe an hour or so or even, hopefully, a day or two.

He glanced at it and said in a neutral voice, 'Try it,' and went on with what he was doing. I was equally neutral. If he'd shot it down I wouldn't have fought for it. I wasn't even sure that the title of the play it parodied would be remembered. John said, 'It won't matter if it isn't.' I wasn't sure about that either.

Later that evening after dinner in the flat the PM, D.T., Hoskyns and I went into the sitting room for coffee and I read her a part of the draft for Brighton. When I came to it she suddenly leant forward and turned to Denis for his reaction but he, wise man, had fallen asleep over the evening paper. (His attitude to speeches, and Party Conference speeches in particular, was to switch off whenever possible.) She made no comment so I carried on reading the rest of the draft.

During the speech on the final afternoon at Brighton I was not expecting any special reaction but when she said: 'To those waiting with bated breath for that favourite media catchphrase, the U-turn, I've only one thing to say. "You turn if you want to. The lady's not for turning", the response was immediate, people glancing at one another as they do when something has suddenly registered and they want to see if their neighbour has taken the measure of it and, if so, to share it.

I thought if the media latched on to the phrase it would be the play on 'U-turn' that they'd go for. In fact they went for the second

sentence and they were, of course, right. 'All great soundbites happen
by accident,' one, says Peggy Noonan. If 'Not for Turning' is, by
great good fortune, one, then as usual Noonan is correct.

I had not consciously asked myself 'What truly typifies Thatcher?
What is the essence of the lady?' Had I done so I might have written
'Once I make up my mind, that's it'. Or 'A conviction politician
doesn't waver or backtrack. She hangs in there and sees it through.'
Or 'Once she's sure, she holds rock-hard to her beliefs'. I might have
put on paper any of a dozen other ways of saying the same thing
and settled for one of them, but it wouldn't have been a soundbite
because none of them has the punch that turns the prosaic into the
definitive and, if you're very very lucky, the not-to-be-forgotten.

Driving back from Brighton with Hoskyns and his wife Miranda I
was astonished to hear the 'Turning' line quoted over and over on
the car radio and even more surprised to hear an experienced political
columnist come on the air and refer to it as 'a good little one-liner'.
No. One-liners are the stuff of a Bob Hope or Victor Borge variety
turn. The best are brilliant but they are not soundbites. They have
no internal life of their own. They don't spring naturally out of a
speech, they are superimposed upon it. A soundbite can't be stuck
on like a stamp.

TLNFT has stood the test of time precisely because it's *not* a one-
liner. In itself it's quite unremarkable but it sprang freshly minted
out of the text and caught on because it pinned the lady's character
down in five short words. It *was* Thatcher and was instantly seen to
be her by the public. I might add that I had not the remotest idea,
when I parodied the title of Christopher Fry's fine play by substituting
'turning' for 'burning', that those five short words would be the
headlines in five national newspapers the following morning; nor
that it in turn would be parodied and come to haunt me down the
years. It seems that the lady is also not for 'spurning, learning,
yearning, returning', not to mention 'vanishing, banishing, cleaving,
deceiving, hissing and kissing'. The last of these is certainly true.

One day at Chequers when, as ever, the first fine careless rapture of
an election victory had passed and the political weather clouded over,
Hoskyns, David Wolfson, her Chief of Staff at Number Ten, and I
were discussing with the PM some way of the four of us getting
together informally on a regular basis that wouldn't call for another
speech or a fixed agenda or a special niche in the hopelessly over-
crowded diary but would enable us to kick the political football
around, foresee trouble and hopefully forestall it and maybe come up

with one or two fresh ideas in a relaxed atmosphere.

Various suggestions were advanced as to when, where and how this could come about and finally Sunday nights at Number Ten were settled on as the most likely time and place. The Prime Minister usually returned to Downing Street from her weekend at Chequers around 9.00 p.m. on Sunday evenings but she said, 'I'll drive back around six and we'll meet in the flat and discuss whatever's in the wind that looks threatening or promising. Now let's see, what about food? I know. I'll bring sandwiches from Chequers and we can eat and talk without bothering with a proper meal. How's that?'

We agreed and she became quite excited at the prospect of still more work to fill the teeming twenty-four-hour day.

Nothing came of it. Something cropped up the very next Sunday and killed the idea before it could take off and the Sunday after that she had a couple of weekend commitments that simply couldn't be broken and somehow the Sunday Night Sandwich Scheme drifted away to wherever political plans that are aborted at birth do drift. Once in a while one or other of us would make a tentative attempt at resurrecting it but without any real belief that it would materialise.

When she heard about it Caroline Stephens, wearing her Diary Secretary hat and already fighting a losing battle against having every minute of the day, and frequently night, spoken for, said: 'It's a non-starter. Won't happen. Forget it.' It was and it didn't and we did.

Might subsequent events have never happened either, if three men and a woman had been able to meet regularly and anticipate, say, the stormclouds of the Community Charge and disperse them before they reached hurricane force? I doubt it, although smaller things have changed the course of history.

Hoskyns was a joy to work with. Like many fundamentally serious people he found it necessary to laugh a good deal. (Asked by a fellow officer from his army days what he was doing now, John said, 'I work for Mrs Thatcher.' To which he received the jolly reply, 'I say, you must be the most frightful shit!') He also shared my view that there was no political problem that could not be helped to a solution over a relaxed dinner at the Travellers' or Brooks's. However, at the Blackpool Conference of October '81, what began as a minor problem suddenly blew up a storm, proved incapable of solution and most regrettably became the final straw that had a lot to do with Hoskyns leaving Downing Street.

The speech had been largely agreed when Clive Whitmore, the

Private Secretary at the time (always a civil servant, never a Party appointment), sitting quietly in a corner murmured gently, 'Do you really want to hit Labour quite so hard, Prime Minister?'

'No!' she cried instantly. 'No, I don't!' And glared first at John and then at me.

A considerable argument ensued in which Whitmore, a first-class man with humorous eyes, who had done no more than offer a tentative comment and even this with no great fervour, took no part but the remark had evidently sparked the Prime Minister who was going through one of those periods when she was under attack for so-called 'extremism' (an idea that was a nonsense) and she grasped eagerly at Whitmore's interjection.

The result was far-reaching. Much of the draft was discarded and a new one written, not by us. It did not fail – nothing Mrs Thatcher did ever failed with the faithful – but for the first time with a Conference speech the press was indifferent to poor.

Worse still, as I walked back along the front to our hotel with Hoskyns and his wife, John, who had been more and more disturbed by what he saw as the PM's increasing tendency towards caution, said, 'I'm afraid that does it. I shall resign.' I had heard this before and brushed it aside but Miranda said, 'No, this time he means it.' What happened at Blackpool was not the only reason for John's departure but it was the crunch.

Although they frequently differed in their approach to politics, the PM was most reluctant to lose the bold and original thinker who was the head of her Policy Unit and asked one or two of us who were close to him, like David Wolfson and myself, to try and dissuade John from leaving but he was adamant and made his reasons clear. Margaret was characteristically generous, recommending him for a knighthood and giving him a fine farewell dinner in the State dining room at which she said how much she regretted his going and what a unique job he had done. ('You brought a whole new dimension to our thinking.')

Number Ten's loss was the Institute of Directors' gain. Hoskyns became their Director-General. The reason for his resignation was not the PM's presumed extremism but, on the contrary, her increasingly moderate approach of which the Blackpool speech of '81 was a classic example. 'There be dragons out there!' Yes, but in her third year in office she was not in the slaying mood and for Hoskyns it removed the reason for his having taken the job in the first place.

His successor as head of the Policy Unit was the witty, diffident, and charming Old Etonian Ferdinand Mount. As a highly regarded professional journalist Ferdy knew all about deadlines. The result was, come Election '83 he was ahead of the game, producing lively first drafts of key sections of several of the Prime Minister's speeches before the 'off'. But I remember him most for the high comedy of 'Ferdy and the Alka-Seltzers'.

We were in the small dining room at Number Ten at work on yet another Conference speech (Brighton '82) when Ferdy suddenly started to sneeze. This went on for several minutes until Margaret said, 'Ferdy, you've got a nasty cold.' Mount mumbled a diffident denial. 'Well, if you haven't, you're about to have one. Now there's only one thing to nip a headcold in the bud. Alka-Seltzer,' and she ran upstairs to the flat and down again.

'There. Take three of these.'

'No, really, I'd rather not.'

'As a precaution, dear.'

'I'm all right, truly.'

'You don't look all right.' And she dropped three white discs into a glass of water and watched them fizz before handing the glass to Ferdy. Like a prep-school matron to the newest of the new boys she ordered, 'Get them down you right away, and it won't be long before you feel quite different.' It wasn't. Half an hour later she inquired, 'Better now?'

'Well, no, actually,' said Ferdy with even more diffidence than usual. He looked ghastly. 'I'm afraid I must go home at once,' and was on his way before any further precautionary prophylactics could be forced upon him.

The PM looked mystified. 'I've never known them fail before. He must be sickening for something serious. Let's hope it's not infectious.' And she dropped two more discs into another glass of water and thrust it at me. 'Just a precaution.'

A delightful man, Ferdy Mount, but running the Policy Unit was not a literary pursuit and, to everyone's regret, he opted to return to the polished political column for which he was famous. (Later he became editor of *The Times Literary Supplement* which has done the TLS nothing but good.)

Come the '83 election I had been working for Mrs Thatcher for more than eight years and we had become close friends. But in the political forest no relationship is roses all the way...

The last big rally a few days before polling day was the Conservative Youth-cum-Showbiz gathering at Wembley. I saw it on TV while waiting to record her final television broadcast of the campaign in a secret makeshift studio in the West End. I was taken aback. The showbiz element was overdoing the hysteria and Margaret's exploding bouffant was over the top in more senses than one. I said to her favourite hair-and-make-up girl, 'You see that hairdo. Do get her out of it as soon as she arrives.' The girl said, 'I can't, it's lacquered. I'd have to wash it.'

'Then wash it, love, for goodness' sake!'

'There won't be time for it to dry and set.'

This was ominous. Women's hair, like their clothes, can be soft and soothing or striking and provocative, the outer image signalling the inner mood. There was no doubt which mood Wembley was signalling.

When Margaret arrived with Ian Gow at the largely unfurnished building hired by Tim Bell of Saatchi's in Maddox Street off Regent Street for recording the broadcast, my worst fears were confirmed. She was on the wrong sort of high, the adrenalin pumping furiously. The hysterical Wembley hoop-de-do, not her style at all, had roused her fighting spirit to an alarming level, her hair made her look formidable rather than appealing, her dress was a harsh, importunate blue and she was making waves of a distinctly combative nature.

'Now then,' she said briskly, sitting down opposite me to tea and cakes with Ian, Tim and Gordon Reece. 'The final political. What have you got? What's it about?' Her tone was militant, aggressive.

'Actually it's not so much about specific political items,' I said, doing my damnedest to coo like a dove, 'it's more of a mood piece.'

'Ha!' she said, thumping her handbag and turning to Gow sarcastically. 'What did I tell you? Ronnie will want me to do a *"mood"* piece, I said.'

'That's right,' I murmured in my Owl-to-Eeyore voice which was probably a mistake. She picked up intonations fast.

'Well, go on, then,' she said, for once not shading her eyes but glaring at me. 'Let's have it.'

At this moment a Salvation Army band appeared at the top of Maddox Street, blasting flat out as it marched along Regent Street summoning the godless to deliverance. I waited. Mrs Thatcher, though devout, looked for a moment positively pagan. In this atmosphere, I thought, 'Never in the field of human conflict' would have fallen flat. Finally I read what I had written and waited for the demolition job to begin. I was not disappointed.

'No! No!! No!!!' she flew at me. 'The end's not all that bad and there's a couple of paragraphs at the beginning but as for the rest – I want facts, not moods. Facts, facts, facts!' The words poured out of her. 'Facts about housing, facts about the economy, facts about the NHS – more nurses, more doctors, more dentists! More of everything! That's what we've given the country and we're entitled to remind people and ask for their support.'

'But, Margaret,' I pleaded, 'we've been reminding them for the past three weeks. They're up to their ears in facts. Don't you feel one can have too much of a good thing?'

'No, I don't,' she said curtly. 'We have an excellent record, let's spell it out. I don't know what you're after.'

'A little warmth, perhaps? A little night music?'

'Night music? Night music? This is the final Party Political before a General Election and you want me to give them *night music*?' I could see if we'd been in the flat she'd have reached for the Alka-Seltzer.

'I was speaking figuratively.'

'Listen, we're heading for the finishing-post. We want people cheering and shouting "Maggie, Maggie, Maggie!" My word, you should have heard them at Wembley.'

'I did.'

'Well, there you are, then.'

'I thought it was vulgar.'

'You what?'

'I'm afraid I didn't like it at all. That comedian shouting "Let's bomb Russia". You shouldn't be associated with that sort of thing.'

'For heaven's sake, it was a joke!'

'In very poor taste.'

'Well, *really!*'

'Believe me, that's not the way to win votes. In fact it could cost you quite a few.'

Fortunately at that moment the make-up girl appeared. 'I'm coming, dear.'

She turned to me, 'I'm sorry but it won't do,' and then to Gow, 'Ronnie's gone wobbly, you'd better find a rewrite man' and she disappeared into the make-up room.

I realised I had gone over the top but – more *dentists*? Hell's teeth, they're indispensable and no doubt out of office hours as lovable as a thousand-and-one dalmatians, but that whoops-a-daisy chair, those hypnotic instruments of torture they thrust into your oral cavity while making conversation so that if you try to answer you choke to death, always assuming you haven't been dehydrated by that insatiable saliva sucker – what was she after, the masochist vote?

Ian cast about for a non-wobbly wordsmith and eventually came up with Brian Walden. After three weeks covering and writing about the election, Walden had been on the town, celebrating with profound relief that the damn thing was just about over before returning home and falling into a deep sleep from which he had been woken with difficulty.

When he finally arrived around midnight he looked wobblier than anyone, staring around him at this strange building, almost devoid of furniture, in which he found himself as though he had no idea where he was or what he was doing there. Strong black coffee was poured down him and eventually a sort of mishmash central section of the broadcast was devised by the two of us. Meanwhile the make-up girl had done a brilliant job on the PM, washing and resetting her hair in record time, shading the flaming cheeks with a delicate pink blush and substituting a sympathetic soft grey dress for the turbulent blue.

The effect on the lady's temperament was immediate. All aggression gone, she emerged gracious and emollient and immediately agreed to record both versions, the original and the mishmash. The mishmash was broadcast.

A few days later Tim Bell ran a video of both for that fine actor and my good friend Anthony Quayle, who had seen neither, without telling Tony which was which. Without hesitation he chose the original.*

* Party Political Broadcasts are a contentious subject. I am indebted to Bill Deedes, former editor of the *Daily Telegraph* and longtime friend and golfing partner of Denis Thatcher, for the following:
'A Member of a Polish ecology party, given five minutes airtime for a Party Political Broadcast, declared: "*I cannot think of what to say. So I will ask my two daughters to sing to you.*"' Now there's an idea for Central Office.

16

. . . .

Luck be a Lady

'Luck be a lady tonight
Never get out of my sight . . . '
Frank Loesser, *Guys and Dolls*

'I wasn't lucky, I deserved it.'
Margaret Thatcher, aged nine,
on receiving a prize for poetry

It's doubtful if Margaret would ever agree that she was lucky. She would say, I'm sure, in that crisp, confident tone of hers, that people make their own luck through hard work. She would acknowledge that she was fortunate on occasions when a successful outcome was essential, but that was only right and proper, being the result of meticulous preparation.

Well, perhaps. Nevertheless a thread of uncovenanted good fortune did run through her life from the beginning. Indeed it played an important part in her receiving a higher education.

Born over a grocer's shop in Grantham, Lincolnshire, of a strict ex-Liberal Methodist father who became Mayor of his home town and a conventional domesticated mother who served behind the counter, Margaret Hilda Roberts went from elementary to grammar school with no particular distinction. However, hard-working and determined to escape from the limiting environment into which she was born and make a way for herself in the wider world, she set her sights on going to university and to Somerville College, Oxford, in particular.

With encouragement from her father she sat the entrance exam at the age of seventeen, hoping for a scholarship and intending to read chemistry. She failed but her name was put on a waiting list in the vague hope that a place might become vacant at some future date. Bitterly disappointed, she went back to school. However, as luck would have it, a place became vacant almost at once and in October 1943 she was off to Oxford and a whole new life.

*

After four years at Somerville, a Second in chemistry, a spell as a research chemist and a period at the Bar specialising in tax cases, she decided on a political career and at a Dartford constituency meeting met and subsequently married Denis Thatcher, a successful businessman.

She twice fought Dartford, a safe Labour seat, but struck lucky when in 1959 the Conservative MP for Finchley stood down. The selection committee stipulated that to be successful the new candidate must live within forty miles of the London suburb. It so happened the Thatchers had just bought a house near Farnborough in Kent that precisely met that requirement. Within weeks of becoming an MP luck was with her again. She came second in the draw for the Private Member's Bills which decided in what order they should be introduced. The luck of the draw led to an early maiden speech in support of her Bill (to give the press access to local Council meetings). The speech was hailed as being of 'front-bench quality' and brought the new Member for Finchley immediately to the attention of the Party hierarchy.

Her rapid advance up the political tree, first to a junior post on the Opposition Front Bench and then via Pensions, Housing, Energy, Transport, Education and Environment to the Shadow Cabinet, was undoubtedly due to a first-class political brain and sheer hard work. But Keith Joseph's unhappy speech at Edgbaston, which led to his decision not to stand for the leadership of the Conservative Party and to Margaret Thatcher doing so in his place, was yet another stroke of luck that was to make her the first woman in British history with the key to Downing Street.

The economy the new Prime Minister inherited was in bad shape. There were no overnight miracles to be wrought and the political honeymoon was brief. By March 1980 Labour was ahead in the polls and the first by-election of the Thatcher Government, at Southend, reduced the Conservative majority from 10,774 to a bare 430. The Government's unpopularity ran on into 1981 and remained so throughout the year, with the Liberals winning the Croydon by-election and Shirley Williams taking Crosby for the SDP with a majority of more than five thousand over the Tory candidate. Then fortune intervened. 'Give me generals who are lucky,' said Napoleon. To which Mrs Thatcher might well have added, 'And give the enemy generals who are not.'

On 2 April 1982 General Leopoldo Galtieri, the Fascist leader of Argentina, launched an attack on one of the British Falkland Islands in the South Atlantic – the remote and virtually uninhabited island of South Georgia – and ran up the Argentine flag. Within days Port Stanley, the Falklands capital, had fallen, the Governor had surrendered, a British task force was mobilised and the first ships, packed with troops, were on their way. After some initial hesitation – she was never gung-ho about this expedition as has been suggested, she was never gung-ho about anything – this immediate and, to many, astonishing response by the Government was the first major test of Margaret Thatcher as Prime Minister. Fully briefed, and indeed encouraged, by the First Sea Lord, Sir Henry Leach – 'If we don't [do it] or if we do it half-heartedly and are not completely successful,' he told her, 'we shall be living in a different country, which counts for very much less' – she took a tremendous gamble, sending some twenty-seven thousand men and valuable warships of the Royal Navy halfway across the world without full air cover or a nearby base with which to supply them.

On the liberation of a handful of British subjects and the recovery of a remote piece of British soil depended not only national pride and dignity but the survival of the Government. It could have gone dreadfully wrong, but the luck that was Margaret Thatcher's time and again throughout her political life was with her, and she was at her embattled best. She was working with warriors. Being by nature one herself, they spoke the same language and although they were not always in agreement she developed a strong affinity with the Service chiefs which had built up during regular contact over NATO and Northern Ireland.

Top brass tend to come straight to the point. So does she. Advice was given, accepted or rejected, that was that. There was seldom prolonged debate, as with politicians. Scientifically trained, she could discuss the X rifle, the Y tank, the Z aircraft with some fluency and, once she had done her homework, almost on equal terms. For a woman to be able to do this was, in the climate of the period, remarkable.

During the Falklands campaign, fired by the Navy's involvement, for the first and almost the only time that we worked together I sent in some unsolicited material which she used for her annual speech to the Conservative Women's Conference in the Queen Elizabeth Hall. Half an hour before she was due to make that speech, word came that the destroyer HMS *Sheffield* had been hit amidships by a French Exocet missile and was sinking, with twenty seamen's lives lost already. I was with her in the study when the news came through.

She made no sound, just stood with her body half turned away, fists clenched, struggling for control. Then, almost but not quite silently, she was weeping.

We cut the forty-minute speech to less than twenty. Wearing black and outwardly composed, she spoke calmly and well. At the end, instead of the usual triumphalist gestures, both hands held aloft like a victorious boxer which had become her trademark in response to applause, she gave an odd little bow, left, right and left again, hands straight down by her sides, to check any untoward enthusiasm from her audience and sat down quickly. She was deeply emotional but it was controlled emotion (just) and the jerky little bow was strangely moving.

Like cold water to a thirsty soul, so is good news from
a far country.
Proverbs 25, v. 25

The Falklands factor did not of itself win the 1983 election, she was beginning to move up again politically before it began, but Galtieri's scalp at her belt was hardly a handicap. The Iron Lady was established as a powerful national leader, a good person to have at the helm in a crisis.

In due course, to the Argentine's scalp was added another nearer home. She had not forgotten what had brought about the defeat of Edward Heath's Government, of which she had been a member, in the General Election of February '74. It was the miners' strike. When, ten years and one month later, on 5 March 1984, the miners under Arthur Scargill struck again, she was ready.

She knew that this was the battle that others had either lost or run away from and that if her government was to survive she must win. The Heath Government's indecision, an on-off-on election, the failure to stockpile sufficient oil and coal in advance to keep the factories turning and the home fires burning were the clearest possible lesson for the Thatcher Government not to do likewise. The lesson was learnt. This time oil and coal from overseas had been imported in bulk and stacked in readiness for a miners' strike if and when it came. She was fortunate to have had her predecessor's experience to guide her, if only in what *not* to do.

Again she was lucky in her adversary. Not only was Arthur Scargill not a popular figure except in the mining industry; for one of her temperament he was the ideal opponent. Violence, mass picketing and intimidation were not weapons she was prepared to accept and, as with the Falklands, her utter determination to gain the day against brute force carried the majority of the people with her.

Although Ian MacGregor, the tough Scots Chairman of the National Coal Board, and Peter Walker, the Secretary of State for Energy, did not always see coalface to coalface she managed to keep them both on her side throughout the many twists and turns of the year-long strike.

During that year I found myself invited to a number of private and confidential dinners that took place at, of all locations, Claridge's Hotel, where one David Hart, a wealthy, right-wing, rumbustious character who was fascinated by the political struggle and whom I had known for some time, had set up camp. Invariably present was Ian MacGregor, to whom I took an immediate liking and whose ex-officio, unappointed and exceedingly impromptu man-in-the-field Hart appeared to be.

Sporting dirty old jeans and a deliberately mud-bespattered face by way of disguise, the streetwise ex-Etonian would set off, at some risk to life and limb, for the scene of skirmishes between the police and the more violent of the Scargill miners and report back. He had a strong theatrical streak and, I think, saw himself as a kind of Blue Pimpernel.

But it's easy to mock. David did a useful job during the miners' strike. While his visits to the scenes of violent conflict were his own idea and in no way inspired by the Prime Minister, he would keep her informed by telephone (by a circuitous route which at times included my flat) and give detailed information to her as well as to MacGregor from what was in effect the front line. He also helped to finance the breakaway Nottinghamshire miners, picking up the tab for experienced legal advice which the Nottinghamshire men badly needed but could not afford.

An unorthodox and complex character, Hart was in constant danger of arrest for trying to be helpful. The result was often confused and hilarious. Although it was plain to me that he was on the side of the angels this was not always as clear to strangers as it might have been and on one occasion I had some difficulty convincing Special Branch that he was neither my chauffeur nor a triple agent.

The result of the miners' strike depended finally on the resolution and willpower of the Prime Minister to hold fast and withstand the heat of the day. When, on 5 March 1985, after exactly twelve months, the NUM Conference voted 98 to 91 for a return to work, Margaret Thatcher had passed the second major test of her premiership.

Harold Macmillan's dictum 'Never upset the Treasury, the Vatican or the National Union of Mineworkers' she had clearly seen as a challenge. Upsetting the Treasury was always a pleasure. ('As its First Lord it's for the Treasury not to upset me.') Now she had seen off the NUM. That left the Pope. One could only pray that the devout Catholic was taking precautions.

Since the result of General Elections depends not only on the present but on people's memories of the recent past, trouncing Arthur Scargill did her no harm politically. However, on the day the miners went back to work the teachers came out on strike. In deciding to remain in the wings, I reflected, rather than set foot formally upon the greasy pole, I may not have been entirely foolish.

In the early morning of 12 October 1984, I was in the sitting room of the Prime Minister's suite in the Grand Hotel, Brighton. The sitting room faced the sea. The final draft of the Conference speech was agreed and we gathered our papers. I glanced out of the windows at the promenade where the night police patrol strolled up and down. All was quiet and still, the sea calm. I looked at my watch. It was coming up to 3.10 a.m.

When the other writers had gone, leaving only John Gummer, who was Chairman of the Party at the time, and myself, I saw she was still tinkering with the text of the speech as Robin Butler, the Private Secretary, came in.

I said, 'Do go to bed, dear. It's all right, I promise you.'

She said, 'I'm going,' and put the speech down. 'I just have this one paper to sign for Robin.'

I went out, waved goodnight to the secretaries in the room immediately opposite and made my way along the corridor. As I started up the staircase to my room on the floor above there was a violent explosion. I was flung against the wall and down a few steps. My briefcase went flying and burst open, scattering the contents in all directions.

Curious how one reacts at such a time. All I could think of was 'My God! The speech!' That people might be dying and that in any case there were at least a dozen copies in the secretaries' room did not enter my mind. I went down on my hands and knees, feverishly gathering the scattered pages of the final draft and shovelling them into my briefcase. Then I hobbled back down the corridor, bruised and shaken but otherwise intact.

There were no cries for help, no sound at all, just dust, clouds of dust, followed by the occasional crunch of falling masonry from somewhere above. Otherwise silence. It was eerie.

As I approached the Prime Minister came out of her sitting room, crossed the corridor and went into the secretaries' room opposite. When I followed she was sitting on an upright chair, very still. The girls were standing on chairs peering out of a side window, bubbling with excitement. I just stood, quiet as a stone.

At length she murmured, 'I think that was an assassination attempt, don't you?' What does one say at such a moment to such a question? I decided it was rhetorical. It was clear that a bomb had gone off, later acknowledged to be the work of the IRA. This year I had been given a room on the same side of the hotel as the Prime Minister's suite, directly in line overhead but five floors up. In the past I had always been along the corridor from her suite on the same floor, as I had to be in and out of my room for reference books and notebooks and the lift was constantly in use which would have meant long waits and time wasted.

When I had found on arrival that I was five floors up I had protested to Reception who said they were sorry but the rooms had been fixed by Central Office, who had as usual been instructed to give priority to the officials of the Party and their wives. I had continued to remonstrate but to no avail until Tim Bell and Gordon Reece, who happened to be near and heard what was going on, said 'Leave it to us.' Evidently they pulled the right strings because my room had been changed to one on the floor above the PM's *but on the other side of the staircase.*

The switch almost certainly saved my life, for the bomb had been a delayed-action device planted in the sixth-floor bathroom immediately above the room that would have been mine.

There was a delay of some forty minutes before we were allowed to leave the building. Presumably this was to make sure that no IRA sharpshooter was waiting on an adjoining rooftop. But what if there were other bombs in the hotel? Indeed, at one point we were told that there were. I mentioned this, first to Michael Alison, her PPS, and then to Bob and Barry, her two Special Branch men who had been with her since she had become Leader. Although they, more than anyone, knew the danger of the Prime Minister remaining in the hotel they could do nothing; security was in the hands of the Brighton police.

Finally all of us – the Prime Minister, her husband, writers, secretaries and the rest of her immediate entourage – went down the main staircase, most of which was still standing, through the front hall, picking our way over the rubble and down another staircase to the kitchens and out through a back door. The Prime Minister's car was drawn up immediately outside. She and Denis got in and the car drove off at speed. The rest of us had been told to wait and eventually a minibus appeared and everyone got in. As I was about to do so Alan Watkins of the *Observer* appeared. He had not been in the hotel but was clearly appalled at what had happened and asked about casualties. I told him that I knew nothing of casualties, that it was all strangely quiet inside the hotel. (There had in fact been five deaths, among them John Wakeham's wife, and serious injury to several others: Wakeham himself, Norman Tebbit and, above all, his wife Margaret.) Watkins was no Thatcher supporter but at that moment we were as one in the face of a murderous attack.

We drove off in the minibus with no clear idea where we were going but eventually found ourselves at Brighton police station. There we were taken down to the basement, past some cells and into a kind of empty storeroom where no one seemed to understand who or what we were except that we'd come from the Grand Hotel. We were given cups of lukewarm chocolate which made me feel sick and asked to sign our names and occupations in a ledger. These the police examined closely and apparently discovered with complete surprise that we were part of the Prime Minister's staff. This caused a stir and we were immediately whisked into a lift and up to the top floor of the police station where we found Mrs Thatcher and Denis, Geoffrey Howe and his wife Elspeth, Leon Brittan who was Home Secretary and John Gummer, the Party Chairman.

Gradually we were joined by other members of the Cabinet. Keith Joseph, immaculate in a Noël Coward dressing gown over his silk pyjamas, was the only one, so far as I could see, who had remembered his red Cabinet despatch box. He had been discovered sitting on it on the promenade immediately opposite the hotel staring calmly out to sea, which I thought was intellectual, sophisticated and entirely apropos for a Fellow of All Souls.

Tepid tea was handed round. There was desultory muttering and a general feeling of bewilderment. No one seemed to know how long we would be there or where we would be going. Into this atmosphere of uncertainty there suddenly strode the commanding and immensely reassuring figure of Charles Price, the United States Ambassador, a handsome giant of a man.

'Charlie!' cried Mrs Thatcher in the tones of Lady Bracknell at a tea party taken aback to find someone she hadn't invited. 'What are you doing here?' The popular Ambassador, who had been staying at the next-door hotel, the Imperial, assumed his most ambassadorial demeanour.

'Prime Minister, I have a message from your friend President

Reagan,' he said gravely. 'He sends you his deepest sympathy and his profound relief that you are safe.'

'Ah, how kind,' murmured Mrs Thatcher, taking the Ambassador's tone and seemed about to say more but he held up his hand.

'The President wants you to know,' he continued even more gravely and choosing his words with care, 'that after due consideration and giving the matter the most careful thought he has come to the conclusion that Mondale is not too old to run.' (Walter Mondale was Reagan's opponent in his campaign for re-election. The President had been under fire from sections of the American press for being too old for the job.)

For a second Mrs Thatcher seemed about to point out that the Ambassador or the President or both had got it the wrong way round but there was an immediate burst of laughter from everyone else and just in time she joined in.

The Ambassador's quip, delivered deadpan, was just what was needed to ease the tension. Two things occurred to me. First, that Ambassador Price had the ability of great actors who can make people laugh in the face of tragedy. Second, that in a crisis the British make tea, the Americans make wisecracks. Which, come to think of it, says something about the special relationship.

The current Political Secretary at Number Ten, Stephen Sherbourne, the secretaries and I now waited for over two hours in a bus outside Brighton police station to be taken to Lewes, the headquarters of the Sussex Police. It was cold. Some optimist had left the sunshine roof open. Penny Gummer arrived in her nightgown with no other clothing and no husband, looking bewildered. Sherbourne gallantly whipped off his jacket and put it round her. Walter Raleigh could not have done more. Stephen's tall, thin build and unobtrusive manner concealed a nice sense of the absurd and a keen political brain.

Finally we drove off to Lewes where the Prime Minister had already arrived, gone straight to bed for a couple of hours and was fast asleep. Extraordinary woman, I thought for the umpteenth time.

As we got out of the bus it was reassuring to see police commandos with rifles behind practically every blade of grass. We were each asked in turn if we'd like to see a doctor. We all declined.

They offered us bunks usually occupied by the police cadets who were trained at Lewes but there was no time for sleep. I went with Sherbourne and the secretaries over to the administration office, where typewriters and photocopiers were put at our disposal, and we

303

began to try and reshape the original speech which would obviously require a major rewrite in the light of what had happened. The secretaries worked nobly and cheerfully through what remained of the night as we cut and rearranged and dictated. None of us was sure that there would be a speech but I couldn't see the PM departing from her rule: 'Whatever happens, business as usual'.

After a huge breakfast in the police canteen – I learnt in the war that danger causes hunger – we went back to Mrs Thatcher's small room where she was up and watching reports coming in on the television. There was much telephoning with Willie Whitelaw, her deputy, about whether the speech should go ahead as planned. Opinions were divided. With five thousand people in the hall security would be a nightmare but, as I thought, she was determined to proceed as though nothing had happened.

At eight-thirty we piled into two cars and a bus. The entire Lewes police staff were lined up to wave us goodbye and good luck as we headed back to the conference hall at Brighton. As we strode quickly through the concourse and into the hall, the first debate of the final day had started. Ironically it was about Northern Ireland, with the Northern Ireland Ministers, including Douglas Hurd and Chris Patten, on the platform.

The moment the small audience recognised the Prime Minister it rose and burst into applause. We hurried backstage without stopping and into a small room where she, Robin Butler, Sherbourne and I continued to work on the revised speech.

There were a couple of interruptions. At about eleven, Harvey Thomas, a huge man who had been Billy Graham's organiser for his mass religious meetings before becoming Presentations Director at Central Office and whom we heard had fallen six floors and been killed, walked in.

M.T.: 'My God! We thought you were dead!'

Harvey: 'Well, no, actually. You see, my wife's just had a baby and I couldn't very well cash in my chips after that.'

Work on the speech resumed. At noon a secretary popped her head round the door and said, 'Excuse me, Prime Minister, but four Bishops have arrived.'

M.T.: 'Whatever for?'

Secretary: 'To convey their sympathies.'

M.T.: 'Good Lord!'

R.M.: 'Precisely.'

M.T.: 'What a nuisance. I mean, how kind. All the same, there's really no time for ... I suppose I'll have to see them. Where can I put on a new face?'

The rest of us withdrew while the Prime Minister applied powder and lipstick in the nearest lavatory, finally emerging to receive the Bishop of Lewes, the Bishop of Chichester, the Bishop of Brighton and Arundel and the Bishop of Winchester. After comfort and consolation a quick sandwich lunch followed and then the speech.

As Margaret came on to the platform the five thousand rose and roared their relief that she was alive. It was a moment of high emotion. The speech was a triumph of triumphs but it wouldn't have mattered if she'd read the Yellow Pages, she was alive and safe. Five close friends had died and others were injured but the principal target and her Cabinet had survived.

After the speech Stephen and I waited outside the Royal Sussex Hospital while the Thatchers visited the injured, including John Wakeham and Norman Tebbit and his wife, a woman, like her husband, of immense courage who was seriously crippled. All three were exceedingly fortunate to be alive.

And so, at last, by car to Downing Street. The two Special Branch men had gone bravely back into the hotel which was largely gutted, picked their way over the rubble, rescued our luggage and brought it to Number Ten. There in the hall we collected it. I felt suddenly dehydrated and gulped two large glasses of water before heading, exhausted, for home.

Two days later I received the following note:

10 DOWNING STREET

24 October 1984
   Ronnie dear –
Just to say thank you for being with us at Brighton –
an experience that will remain with us for the rest of our
lives and which has cost our friends *so dear*.
Margaret

It was only then that I remembered Robin Butler coming into her sitting room at the hotel with a last-minute paper for her to sign. Had he not briefly delayed her she would have been in the bathroom, which lay between the sitting room of her suite and her bedroom, on her way to the bedroom at the moment the bathroom suffered a direct hit. It was the most blessed of all her strokes of luck.

Writing of 'the Scottish Play', Benedict Nightingale, the dramatic critic, vividly describes how 'On the night of Duncan's murder lamentings and strange screams of death were heard in the air and there was prophesying with accents terrible of dire combustion and confused events'.

So it was, or very nearly, with the Astonishing Affair of Michael Heseltine and the Helicopter Company, which in its final manifestation turned out to be as unpredictable and theatrically exciting as its flamboyant central character.

In the teeth of this phenomenon and Heseltine's sudden noonday exit from Downing Street the question that absorbed the nation in January 1986 was, would the Government survive? I put it another way: would the lady's luck hold good? Not being *parti pris* to any facts behind the facts, if such there were, I cannot comment on the tittle-tattle spiced with wishful thinking from Tom, or rather Tam, Dick and Harry current at the time, except to observe that, when challenged, not an iota of solid evidence, let alone politically inspired proof, ever emerged to substantiate the rumours swirling through Westminster and Whitehall. However I recall vividly the final eighteen hours or so before the crucial vote of confidence debate which brought the affair to a climax, having spent the greater part of them in Downing Street. But to begin at the beginning.

In the autumn of 1985 Westland, a comparatively small English company which made armed helicopters for the Ministry of Defence, found itself in financial difficulties and began negotiations to merge with the American Sikorsky company which was in the same line of business. At the same time Michael Heseltine, who was Secretary of State for Defence and passionately pro-Europe, was resolved that Westland should join a European consortium and began to pull the necessary strings that could bring such a union about.

However, of the two options the Government, through the Department of Trade and Industry (DTI) – Secretary of State Leon Brittan – preferred the American Sikorsky connection. The result was a clash between the two Secretaries of State, both senior members of the Cabinet, which by mid-December had become public property. There was a brief armistice over Christmas, after which guerrilla warfare between the two Cabinet Ministers was resumed. Almost at once the plot thickened. In early January a letter from Heseltine to the managing director of Lloyds' Merchant Bank appeared in *The Times* newspaper. In it the Defence Secretary claimed that Westland might lose European contracts if it joined forces with the American firm. Over the weekend Mrs Thatcher's Foreign Affairs Adviser, Charles Powell, informed the Chief Press Secretary, Bernard Ingham, that the Prime Minister was concerned about the accuracy of the Heseltine statement and that the Solicitor-General, Sir Patrick Mayhew, had been asked to look into the matter. In a confidential letter to Leon Brittan, as Minister responsible for Westland at the DTI, the Solicitor-General referred to 'material inaccuracies' in the Heseltine letter. The letter was to become political dynamite.

There are various versions of what happened next, some motivated by a desire for objective truth, others driven by a passion for Party advantage. It appears that at lunchtime on Monday 6 January, the DTI Head of Information informed Ingham by telephone that ministerial permission had been given to 'leak' the Solicitor-General's letter and asked Number Ten's advice as to how to proceed.

Ingham, in his vivid account of these events, regrets 'to this day' that he did not advise the Head of Information at DTI, the Secretary of State's permission notwithstanding, 'to have nothing to do with the ploy'. In the event, when the DTI released the letter containing the so-called 'material inaccuracies' and subsequently appeared to claim that Number Ten had agreed to the disclosure, the fat was in the fire.

A further development stoked the flames. Around noon on 9 January Heseltine swept out of Number Ten in the middle of a Cabinet meeting with all the brio of Ronald Colman as Sidney Carton on his way to the guillotine. Whether it was a far, far better thing he did than he had ever done before one must leave to history, but walking tall and handsome up Downing Street with the press and television cameras in close pursuit he let it be known that he had resigned. Apparently he had not formally done so when he strode out of the Cabinet Room, leaving Mrs Thatcher momentarily uncertain whether he had gone for good or merely to the lavatory (or 'facility' as she sometimes called the smallest room in the house).

Early that afternoon Heseltine held a press conference, giving his version of events in full. At which the Labour Opposition, seeing a golden opportunity of involving the Prime Minister, insisted that there *had* been agreement from Number Ten to disclose the Solicitor-General's letter and that this could not have been done without her permission or, at least, her knowledge.

Mrs Thatcher countered by ordering an official inquiry. This was conducted by Sir Robert Armstrong, the Cabinet Secretary and head of the Civil Service. After interviewing everyone concerned Sir Robert concluded that there had been no breach of the Official Secrets Act and so far as Downing Street was concerned that was the end of the matter. But it was not the end of the matter.

Scenting blood, Labour tabled a motion of no confidence in the Government and what had originally been no more than a storm in a helicopter was now a full-scale political tornado in which the Prime

Minister's word was in question and the survival of her government at stake.

The crucial confidence debate was to begin on Monday 26 January, at 3.30 p.m. On the morning of Sunday 25 January, Michael Alison, the Prime Minister's PPS, telephoned me to say that the PM was working on her speech for the debate and had asked if I would be available to lend a hand if needed. I said I had planned to be out of town for the day but could cancel or alternatively could be reached by phone at any time and back in a little over an hour. The PPS said go ahead but he might call me around teatime. I gave him the phone number and left for the country. At 4.30 p.m. he telephoned and asked if I could come as soon as possible. I made my excuses and drove back to town, reaching Number Ten shortly before six, and was told to go straight to the Cabinet Room.

Around the table were the Prime Minister, in her usual seat at the centre, looking grim but calm, with Sir Robert Armstrong on her right, Charles Powell and Bernard Ingham sitting opposite side by side, saying (quite rightly, as civil servants) not a word from start to finish and David Wolfson, her former Chief of Staff and man of wise counsel in time of trouble. A huge pile of reference books and copies of Hansard occupied the centre of the Cabinet table.

'Come in, dear, come in,' said Mrs Thatcher. 'We've had a thoroughly unprofitable day.' She sounded exasperated, as well she might be. I gathered that the Downing Street view was that the facts had been clearly established by Sir Robert's inquiry and that should have been final, since there was no question whatever of changing or modifying an official report. Further, that even had such an outrageous course been contemplated it would not have been possible since the result of the report of the Secretary to the Cabinet which had established the facts was widely known. Nevertheless the Prime Minister was fully aware that the ruffled feathers of two of her senior Cabinet Ministers, on the one hand, and the muddying of the waters by the Opposition, on the other (a legitimate ploy in the circumstances), could bring down her government and regarded such elements in the equation as both absurd and below the level of events. At the centre of it all was a dispute about the future of a small helicopter company in the West Country. Was it possible that the fate of her Government depended on such a minor matter? Incredible!

I too found it hard to believe. The more I listened to the various suggestions as to how the following day's vital debate should be conducted the more astonished I became that such a little thing could be the instrument of what would undoubtedly bring about the Government's resignation if the vote of no confidence were to be carried. But perhaps history is often thus. What followed was certainly high drama. Although, not being a civil servant and never having been asked to sign the Official Secrets Act, I was not bound to silence either by protocol or practice, I nevertheless took my cue from Ingham and Powell and said nothing until the following morning and even then not until the last few minutes, by which time it seemed to me that the solution to the problem had already emerged.

The key was the Prime Minister's furiously denied involvement in the affair. If both Heseltine and Brittan, from their opposite points of view, were to close ranks and, whatever their differences, come out publicly in support of the Prime Minister during the debate, that would show a united Cabinet and clear her and her government of the wholly unsubstantiated charge of duplicity. The opposing views of the two Secretaries of State obviously made this far from easy to bring about but if it could be achieved and ruffled feathers soothed the Conservative backbenchers would be reassured, the Opposition discomfited and the Prime Minister absolved of any conceivable involvement.

Neither of the two principal protagonists appeared in the Cabinet Room that night or the following Monday morning when we reassembled but I gathered they were both in the building or in Number Eleven, though in different rooms, where Willie Whitelaw, as Deputy PM, and the Chancellor, Sir Geoffrey Howe, were attempting to mediate. But finding a formulation agreeable to the two dissenting Ministers was proving stubbornly intractable. Political fortune and personal pride were involved and there was much toing and froing between those urging Brittan, who leant one way, and those pressing Heseltine, who leant the other, each from honourable motives, to meet in the middle. Everything now seemed to rest on how to satisfy the integrity and dignity of these two central figures.

Meanwhile, in the highly charged atmosphere of the Cabinet Room the clock was ticking away the minutes and time was running out. To an outsider who also happened to be a playwright, it was pure C. P. Snow: eighteen hours of riveting drama in which the stakes could not have been higher nor the insight into the political process more engrossing.

Just after 3.00 p.m., with less than a quarter of an hour to go and nothing decided, the PM suddenly said, 'Does anyone realise I have to be in my seat in the House in twelve minutes?' At this Sir Geoffrey Howe, seated on her immediate right, suggested, in that disarmingly mild susurration that not quite five years later was to prove so deadly, a minor variation in the draft that was before her.

For a moment she seemed to think he was proposing a change in

309

the text of the official inquiry and, jabbing him in the chest with the forefinger of her right hand, berated him, '*You* make such a proposal! You, a silk, a silk!'

The silk in question made clear that no such thought had entered his mind, all he wanted was to get the two recusants to unite in support of their Prime Minister. As this was precisely my view I ventured, 'Surely that's not beyond the wit of man. I mean, it's common sense.' This was greeted by the Prime Minister with a sharp look at me, followed by a moment's silence, followed by a deep sigh. 'Well, what is it everyone wants me to say?' What it amounted to was that in the name of unity she should, in the debate, apply the healing touch of understanding to both Brittan and Heseltine, which in turn would surely be reciprocated and the Government would be seen to be as one. This would lift the backbenchers and unite them against the Opposition. The Prime Minister looked far from satisfied but I had the impression that, *faute de mieux*, she would do as had been suggested.

There was a quick flurry of senior Ministers and civil servants coming in and out and a reference to a possible meeting at six o'clock. Mrs Thatcher said, 'I may not be Prime Minister at six o'clock' in a tone that left open whether or not she meant it. Then she gathered her papers, took her hand-mirror from her bag, patted her hair and everyone was away in a whirl of limousines as the centre of gravity moved rapidly from Number Ten to the Commons. With three-line Whips out on both sides, Members who had failed to get a seat were standing three deep at the entrance to the crowded chamber.

For the record, Brittan and Heseltine did finally agree to support the Prime Minister in the House from their different viewpoints and this had the desired effect on the packed assembly, as I had believed it would. However, something had already occurred that none of us could have foreseen, which, coming when it did, had an even greater influence on the outcome and which only two newspapers mentioned (or perhaps noticed).

The Opposition Leader, Neil Kinnock, who moved the vote of no confidence, nervous and highly strung on the big occasion, recited an early section of his speech *twice*. By so doing he quickly lost the attention and sympathy of the House which began to mutter and, despite some notable contributions from both sides, the debate was virtually over before it began. He is not, of course, the first politician to have committed this simple human error but he was probably the first Leader of Her Majesty's Opposition to do so when bringing down the Government of the day in a matter of hours, however unjustified it would have been, was very much a possibility.

There are two further points worth noting. It was not the last time that Michael Heseltine would be responsible for putting Margaret Thatcher's future on the line – but this time luck was with the lady. As for my political innocence, I was learning fast.

The Westland Helicopter Affair continued to hover politically above the Government throughout 1986, its rotor-blades throwing up unattested clouds of doubt from time to time despite the departure of its two principal protagonists, Heseltine's resignation being followed by that of Leon Brittan who never returned to the Government but in due course went to Brussels as a Commissioner and later became a Deputy to the President of the Commission, Jacques Delors.

In February, unemployment headed for three-and-a-half million, and the March Budget cut a penny off income tax. In April the United States bombed Libya from British bases and the Conservatives lost the Rydale by-election and only just clung on to West Derbyshire.

Midsummer saw Mrs Thatcher in hospital for an operation on a displaced finger-joint. The operation successfully concluded, her touch came back as she triumphantly demonstrated in October at Bourne-mouth where she tore into the Opposition on defence.

> Last week ... in a decision of the utmost gravity, Labour voted to give up Britain's independent nuclear deterrent unilaterally ... an absolute break with the defence policy of every British Government since the Second World War ... I believe the interests of Britain can now only be served by a third Conservative victory.

With the Liberal rank and file rejecting their official Party line, the defence of the realm was now firmly at the centre of the political battleground and for the first time since Westland the December polls had the Conservatives ahead.

They remained there. In March the 1987 Budget cut another two pence off income tax and the Prime Minister made her first trip to the Soviet Union. For this she bought the latest Aquascutum fashion range and, to point a moral and adorn a tale, not for the first time used her sex, and sexuality, to political advantage. The Russian people loved the clothes that weren't available to them and loved her for wearing them. The embodiment of the free world, she came on like a modern Tsarina, hailed in triumph by a Communist people. It was the first popular breakthrough to the East by a Western leader and it was the British Prime Minister who made it.

If one object of her visit was to strengthen Anglo-Soviet friendship and another to advertise the prosperity and brilliance in design of a free Britain, there was a third. It's always a good political ploy to be seen as a leader on the world stage when you're approaching a domestic judgement by your fellow countrymen. It grabs the head-lines, broadens the canvas against which you are judged, and the difference between a Prime Minister and a Leader of the Opposition is seen by the electorate to be poles, and hopefully polls, apart.

With the local elections of 7 May continuing to favour the Tories, four days later Margaret Thatcher called her third General Election.

The lady disliked elections, not because she feared a fight, on the contrary she revelled in any kind of clash, ideological or otherwise, but because they were a massive interruption to the Government's work, bringing everything to a halt for three distracting weeks and even (heaven forbid, but the possibility was there) for ever. The continuance in office of a radical Conservative government was in her view vital to the future of the country and feeling her task no more than half done, if that, the possibility, whatever the polls were saying, of having chosen the wrong date (and the choice is the Prime Minister's alone) or some unforeseen event changing the Government's prospects in mid-election, hung heavy on her mind as usual and haunted her almost until the last result was in.

General Elections also had a marked effect on her personality. What the voters saw was all-conquering mega-Maggie in peak form crisscrossing the country by plane, car and campaign bus in an apparently tireless and confident quest for a renewed mandate. An international figure now, and a 'draw' of immense pulling power, excitement followed wherever she went and the idea of losing seemed unthinkable. But not to the lady herself. She never took anything for granted.

To those close to her General Elections (apart from the first) meant that an edgy, difficult, even at times irascible character had temporarily taken over and, although the reason was understood by all of us, the edginess was infectious and one longed for the inevitable tension to be over and normal business to be resumed. The '87 election was particularly stressful as, in addition to the ritual exertion and fatigue of any election as well as the minor matter of running the country, she had toothache throughout the campaign.

Nevertheless I felt reasonably optimistic about the result. The speeches were going over well and the political journalist John O'Sullivan who, along with John Redwood, had become an invaluable member of the writing team, had done an admirable job on the manifesto under the guiding hand of Brian Griffiths, now head of the Policy Unit. To this I had contributed little except to change the order here and there and, together with O'Sullivan, to simplify the language and make it more readable. Press and politicians apart, does anyone read manifestos?

Despite the vital importance of the election result, cheerfulness, not to say a welcome touch of farce, occasionally broke through. One afternoon in the middle of a speechwriting session in the study at Number Ten Cecil Parkinson, who was again standing for his Herts-mere constituency, telephoned and asked for the Prime Minister. 'Oh dear,' she muttered, 'is it urgent?' Apparently it was. He was put through. After saying that the Conservative Party was the smart party – he meant in dress rather than intellect though no doubt both were implied – he complained that certain Tory Ministers on the stump and on television were letting the side down by looking either thoroughly scruffy or too ornate. When she asked him to be specific he named the Chancellor of the Exchequer Nigel Lawson who, he said, badly needed a haircut, and Kenneth Clarke whose dashing yellow waistcoat, said Cecil, appearing in colour on the nation's television screens, struck a note of levity that was inappropriate at this grave moment in our island story.

'Right ... Yes ... Right,' sighed the lady, taking notes, and eventu-ally hung up with a certain impatience.

'Well, *really*,' she muttered, 'I hardly think hair and coloured waistcoats will mean the difference between victory and defeat. However ... ' and she went to her desk, picked up the phone and asked for the Chancellor.

As he was only next door at Number Eleven, which like Number Twelve has a corridor connecting with Number Ten, it seemed to me that he might be requested to pop in for a moment and an entertaining little diversion on 'Hairstyles: how to win a third term' could be enjoyed by all.

When he came on the line he was requested to see a barber at his earliest convenience. There was some confusion while it was estab-lished that no, she did not want him to see A for Anthony Barber (Ted's Chancellor) and that no, what she wanted cut was not the fiscal deficit or the Health Service but his hair. He evidently agreed to at least a trim because she said, 'I would be grateful' and rang off. 'Well, that's all right, then,' she sighed (ah, but on a point of order, Madam Speaker, was it? Or was the memory of that trichological indignity stored up in the Chancellor's subconscious, one day to surface unforgotten and to play a crucial part in his dramatic resignation? We shall never know).

313

She next telephoned David Young (Secretary of State at the Department of Trade and Industry) and asked him if he would be kind enough to speak to Ken Clarke about his waistcoat. (Clarke was Young's Number Two at the DTI.)

Clearly, at such moments, to be Young was *not* very heaven because he declined the assignment, presumably on the grounds that this was a matter of such delicacy and national importance that only Prime Ministers could handle it. Who finally got the job I don't know but the waistcoat duly vanished from the nation's screens. Which I thought was a pity. Anything that lightens our political darkness is to be welcomed. Indeed, catching the mood of the moment, I felt a powerful urge to suggest that she had a word with Ted Heath, who at that time favoured the fuller fashion in hair, and warn him Old Bexley might go Labour if he didn't do something about his locks. Happy days, which acted as a sedative to the nerves induced by yet another election.

The final week of the campaign, which began with the much-exaggerated 'wobbly Thursday', put an added strain on the Prime Minister as she had to interrupt her election tour to fly to Venice for two days and the latest in the round of nonstop Summitry. This meant that she could play no part in the writing of the last crucial speech of the campaign, which was written by John O'Sullivan, Stephen Sherbourne and me in the small dining room at Number Ten from 7.00 p.m., with a break for dinner, until 4.30 the following morning.

When it was done Stephen drove me home through the rain and later went off to Northolt to meet the PM's plane on her return from Italy. The speech had been faxed to her and, understandably nervous about her reaction, Stephen stood fidgeting on the wet tarmac, prepared for the worst. However, when Charles Powell appeared at the top of the aircraft steps he was waving the speech, smiling broadly and giving the thumbs-up sign. Tiresome people might draw a moral from this ('Tell the writers what you want and let them get on with it') but for my part I wouldn't dream of making such a deplorable suggestion.

The final rally of the campaign was, as in 1983, at Wembley but this time I was taking no chances. I rode out with Mrs Thatcher in the campaign bus, but the dress was fine, the hair was fine, and knowing that tomorrow was a rest day before the tension of Polling Day she was in good fettle and on the way worked cheerfully with me on a few final thoughts for the speech. Knowing that David Steele and David Owen's Alliance Party was divided on all but the Christian names of the joint leaders I suggested she half-speak, half-sing

David, David, what are we going to do?
I'm half craz-ed trying to be like you ...

This she did, and it went down happily with the vast audience that was raising the roof to the accompaniment of Lloyd Webber fortissimo, showers of streamers, coloured balloons and laser beams as though it was an American presidential convention. Over the top but at least this time nobody made jokes about bombing anybody.

When Norman Tebbit, the Party Chairman, saw us arrive he grinned and said to me, 'So they've called up the cavalry, have they?' If they had, I doubt it was necessary.

The result of the General Election of 1987 was:

Conservatives	375 seats
Labour	229
Alliance	22
Others	24
Conservative overall majority	100

Two days later, as a typically thoughtful gesture of thanks, Margaret invited O'Sullivan, Sherbourne and me to watch the annual Trooping the Colour ceremony in Horseguards Parade, which takes place in June, from the Prime Minister's stand immediately outside the back entrance to the garden of Number Ten. This was the first time the Queen arrived to review her Guards in a low-slung open carriage rather than in uniform and on horseback. She wore a light blue summer dress and looked enchanting. The morning sun shone brilliantly and after the long ceremony there was the traditional reception at Number Ten for the various High Commissioners to the Court of St James, several of whom wore the colourful yellow, green and red robes of their native lands. It was at this gathering that one of the British guests uttered the memorable, if reprehensible aside, 'Now I know why it's called Trooping the Colour'.

After a merry champagne and buffet lunch in the State dining room while the PM darted in and out reshuffling her Cabinet by telephone, John O'Sullivan and I, in full morning dress, strolled slowly, happily, up The Mall towards the Palace, tired to our boots and glad it was over but quietly celebrating that in pulling it off yet again the lady had been third time lucky.

17

. . . .

Random Harvest

Watching the political parade go by over a period of two decades, not all passing thoughts, or people, not every experience stayed with me. However, sifting through the bank of memory, here are one or two that did ...

'Supergrass'

There was something of the soldier about him. Robust, twinkling, a clean-shaven Dickensian character, Ian Gow was a serious, irre-pressible, and warm-hearted man, and a brilliant PPS to the Prime Minister. Known affectionately to the House of Commons as 'Super-grass', he had a knack of reporting back to the lady everything she needed to know about the gossip of the bazaars without ever betraying a confidence, a rare feat in the political world.

Although devout and a regular churchgoer, Ian also needed human icons to look up to and worship. He found two in Margaret Thatcher and General de Gaulle, an improbable duo but warriors both.

Given to expressions such as 'Have you fire?' when he saw someone with an unlit cigarette, Ian was a family man with two fine sons and a loving, professional pianist wife.

There was no more loyal friend to be had in politics. On my receiving a K in the 1980 New Year's Honours he immediately organised a celebration at his Lambeth home. There was a wide variety of music at the piano from his wife Jane (beautiful and sober) and myself (not so beautiful and not quite sober) followed by dancing

317

in the streets into the small hours. Rejoicing in someone else's good fortune was typical of Gow.

His deadpan humour was a splendid safety-valve at Party Conferences. One year at Blackpool the writers' room at the Imperial was the smallest ever. To obtain entry one had to squeeze through the door. Having negotiated it, Ian took one look and rang the hotel manager. 'I'm in the writers' room,' he said. 'Would it be possible for them to have something smaller? I did say smaller, yes. It's essential that they concentrate instead of rolling about all over this huge arena you've provided. Thank you, but quite frankly if we'd wanted Wembley we'd have asked for it. See to it forthwith, would you?'

Ian was shrewd about people. Hearing that a friend of his was taking Tessa Jardine-Patterson, one of the Number Ten super-secretaries, to dinner, Ian left a note on her desk. 'If tonight he asks you to marry him, say yes.' He did and she did and Mr and Mrs Gaisman and their children continue to live happily ever after.

I believe Ian knew that he would die at the hands of the IRA. As a former Northern Ireland Minister he had Special Branch security but brave, bursting with life and determined not to have his activities circumscribed, he refused to take the usual precautions.

When the Anglo-Irish Agreement was signed by Margaret Thatcher and Garret Fitzgerald he could not stomach it, regarding it as a betrayal of Ulster, and despite his closeness to the PM (no one was closer) his integrity was such that he voted against it in the Commons and resigned from the Government. Despite this, and to the lasting credit of both, Ian and Margaret remained firm friends and she continued to be a regular guest at his dinner table to the end.

Willie's Way

In the musical *Camelot* there's a song in which King Arthur, who is having wife trouble with Guinevere, his queen, meditates musically on 'How to Handle a Woman'. He comes to the conclusion that the answer is 'To love her, simply love her, love her, love her'.

The acknowledged expert at handling Mrs Thatcher was her deputy, Willie Whitelaw. Whether he followed Arthurian practice and simply loved her, loved her, loved her, I am unable to say, but it was Willie (as he was to everyone), a large man in every sense, who came closest to solving the problem. I would guess that a somewhat subtler approach was brought into play: the more she tried to behave like a man the more he treated her like a woman. Willie's great strength was his loyalty which enabled him to say things to her that others couldn't, not by virtue of his seniority, though that helped, but by a special kind of gallantry, the knightly suit of armour that he threw round her whenever she was under fierce attack, which was rather more than seldom.

One day at Blackpool during a speechwriting session Margaret said, 'Every Prime Minister should have a Willie.' I've never been entirely sure whether this was a Rabelaisian sally or a slip of the tongue. I think the latter has the edge because, when the explosive burst of laughter that greeted this observation subsided, she frowned and said sternly to her wordsmiths, 'Everything that's said in this room is confidential. You realise that.' 'Oh, absolutely. Rather. No question,' we chorused, crossing our fingers. I think she knew it would go the rounds, as of course it did. We owed it to Willie as well as to history and when it was leaked to him (not by one of us, as it happened) he roared his delight until he wept.

A Special Relationship

Dark, handsome, loyal and charming, Charles Powell, her Special Adviser on Foreign Affairs, was lent by the Foreign Office and never returned. Officially neutral, like all civil servants, he would not, I fancy, swear to it on all occasions. The Prime Minister kept him at her side, as much at home as abroad, for his contribution was outstanding. A high-flying diplomat who was not a professional speechwriter, Charles became one *par excellence*. He was the prime architect of the address to the Joint American Houses of Congress, the Bruges speech, the Prague speech, the Aspen, Colorado speech and dozens of others over the years. It was a privilege to be asked to take a polishing pen (which scarcely required it) to some of the many speeches of which the Prime Minister and Charles (now Sir Charles) Powell were the joint originators.

On Green Leather

I'm glad I never became an MP. It's a stressful, often exhausting job, attending the House at all hours, nursing constituencies, holding surgeries, answering mail, opening fetes, obeying three-line Whips, getting lost on British Rail and in many cases having to cope with two homes, one wife, children, staff, mistresses, mortgages, overdrafts and bar bills. The hours are long and frequently tedious, excitements occasional rather than regular, and if it's tough at the top it's also tough in the middle and at the bottom.

Politicians shouldn't be hamstrung by money problems. I know it's easy to say and hard to achieve but in an ideal world money worries shouldn't come in.

What happened to Mrs Thatcher might just possibly not have done so if her backbenchers with marginal seats had had other means than their MP's salary to provide for their families (some do, but not the majority). They should be free to fight through periods of their Party's unpopularity without being haunted by fear of losing their source of income. The wonder is that most remain dedicated, honourable men and women who serve this democratic country well and are largely unappreciated when they're not being insulted.

Tatler Time

A gushing lady at a Chequers cocktail party: 'Such a beautiful house, Prime Minister, so elegant yet so friendly. How is it run?'

M.T. (eyes flashing): 'On a shoestring!'

Dancing in the Dark

If life with the Thatchers was sometimes surprising, dull it wasn't. On one occasion, talk in the flat had turned yet again to those who were 'one of *us*' and those who were not. Lord Carrington, the Foreign Secretary, though liked and admired by both Thatchers, was regarded by Denis as a 'not'.

M.T.: 'Be fair, dear. He was very good over Rhodesia.'

D.T.: 'Yes, but he didn't dance with Kaunda.'

M.T.: 'I should hope not.'

D.T.: 'You did – and that's what turned the trick.'

M.T.: 'I doubt if that's what history will say.'

D.T.: 'History wasn't there. I was.'

A shrewd man, D.T.

Unofficially Yours

I never got around to joining the Conservative Party, I don't know why. No, that's not true. I do know why.

I have an instinctive dislike of labels and have always found being pinned down claustrophobic. I empathise and wear a blue rosette, if pressed, during elections but that's about the strength of my official contribution. (Unofficial is another matter.) Of course if everyone took my independent line the Party would have no members, which would be nice for Labour but bad for democracy and political life would be impossible. However, most Tories are happy to sign on the dotted line so perhaps the occasional oddball can be indulged without totally wrecking the system.

Upstairs, Downstairs

In Mrs Thatcher's time there was no 'Kitchen Cabinet' in the sense that there was when Harold Wilson ran Number Ten. There was a small circle of friends she could relax with, confide in and trust but there was no cabal or group with the kind of influence that the words 'Kitchen Cabinet' imply and that suggest something secret going on that bypassed the Cabinet proper, as in Wilson's day.

When the Cabinet was bypassed under Thatcher it was by the official committees that were made up of a handful of Ministers and civil servants and were essential if the Government was to get through the ever-growing workload of running our country in our time. Over most of them the Prime Minister herself presided.

These committees had numbers and what they did was supposed to be known only to those who sat on them, though some were really secret and others more secret still and finally there were those so secret that officially they didn't exist. Today there is talk of more open government. There is always talk of more open government. But under Margaret Thatcher there was no atmosphere of hush-hush or everyone watching everyone else's eyes and wondering what was going on behind them. (With hindsight, perhaps in the later years there was something of the sort but if so I failed to notice it.)

The Engine Room

You knew you were at the heart of things in Downing Street, that here was ultimate political power, but there was nothing stuffy or pompous about Thatcher's Number Ten. The building doesn't lend itself. The State drawing rooms and dining room are elegant and beautifully furnished but the working rooms are just that – rooms where people work as in any other office building, unglamorous, almost plain. If you walked into Number Ten and didn't know that it was Number Ten you wouldn't know that it was Number Ten.

But if you know its story and think of the men – and one woman – who have run Britain from those premises and more than once saved it from its enemies, then it acquires a wonder and a magic.

And if you walk down its long corridor from the black front door to the white one at the end of that corridor which opens on to the Cabinet Room, and stand in the doorway and look about you and remember those who have sat and taken the big decisions – not precisely in the room in which you are standing, for Number Ten has been there for two hundred and fifty years and is now three buildings knocked into one, but symbolically the same – why, then you are a dull stick if you are not stirred and humbled by the experience, for you are standing in the engine room of our country's history.

32 Smith Square

Central Office, the Conservative Party HQ, is a building with no distinct personality. I suspect this is deliberate. People are there to work for the Party, in government and out, and it concentrates the mind not to think about the environment in which you are doing it. Although recently refurbished and much improved, the walls are for the most part bare and so is the cash box.

In wartime (elections) the Party is flush but only for the run-up and the election itself and every penny is needed for the campaign. In peacetime (between elections) the Party is broke because the big donors don't start to worry about donating until the next election looms and the possibility of a Labour government keeps them awake at night.

The Labour Party, which is largely financed by the unions, is even worse off, for roughly the same reasons. The unions don't like parting with their cash until they have to and then do so only out of fear of yet another Conservative government. This should be a comfort to the Conservatives but isn't.

Either way, Central Office is a nervous place. Chairmen come and Chairmen leave and naturally bring their own ideas and choose those sympathetic to them to carry them out, so it's easy come and easy go and hello, who are you, then? Have a nice day.

Those who work there appear cheerful – there's a lot of smiling done, especially when the polls are bad – and on the whole people are there because they are genuinely dedicated to the cause. It's certainly not for the remuneration, which varies from moderate to no great shakes to you must be joking.

Try This for Size

On one occasion I stayed the night at Chequers in the great canopied four-poster that the WRAF sergeant on duty told me General de Gaulle had once occupied during Churchill's wartime premiership. Churchill is said to have likened de Gaulle to a female llama surprised in her bath. Had I known this at the time I might have been less overawed. As it was, I lay there wide awake reliving history, with what I imagined was Mon General alongside me, the exceptionally tall cadaver stiffer even than usual with infuriated pride. The bed was extra-long and so, despite the luxury and comfort, was the night. I thought that, like the General, it would never end. I didn't sleep a wink.

When You Wish Upon a Star

Alexander Cohen, a well-known New York theatrical producer whom I have met from time to time over the years, is in charge of the opening of the Disney Theme Park in Orlando, Florida.

He telephones one day from California saying that he's getting a group of world leaders of the time – Ronald Reagan, Mikhail Gorbachev, François Mitterrand – to appear briefly on television and say a few words on a subject of their choice to mark the grand opening, and do I think that Mrs Thatcher would speak for the UK and if so will I ask her? Of course there'll be a fee which he suggests should be paid to the Wishing Well Appeal for the Great Ormond Street Hospital for Sick Children. I say she doesn't do this sort of thing as a rule and what fee does he have in mind? He suggests £1000. I say I couldn't even bring the subject up for less than £10,000. He says he'll have to ask the Disney people and he doesn't know what they'll say. I say I do, that it's cheap at the price, and sure enough they agree at once. When I ask Margaret she says, 'What is a theme park?' I say, 'I'm not entirely sure but if it's Disney it's probably for children of all ages.' She says, 'If it's for charity of course I'll do it' and a few days later a camera crew arrive at Number Ten and set up their apparatus in the Blue Drawing Room.

While we're waiting for the lighting arrangements to be finalised she says casually, 'I was wondering . . . I happen to know of a hospital which needs a special piece of expensive high-tech equipment. By an odd coincidence it costs around ten thousand pounds. Do you think Mr Cohen would mind if I gave my fee to them?' I say I'm sure he won't mind as long as it goes to a deserving cause and ask which hospital is in need of this special piece of expensive equipment that by an odd coincidence costs around ten thousand pounds and how does she know about it?

'Funnily enough,' she says, gazing at the ceiling, 'it's in my constituency.'

No wonder they call her Mrs Finchley.

Free to be Free

In all the years that I have led a political life I have never taken money for it. Not that I don't care for the stuff but, valuing my independence and wanting to be clear of any commitment to remain if I was fundamentally at odds with what was afoot, I decided from the beginning that any contribution I might make should, like the Health Service, be free at the point of delivery. I also had a feeling that, if my opinion was worth anything, it was more likely to be listened to if I hadn't been paid for it. I had royalties from plays past and present coming in from time to time and financial independence gave me one of the two freedoms open to a writer. The other, of course, is bankruptcy.

Charles Snow once asked me how much I was paid and when I said, 'Nothing. I don't want it,' he said, 'Cleverest thing you ever did.'

'Why clever?'

'You're not a burden to the State or a threat to anyone else's job.'

Charles was a wise old bird and although those were not my reasons I daresay there was something in them.

A Whole New World

My extended involvement in politics was unintentional. I had in mind to be a short-term foot soldier for one campaign, not a long-term aide to the General Commanding. Although I felt personally committed to helping Margaret whenever she needed me, wall-to-wall politics has never been a passion. Politics was one more string to a bow that had already brought an entertaining life and what my mother used to call 'a reasonable income'. Not depending on it for a living, I knew that I could walk away from it, nor would I be unduly dispirited if it walked away from me. Perhaps this helped me to view the political scene through a different lens from those whose very being revolves around it; with sympathy and affection but also with a measure of detachment.

Apart from its intrinsic fascination, one of the bonuses of political life was that it brought me an entirely new circle of friends. These were not only my fellow writers but Ministers, MPs and civil servants, mainly high-flyers, who were for the most part quite unlike what one might expect. I think particularly of the surface irreverence that was to be found in people like Willie Whitelaw, Peter Carrington, Keith Joseph, John Wakeham, Ian Gow, John Hoskyns, Robin Butler, Charles Powell, Nigel Wickes, Bernard Ingham, Stephen Sherbourne,

John Whittingdale, and many others who were wisely and shrewdly in the frame. I took for granted their loyalty and dedication to the job. What surprised me was that they walked so easily in their power base. For all their heavy responsibilities these men were light of heart.

In addition to the indispensable Charles Powell, others at Number Ten who cheerfully submitted their basic work for my occasional burnishing were Andrew Turnbull, her last Private Secretary, and Paul Gray, her Economic Secretary. In their shoes I can't see myself taking kindly to interference from a political layman but these admirable civil servants were encouraging and supportive throughout, and even gave every appearance of being grateful. Down the years our Civil Service has been accused of every kind of infamy, from frustrating the will of the people to sabotaging government policy to adopting a negative approach whenever possible. That is not how I have seen civil servants through four administrations. They made me welcome and did what they were asked to do with flair and the utmost good humour. At the highest level the British Civil Service is still the best in the world.

Romeo Y Julieta

After every Party Conference speech a gift would arrive from Number Ten – usually a box of cigars. On one occasion it was a box that had been given to Denis with his name stamped on each stogie but he doesn't smoke them so they came to me. Only once was there a variation of this annual gift. After the Brighton bomb anything celebratory would have been inappropriate. The lady's sense of the fitness of things was as usual impeccable and a few days later a dark grey pullover arrived instead.

My Word, but He Was Old

What I feared would be a melancholy occasion turned out to be close to carnival-time. I was one of four close friends of the C. P. Snows who were asked by their son Philip to give a short reading from a favourite author of Pamela Snow's (novelist Pamela Hansford-Johnson), at her memorial service. Somewhat to my alarm I was allocated a passage from Proust (not the least arcane of authors even in translation).

The service took place at St James's, Piccadilly, and the church was packed. Three of us waited in the front row for the proceedings to begin but nothing happened. Apparently the fourth reader had not shown. It continued not to happen for a good ten to fifteen minutes while the organist ran softly, sweetly, through his repertoire in that hushed way they have when pretending that this is part of the order of things and they're not ad-libbing to cover a mishap. It was like waiting for the bride to arrive for her wedding but surely there could be no question of a last-minute change of mind on this occasion. The reason for the delay was made clear when the fourth reader at last appeared in the portico.

The ancient and familiar hunched figure of former Prime Minister Harold Macmillan came slowly, step by careful step, up the aisle leaning heavily on Philip Snow's arm and a stout country walking stick before sinking with relief into the aisle seat on the front row. A murmur of appreciation ran through the church at this gallant if belated entrance and the sound of handkerchiefs being discreetly blown rippled along the crowded, sympathetic pews.

Macmillans had been Charles and Pamela Snow's publishers for most of their writing lives and one felt it was damn decent of the old boy to make what was plainly a Herculean effort and turn up for Pamela's farewell function.

When his turn came he was again escorted with loving care by Philip Snow to the lectern where he was to read one of the Psalms of David. Once more his progress was executed with evident pain and one began to pray he would survive the service. Philip switched on the microphone and the light above the lectern before returning anxiously to his seat.

The distinguished old gentleman read the psalm with a gentle quavering charm. The carefully enunciated diction made the reading especially moving. I doubt if there was a dry eye in the church.

When he had done Philip reappeared swiftly at his charge's side to escort the grand old man of British politics back to his seat. However, this was not what Macmillan had in mind at all. With a sudden dismissive wave of his hand he shooed the young man away as though he couldn't imagine what he was doing there, switched off the microphone, turned off the lectern light, cleared his throat, straightened his spine and, an erect martial figure, marched briskly back to his aisle seat unaided, sat down and looked about him with the mischievous grin of one who has just pulled a number of legs to his considerable satisfaction.

At this *coup de théâtre* all the ranks of Tuscany could scarce forbear to cheer – or, in my case, burst into immoderate laughter. Harold Macmillan had staged the performance, from carefully delayed entrance to final delivery, quite beautifully – but then he had always been one of the great performing Prime Ministers. How Charles and

326

Pamela would have enjoyed it, had they been there. Perhaps they were.

The Wrong Way Round

Many of the intellectual Left seem to spend a lifetime trying to explain events in the light of their political beliefs, rather than relating those beliefs to a world in constant flux. Ladies and gentlemen, it can't be done.

A Question of Priorities

Luncheon at Chequers was proceeding in the normal manner. That is, peacefully, country-style. Suddenly one of the Service girls slipped, juggled desperately with the plate she was carrying, lost control and finally tipped the entire contents – hot soup – into Sir Geoffrey Howe's lap. The Foreign Secretary gasped. The Prime Minister leapt to her feet.

'There, there,' she cried. 'Now you mustn't be upset. It's the sort of thing that could happen to anyone.'

No, it wasn't the Foreign Secretary she was addressing, it was the girl. With hindsight, was it altogether wise to treat Sir Geoffrey any old how?

A Straw in the Wind

Another Chequers lunch celebrated Margaret Thatcher's tenth anniversary in office. She didn't care for anniversaries. Trumpeting one's success, she felt, was tempting Fate but other people liked them so she went along. On this occasion there were Party grandees, members of previous Cabinets and one or two from the current one. John Major, the Chief Secretary to the Treasury, and by no means the most senior politician present was the only Minister who hosted a table. It was suddenly clear to me that this was a signal: here was her chosen successor and she was presenting him as such for the first time. If it was not quite the young Prince of Wales's investiture at Caernarvon Castle it was its political equivalent and, in its unobtrusive English way, equally significant.

An Ideal Husband

Denis Thatcher was the perfect partner who played the media at their own game, pretending to be the *Private Eye* cartoon figure, glass in hand on all occasions, rather as Churchill was seldom photographed minus cigar in mouth, which we now know half the time was unlit. 'If that's the character they want … ' D.T. seemed to be saying, 'Anything that takes the flak away from you-know-who is fine with me.' His phlegm and her fireworks were an ideal combination. He was also politically shrewd, combining a knack of hitting the nail on the head with reducing the complicated to basics. His comment on his wife becoming caught up in the bedlam of yet another General Election can scarcely be bettered. 'I don't know why we have to go through all this carry-on for three bloody weeks. I mean, it's either "Hello, it's me again" or "Goodbye".'

Sorry, but Your Slant is Showing

I realise that even to mention the British Broadcasting Corporation in a political context is to plunge into deep, fermenting waters but some things should be said before everything becomes blurred and out of focus, so let us take a deep breath and zero cautiously in.

During the Thatcher years one had to watch and listen carefully, over a period, to understand the subtle techniques employed by some of the news and current affairs programmes of the BBC: the nuances, the delicate juxtapositions, the creative editing, the occasional making of news rather than the reporting of it that leant Left because that was the right way to think. These sinuous manoeuvres came from below rather than above, though above seemed to catch the infection and either refrained from intervening or went native on arrival.

It was said that the Corporation was misunderstood, that it was not anti-Conservative, merely anti whichever party was in power, a watchdog barking impartially on behalf of the people, which simply made it anti-authority. This jolly little equivocation reminds me of the intimate revue in which H. Gingold, on being informed by H. Baddeley that her birthday made her a Virgo, remarked 'Does it? That's clever of it.'

Of course the manipulations were subtly done and hard to pin down, and it was difficult to convince those who did not wish to be convinced of what was going on, but to those who marked, learnt and inwardly distressed the slant was unmistakable. While throughout the continent of Europe socialism was on its way out, Britain's most powerful media source tended to paint a picture that was not only critical of the Right, which it had every right to be, but Left-inclined whenever possible and sometimes blatantly so, thus tilting a balance that should by statute be politically neutral. The left-wing stance was, and at the time of writing still is, unmistakable.

I have little doubt that it was the clever young high-flyers in current affairs who over the years powered the anti-Thatcher campaign into every home. Their chosen method was the wearing-away-at-a-stone technique, a noun here, an adjective there, sometimes a paragraph tucked into an otherwise harmless sequence of words and a visual impact brilliantly deployed. In addition, for certain political pro-grammes there was that unique agglomeration known as the studio audience which, it was claimed, was carefully balanced. One can't help feeling that, if this was so, whoever did the balancing had an original pair of scales. Mrs Thatcher was fully aware of the position – she was certainly told often enough – but for some reason, perhaps because much of what was happening was aimed at her and if she complained she could be accused of a purely personal reaction, she turned a deaf ear and a blind eye.

Her husband was different. He deeply resented the BBC's treatment of his wife and frequently blew his top on the subject. This was no empty prejudice, he was well-informed and articulate and could give you chapter and verse in language that was fruity and pulled no punches. His wife denied nothing but took no public action, possibly with memories of Harold Wilson and the Radio Doctor.

Those who did these things did not do them all the time. There were weeks, even months, when they laid low and played fair, but after a suitable interval the piranhas would be back in business.

The danger did not depart with Mrs Thatcher. At his first Party Conference as Prime Minister (Blackpool '91), John Major, watching the Nine O'clock News, became aware of a gross imbalance in the reporting of the Health Service debate and let his anger be known, sufficiently to cause alarm in the higher echelons of the BBC. The Corporation says firmly that it won't be bullied by politicians. Nor should it be, but the boot is on the other foot. It was not perhaps the brightest of ideas virtually to write off John Major during the election campaign of '92. The bewilderment, not to say dismay, on the faces of some of the television familiars as the results came in was one of several visceral pleasures on election night. There were only the Liberals left to turn to ('and now once more over to Alan Beith').

There is nothing wrong with the BBC (the best orchestras and music in the world of broadcasting) that restoring balance and burying bias in its news and current affairs programmes wouldn't cure. With respect, ladies and gentlemen, propaganda is not your business.

A Small Celebration

She has learnt on the grapevine that Stephen Sherbourne and Colette Bowe are organising a small dinner party for my birthday with a few close friends who have been a part of my political life for many years. At once she says that she and Denis would like to drop in for a pre-dinner drink. I'm not supposed to know about this but I get to know and am touched and flattered.

The dinner is to take place in a small hotel off Sloane Street and the Thatchers arrive exactly on time.

D.T.: 'When the Boss said "It's just a pre-dinner drink" I said to her "What, only one?"'

There is more than one and they don't just drop in, they stay well beyond the statutory minimum, chatting away and obviously enjoying themselves as we enjoy their taking the trouble to be there.

They present me with a silver salver inscribed 'Ronnie – on your 70th birthday from Denis and Margaret'. This unexpected and much treasured gift is typical of their thoughtfulness and generosity.

Eventually the PM looks at her watch and says to Denis 'We must go', but he takes no notice. She has to say it several times. Finally she rises from the sofa and in a commanding tone says, 'If you want me to poach your egg, come *now*!'

He sighs and turns to me. 'Good luck, my old. Boss says I've got to go and eat some bloody egg or something. Have a lovely life. I have.' Lovely man.

This is My Life

Margaret Thatcher was married to politics as no other politician I have known. Luckily she had a husband who understood, was tremendously proud of her (she was his second wife) and at all times put her wishes first. But from the tenth anniversary onwards his longing for a little private life occasionally broke through and he would jest, 'Let's go on Tuesday.' Half-amused, she would wonder aloud, 'Why does it always have to be a Tuesday?'

In the event it was a Thursday.

18

. . . .

A Woman of Some Impatience

As with actors in a play, so in politics one gets close to people, until all at once the run is over, the final curtain falls, the players disperse.

If looking back is agreeable, misty-eyed is a mistake. No rose-coloured spectacles. See it clear, tell it true, otherwise no point.

Here then, before the grand finale – if grand is the word – is Britain's first woman Prime Minister as the writer saw her, in close-up, without filter or soft focus, over sixteen years.

Margaret Thatcher evoked extreme feelings. To some she could do no right, to others no wrong. Indifference was not an option. She could stir almost physical hostility in normally rational people while she inspired deathless devotion in others. Both reactions were for the most part based on a strictly limited knowledge of the lady. The chatterers, of course, abhorred her because she was right-wing and kept them away from the strawberry beds for more than a decade, but others with no axe to grind reacted with equal violence for or against.

None of this surprised me. As Sir Peter Hall described the actress Dame Peggy Ashcroft, she is a woman of 'seductive contradictions'. Sometimes she was Mrs Miniver, sometimes Mrs Danvers, sometimes a riveting mix of those celebrated characters of the fictional forties. (Later, and very occasionally, there was an interface with Anna Neagle in *Sixty – sixteen? – Glorious Years*.) Sulphurous or enchanting, blazing or controlled, sensitive or less than tactful, she had something else in common with Dame Peggy: star quality. Even her most implacable opponents acknowledged that and many envied it.

When I first met her it was far from clear to me that here was a woman who would become the outstanding political figure of her time. I liked and admired her. I thought she would probably go far. But not that far. I misjudged what single-mindedness could do. She was shrewd but so are most politicians who make their mark. Here was something special: an at times explosive mix of steel, will-power, a cool brain, feminine charm when it was called for, and a masculine determination, come what may, not to be deflected from her chosen path. There was also, it seemed to me, a simplistic side to her nature.

She understood well the environs of the House of Commons and the small change of domestic life but appeared to have few, if any, other interests. She had not only dedicated herself to politics to a degree that left little time for other pursuits, she also had no apparent inclination to seek them out and indulge them.

The Arts? She enjoyed the classical paintings lent by the Ministry of Works that covered the walls of Chequers and Number Ten but she was not a connoisseur. She had some fine pieces of china, many of them gifts from admirers, which she cherished but she was not a collector. Music? The theatre? Hardly a devotee. Literature? A keen appetite for Kipling (she knew whole poems by heart), the speeches of Churchill and Enoch Powell, and political biography. Otherwise, from first to last her profession was her hobby and her hobby her profession. Her passion for work was insatiable. This was both the key to a great political career and a massive hostage to fortune when that career came to its sudden discordant end and left her stranded. For a whole year one was deeply worried for her.

As late as 1975 when she was fifty, she was still, it seemed to me, something of a stranger to the ordinary pleasures of human experience. In her youth 'abroad' had not been available to the man and woman in the street, only to the rich or nearly rich, and until it became a part of her job she had rarely travelled overseas and not at all before her marriage.

Outside the political arena there was an attractive vein of innocence. (I can hear now her streetwise daughter's affectionately exasperated 'Oh, *Mum!*' whenever it surfaced.) It was one of the nicest things about her. Years later, despite all the contacts and the travel, the exposure to the wide range and variety of life that supreme power brings, she remained in many ways surprisingly, and pleasingly, unsophisticated.

In his play *Design for Living* Coward describes a character as 'upright, forthright and downright'. His tongue is firmly in his cheek, but Mrs Thatcher really is those things. She actually believes in right and wrong and that the difference can't be fudged. There were those who thought her a prude. They were wrong. She was morally quite unshockable, though in provincial Grantham in the twenties and thirties, with a Victorian grandmother and a much-loved father who was a Methodist lay preacher her most formative influence, she may well have been straitlaced.

Her strict Methodist upbringing – Sunday school and church in the morning and nothing more suggestive than homework in the evening – can hardly have brought a good-looking young teenager to the attentions of the opposite sex as was customary even in the thirties. She believes she was the only person at school who went to church quite so often. 'I think it would have been a little bit better to have been a little bit less,' she said later with remarkable restraint.

But Oxford, the Bar and, above all, marriage to Denis Thatcher – they were married in Wesley's Chapel in the City of London – sent Mrs Grundy packing, if there had ever been a tendency to give that tiresome woman house room. With D.T. for a husband, prudery was not possible. His vocabulary, uninhibited and vividly educational, would have laughed any such over-refinement out of court and, contrary to almost universal belief, Mrs Denis Thatcher became what Americans called 'a broad-minded broad without hang-ups'.

Also without vanity. Those who could not bear to look at her on television had an unexpected ally – the lady herself. When she appeared on screen she would immediately switch off or, if others were watching, take a quick look, wince, and leave the room. This was something of a handicap in the early days when it would have been helpful for her to have seen for herself her mistakes of presentation without the need to have them explained to her second-hand. As it was, even after becoming an experienced communicator, she remained constantly dissatisfied with her performance and felt that she could have done better, an attribute not common to every politician.

Just as there are two kinds of Labour Party – Left and loony Left – so there are two kinds of Tory – consensualist and dissensualist. Although Margaret Thatcher is of the latter persuasion she never seemed to me a Party person. I saw her as a pragmatist with principles who paddled her own canoe much as Churchill did and, like Churchill, did not always find the Conservative Party to her taste.

If a two-Party system meant being a Conservative because the alternative road to power – to be a Socialist – was unthinkable, then of course she was a Conservative. But the old familiar precepts of the Tory grandees were never the heart and centre of her political philosophy, any more than they are her successor's. Nevertheless she recaptured Downing Street for them in 1979 and held it in '83 and '87 with an appeal that was not so much classless as across the classes. There were those who claimed that in her middle and later period she made up policy as she went along. I wouldn't quarrel too much with that assertion. Nor did her Party, so long as she continued to win elections. But bringing home the bacon did not stop intellectuals and snobs from patronising her as politically naïve.

Naïve she was not but, a true radical, she was impatient. Impatient with the gurus of the status quo. Impatient with those who knew that a willingness to change was at the heart of true Conservatism but had failed to act upon that knowledge with sufficient resolution at a time when it was never more necessary. (She once said, 'If a political leader floats an idea five years ahead of its time he could kill that idea. But if it's two years ahead of its time it could work.')

She believed that socialism was halfway to a fully controlled and planned society and there could be no meeting-point with such a doctrine. A government existed to serve individuals and their desires, not to instruct them in what those desires should be. Therefore the tasks of government should be limited. On a Scottish tour during the Opposition years she had met a young manager who spelt out what he considered were Britain's three main problems: inflation, taxation and regulation. This exactly mirrored her own perceptions.

She believed the fruitless attempts by the Labour governments of Wilson and Callaghan to make and mend the political patchwork quilt by buying off, in one case the unions, and in the other a handful of Liberals, had simply wasted time. If she was impatient it was with good reason. 'Steady as she goes' might be a philosophy for a country enjoying a prosperous present with expectation of a similar future but Britain was 'the sick man of Europe'. You didn't turn round a nation in decline by applying a political poultice. Therefore the road to the future must begin with a break with the past, which implied new blood, a fresh approach and a fundamental change of direction. She knew where she wanted to go, it had all been worked out in Opposition, and the moment she had power she set to work to put her policies into practice with, like her predecessors, varying success.

The workload of a modern Prime Minister is prodigious but the heavier the load, the happier the lady. Larger than life with the will to turn tides, she led from the front and, with the exception of the wartime Churchill, was the definitive hands-on Prime Minister, leaving nothing to chance and seldom to others. Her Ministers were labelled 'wet' or 'dry', a not always accurate shorthand. There were wets who were dry as a bone on some issues and dries who were soaked to the skin on others.

For years she galvanised the nation by the sheer force of her resolve. There was no stopping her once she had a policy between her teeth. Here was *perpetuum mobile* incarnate. Yet she once said to me, 'I can only do one thing at a time.' When I ventured, 'Didn't you have twins?' she neither laughed nor frowned but changed the subject. The caricature Thatcher of the cartoon and the rubber puppet – the Iron Lady, inflexible, furious, tough as blazes – had little grains of shrewd perception but missed the private person who was none of these things. The Iron Lady tag had been pinned on her by the Russians. What they intended as a jibe she took as a compliment and political asset which she used to her advantage, but it was no more than a device that established her as a warrior for foreign consumption. Under a bold and militant exterior she was as sentient and vulnerable as the rest of us. (Who else left Number Ten in tears?)

During the Reagan years and the Bush presidency the United States frequently beckoned. Margaret Thatcher needed no persuading. When she stepped on to American soil she became a new woman. It was as though the very air of this still young land of freedom and enterprise was a tonic. The slightest feeling of fatigue, if she ever knew such an experience, or a headcold (almost her only physical weakness, to which she paid no attention whatever) was gone in a flash and she looked ten years younger. She loved America: its tempo, its thrust, its impatience with yesterday, even its crudities which are often the price to be paid for being a pioneer. And America loved her back. There's nothing like the chemistry of mutual admiration.

Stepping off the RAF VC-10 at 6.30 a.m. on the overnight flight from Northolt she would go straight from the aircraft and do four or five television interviews before breakfast, among them Barbara Walters, the toughest, with whom she had an immediate rapport.

The American perception of Margaret Thatcher was very different from that of her homeland. It wasn't just that the United States is a matriarchal society, it went deeper than that. There were millions of Americans, who had only read about her or seen her on television, to whom she was a legendary figure who could speak the language of a free society with more passion than many of their own politicians. Here was a crusader, an original fresh out of the old country, and the sons and daughters of the American Revolution identified with her and believed that, had she been qualified by birth, she could have been their first woman President. In lieu of the White House, Britain's

335

Prime Minister on her many journeys to the United States became
an ambassador without peer in peacetime. With the people of America,
only Churchill at his zenith surpassed her popularity. It made a nice
change from things at home.

At the other end of the political map it was Margaret Thatcher
who first recognised in Mikhail Gorbachev a leader of the Soviet
Union as it then was (how extraordinary to be able to write that)
quite unlike his predecessors and went public on it. At their first
meeting at Chequers, despite having to communicate through
interpreters, there was an immediate meeting of minds. They got on.
She sensed that he liked women – he had an attractive wife who
always travelled with him – and at the traditional photo-opportunity
in the front drive she famously declared that here was a man with
whom she could do business. No other Western leader had said
anything like that about a Russian leader before, but she believed
that to expose the so-called 'Evil Empire' of the East to the influence
of the democratic West was a more sensible policy than for potential
enemies to continue to stockpile the weapons of mutual destruction.

It was a breakthrough that anticipated Reykjavik and began the
switch from 'niet' to 'da' in Soviet responses to the West which today,
the Middle East and Baltic States permitting, is leading to the step-
by-step abolition of the world's nuclear arsenal. If that finally happens,
if the great powers, as they destroy their armaments of no recall, are
not threatened by small ones with an undiscovered nuclear capacity,
then it was during a weekend at an English country house in
Buckinghamshire that an Englishwoman and a Russian built the first
bridge to the safer, saner and more peaceful world that the twentieth
century has not experienced but the twenty-first may not only come
to know but take for granted.

Over the years Margaret Thatcher's appearance changed from
what, if you didn't know otherwise, you might have thought was a
pretty, small-town schoolmistress with rather good cheekbones who
had neither time, money, knowledge nor inclination to bother about
clothes, to a person of immense authority and style who was the first
woman Prime Minister of her country and looked every inch the
part. She acquired glamour, a quality that is partly physical, partly
a glow that comes from within and often grows with the job you do
and the awe with which you are regarded.

When society airheads asked 'Does she think she's the Queen or
something?' it was no more than a snobbish attempt to be superior,
but as time went by there *was* a touch of the regal about her,
especially after she got the clothes right, the walk right, the hair
right, and the smile right. The jester who remarked that the Treasury's

MTFS (Medium Term Financial Strategy) really stood for 'Margaret Thatcher For Sovereign' had a crumb of observation going for him. Both Monarch and Prime Minister could afford to be amused.

The need to take unpopular measures toughened Mrs Thatcher. In a man toughness can be agreeable, even admirable; in a woman it is unalluring. Once the novelty of being the first elected member on the distaff side to run Britain began to fade she would, I think, have liked to cancel the gender factor, but she was shrewdly aware that being the sole female on the international circuit had its advantages.

As a woman she had no need to pull punches, while the male response was partly neutralised by the demands of courtesy. At the ever-growing number of European Community gatherings that filled her diary year after year, she stood out from the men. In the statutory photographs that are routine on these occasions there she was, front and centre, the one with the handbag, surrounded by what looked like a clutch of supporting and admiring males. The fact that some were less than admiring and others not at all supportive was not captured by the camera which, with the possible exception of M. Delors, registered only smiles all round. At these Summits, as at home, she was feared, respected, hated, admired, an increasingly formidable statesman with whom, until the latter years, it was dangerous to cross swords if you didn't want to end up with still more rebates for the United Kingdom.

'Speak softly and carry a big stick' may be sound political advice. 'Talk tough and carry a handbag' was the Thatcher method. In exclusively male preserves perhaps it had to be. A resolute woman in charge of a country is unlikely to be collegiate and therefore more difficult for men to live with at close quarters than an equally resolute male. The latter is a familiar figure and there's always Annie's Bar to mend fences, the former unknown territory to be approached with care. Though technically *primus inter pares* she became increasingly presidential in her dealings with her Ministers. I never had the pleasure of attending one of her Cabinets but the word was, if somebody hadn't mastered their brief, she didn't take prisoners.

Nevertheless, the received wisdom that she was less inclined than most to try a little tenderness, like much else that was thought, said or written about Mrs Thatcher, is a myth. Whatever the demands of the diary, when some disaster, national or personal, struck, she would ignore, cancel or postpone her commitments and rush to the side of whoever was in distress.

A group of us were gathered at Chequers for work on a major speech when an IRA bomb went off outside Chelsea Barracks, killing or maiming a busload of soldiers. She dropped everything, went rushing round the terrace gathering spring flowers by the basketful and was gone to London with a hurried 'Carry on. I don't know when I'll be back.' It was late in the day before she reappeared.

This sort of thing was not done for show. When her personal chauffeur died she slipped quietly away to his funeral in the suburbs and the press knew nothing of it. She always went to the funerals of friends unobtrusively, hoping to give what comfort could be given, a woman in a church pew or at the graveside who just happened to be Prime Minister.

At official funerals – the victims of the IRA or terrorist attacks in St James's Square or the skies over Scotland – this was not possible. There was the woman in the plain black dress and the unprepossessing black hat, brim pulled well down but impossible to hide from the cameras the drawn face and the look that said, more eloquently than any speech, 'Perhaps if one had done something more ... ' Iron Lady? Yes, for the media, for public consumption. But the private pain, that was just like anyone else's at a funeral – raw and poignant and exposed.

Watching the rise and rise of Margaret Thatcher, one thing puzzled me.

No one could be less class-conscious. She was genuinely anti-class. (When she used high fashion it was as a political weapon, though in my view, like many pretty women, she looked her best when she wasn't trying.) And yet, as she progressed from lower-middle-class Grantham girl to a world figure whose every word commanded attention, it wasn't just her progress up the political ladder that was engrossing, it was the social advance to which she appeared to take quite naturally, as though it sprang from birth rather than an astonishing career. She seemed to acquire an air of – I can't avoid the word – breeding (come to think of it, why should anyone? Animals that have it are admired, win prizes). It was as though somewhere in her family tree the genes had skipped a couple of generations and were now reborn in her.

When John Major calls for a classless society it's what one expects to hear. He typifies the Brixton boy whose brilliance, warmth and underlying toughness have taken him to the top and sensibly he makes no effort to seem otherwise. But the more Margaret Thatcher cried, in effect, 'Class, dismiss!' the more she seemed to embody class distinction. I can't explain this. I merely report it.

On 26 May 1989 at Guildhall she received the Freedom of the City of London. This by no means automatic honour was bestowed on her as Prime Minister rather than Party Leader so the excellent draft of her speech of thanks had been written by the Private Secretary, Andrew Turnbull, with the final fretwork down to me.

The morning after this was approved Amanda Colvin, then her Personal and Diary Secretary, called me to say there was a spare ticket for the Guildhall ceremony and the lunch at the Mansion House that was to follow and the PM wondered if I would like it. This invitation was typical. Knowing that I had declined any kind of salary she was always thinking up ways of saying 'Thank you for helping.'

It was a grand occasion with the Establishment in full attendance. Margaret was in excellent form, relaxed and happy on the raised section at one end of historic Guildhall, surrounded by senior officers of the City of London in their official robes and their ladies in their sparkling spring outfits. After the ceremony, as we shuffled along in the crowd going out I found myself next to Dr Runcie, then Archbishop of Canterbury. He murmured, 'I'm just off to the United States to give an address. I was looking forward to it but that speech of the PM's has given me an inferiority complex.' I had met him once before at Chequers but I doubt he remembered. The most agreeable compliments come from people who are unaware that they are giving you one. At the Mansion House lunch she was scheduled to give another speech to much the same audience. She did eighteen minutes off-the-cuff without a note. Who needs 'helpers'?

Most people recharge their batteries by going on holiday. With Mrs Thatcher the opposite was the case. She actively disliked holidays (actively is the word), regarding them as a waste of a good engine while it was still capable of peak performance, and virtually had to be bullied into taking them.

One of those who twisted her arm on these occasions was the redoubtable Lady Tilney, who used the privilege of long-standing friendship and the authority of a DBE to speak her mind with a candour that could be awesome. If Margaret could be tough, Guinevere was tougher. In this, as in all things, she was supported by that verray parfit gentle knight, her husband, Sir John, in his time a fine soldier and a Liverpool MP widely respected on both sides of the House. To them and others Margaret would reluctantly defer but, after approximately twenty-four hours of enforced leisure and not a crisis in sight calling for her instant return to Downing Street, she tended to grow desperate. The picture of her supposedly lugging Denis's golf clubs round whatever course was adjacent to the holiday home with an expression that says 'I'd like to grab a four-iron and clout whoever talked me into this' is a photo-opportunity to be treasured.

Goodness knows where the wellsprings of her extraordinary energy were located. They said she took Royal Jelly. They said a lot of things. There are those who believe she literally recharged her batteries from time to time by slipping quietly out of Number Ten by the back door to take some sort of ionised bath through which a special current of electricity had been passed by an Indian lady living in Shepherd's Bush. Such mysterious goings-on sound more like Mrs Christie in paperback than Mrs Thatcher in the buff but, people being passing strange, I suppose they could be true.

However, since so far as I am aware no one ever saw her entering the bath exhausted and emerging half an hour later bright as a button, fit as a fiddle and fresh as a daisy, I can offer no explanation of these alleged immersions, other than to say the theory that the electric current in the water recharged Margaret seems to me most improbable. It's much more likely that Margaret recharged the water.

When the popularity that had sustained her in the early years began to fall away and the attacks grew apace they said, 'She's used to it, she doesn't feel it.' She felt it. She knew the strength of the hostility of those who saw in her the enemy of everything they believed in. It failed to weaken her resolve or soften her policies but it got to her all right. Being up there where the buck stops, on your own, doesn't make unremitting denigration and abuse any easier to take.

'Come now,' you say, 'she wanted the job and went flat out for it, she must have known what it would be like – the stress, the pressure, the massive responsibility that goes with the territory, there never was anyone who revelled in it like Mrs T. She had the constitution of an ox and almost perfect health and could manage with half the sleep the rest of us require. So no one likes to be a target and it's lonely up there on the mountain-top. It must be worth it or there wouldn't be such a cluster on the rockface challenging for the peak.'

All right. It's true she was blessed with the equipment, physical and psychological, to take the strain of the job that she felt she was born to. She none the less struck me as a solitary who was always with people, a loner whom her working life obliged to appear gregarious. For all the flying to and fro across the globe, the Summits and the Cabinets, the committees and the diaries overflowing with engagements, some as much as a year ahead, with a single exception (her husband) the woman in the Downing Street emplacement, who made mistakes like most of us do but did great things like most of us don't, was very much alone at the heart of the maze – and never more so than when her political career moved suddenly to its unimaginable climax.

19

. . . .

'That Thing in November'

The days dwindle down
to a precious few
September, November . . .
Maxwell Anderson, *'September Song'*

Friday 12 October, 1990, the day before her sixty-fifth birthday, and her sixteenth Party Conference speech (and mine) is coming to a close . . .

The speechwriting team had once more spent the week holed up in the customary seaside hostelry – this year the Highcliff, Bournemouth, under the maximum security enforced at all Party Conferences since the Brighton bomb six years before.

I had driven down from Number Ten with Andrew Turnbull, to join veterans Robin Harris and John O'Sullivan (who had flown back for the occasion from New York where he was editor of the *National Review*), and the young and personable Political Secretary, John Whittingdale, whose way it was to greet my more light-hearted contributions with loud and apparently spontaneous laughter (only one of many reasons why he is an excellent fellow).

Also in attendance, in addition to Turnbull, were her most recent Parliamentary Private Secretary, Peter Morrison (tall, florid, amiable and ample), who was both fascinated and mystified by the speech-writing process. Well, to a newcomer it *is* one of life's more memorable experiences. On parade on the final morning was one more auxiliary brain, the admirable Stephen Sherbourne who had volunteered – yes, he *volunteered* – to join us for the last few hours of this uniquely punishing event and whose deep-rooted addiction to it I understand and share.

The Party was in apprehensive mood and the Leader's annual boost was badly needed. Since last year's Conference a number of Cabinet Ministers had resigned. The Chancellor, Nigel Lawson, had gone, ostensibly over his insistence that the PM should dispense either with his services or those of Professor Alan Walters, her economics adviser, but fundamentally over Europe. The experienced and long-serving Norman Fowler at Employment and the even longer-serving Peter Walker in charge of the Welsh Office had departed 'to spend more time with their families' (a delightful euphemism for 'enough is enough'). Worse, her friend and close political ally, Nicholas Ridley, had been obliged to step down from Environment, again over Europe, when part of an interview he had given the editor of the *Spectator* (Dominic Lawson, son of Nigel) in which he had spelt out some typically trenchant views regarding our German continental colleagues and which he had thought were off the record, turned out not to be.

With all this on her mind and an imminent challenge to her leadership almost certain, I expected Margaret to be showing signs of strain but, as always, she led from the front and had been, at least on the surface, in excellent humour throughout the week. The Bournemouth weather was mild and clement and that esoteric exercise, the writing of the Leader's Conference speech, had for once proceeded on its way with a remarkable lubricity. Even the last-minute fight against time was missing. We were up to schedule.

When, in my occasional role as court jester, I had started a minor tussle with the lady to enliven the proceedings and the others stopped work, leaning forward eager for the joust, she had smiled with the utmost good nature and said, 'Relax. This is just Ronnie and I having our annual fight.' The sea had been calm all week and in the Prime Minister's suite an equal calm had prevailed. That this was the calm before the final storm was in no way apparent . . .

In the conference hall, where she rouses the faithful to a final frenzy, her peroration rings down the curtain on the predictable Roman triumph. How many more, I wonder, my mind going back to fifteen unique Octobers on the waterfront. If this is to be the last of the series her final words, the very essence of her political philosophy, may perhaps be remembered.

Labour's vision has been shattered.
Beneath its contrived self-confidence lies a growing certainty that the world and history have passed it by; and that if Britain rejects them yet again, as I believe it will, socialism must return for ever to its proper place – the Reading Room of the British Library where Karl Marx found it. Section: History of Ideas; Sub-section: 19th Century; Status: Archaic.

The new world of freedom into which the dazzled Socialists have stumbled is not new to us.

What to them is uncharted territory is to us familiar and well-loved ground.

For Britain has returned to those basic truths and principles which made her great – personal liberty, private property and the rule of law, on which democratic freedoms everywhere are based.

Ours is a creed which travels and endures. Its truths are written in the human heart.

It is the faith which once more has given life to Britain and offers hope to the world.

We pledge in this Party to uphold these principles of freedom and to fight for them.

We pledge it to our allies overseas.

And we pledge it to *this* country we are proud to serve.

The reception is, if anything, even more delirious than usual. On the platform, surrounded by her applauding and apparently adoring Cabinet, the star acknowledges the rapturous acclaim of her public, both arms held aloft as they have been every year since 1975. In the body of the hall 'TEN MORE YEARS!' roar the faithful five thousand, stamping their feet in time with the words. 'TEN MORE YEARS! TEN MORE YEARS!! TEN MORE YEARS!!!' they cry fortissimo. The floor trembles. The rafters shake. It is as though by the sheer force of their utterance and its constant repetition they feel they can compel the future. Even by the Leader's standards it is a salute to end all salutes. As it turns out to be ...

Forty-one days later, shortly after nine-thirty on the morning of 22 November (an ominous date in the political calendar: it was on 22 November 1963 that President John F. Kennedy of the United States was assassinated), after eleven and a half years as Prime Minister, Margaret Thatcher resigns.

There are those who hold that, metaphorically, Mrs Thatcher too was the victim of political assassination. She would not, I think, dissent from that, though strictly speaking the denouement was a voluntary act of abdication. At which I fancy she would give a wry smile and ask, 'Does anyone believe that?'

There are numerous versions of the lead-up to the downfall of Britain's longest-serving Prime Minister this century and the second-longest ever. From my observation post it was clear that a sequence of events that was to move with the inevitability of Greek tragedy to its riveting conclusion had been set in train more than a year before by an obscure backbench Conservative.

Once a year in November, when Parliament reassembles after the summer recess, the Leader of the Conservative Party is subject to re-election and may be challenged by any Member of the Parliamentary Party in good standing. Since 1975, when Margaret Thatcher had successfully challenged Edward Heath for the leadership, no one had come forward to challenge her. As Conservative victory followed Conservative victory her position had become steadily more entren-ched. When the chips were down she had delivered. Three times.

However, throughout the early summer of '89, backbench Tories were becoming restless. The so-called Poll Tax, the economy, and Europe were three flashpoints showing red for danger and for the first time there were enough voices, hushed or overt, raised against the Leader to encourage rumours that a challenger would emerge in the autumn. When he did emerge it was in the improbable form of Sir Anthony Meyer, a Conservative MP of less than outstanding acuity. He was seen as a stalking-horse for Michael Heseltine but that November Heseltine held back and Meyer's name went forward alone.

There was, of course, no serious threat from such a candidate but it was a reminder that, ten years at the top notwithstanding, the Leader was not impregnable and, under the Byzantine formula devised by Humphry Berkeley and implemented by Edward Heath and Alec Douglas-Home, could be challenged. That the rules had not specifically been intended to apply to a Prime Minister in office was not spelt out. A challenge was therefore not *ultra vires*.

The Thatcher campaign was officially run by that sturdy Scot, George Younger, but Ian Gow, Richard Ryder and Tristan Garel-Jones, the astute Deputy Chief Whip, were all privately active on her behalf. The result – Thatcher 314, Meyer 33, abstentions 24 with 3 MPs unable to vote – was the expected walkover. Nevertheless a total of sixty Tory MPs had failed to endorse their Leader. It was a litmus test of what was possible against even such a towering figure and its implications were not lost on political enemies and friends alike. Garel-Jones in particular was alarmed and sought a private meeting with the Prime Minister.

Over a drink in the flat at Number Ten he warned Mrs Thatcher that, in addition to the sixty who had not supported her against Meyer, there were a hundred more, a mixed bag of the genuinely uneasy at the way things were going and the disaffected who had been passed over for office or honours, who might well have rallied to a more substantial challenger. As it was, a marker had been put down that had opened the door, and quite a few minds, to future possibilities. The Prime Minister listened, took notes and was grateful for the information, but while Garel-Jones could warn he could not demand action. None followed. It wasn't complacency. She was counselled by others who had her ear to watch her back. But three times she had bucked the political trend and felt there was no compelling reason why she could not manage a fourth triumph at the polls. One mo' time was surely possible, followed by a grand goodbye at the moment of her choice. In mid-Parliament perhaps. Perhaps not. Was she as confident as she seemed? I wasn't sure. I recalled an incident earlier that year at Chequers.

A few of us were sitting in the private garden. It was a lovely summer's afternoon, the birds were in full song and Chequers was looking its very best, than which there is no finer sight in all the English shires. The Prime Minister, however, seemed distrait, her eyes wandering from tree to tree and flower to flower as though to remind herself that nothing is for ever. Suddenly she sighed, 'Oh well, there's always the mashed potato circuit.' (The mashed potato circuit is an Americanism referring to the meal that goes with the lecture tour.) I was taken aback. High summer in England, Chequers and the weather obliging: hard not to feel all's right with the world. But clearly for Margaret it wasn't. Although her personal crisis was eighteen months ahead there were moments when she seemed to contemplate the shape of things to come with a sense of foreboding. This was one of them.

Another, even more unmistakable, occurred the following year at the dinner to celebrate her husband's seventy-fifth birthday: a sparkling occasion – black tie, glittering silver, some forty people round the State dining table at Number Ten.

After the meal was over and toasts had been drunk the guests were taking coffee and chatting in the Pillared Room when I spotted Margaret sitting on a sofa in a far corner, quite alone. She was usually an exemplary hostess, moving from group to group, making sure the conversation was flowing and no one was being mortified, but now she was apart, looking slowly round the room, lost in a kind of melancholy which I sensed without knowing the reason for it. For such a cheerful gathering she seemed withdrawn and sad, as though troubled by something not visible to the rest of us. I wondered what was wrong and went over and sat beside her. She said nothing for quite a while, then murmured, more to herself than to me: 'Sometimes I think all that really matters is one's friends.'

There was something going on here I didn't understand. I felt suddenly concerned for her and thought of the tender little song that ends Stephen Sondheim's musical *Into the Woods* which was running at London's Phoenix Theatre, the song called 'No One is Alone'. I was about to say, 'Go and see it. I think you'd like it' when someone gushed noisily up and the spell was broken. She gave me a wan half-smile, then, collecting herself, rose and walked briskly away into her friends.

It is noon on Monday 22 October, 1990, and the Great and the Good, and the not so good, are assembled at St Margaret's, Westminster, for the memorial service for hugely popular Ian Gow, recently murdered by the IRA.

Sir Geoffrey Howe's address – he was a close and loyal friend of Ian's – strikes just the right note: moving, at times hilarious, deeply felt and beautifully delivered. How Ian would have loved it – and how deeply shocked he would have been at what Sir Geoffrey was to precipitate exactly one month later: the political liquidation of the woman for whom Ian's love and devotion was second only to that for his wife (I seem to hear the primal screams of intellectual snobs – Lady Warnock, former Mistress of Girton College, Cambridge, comes to mind – but Margaret could as easily inspire devotion as its opposite).

After the service Conservative and Labour Front Bench file out of the church, side by side. 'I must say, Geoffrey was very good,' says Margaret to Neil Kinnock as they go past me down the nave. I raise an eyebrow. She has not, for quite some time, been in the habit of praising the sole survivor of her first Cabinet and their working relationship, never close, has not been helped by her regular deflating of him in her last.

As he is temperamentally pro-Europe and she the opposite, they have found themselves not infrequently at odds at the various European Summits that they perforce attended together. Since Madrid in the summer of '89 neither has been at pains, and especially not Sir Geoffrey, to conceal their differences on Europe in general and on economic and monetary union (regrettably known as EMU) in particular. For a Prime Minister and until recently her Foreign Secretary – much to his chagrin he has been reshuffled sideways and is now Leader of the House and Deputy Prime Minister – to be known to be divided has not strengthened her position or diminished his disquiet. It is her report to the House on the Rome Summit a few days later, in which she cries 'No! No!! No!!!' to Europe, that finally triggers his decision to resign, and after a Cabinet at which she has been even harder on him than usual he goes straight to his office and writes his letter of resignation. It is Thursday 1 November. Time is running out. Now her Deputy has gone. The impression grows of a government gradually disintegrating. The pieces on the political chessboard are moving into position for the endgame.

Any Minister who resigns is entitled to address the House and give his reasons, or what pass for his reasons. Sir Geoffrey's resignation letter has been courteous and careful but not too careful. Will he leave it at that? Surely not. But nothing happens. Day follows day and still Sir Geoffrey Howe stays silent. Curiosity mounts. What is he up to? In the corridors the word is that he is writing his speech and having difficulty with it. Meanwhile Michael Heseltine, expected daily to announce his candidacy for the leadership, drops broad hints in a letter to his constituency chairman without actually taking the plunge. He then goes off on a trip to the Middle East, leaving the media agog and Westminster bewildered.

At Number Ten the Prime Minister has no illusions. 'It'll be a fortnight's agony. Oh well. Never mind,' she says matter-of-factly in the only reference she makes to me about what she regards as the coming contest. I remind her that the challenger hasn't specifically declared himself and may not do so. I don't believe what I am saying. Nor does she.

'He'll stand. He's waiting for his moment.'

The writing of the annual Lord Mayor's Banquet speech, due on Monday 12 November, continues according to schedule. As it is a Government rather than a Party occasion Andrew Turnbull and Charles Powell, the senior civil servants, supply the backbone of the speech which is sent to me for polishing. On Sunday 11 November, we work until ten in the Cabinet Room. If she is anxious it doesn't show. Indeed she is positively cheerful. At times like this, when the Lord Mayor and his banquet can hardly be uppermost in her mind, one's admiration for her ability to concentrate on the matter in hand is unstinted.

In this she is as ever helped by Bernard Ingham who, taking no risks with her self-confidence, continues to shield her from the worst of the mounting speculation and personal attacks by confining his morning press reports to the usual summary. It is kind of Bernard – who has made scowling an art form but is really a sentimental old duck – though perhaps it makes the shock that much more traumatic when finally she is faced with what she comes to call 'That thing in November'. (I am aware that Mr Enoch Powell says there is no such thing as a thing but, as an expression of supreme contempt for something one cannot bring oneself to refer to in any other way, I would dare to say I think there is.)

The audience for the Lord Mayor's Banquet speech at Guildhall – white tie, tails, curling cigar smoke – has never been a favourite of hers, although the majority are Conservative supporters, but she gets off to a bold start, taking the intense interest in the coming fight for the leadership head on with a light-hearted promise to knock the bowling all round the ground. 'That's my style,' she affirms. This draws immediate applause from the City gentlemen and their ladies and by the time she sits down twenty minutes later there is a growing feeling of relief that Margaret Thatcher, who has survived so many alarums and excursions, will once more come triumphantly through. 'She always does' is the general feeling.

The following afternoon, Tuesday 13 November, at four-twenty, Sir Geoffrey Howe rose in an emotionally charged House of Commons to make his long-awaited resignation speech. If expectations were high he did not disappoint. Never in my lengthening experience of the political scene was a demolition job done with such meticulous artistry. He had taken his time to write it but from his point of view, and that of others on the Conservative benches who felt as he did, it was time well spent. In a crowded, electrically silent House he began what was and will remain for ever an historic speech with a surgical precision, each word honed with Aesculapian skill for maximum effect. This was no passionate philippic. It was much more subtle. Four rows behind and slightly to the right of the Front Bench on which for so long he had been a fixture, he began by poking fun at those in the Government who had attributed his resignation to no more than stylistic differences. 'If some of my former colleagues are to be believed, I must be the first Minister in history who has resigned because he was in full agreement with government policy,' he said to loud laughter from all parts of the House. (Relax them first with a joke.) And then, 'The truth is that in many aspects of politics, style and substance complement each other.' (Impossible to quarrel with that.)

Moving on to the inflation factor, he attributed the failure to control it to the Prime Minister's delay in joining the Exchange Rate Mechanism (ERM). 'The real tragedy is we did not join [it] at least five years ago.' He referred to his 'Rt. Hon. Friend dismissing ... the very idea that the hard ecu proposal [for a single European currency] might find growing favour among the peoples of Europe ... How on earth are the Chancellor and the Governor of the Bank of England, commending the hard ecu as they strive to do, to be taken as serious participants in the debate against that kind of background noise?'

Background noise? No one had ever referred to Mrs Thatcher as background noise, they wouldn't have dared. 'It is rather like sending your opening batsmen to the crease only to find, the moment the first balls are bowled, that their bats have been broken by the team captain.'

The mockery was merciless. Margaret Thatcher, in her usual seat on the Government Front Bench facing the Despatch Box sat listening, apparently relaxed, her head half-resting on the green leather, a suggestion of a smile at her lips, while her former colleague's scalpel continued to carve and dissect with the utmost delicacy. 'The tragedy is – and it is for me personally, for my party, for our whole people and for the Prime Minister herself, a very real tragedy – that her perceived attitude towards Europe is running increasingly serious risks for the future of our nation.'

This was scorching stuff. In a reference to his 'commitment to Government by persuasion' he pressed home the impossibility of a convincing and united approach to political problems in the face of repeated interjections from offstage. 'I realise now that the task has become futile, trying to stretch the meaning of words beyond what is credible, and trying to pretend that there was a common policy when every step forward risked being subverted by some casual comment or impulsive answer.' The unrelenting attack went on, but he did not raise his voice. Indeed, as this gentle surgeon went for the jugular he lowered it slightly.

'I have done what I believe to be right for my party and my country,' he concluded in the velvet monotone of which he was a master and which was so much more destructive than a blistering attack. 'The time has come for others to consider their own response to the tragic conflict of loyalties with which I myself have wrestled for perhaps too long.'

I sat forward sharply. His closing words had gone suddenly, daringly, beyond the parameters of a personal resignation statement. This was a calculated invitation to Cabinet and Party by her former Chancellor, Foreign Secretary and Deputy Prime Minister to join him in removing the Head of Government from office. ('Right. Sew her up, Sister.') He sat down to a stunned House. The mildest of mortals, widely regarded as a natural conciliator, almost cuddly, had been translated into a hanging judge.

As a parliamentary performance it was superb. As political subversion it was deadly. In content, timing and delivery it was a killer of the highest class, in turn witty, factual, regretful and lethal, designed for his Party rather than the Opposition but also for the wider audience in the country. He had come, not to praise Margaret Thatcher but to bury her, and in eighteen remorseless minutes he had dug her political grave, filled it in beyond possibility of exhumation and conducted an autopsy while the victim was still alive and listening.

Nothing subsequently said or done by others approached the impact of those eighteen minutes. They were the catalyst of all that followed, as their speaker surely intended them to be. To pretend otherwise is to underestimate Sir Geoffrey Howe, a mistake that Margaret Thatcher had perhaps made once too often and for which she was to pay the ultimate price.

What to me was incongruous, as well as fatally damaging, was that the knife had been wielded by, of all people, a deceptively grey and unobtrusive politician – not a trace of the killer instinct, one would say – who for years had padded peacefully about the corridors of government, albeit in the highest offices of state (bar the one that mattered most) giving the impression behind the glasses that he lacked ambition and regarded life as, on the whole, a bit of a disappointment.

Had this honourable and decent man really done what he did solely 'for my party and my country'? Or was there a sub-text, a part-reprisal for the humbling he had endured over the years in the killing fields of Cabinet (I had witnessed it myself once at the time of the Westland Affair) as well as what he saw as the need to remove the Leader who, if she was still there at the next election, would according to the opinion polls lose it?

Whatever Sir Geoffrey's motive, or combination of motives, conscious or subliminal, if it was Margaret Thatcher's tragedy, it was, as he admitted, also his. For despite all the offices he held and the outstanding gifts he brought to a career of the highest distinction, Geoffrey Howe will assuredly go down in history as the Brutus figure whose carefully-timed stab in the back set the stage and provided the ammunition for others to complete the political destruction of Margaret Thatcher. Compared with that single act of brilliantly executed matricide all else, in a lifetime of service, will be chaff before the wind. I wondered what Ian Gow would have thought, had he been there. But then if Ian, who was close to both of them, had been there it might never have happened. As for me, whatever political innocence I had left vanished for ever that afternoon. So this was politics, naked and unashamed. I had learnt at last.

*

Intentional or not, the immediate effect of Geoffrey Howe's rever-berating intervention was to give Michael Heseltine the green light for which he had been waiting and within twenty-four hours, to nobody's astonishment, he declared that he was standing for the leadership. He was duly proposed and seconded by two of his supporters while Douglas Hurd and John Major stood for Margaret Thatcher. The first, and indeed the only ballot should there be an outright winner, was set for Tuesday 20 November.

Meanwhile the Prime Minister carried on with her engagements as though nothing untoward had happened and this tiresome business was no more than a distraction from her essential job of running the country.

On 16 November she visited the troops in Northern Ireland. Two days later she flew to the Paris Summit for the signing of the CFE (Conventional Forces Reduction in Europe) Treaty and the Conference on Security and Cooperation in Europe (CSCE) that marked the end of the Cold War.

With her leadership at the hazard it was her own security that she should have put first. That shrewd observer Alan Watkins comments, 'If Mrs Thatcher had stayed at home instead of going to Paris she would certainly have seen off Mr Michael Heseltine and might still be Prime Minister today.' I have no doubt about the first half of that proposition. To be out of London for the forty-eight hours before the ballot was an extraordinary decision. Had she cut the Summit the Presidents of the United States, France and the Soviet Union and the German Chancellor would surely have understood. They knew, if anyone did, that when fighting for one's political life it's imperative to be where the action is. But as ever she bowed to the demands of world statesmanship, regarding it as the higher duty. I believe it was her undoing.

It could be argued, perhaps it was, that duty was not the sole consideration: that it was clever tactics for the Prime Minister to be seen on the world stage chatting and dining in French palaces on equal terms with Messrs Reagan, Mitterrand, Gorbachev and Kohl while at home her backbench challenger, albeit a former Secretary of State, had no comparable photo-opportunities. It's an argument that might have been valid in a General Election where the electorate runs into millions, but not when all depended on 372 MPs gathered at Westminster who held her fate in their hands and whose weaker brethren needed to be evangelised by their Leader in person. At such a time her place was surely in the purlieus of the House of Commons, rallying the faithful, reassuring the doubtful and showing the flag.

As it was, gently twisting the necessary arms was left to her campaign team, which was not as sharp as it had been the previous year. It was again led by George Younger, though this time with a certain reluctance. Apparently he had difficulty tearing himself away from his duties as chairman of the Royal Bank of Scotland, which was unhappy at the prospect of being without him for even a wee while. A key figure in those critical days was her PPS, Peter Morrison, a dedicated Thatcherite whose task it was to assess, insofar as it was possible, the strength of her political support. The calculations of the leadership poll being as finespun as the rules that governed it, this was far from easy. If all those who assured him they were body and soul with the Prime Minister were to be believed, she was home and dry, but Morrison formed the view that a number were being economical with the truth of their intentions. The question was, how many? He estimated approximately 15 per cent were not to be relied upon and built the figure into his head count. It was a good guess.

Just after 6.30 p.m. on Tuesday 20 November the result of the ballot was phoned through from the House of Commons to the British Embassy in Paris where Margaret Thatcher was waiting in an upstairs bedroom with Charles Powell, Bernard Ingham, Peter Morrison, Ambassador Sir Ewan Fergusson and Crawfie (Mrs Crawford, her wardrobe mistress).

The figures were:

Thatcher	204
Heseltine	152
Abstentions	16

To those unacquainted with the mysteries of how the Tories elect their Leader this would appear to be a clear victory for the Prime Minister. Not so. The rules for the first ballot are double-jointed. They require – or did then, they may have been changed since for they are arbitrary and slightly dotty – *first* a minimum of 50 per cent, plus one, of the Parliamentary Party. That was, at the time, 187 votes, a hurdle she cleared with ease. But then came the second leg of the equation. Under the convoluted formula she *also* needed a lead over her challenger of 15 per cent of the Parliamentary Party. That was, at least 56 votes.

Mrs Thatcher was only four votes short of the fifty-six that would have given her outright victory but under the peculiar party arithmetic a miss was as good as a mile. If she was to remain Prime

Minister, a second ballot was inevitable. True, the deficit was small but significantly, abstentions included, as many as 168 of her MPs – exactly a hundred more than the year before – had failed to rally to her cause. (Garel-Jones had been precisely right.) The effect of the missing four votes was a psychological setback out of all proportion to their number. This was no flesh wound. The political furniture that had supported Margaret Thatcher in office for over eleven years was collapsing.

Although she went straight out on to the Embassy steps and announced to an astonished BBC correspondent and the waiting world that she was very pleased she had more than half the Parliamentary Party vote and that it was her intention (a word that was deliberately not a commitment) to let her name 'go forward for the second ballot', there are those who believe that in her heart she already knew that it was over.

WEDNESDAY 21 NOVEMBER
Back in London by lunchtime the following day she summons her most senior advisers to sandwiches in the Cabinet Room. There is little for her comfort. George Younger has finally succumbed to the piper's lament from the Bank of Scotland and withdrawn across the border. John Wakeham is now her campaign manager. Wakeham is highly experienced and widely trusted but serious damage has been done and it's late in the day to turn the tide. Meanwhile the reverberations of Geoffrey Howe's deadly speech continue their corrosive effect on the Parliamentary Party and the vigorous and well-organised Heseltine camp, elated by the Prime Minister's stumble at the first fence, is steadily gaining strength.

Will she really go ahead with the second ballot? Rumours whistle down the wind. Sums are done. Figures fly. Politicians gather in houses, clubs, bars and corridors to confer, to swap notes, to assess the position. Wakeham urges the Prime Minister to consult her Cabinet colleagues. It's the Cabinet, not the Party, that she needs to hear from, he tells her. If the colleagues are with her, or at least a majority of them, then she can continue the fight with a measure of confidence. If not...

The members of the Cabinet – all but John Major who is at home in his constituency nursing an impacted wisdom tooth – are summoned to the Prime Minister's office in the Commons. They are to go in one by one at roughly five-minute intervals so that each can speak privately without being influenced by his colleagues. In theory, this is admirable. In fact, as they gather in the corridor outside the

354

office, there is ample time for an exchange of views and a body of concerted opinion to build up. Thus each individual opinion offered to the Prime Minister becomes in fact a collective judgement.

The majority, in most cases with deep regret, in one or two with undeclared relief, tell her that in their view, if she goes forward to a second ballot, she cannot win. That they will – errors and omissions excepted – support her if she does, but that Conservatives in the House and key constituencies are running scared and if she continues to fight on there is a grave risk that not only will she be humiliated but the Tory Party will be torn apart. 'Finish, good lady, the bright day is done, and we are for the dark.' Antony's farewell to Cleopatra, with the crucial substitution of '*or*' for '*and*', is the advice the colleagues are urging their leader to accept. The unmistakable implication is that, if she goes, the Party will recover nationally. If not, not.

She listens quietly and with dignity to what her Cabinet are telling her. What if they are wrong? True, the Thatcherites among them are a dwindling force, the pragmatists are dominant, but there is nothing so febrile as political opinion and she is a born fighter. To go down fighting is one thing. To throw in the towel before the bell for the last round is against her deepest instincts. After all, a switch of two votes – just two, dammit – on the first ballot and there would have been no need for a second. On such minutiae hang political fortunes and the fate of nations. Even now all might just possibly come right, mightn't it? Mightn't it?? But even as she ponders her dilemma, reports filtering through to her office tell of support breaking up and draining away. By early evening it is clear the position is terminal. Ah well. She has thanked each of her Cabinet in turn and told them she will sleep on it. She returns to Number Ten, to consult her husband and decide her future.

THURSDAY 22 NOVEMBER

Throughout the night and the early hours of the morning her staunchest friends in the Party send messages of support, some even go round to Downing Street and try to see her, to beg her to stand firm and continue the fight. But to her husband's intense relief – the last thing Denis Thatcher wants is to see his wife humiliated – she has made up her mind. Morning brings a highly emotional final Cabinet at which she formally confirms what its members already know and at 9.41 the Press Association announces that the Prime Minister has resigned. The Thatcher era is over.

As the news flashed round the world huge bouquets of flowers, cables, letters and messages of condolence and comfort, of distress and goodwill and total disbelief, began pouring into Number Ten. She barely glanced at them, not daring to let emotion take over, and drove to the Palace to confirm her decision to the Queen. But until a successor was chosen the nation's business had to go on and, as though to confirm that when the gods are against you there is nothing to be done, a no confidence debate tabled by the Opposition – to which she was required to reply on behalf of the Government – was scheduled to follow Prime Minister's Questions that afternoon.

Again, as with Geoffrey Howe's speech, a packed House of Commons. Again the tension, this time laced with sympathetic embarrassment, much of it coming from the Opposition benches. After the standard fifteen minutes of 'Questions to the Prime Minister' Neil Kinnock opened the debate with a spirited attack on the Government which failed to grip. He was not to blame. From the moment she came in all attention had been focused on the woman in blue on the Government Front Bench who now rose to reply.

She began quietly, professionally, under iron control. (She had told her staff, who as usual had briefed her for PMQs, that she would be all right provided everyone wasn't too nice to her.) As the speech proceeded there were polite murmurs and the occasional 'Hear, hear' but nothing remarkable took place until she made a passing reference to, of all things, the prospective European Central Bank and who might be its Governor.

'She's going to be the Governor!' said extreme left-winger Dennis Skinner from his corner seat on the Labour front row.

A great gust of laughter broke the tension. The lady stopped in mid-sentence, took a step or two up and down the gangway separating the Government and the Opposition benches and appeared to consider the matter gravely, then with a broad grin and perfect timing said, '*What* a good idea! I hadn't thought of that.'

The House exploded into something approaching hysteria. The laughter of relief at this response to misfortune went on and on. Margaret Thatcher went on smiling. Eventually she tried to get back to basics. 'Now where were we,' she began and then a sudden burst of euphoria seized her and she cried out, 'I'm enjoying this! I'm enjoying this!'

Her transparent pleasure – she really *was* enjoying it – seemed to take her as much by surprise as her audience and from that moment the speech was an unqualified triumph. It was not so much what she said as the spectacle of an irrepressible human spirit, resilient in the teeth of personal disaster, that gripped and moved the House. She had never shown to such superb effect in all the days of her supremacy. It was great theatre, gallant, without a trace of self-pity, and was seen as such by the House which is at its best when, irrespective of Party, it recognises and salutes courage.

Margaret Thatcher's valedictory appearance in the role of Prime Minister was the finest of her career and will not be forgotten by those who were privileged to see and hear it. By the time she sat down her domination of the House was so complete that her downfall seemed to some to have been a madness of the moment. Others who, in the ballot, had voted for her opponent began to wonder what they had done.

What *had* they done? Was the Prime Minister the victim of a carefully contrived political plot, as she and others came to believe and indeed many still believe? Having dug deep in inner and outer circles I have to say I do not believe there was a conspiracy to bring down Mrs Thatcher, in the sense of a clandestine intrigue or planned betrayal by her Cabinet colleagues and others in the higher reaches of the Conservative Party.

I think what happened was this:

After a year and more of adverse opinion polls a growing number of Conservative MPs, notably those with marginal seats, became convinced that if the next General Election was not to be lost, and their seats with it, the Leader must be changed. This view was correctly reported to the Cabinet and by them to the Prime Minister, confirming her own reports from the Chief Whip and the chairman of the 1922 Committee. She was faced with a consensus of opinion and she bowed to it. When is a consensus a conspiracy? I would say, when consensus is not enough to bring about a result profoundly desired by those determined to achieve it. In this case it *was* enough. However reluctantly, she accepted the opinion of the consensus. There was therefore no need to conspire.

To put it crudely: Margaret Thatcher came into politics to change the nature of society. Her chosen instrument was the Conservative Party. Her policies were radical and the hierarchy didn't really care for them but she delivered the vote so they went along. They were the Conservative Party. They were there to conserve. There was a radical wing but it was a wing, not the whole bird. 'Time for a change,' she had said in 1979. Up to a point, they agreed. They are the Up-to-a-Point Party.

She knew this. She had always known it. But there was much to

357

be done and to settle for half measures was not in her nature. However, her political antennae were acute, so after a time she called a halt and trod water to see what would happen. What happened was people began to say she had run out of steam. So she stirred things up with a controversial measure that would show there was plenty of steam left where the rest had come from. She called it the Community Charge and they didn't like it. They called it the Poll Tax and the other kind of poll said more than half the electorate detested it.

Traditional Conservatives wanted her to call it off, to turn back the tide of unpopularity before it engulfed them. But she was the lady who wasn't for turning, especially when she believed that she was right and that in due course time would prove it. The Party read the runes, however, and saw that time was running out. It refused to follow the Leader and the Leader was determined to carry on leading. So they turned her out.

There were other reasons, one in particular: the great landmass across the Channel. If Mary Queen of Scots had 'Calais' written on her heart, then Margaret Thatcher will surely one day find 'Europe' carved on hers. She believed in a Common Market but not a Common Country. Sovereignty, whether in small or large amounts, bit by bit or one fell swoop, was not to be surrendered. 'O Island in the rain, solo and safe shalt though remain.' But even she couldn't handbag the European idea into oblivion. The Treaty of Rome, of which Britain was a signatory, had given it binding jurisdiction. Something, or someone, had to give. Under extreme pressure she gave.

There was also, in my view, a third reason. After eleven and a half years of change people wanted a little peace and quiet. But reformers are not peaceful, quiet people. It is their function to challenge the status quo, not to bestow the tranquil life. Well and good, but an excess of innovation can induce political odium. To be unpopular is not *ipso facto* to be wrong, indeed frequently the reverse, but when the grumbling appendix of dissent led to a conviction that Margaret Thatcher could no longer guarantee the vote, the Party did not hesitate. Moving with a ruthlessness worthy of its history it dumped the pilot, an inconvenient woman whose time, they felt, was up.

But the pages of history are studded with the inconvenient who are retrospectively seen to have been indispensable.

To the Prime Minister the shock, not so much of going but the manner of it, was right at the top of the Richter scale. She had fought right to the edge of the envelope but had underrated the determination of the Conservative Party to remain in power at all costs and its resolve to remove anyone or anything that it considered a let or hindrance to its retention of that power. Thankfulness for three election victories did not come in. If the barrier to a fourth was the person who had delivered the previous three, then, past successes notwithstanding, that person must go. Rightly or wrongly that is what a majority of the Parliamentary Party and subsequently of the Cabinet came to believe and they acted accordingly. There was no long-distance planning, no conspiracy. They simply seized the hour and grasped a sudden, unexpected opportunity.

Margaret Thatcher was brought down by a combination of:

1 The Poll Tax.

2 Europe, to which she had never been more than lukewarm and became progressively cooler as the EEC became the EC.

3 The Paris Summit with which the leadership ballot fatally coincided.

4 The comparative weakness of her campaign team who, Norman Tebbit excepted, were outgunned until John Wakeham took over and then it was too late.

Lord Home, in his charming book *The Way the Wind Blows*, writes: 'Politics do not spare those who make mistakes or those for whom the luck does not run.' Like all who ever held her office Margaret Thatcher made mistakes but she was her own lucky general and her luck ran on and on until at last, in November 1990, it had run its course and, as the autumn leaves began to fall, an outstanding British Prime Minister fell with them.

20

. . . .

Margaret –
Then Suddenly John

With the end of her premiership there was a single overriding priority for Margaret Thatcher: that everything she had fought to achieve should go forward under her successor. This meant Michael Heseltine had to be stopped. If she could not do it, others must.

Her former sponsors, Foreign Secretary Hurd and Chancellor Major, took up the challenge. Major, her protégé and next-door neighbour, had long been her choice to succeed her but Number Ten was not in her gift. However, she could and did use the five days until the second ballot on Tuesday November 27 to telephone her supporters in the Parliamentary Party and urge them to vote for him. Between calls she collected together, packed and supervised the removal of the accumulated personal and official impedimenta of eleven years' tenancy of Number Ten, a task which once in a while for a few moments took her mind off what had happened to her life.

Meanwhile the three-handed contest for Party Leader and Prime Minister, largely conducted by individual interview on television, took place in a remarkably urbane atmosphere. The contestants did not disparage or belittle one another. Perhaps because each knew that whoever gained the palm would require the services of the other two, or perhaps just because they were made that way, no aspersions were cast, there was no opprobrium, not a whisper of ridicule. Throughout the weekend, facing tough questioning by the usual broadcasting inquisitors, each spoke positively of his political philosophy and how he would handle the premiership, should it fall to him. It was all done with a civility and moderation that in a political fight for the top of the tree was in my experience unique. Indeed, if courtesy and good temper were the key to victory the result could well have been a tie.

A depressing day in Downing Street, damp with drizzle. The Thatcher luggage is coming out of Number Ten piece by piece – trunks, suitcases, packages, personal effects, secretaries with file after file of private papers, Denis with his golf clubs; everything that time and the years have gathered is loaded into cars and vans. And it's all there live on television.

I wonder, not for the first time, must we do it like this? No privacy. No quiet back-door exit (although there is one; the Douglas-Homes went that way) but right here on the box with the nation looking on, some sad, some glad, some shocked, some gloating. Democracy in action? Yes. But does it have to be so unfeeling? I remember Ted Heath's piano being upended and chucked into the back of a lorry as though it were junk. Again the nation rubbernecking.

Can we not allow those whom we elect to the highest office a breathing-space to go in dignity and peace? We dismiss them so curtly with maximum despatch. There's something almost ghoulish about it, as though the nation is rubbing its hands. Conservative, Labour, no matter which Party they belong to, they have led their country and that's no small distinction. For a time they have spoken for us all. Surely they deserve better than an instantaneous 'over and out' with the raree-show recording the final rites.

It is evening and the farewell party is under way at Number Ten. The entire Downing Street staff, together with friends, relatives, everyone to whom the Thatchers have become what had seemed to be a fixture, are gathered in the State reception rooms. I had feared it might be a wake but although there is a strong undercurrent of emotion there is also a feeling of achievement. We have most of us known each other and worked together a long time for the lady: the comradeship has inspired affection but for a time the wine takes care of any lump in the throat before it can tangle with the canapés.

Official photographs are taken of the Prime Minister surrounded by all the various groups that have served her. When it's the turn of the Political Office she calls to me to come and join them. I mumble something about not being official but she says crisply, 'Don't be silly, dear' and the others say, 'Come on, come on.' So we have our picture taken.

There are speeches, well-judged and mercifully brief, by the lady and her husband and goodbye gifts for both of them. Andrew Turnbull, on behalf of the staff, presents Margaret with some fine books. He keeps till last a small high-frequency transistor radio. 'So that, wherever you are in the world, you can continue to be cross with the BBC.'

Peggy Noonan's discovery of certain truths of political life constantly parallels my own experience and that evening one of them keeps running through my mind.

'If you join government, calmly make your contribution and move on ... do your best and when you have to – and you will – leave and be something else.' For a maverick like myself that is one for the shaving mirror. Even so I find it hard to say goodbye with the requisite detachment. Finally I manage it and walk slowly down the familiar staircase where the walls are lined with the photographs of every Prime Minister who has held that great office since Sir Robert Walpole. There are forty-eight of them. Soon they will be joined by the forty-ninth. I wonder what they will think when they find that it's a woman.

At the top of the long, deserted corridor that ends with the Cabinet Room I stop a moment and look up at the fine portrait of Churchill by Frank Salisbury. A challenging presence who looks down at you and wherever you stand catches the eye, he appears to be brooding on the nation's future. Upstairs the sound of the party breaking up mingles with sudden shrieks of laughter. If this is goodbye to Margaret Thatcher they are certainly doing it in style. I make my way down the corridor to the front door and collect my overcoat and umbrella.

As I put on my coat the police doorman, an old friend, grey-haired, white-shirted, always smiling, appears from the security room. He is smiling now and to my surprise puts out his hand. 'It's been a pleasure, sir.' I'm puzzled. 'All these years. May I wish you the very best?' I suddenly realise he's saying goodbye, that he takes it for granted that as she is going I'll be going also. He's right, of course. I shake the proffered hand. 'Good luck to you too, my friend.' He opens the front door. It's still drizzling. 'You know, sir, you ought to write a book about all this. While you remember.'

'Oh, I shall remember.' How does one forget a seminal time of one's life?

I wave and walk out into the damp November night and the usual clutch of press photographers and television cameramen whose second home is Downing Street. I recognise one or two.

'Good party, sir?'

'How was the party?'

'Sad?'

'No. Triumphant.'

In a way it had been. Certainly she had shown no sign of the psychological trauma that many, myself included, feared was to come. Indeed it might well have started and was only suppressed in public by her rigid self-discipline. I put up my umbrella and walk on down towards the iron gates. A few of the press boys run alongside, microphones at the ready.

'Any speeches?'

'Did she make a speech?'

'A short one, yes.'

'How was it?'

'Fine.'

'Did you write it?'

The idea that for a Prime Minister everything has to be scripted has evidently taken root. 'Lord, no. No more speeches.'

I continue on to the gates and out into Whitehall, hoping for a cab. But the rain is heavier now and the taxis splash by, engaged or hurrying to get home and into the warm. One of the spikes of my umbrella snaps. I put it down, turn my coat collar up and head for Trafalgar Square, my mind still focused on the woman spending her last night in Number Ten. A jumble of disjointed thoughts crowd in elliptically, in no special sequence...

She must have been confident she would still be in office, invitations to the traditional Chequers Christmas lunch had already gone out... Had she called it a day at the tenth anniversary, she could surely have gone in triumph ... what was to come was in nobody's tea-leaves. Hindsight is a gift only granted historians... Did people really want the changes she brought about?... What people really want is to have it both ways: low taxes, secure defence, the best health service in the world – without of course having to pay the market price for any of it... One minute, senior statesman on the world circuit, the next, diary wiped clean overnight ... Everyone faces sudden cutoffs. How will she cope ...? Happens all the time in the theatre... But centre-stage for sixteen years, what do you do when the curtain falls?... Write your memoirs ... Writing history is no substitute for making it. Even Churchill found it hard 'to change over so quickly from a life of intense activity and responsibility to one in which there is nothing to look for but anticlimax'... Well, he came back. Perhaps she ... No, that's not an option ... It could change her – and perhaps not for the better... She's a fighter, not a sulker. 'Better to light candles than curse the darkness.' F.D.R., wasn't it?... No. Another lady of some distinction. *Eleanor* Roosevelt.

*

I'm past Nelson's Column and heading for St James's Street and Brooks's. On a sudden impulse I turn up Suffolk Street to the stage door of the Haymarket Theatre. The stage-door keeper is in his cubby-hole.

'Hel*lo*, sir. Haven't seen you for quite a while. Coming back to us, are you?'

'I never really left, you know.'

Over the tannoy I can hear the audience laughing. 'That sounds all right.'

'Yes, sir. Good house. Going in front?'

'Er – no. I think I'll just watch a little from the side.'

'Right, sir. You know your way.'

'Yes. Oh yes.'

I slip quietly into the wings. On stage there are the actors, moving about under the coloured lights, just as I have known and been captivated by them since early childhood. Dimly in the dark beyond the proscenium arch I can make out the audience, suspending their disbelief, playing their part in the masquerade. I stumble against the props table. In the prompt corner, on the book, the ASM looks round sharply, 'Ssh!' She sees me, smiles hello. I smile back, feeling the warm glow of recognition and belonging that the theatre always generates in me.

The familiar smell of canvas, resin, paint and wood comes at me like an aphrodisiac. Suddenly my world is back in balance. If this is political journey's end, why then, it's been a great adventure. And now it's over.

21

. . . .

Man Proposes

The Friday before the Conservative Party Conference '91 at – where else? – Blackpool, my telephone rang.

'This is Number Ten. I have a call for you.'

Click.

'Good morning. This is Judith Chaplin. I'm John Major's Political Secretary.'

'Good morning. Yes, I know.'

'How are you?'

'I'm managing to maintain an interest. How are you?'

'I'm fine.'

'Good. That's very good news.'

Pause.

'Sir Ronald, the Prime Minister was wondering if by any chance...'

The first rough outline of John Major's speech to Conference, to be given the following Friday, 11 October, arrived within the hour.

It had been arranged that I would study it, feel free to add, subtract, amend or modify at will and come into Number Ten with the result the following morning, prepared to work through the weekend with the PM, Sarah Hogg, head of the Number Ten Policy Unit, and Major's speechwriter, Nicholas True, and if all went well travel up to Blackpool on the Monday and spend the week there working with the new team. The speech was particularly important, Mrs Chaplin had confided, it would be the PM's first chance since succeeding Mrs

Thatcher to establish himself with a mass constituency audience, so not only the content was important but its reception. Would this programme, or any part of it, be possible?

Er – well – er – yes, it would be possible. Of course it would mean missing the opening of Anouilh's *Becket* at the Haymarket, with Derek Jacobi and Robert Lindsay, of which we had high hopes – on the other hand, there's the new Leader, of whom everyone in the Party, and not a few outside it, have expectations. Indeed, I'm one of them.

'Right, then. Till tomorrow.'

I was more than a little surprised to be recalled to the colours. Almost a year had gone by since Margaret's departure and I had assumed I was permanently linked by the *nouveau* with the *ancien régime*, but within minutes of entering the Cabinet Room on the Saturday morning it was clear we were not only on the same side but the same wavelength.

For a moment it was strange, seeing a man sitting where she had sat for so long, at the centre of the Cabinet table, but it was hard not to feel at ease with such an unassuming and relaxed personality. His team – Sarah Hogg, Nicholas True, Jonathan Hill and Judith Chaplin – were more or less strangers to me and behaved at first with the respect they evidently felt was due to an elderly gentleman (which I mostly do not feel but am). However, they must have decided on second thoughts that all this deference to a theatrical person was inappropriate because they quickly switched to treating me as one of themselves, an attitude I'm glad to say they have adopted ever since.

The Prime Minister had begun by saying he knew I was used to all-night sessions at Party Conferences but he was in favour of a good night's sleep and he hoped I wouldn't find the idea too eccentric. I said I would do my best to adjust to this bizarre caprice and he gave the smile and seemed relieved.

The first thing one notices about John Major – apart from the smile which is like being hit by a follow-spot at twenty paces – is his natural courtesy, which is exceptional. When it's time to go he actually sees you to the front door, as though Number Ten were a private house and you were his personal guest. No, it's *not* to make sure that you leave the premises. At least, if it is, it's beautifully done.

And so, after a weekend during which an easy rapport had been established, it was once more unto the beach . . . Even before I arrived British Rail had made sure it was like old times. The train from Euston to Blackpool North broke down twice and when we finally pulled into the station on the Monday evening, over an hour late, the rain was tropical.

So far, so sentimental. Lavender Patten, Chris's wife, had been on the train and was met by her husband's car so I was given a lift to the Imperial Hotel of a thousand and one days and nights, to be greeted by her husband with a welcoming slap on the buttocks. (I suspected it was he, now Chairman of the Party, who had recommended my recall.)

Work on the speech, with regular descents into the bowels of the hotel for rehearsal, proceeded smoothly, often light-heartedly, until the Wednesday when, despite the steady rain outside, the temperature in the Winter Gardens rose several degrees. This was the day, and noon the hour, when Mrs Thatcher was due to appear and receive the homage of the faithful.

The possibility of things getting out of hand was considerable and a lot of nerves were taut when at precisely one minute past twelve John Major escorted Margaret on to the platform. At which bottled rapture burst its bonds and collided with a massive fallout of nostalgia.

'Speech! Speech!! Speech!!!' screamed her people – and these were still supremely her people. For me time seemed first to stand still and then to go into reverse, for it was in this hall in 1975 that it had all begun for her, and many others present then, besides myself, were present now. Through the uproar and the acclamation, which even Bonnie Prince Charlie's return to claim his birthright could surely not have rivalled, the lady smiled and smiled and carried on smiling. In the audience stiff upper lips were at a premium and one felt boxes of Kleenex might usefully have been passed along the rows of the devoted by the watchful stewards and security men. Finally, after what seemed like eternity, she sat down in a carefully prearranged seat, tightly wedged between the Prime Minister and the Chairman (Central Office had been scrupulous in ensuring that Party unity should be visible and unmistakable), half rose, nodded several times in all directions, gave a little bow and, as collective emotion at last exhausted itself, resumed her seat, and remained seated.

By now four important points had been established.

First, no one had been upstaged. Second, the faithful had demonstrated that they still loved her to distraction. Third, John Major gave the smile to signal that he understood how they felt and agreed with them. And fourth, the lady, who had promised not to speak despite demand that predictably became a frenzy, kept her word and didn't utter.

A small private luncheon in the hotel with a few old friends, hosted by John and Alison Wakeham, followed. Margaret had obviously been moved by the events of the morning and took time to relax but as the whisky went down she was soon in her best didactic form. I had seen her several times during the eleven months since she had left office and it was clear that the hurt of rejection had been intense. It wasn't just the loss of a job she loved, it was as though someone had pushed her off the planet. (There were, of course, one or two who would have liked nothing better than to lend a hand at the edge.) But the healing process had finally been successful. She was back to her old self and was soon, as Jennifer's Diary inimitably describes such moments, 'sharing a joke' with the eight of us round the table.

By the time we reached the coffee stage the Iron Lady had returned, cannonballs raking the political spectrum from end to end. I was reminded of Coriolanus telling the Romans who had banished him, '*I* banish *you.*' All of which was most enjoyable and thoroughly reassuring. As Prime Minister she had frequently to suppress her emotions, at least in public. In what I think she still regards as exile she no longer has that obligation and plainly has no intention of being restricted by it. We have been warned!

After the Adoration of the Maggie John Major's keynote speech on the Friday could well have been an anticlimax. It wasn't. By Thursday evening I had known he was going to be all right. There was a difference in style from the lady but the principal essentials of policy were unchanged. As the speech proceeded he handled her audience with growing confidence and, by the time he was done, the Party, with all the affection they had given year on year to Margaret, gave their unqualified approval to the new Leader, who wears the cares of State with humour and resilience, who is a great deal more than sugar and spice and all things nice, is dedicated to shepherd's pie and sausage and mash, and in his own down-to-earth manner had shown that he could be as effective as the high octane lady whose choice he was. In this country we like having the best of both worlds. That week in Blackpool, with tact, finesse and some crafty stage management, the Tories gave a lesson in how to have the best of two very distinct Prime Ministers, though in their generosity to me they were identical.

10 DOWNING STREET

28 October 1991

Dear Ronnie

I am writing to say how very grateful I am for all the help you gave me with my speech to the Party Conference.

It was enormously reassuring for my first Conference speech as Party Leader to have your help and advice, not only with the words of the speech, but also with the delivery. Your humour and patience were tremendous.

Thank you so much for stepping in and working so hard at such short notice – I believe that it was finally a very successful speech.
With best wishes.
Yours ever
John

– And wasn't it fun to do – despite the work. I am *very* grateful.

Fun? Yes, it *had* been fun. Margaret got it right, I thought. This is a most unusual man.

Throughout the winter and early spring Britain and the free world waited with growing impatience for the General Election. Most of these quinquennial upheavals are labelled 'watershed' elections – it helps to sell newspapers and brings out the vote – but this one, finally set for 9 April 1992, was acknowledged as genuinely seminal by the Conservatives and above all by the Labour Party. After three consecutive Conservative governments it was, claimed the Opposition, 'Time for Labour'. Over the weekend of 20 March, along with the tirelessly resourceful and sure-footed Nick True, Stephen Sherbourne the professional who had been a friend for years, and the quietly supportive Dermot Gleason, another friend from the 1970s Research Department, I moved into the large Political Office room in Number Ten and dropped anchor. There the four of us set up camp for the duration, assisted by yet another secretarial support group.

Today Labour still asks fretfully, 'What was the mysterious X-factor the Tories had that we hadn't?' I can now reveal that it was, of course, Debbie, Claire, Rachel and Alice (where does Number Ten find generation after generation of these super-secretaries?) who nursed us day and night through three gruelling weeks with good cheer, patience, sympathy and charm, backed up by a gallimaufry of word processors, printouts, tea, coffee, Scotch, Mars bars, Marathons, KitKats, soups, a variety of sandwiches and every known brand of biscuit. It was like being in Intensive Care which, in the non-clinical sense, it was.

From time to time the comforting figure of Sarah Hogg descended from her office along the corridor from the top-floor flat, like Sister-in-Charge (except that she brought champagne, not camomile) to check that all was well in the writers' ward, that we were properly fed and irrigated, still reasonably sane and keeping the words and ideas flowing to wherever in the UK John Major's Battlebus was to be found, with Prime Minister, his aide-de-camp for the campaign, the shrewd and likeable Sir Norman Fowler, the bright young Political Secretary, Jonathan Hill, Central Office staff, members of the press, a sprinkling of secretaries, a battery of mobile telephones and a soapbox.

An odd little by-product of Election '92 was a subtle change in the atmosphere at Number Ten. Some of the civil servants who ran the Private Office, normally the friendliest and most helpful of colleagues, had begun distancing themselves from those who belonged, or were attached, to the Political Office.

Those of us who were helping a government that, though still the Government, was seeking re-election and might not, who could tell, be accommodated, began to be treated in a neutral fashion, like Switzerland to the Allies in World War II (until it was clear that the Allies were going to win).

'You're only here by the grace of God, you know,' said one of the neutrals, giving us, if not the cold shoulder, one that was decidedly on the cool side. Making clear its neutrality in what was a transitional period, the Civil Service was behaving strictly according to the book and I doubt if some of its members were even aware of the standoff that had occurred. I mention it only because I failed to notice a similar separation of powers during the elections of '83 and '87.

The reason was plain. Whereas the Private Office had regarded Mrs Thatcher's governments as virtually certain of re-election, they were far less sanguine about her successor's. Indeed, it seems this attitudinal shift had begun when the election was only looming, causing decisions that needed to be made by Government to be politely postponed, on one excuse or another, until a later date. This was instructive. The Office clearly thought that Labour would be making them.

For the best part of three weeks, while the opinion polls went obstinately Labour's way, the secretarial corps exuded optimism and Norma Major, beautifully groomed and with a smile to match her husband's, came attractively in and out, the indefatigable Nick and I contrived some nine speeches for the Prime Minister (one felt quite chuffed until a friend pointed out that Mozart wrote *Così Fan Tutte* in seven days).

Meanwhile there was much talk of a hung parliament, most of it emanating from the Liberal Democrats' Leader, Paddy Ashdown. Taking time out from leaping over five-barred gates, the gallant Paddy issued warnings to the Leaders of the two main Parties, 'Not to phone [the morning after the Election] without PR'. This vision of a

370

borderline result in which P.A. would hold the PR strings was greeted by John Major with 'Hung parliament be hanged, we're going to win!'

Still the polls remained intransigent. 'When I make a mistake,' said New York's Mayor La Guardia, 'I make a beaut!' Did the pollsters make a beaut with their predictions or was there a late swing that dramatically changed the picture in the final days or even hours? While there are subtle influences that sway elections, there are others that stare you in the face. When John Major spoke with real fervour of the danger to the Union of Labour's views on Scotland and Scottish devolution, making clear that he stood for a United Kingdom not a *dis*united Kingdom, a united Europe not a United *States* of Europe, he struck two powerful patriotic chords that had maximum impact.

Not a man openly passionate except on rare occasions, his emotions were on this issue deeply engaged and they surfaced in his final speech at the Wembley Rally on Tuesday evening, 7 April, which wound up the Conservative campaign. It was his best speech and the best delivered. It had every Major belief packed into it and was rapturously received. His last television broadcast, which had been recorded in the morning, also went out that evening and again thrust home the danger to the Union. The speech and the broadcast together, delivered with all the authority of a Prime Minister who, to paraphrase Churchill, 'Had not taken office as Her Majesty's First Minister to preside over the dissolution of the United Kingdom', had an effect that Neil Kinnock could not match. The feeling that the Conservatives were on a roll was confirmed by the final opinion polls which at last put them ahead of Labour.

Soon after 10 p.m. on the evening of 9 April it was clear that the Conservatives had won a fourth unprecedented term and John Major was safely back in Downing Street, with an overall majority – twenty-one – that was just enough for a reasonably-safe-but-watch-it administration.

Only one cloud cast a shadow. Party Chairman Patten, who for three crucial weeks had divided his twenty-four-hour day between running the national campaign from Central Office and helicoptering to Bath and back to save his marginal seat – a virtually impossible task – lost it. However, if Chris lost Bath, Hong Kong found a Governor, its twenty-eighth and last before the Chinese takeaway. Come '97 His Excellency will only be fifty-three. There is no reason why he should not then return to the commanding heights of British politics.

Why did the Tories win again? In a perceptive analysis two days after the election the *Guardian* wrote, 'So much of Britain has changed over the last thirteen years. The rhythms and patterns of its society have become attuned to Conservatism.' Harry Truman's adage, 'Where there is a choice between conservatives and those in pragmatic approximation thereto, the voters will always opt for the real thing' also found its mark. Labour tried hard but in politics to pretend to be what fundamentally you are not is to invite rejection. 'Meet the challenge, make the change' was Labour's battle cry. But if the difference between the Parties is not self-evident, the uncommitted will scorn change and stick with the devil they know. Between Thatcher and Callaghan it had been plain. Between Major and Kinnock, the gap was smaller.

Elections leave behind a lot of scar tissue and there was much sympathy for Neil Kinnock. A pleasant man to meet, he had done everything possible to reform his Party, cobbling together the splintered elements with considerable skill. But trying to persuade the neutral voter that what you believe today is heartfelt and sincere, when this has involved renouncing so much that you believed yesterday with equal fervour, inevitably raises doubts about what you will profess tomorrow.

There was something else. Kinnock is a patriot who loves his country but with socialism gone or on its last legs the world over, it would be strange if Britain had reembraced it. At the crunch, despite the Shadow Chancellor's Shadow Budget, people did not believe that the underlying Socialist philosophy – that wealth can be spent on welfare before it has been earned – had genuinely been abandoned.

'Wealth and welfare *hand in hand*,' said John Major, 'those are the twin pillars of the Tory temple. You can't have the second without the first.' Socialism's failure to grasp this truth is central to its global collapse.

Finally, and eternally, once man has been given the right to be master of his own destiny (for many the tangled root of the European dilemma) he will never willingly surrender that right. Unless Labour learns the pervasive strength of that emotion, change Leaders and Deputy Leaders as it may, there is no reason why it should ever again be chosen to govern the British people. Another mainstream party will no doubt arise as an alternative to the Tories but the Labour Party – its ally the unions no longer the power they were and its exclusive writ to speak for the working man invalid and outdated – will become an increasingly irrelevant political force.

Playout Music
1993 – ?

. . . .

I have had the privilege of close encounters of a political kind with three Prime Ministers.

I

Ted Heath, now Sir Edward, Knight of the Garter and Father of the House, is a new man since Margaret Thatcher's resignation and departure to the Lords. What was for so long the face of acrimony and high dudgeon has acquired the benevolence of *A Christmas Carol*. One feels that should he meet Tiny Tim he would push the boat out. The old cold eyes positively twinkle and, to coin a phrase, 'Rejoice, rejoice', while those celebrated shoulders heave with delight at the turn of the wheel of fortune. This is the second springtime of Ted. In the old days he could be good company and an entertaining host. But the camaraderie was lost with his rejection by his Party and his bitterness at the coming of Margaret. Now at last the animus is over (I think). I wish him long and happy days.

II

There are at least two, possibly more, Margaret Thatchers. Part of the fascination of this remarkable woman is that one can never be entirely sure which is in the ascendant and therefore how she will react to the latest political development. One thing is clear. Not for the lady the silence of the lambs. Her belief in certain absolutes remains immutable and highly vocal and, when the mood takes her, there is still a correlation with Miss Bette Davis in one of her more radioactive characterisations. As for the question of retirement, like Queen Victoria's 'possibilities of defeat' it does not exist. For all that, or perhaps because of it, she remains a leader touched with greatness, whose courage never failed her, who in her heyday pulled her country back from the brink of terminal decline and pointed it toward a reborn, Socialist-free society. I don't recall any timbrels and dancing – the job is not yet finished – but who can deny that Margaret led the way?

A minor cavil: latter-day Conservative Prime Ministers seem to have little local difficulties adjusting to their successors. Before his welcome apotheosis Edward Heath was given to sniping at *his*. Now it seems the lady is after all for turning – against *hers*. And indeed (and this is untypically ungenerous) is distant, even cold, to some of us who stood with her all the way and now stand with him. The implication that to support him is somehow to disavow, if not betray, her and all that we worked for together for sixteen years is of course a nonsense. Yet, from a brief encounter, I can testify that is undeniably how she feels. The resentment was unmistakable.

But, you say, she *chose* him. She *acclaimed* him ('the future is assured'). Quite. But as someone almost said, politics is a funny old world and these days the problem of Britain and Europe – in, out or at the heart of – can shatter friendships.

'Did he create the problem?'

'No, indeed he didn't. He inherited it.'

'And is dealing with it in his own way?'

'There's the rub. It may not, you see, be her way.'

'Are you suggesting that a woman built on the grand scale, practically a force of nature, would sooner be succeeded by an echo?'

'I said there's more than one Margaret Thatcher.'

After she had gone, the Italian leader who had been with her at the Rome Summit commented: 'Sometimes she was witty, sometimes she was right, sometimes she was foolish, but she was always great.' Amen to almost all of that.

John Hoskyns, the first head of her Policy Unit, had his differences with Margaret but he surely spoke for all of us who served the lady when he asked: 'What would we have done without her?'

III

John Major, the Clark Kent of the democratic West, may not be Superman but since winning an election in his own right something important has happened. While he is Leader the canard that to vote Conservative is to vote for the selfish society won't stand. He has concern, warmth, cool, tact and, as Mrs Christie said of Miss Marple, a mind like a meat cleaver.

On 9 April I do not think 'holding on to Nurse for fear of something worse' came in but if it did, then Nurse was inspired casting. The hour found the woman for the eighties and the woman found the man for the nineties. The captious with their instant negative responses to the principal political prey, will of course always be there. It goes with the territory. (History has a different perspective.) What he needs now is a little of the lady's luck and a lot of the loyalty that for so long was accorded her and which for the moment she would seem to have mislaid.

The chalice she handed him was not poisoned but the cocktail it contained was politically potent. He will, I think, continue to react *not* by throwing the cup away but by modifying the mixture to suit the times. Meanwhile he deserves support and should increasingly receive it as he comes to grips with his troubled inheritance and restores the nation's belief in itself, as did his predecessor in her lustrous days.

I have heard him referred to as a Parsifal figure: 'Knowledge with compassion.' My definition is a distinction. Where Margaret would ask 'Is he (she) one of us?' her successor turns the coin over. The other side reads '*I* am one of *you*.'

Index

. . . .

MT stands for Margaret Thatcher, RM for Ronald Millar. A figure 2 in brackets immediately after a page reference indicates that there are two separate references to the subject on that page.

Index

Millar, Dorothy Ethel (née Dacre-
Hill; RM's mother)
her name, 11–12, 17–18, 18–19
marriage, 12–15, 16–17, 28, 184
theatrical career, 17–22, 25, 37,
56, 68, 82, 112
admirers, 25–8
and RM's theatrical ambitions,
22, 39, 40–2, 47, 53, 57, 61,
68, 77, 112
and RM's school career, 30, 33–7
and RM's war service, 77, 78, 89,
96–7, 103–4
and RM's trips to America, 128–
30, 158–9, 161, 162, 164–5,
167
last years, 266, 273
death, 5
mentioned, 117
Millar, Commander Leslie (RM's
uncle), 65, 86
Millar, Max (RM's uncle), 17
Millar, Sir Ronald Graeme
childhood, 13–15, 21–2, 25–7
in love with the theatre, 21–2,
39–40, 47, 53, 72, 77
school, 22–4, 28–30, 31–9, 43–
50
writes, *The Lion's Skin*, 40–2
not interested in politics, 48, 77,
117
and prospect of war, 49–50,
51–2
at Cambridge, 52–63, 68–73
in *Antigone*, 54–62
and Second World War, 63–8,
73–4, 75–6, 77–98
meets Ivor Novello, 69–73
in *Swinging the Gate*, 74–6, 77–8
invalided out of the Navy, 98–100
decides not to return to
Cambridge, 103–5
actor, 105–12, 116, 117–19; in
films, 112–15
playwright, 109–10, 115–17,
119–20, 120–1, 122–4;
screenplay, 124–6, 141–3

and Hollywood, 127–41, 142–61,
162–71
adapts Nigel Balchin novel,
172–4
his *Bride* plays, 174–8
adapts C. P. Snow novels, 178–
83, 224
his *Barretts of Wimpole Street*
musical, 183–90
writes *On the Level*, 190–2
adapts *Number Ten*, 192–5
speechwriter to Edward Heath,
201–5, 206–9, 212–13,
223–4
writes *Abelard and Heloise*, 209–
12, 216–17
first official visit to Number Ten,
214–15
first meeting with MT, 218–19
visits to Chequers, 3–6, 219–22,
272–3, 322–3, 327
speechwriter to MT, 225–9, 231–
49, 251–2, 256–73, 274–94,
297–305, 308–11, 312–16,
342–4, 362–4
takes MT to the theatre, 229,
252–6
becomes deputy chairman of
Theatre Royal, Haymarket,
229–30, 262
knighthood, 273, 317
relationship with MT, 287, 343
not an MP, 319
never joined the Conservative
Party, 320–1
not paid for his political work,
324, 339
his political involvement, its
bonuses, 324–5
at Pamela Snow's memorial
service, 325–7
his seventieth birthday, 330
speechwriter to John Major, 365–
7, 368, 369–70
Millar, Ronald Hugh (RM's father),
11, 12–15, 16–17, 28
Miller, Hugh, 118

382

Letter 1 (top left, partially visible):

10 DOWNING
LONDON SW1

THE PRIME MINISTER

Dear Ronnie

I should just like to
so much of your time
on my speech to the W
the Guildhall. To ha
together created add
usual, your help was

I was sorry that th
get the attention
it merited, but it
received. The Fr
was a most

The Rt. Hon. Mrs. Margaret Thatcher, M.P.

HOUSE
LON

26

Letter 2 (top right, main):

10 DOWNING STREET
LONDON SW1A 2AA

THE PRIME MINISTER   19th May 1989

Dear Ronnie,

I should just like to thank you, as always, for your enormous
help with my speech to the Scottish Party Conference last
week. It was very good of you to give up so much time, and
your contribution was invaluable. Indeed, it was widely
remarked that the humour contained within the speech played
a major part in its success.

I very much hope that you will be able to help us with the
Women's speech which I am afraid is all too soon, and I know
John Whittingdale will be contacting you about this shortly.

Yours ever

Margaret

Sir Ronald Millar

Letter 3 (bottom left):

Dear Ronnie,

I felt that I must write to
you to thank you most warmly for
the very great help that you have
been to me recently. I used a
great part of your speech at the
IPA last night and I know that you
are looking at something for my
Lobby speech. I am indeed grateful
to you.

Also let me say how very much
I enjoyed your play last Saturday.
I really do congratulate you.

We all had a wonderful evening
and the Thatcher family has become
a Ronnie Millar fan club — will see in
we than.

Yours ever
Margaret

Ronald Millar Esq

Letter 4 (bottom right, partially visible):

THE PRIME MINISTER   LONDON SW1A 2

Ronnie

d just like to thank you once agai
n my speech to the Central Counci
nt, it was very well received an
large part due to the help and
es.

nday morning we go
Malawi